1993

Reforming Libel Law

THE GUILFORD COMMUNICATION SERIES

Editors
Theodore L. Glasser
Department of Communication, Stanford University

Howard E. Sypher
Department of Communication Studies, University of Kansas

Advisory Board

Charles Berger   Peter Monge   Michael Schudson
James Carey   Barbara O'Keefe   Ellen Wartella

Reforming Libel Law

Edited by

John Soloski and Randall P. Bezanson

THE GUILFORD PRESS
New York · London

© **1992 The Guilford Press**
A Division of Guilford Publications, Inc.
72 Spring Street, New York, NY 10012

Chapter 1 © 1991 University of Pennsylvania Law
Review; Chapter 2 © 1986 California Law Review;
Chapter 3 © 1976 California Law Review; Chapter 4 ©
1981 The American University Law Review; Chapter 5
© Pierre N. Leval; Chapter 6 © Rodney A. Smolla.

Printed in the United States of America

This book is printed on acid-free paper.

Last digit is print
number: 9 8 7 6 5 4 3 2 1

Library of Congress Cataloging-in-Publication Data

Reforming libel law / edited by John Soloski and
  Randall P. Bezanson.
      p.   cm. — (The Guilford communication
series)
    Includes bibliographical references and index.
    ISBN 0-89862-317-0
    1. Libel and slander—United States.
I. Soloski, John, 1952–   . II. Bezanson, Randall P.
III. Series.
KF 1266.L53   1992
346.7303'4—dc20
[347.30634]   92-5660
                          CIP

Contributors

David A. Anderson, Thompson & Knight Centennial Professor and James R. Dougherty Chair for Faculty Excellence, School of Law, University of Texas, Austin, Texas

David A. Barrett, Senior Partner, Duker & Barrett, New York, New York

Randall P. Bezanson, Dean and Professor of Law, Washington and Lee University, Lexington, Virginia

Gilbert Cranberg, George H. Gallup Professor, School of Journalism and Mass Communication, University of Iowa, Iowa City

Marc A. Franklin, Frederick I. Richman Professor of Law, Stanford University, Stanford, California

James H. Hulme, Partner, Arent Fox Kintner Plotkin & Kahn, Washington, D.C.

Pierre N. Leval, judge of the United States District Court for the Southern District of New York, presided over Gen. William Westmoreland's libel suit against CBS

Brian Murchison, Professor, School of Law, Washington and Lee University, Lexington, Virginia

Rodney A. Smolla, Arthur B. Hanson Professor of Law and Director, Institute of Bill of Rights Law, Marshall-Wythe School of Law, College of William and Mary, Williamsburg, Virginia

Steven M. Sprenger, Associate, Shook, Hardy & Bacon, Kansas City, Missouri

John Soloski, Professor, School of Journalism and Mass Communication, University of Iowa, Iowa City

Roselle L. Wissler, Director of Research, Iowa Libel Research Project, College of Law, University of Iowa, Iowa City

Preface

For most of its history, libel law favored plaintiffs. Before 1964, plaintiffs could win a libel suit by showing that the allegedly libelous statements had injured their reputation.[1] For all practical purposes, the falsity of the allegedly libelous statements was assumed, and the burden fell on the publisher to prove that the statements were true. "If publication, defamation (reputational disparagement), and injury could be shown, the publisher was liable, even if there was an honest mistake or understandable oversight."[2] Because money damages were the remedy available to libel plaintiffs, there was a fear that the prospect of having to pay large damages would have a "chilling effect" on the media's willingness to report controversial news stories.

In 1964, the U.S. Supreme Court radically changed libel law and in so doing seemingly provided the media with enormous protection from libel suits. In *New York Times Co. v. Sullivan*,[3] the Court ruled that public officials had to show that an allegedly libelous statement was published with knowledge of its falsity or with reckless disregard of the truth. In *Gertz v. Robert Welch, Inc.*,[4] the Supreme Court extended the media's protection by requiring private plaintiffs to show that the media acted at least negligently when publishing false statements. The Supreme Court's purpose in *Sullivan* and *Gertz* was to provide the media protection from liability for inadvertently publishing false information so as not to fetter the free and robust discussion of issues of public importance. To prevail in a libel suit today, plaintiffs need to show not only that the information published about them is false, but that the media published the information with some degree of negligence, with actual knowledge of its falsity, or with reckless disregard of the truth. Despite the substantial barriers erected by the Supreme Court, plaintiffs continue to sue the media for libel.

The biggest danger the media face in a libel suit is losing and having to pay large damage awards. But this does not happen often. The media lose very few libel cases, and when they do lose, damage awards are often reduced on appeal. The real economic impact of libel on the media is the high cost of defending a seriously litigated suit. Because of the high cost of defending a libel suit, the fear of suit, despite the media's knowing that a plaintiff is unlikely to prevail, is seen as deterring the media from pursuing or publishing controversial stories of public importance. From the media's point of view, the problems with libel law are a serious threat to their journalistic freedom.

From the plaintiffs' perspective, libel law is frustrating and unfair. Libel law provides little opportunity for plaintiffs to repair their reputation. Very few plaintiffs prevail in a libel suit because they are unable to meet the level of proof required by constitutional privileges. Plaintiffs who are able to prove that the information published about them is false and that it damaged their reputation cannot succeed in a libel suit unless they can also show that the media published the information negligently or with actual malice.

The problems with current libel law have led a number of legal scholars to offer proposals for the comprehensive reform of libel law. The proposals are highly controversial. They have been debated and criticized at numerous professional meetings over the last several years.

The purpose of this book is to bring together what we believe to be the most significant libel law reform proposals. Four of the proposals were originally published as articles in law reviews, but three have only been available previously in abbreviated form: the Annenberg Libel Reform Proposal, the Iowa Libel Research Project's Libel Dispute Resolution Program, and the Uniform Defamation Act of the National Conference of Commissioners on Uniform State Laws.

Chapter 1 sets the stage for the proposals discussed in the book. In this chapter, David A. Anderson succinctly explains the problems with current libel law. He also discusses the problems faced by attempts to legislate libel law reform. He argues that the best hope for reform lies with the U.S. Supreme Court.

In Chapter 2, Marc A. Franklin presents his reform proposal. Franklin's proposal is a milestone in the libel law reform movement. Not only was it one of the first reform proposals, the major ideas of his proposal have been incorporated in most of the other reform proposals. In this chapter, Franklin compares his proposal with the libel reform bill introduced by Rep. Charles E. Schumer (D-N.Y.) in the U.S. House of Representatives.

Chapter 3 focuses on the first major legislative attempt to reform libel law: the Schumer bill. David A. Barrett, who helped draft the Schumer bill, examines the bill in light of Franklin's proposal and his criticisms of the bill.

In Chapter 4, James H. Hulme and Steven M. Sprenger offer a vindication proposal for reforming libel law. The legislation they propose would provide a way for plaintiffs to repair their reputation though a judicial determination of the falsity of the allegedly libelous statements. If the statements were found to be false, the media defendant would be required to publish or cause to have published the court's findings on the falsity issue.

In Chapter 5, Pierre N. Leval suggests that it may be possible to obtain a declaratory judgment on the truth or falsity of allegedly libelous statements under current libel law. Judge Leval argues that the constitutional privileges of *New York Times Co. v. Sullivan*[5] apply only to libel suits in which money damages are sought and may not apply in a libel suit in which a plaintiff is seeking only a court determination of the truth or falsity of the challenged statements. If Leval's theory is correct, there may be no need to reform libel law.

Chapter 6 presents the most well-known of the libel reform proposals: the Annenberg Libel Reform Proposal. Rodney A. Smolla, who directed the Annenberg project, discusses the Annenberg proposal and criticisms of it and offers his thoughts about the problems legislative reforms face.

The Libel Dispute Resolution Program discussed in Chapter 7 is not a legislative proposal for reforming libel law. Rather, it is a voluntary, nonlitigation program for resolving libel disputes involving the media. The Libel Dispute Resolution Program was implemented in 1987. This chapter examines the program and presents the results of a three-year experiment with the use of the program.

The Uniform Defamation Act of the National Conference of Commissioners on Uniform State Laws discussed in Chapter 8 is the latest legislative proposal for reforming libel law. The Act draws on aspects of many of the proposals discussed in earlier chapters. The Act is possibly the most comprehensive proposal for reforming libel law. It will come before the Conference for a vote in 1993.

While the various proposals to reform libel law have been debated by legal scholars and media attorneys, there have been numerous bills introduced in state legislatures to reform libel law. Chapter 9 examines the most significant of these legislative efforts and the media's reaction to them. None of the legislative efforts to reform libel law has been supported by the media.

NOTES

1. R. BEZANSON, G. CRANBERG, & J. SOLOSKI, LIBEL LAW AND THE PRESS: MYTH AND REALITY (1987). *See also* Bezanson, *The Libel Tort Today*, 45 WASH. & LEE L. REV. 353 (1988).

2. Bezanson, *supra* note 1, at 1.

3. 376 U.S. 254 (1964).

4. 418 U.S. 323 (1974).

5. 376 U.S. 254 (1964).

Contents

Reforming Libel Law

chapter 1

Is Libel Law Worth Reforming?*

DAVID A. ANDERSON[†]

The remnants of American libel law provide little protection for reputation. The actual-malice rule of *New York Times Co. v. Sullivan*[1] does not adequately protect the press, so courts have imposed many other constitutional limitations on the libel action.[2] Cumulatively, these make the remedy largely illusory. Most victims of defamation cannot meet the actual-malice requirement and many who can are thwarted by other constitutional obstacles.

Nonetheless, libel law continues to exact a price from speech. The constitutional protections are designed to, and often do, encourage the media to defame. Outraged juries frequently return six- or seven-figure verdicts. Although such verdicts are usually reversed on appeal, defamation victims continue to sue. While the likelihood of success is minuscule, the amount at issue is usually large, so the media defend vigorously. Because many of the constitutional issues do not lend themselves to preliminary disposition, even the least meritorious cases can require extensive discovery on both sides. Those actions that go to trial often produce plaintiffs' judgments that are eventually reversed on constitutional grounds. Libel law, as modified over the past twenty-five years, produces expensive litigation and occasional large judgments and therefore continues to chill speech.[3]

As it stands today, libel law is not worth saving. What we have is a system in which most claims are judicially foreclosed after costly litigation. It gives plaintiffs delusions of large windfalls, defendants

---

*This chapter was originally published in 140 U. P. L. REV. 487 (1991).
†Thompson & Knight Centennial Professor, University of Texas Law School.

nightmares of intrusive and protracted litigation, and the public little assurance that the law favors truth over falsehood. If we can do no better, honesty and efficiency demand that we abolish the law of libel.

Much can be said for that course. Since our forebears abandoned licensing, libel has been the principal legal threat to freedom of the press. Abolishing libel law is the only way to completely eliminate the chilling effect that it exerts on the press. To paraphrase Judge Edgerton, whatever is subtracted from the field of libel is added to the field of free debate.[4] Abolition would leave victims of defamation little worse off than they are today. A few would give up recoveries, but many would be spared the costs, emotional as well as financial, of hopeless litigation. The public would get the benefit of information that is now suppressed by the chill of libel law and would be disabused of the inferences that may be drawn from a mistaken belief that defamatory falsehoods are generally actionable.

No matter how much it values speech, however, a civilized society cannot refuse to protect reputation. Some form of libel law is as essential to the health of the commonweal and the press as it is to the victims of defamation. Without libel law, credibility of the press would be at the mercy of the least scrupulous among it, and public discourse would have no necessary anchor in truth.

From the point of view of the defamed, the defamers, or the public, the law of libel is obviously ripe for reform. Many proposals have been offered over the past decade,[5] but so far all have been stillborn because of opposition by the media bar[6] and the absence of any organized support. Now, however, the reform movement has, if not a political constituency, at least an institutional protagonist. The National Conference of Commissioners on Uniform State Laws is preparing a proposed Uniform Defamation Act, to be voted on by the Conference in 1993.[7] In the pattern of previous reform proposals, the proposed uniform act (1) retains present constitutional restrictions on monetary recovery, (2) further restricts the availability of presumed and punitive damages, and (3) requires many defamation victims to accept alternative remedies, namely, retraction or a declaratory judgment of falsity, in lieu of damages.

Like its predecessors, this approach to reform is too modest. Instead of correcting the evils of the present libel law, it seeks to circumvent them through alternative remedies that are likely to prove ineffective. If libel law is to be worth saving, it must provide not merely nominal remedies but remedies that protect reputation effectively, at the least possible cost to speech. Vindicatory declarations and other alternative remedies could supplement an effective and efficient system of libel law. But because of the realities of financing litigation against the legal and financial might of the media, monetary awards must continue to be the primary remedy. The principal opportunities for reform lie in abandoning some shibboleths about jury trials and in reducing the scale of libel litigation.

The objective of this chapter is to show how the current law of libel affects the media, the victims of defamation, and the public and how it might be changed. To appreciate these matters, one must come to grips with some arcana that is stock in trade to the libel bar but is little known to others. To understand that the constitutional law of libel is a rule requiring public officials and public figures to prove actual malice, or even that it is a system of fault-based rules that vary for different classes of cases, is to have an illusion of understanding. The constitutional law of libel has evolved far beyond the well-known fault requirements. The actual-malice rule of *Sullivan* has been subsumed into an intricate complex of substantive, procedural, and evidentiary rules, some of which have little to do with "actual malice" and much to do with judicial power to reject jury findings. Virtually all libel litigation is now governed by the strictest constitutional limitations, rules conceived for libel suits by public officials. The perception that the actual-malice regime is an exceptional one, applying only to a few libel plaintiffs, is a myth. Because of expansive definitions of "public official" and "public figure," and because financial realities compel even private plaintiffs to seek presumed and punitive damages, the actual-malice standard, with all its ancillary restrictions, is the rule rather than the exception. The first section of this chapter explains how little protection of reputation remains under this system.

Understanding how these rules work in litigation is essential to understanding why they fail to adequately protect freedom of speech (the subject of the second section) and why they exact too great a sacrifice of the individual and societal interests in reputation (the subject of the third section). The last section of this chapter discusses the directions reform might take and the obstacles it faces. I conclude that only the Supreme Court can bring about the reform of libel law.

THE CONSTITUTIONAL LAW OF DEFAMATION

Actual Malice

The rule created by *New York Times Co. v. Sullivan*,[8] still the cornerstone of constitutional defamation law today, is that the First Amendment "prohibits a public official from recovering damages for a defamatory falsehood relating to his official conduct unless he proves that the statement was made with 'actual malice'—that is, with knowledge that it was false or with reckless disregard of whether it was false or not."[9]

From the outset, the Court made it clear that this requirement would not be easy to meet. It was not met by evidence that the *New York Times* had in its own files showing the falsity of some of the charges against Sullivan, by the *Times*'s secretary's admission that he suspected one of the charges was false, or by the fact that the newspaper failed to retract at Sullivan's demand, though it had retracted the same charges on the demand of the governor of Alabama.[10] Gradually, the Court made it clear that neither malice nor recklessness, in the common law sense of those terms, suffices. Proof of ill will is not enough,[11] nor is proof that the defendant published without investigating despite an obvious risk of serious harm to reputation.[12] Instead, what must be shown is a subjective awareness of falsity: that the defendant knew what he was saying was false or "in fact entertained serious doubts as to the truth of his publication."[13] Moreover, knowledge of a merely technical falsehood is not enough; thus, deliberate alteration of quotations is not proof of knowledge of falsity unless the alteration materially changes the meaning of the quotation alleged to be defamatory.[14]

Convincing Clarity

To reinforce this constitutional fortification, the Court greatly expanded judges' control of juries—a development that has had far greater practical effect than the actual-malice rule itself. This expansion of judicial control began in *Sullivan*, which intimated that "actual malice" must be proved with "convincing clarity."[15] This means the jury must be instructed that although other issues are controlled by the usual preponderance-of-evidence standard,[16] actual malice must be shown by "clear and convincing proof."[17] The importance of this rule lies not in its effect on juries, however, but in its effect on judicial review. *Sullivan* also held that judges—from the trial judge to members of the Supreme Court—must engage in independent review of a jury finding of actual malice to satisfy themselves that the evidence is constitutionally sufficient.[18] In making this sufficiency judgment, judges must determine not merely that the finding is supported by competent evidence, or that a reasonable person could find actual malice, but that it is shown with convincing clarity. The Supreme Court has never explained what that phrase means, but it obviously enhances judges' power to overturn jury verdicts that under usual rules would have to be accepted. The convincing-clarity standard also provides the measure by which the genuineness of the actual-malice issue must be judged on the defendant's motion for summary judgment under the Federal Rules of Civil Procedure.[19]

Independent Review

The independent-review requirement abrogates the usual rule that jury determinations are not to be set aside unless clearly erroneous.

> The question whether the evidence in the record in a defamation case is of the convincing clarity required to strip the utterance of First Amendment protection is not merely a question for the trier of fact. Judges, as expositors of the Constitution, must independently decide whether the evidence in the record is sufficient to cross the constitutional threshold that bars the entry of any judgment that is not supported by clear and convincing proof of "actual malice."[20]

Lower courts sometimes refer to this as de novo review,[21] but the Supreme Court has never used that term and it is clear that jury findings are not to be disregarded entirely. Indeed, in its own review of actual-malice findings, the Court seems to take some pains to avoid contradicting jury findings.[22] But whatever the Court means by "independent review," there is no doubt that it invites judges to set aside jury determinations.

Although the Court once stated that findings of fact other than actual malice are not to be disturbed unless clearly erroneous,[23] the Court has decided for itself several other issues that normally would be considered fact issues. One is whether the defamatory statement refers to the plaintiff. The common law notion of colloquium allows an unnamed person to prove that readers nevertheless would reasonably infer that the statement was "of and concerning" the plaintiff.[24] The jury in *Sullivan* found that readers would infer that the accusations of misconduct made against police officers under Sullivan's command implicitly defamed him. The Court said basing a verdict for the plaintiff on such an inference was tantamount to seditious libel, "transmuting criticism of government, however impersonal it may seem on its face, into personal criticism, and hence potential libel, of the officials of whom the government is composed."[25] Because such an inference was the only basis for the jury's finding that the publication referred to Sullivan, the Court held that "the evidence was constitutionally . . . incapable of supporting the jury's finding that the allegedly libelous statements were made 'of and concerning' respondent."[26]

The Court has also reviewed the substantiality of a media defendant's factual error. In *Sullivan,* the Court noted that some of the advertisement's allegations were false only in degree; "[t]he ruling that these discrepancies between what was true and what was asserted were sufficient to injure respondent's reputation may itself raise constitutional problems, but we need not consider them here."[27]

In *Time, Inc. v. Pape,*[28] the Court did consider the matter. *Time* magazine reported that the Civil Rights Commission had concluded that Pape had committed acts of police brutality; in fact, the Commission had concluded only that the allegations against him appeared substantial enough to warrant inclusion in its report. The Court held that such a minor discrepancy could not support a finding of actual malice.[29] The inquiry, however, seems to relate more to the issue of falsity than to proof of actual malice. Whether the defendant had knowledge of falsity or serious doubts as to the truth is not dependent on the magnitude of the error. Rather, the issue seems to be closer to that mentioned in *Sullivan*: Was the difference between the truth and the defamatory allegation substantial enough to justify a judgment that the latter harmed the plaintiff in some way that the former did not. In any event, it involves the Court in a constitutionally based review of matters that normally would be resolved by the common law doctrine of substantial truth.[30]

The Court has also intervened aggressively in cases involving hyperbole or satire, sometimes deciding for itself whether the words used can be construed as defamatory.[31] Whether other issues may also be subject to independent review is open to question. The rationale—that judges must determine whether the evidence is constitutionally sufficient to surmount the constitutional barrier erected by the actual-malice standard—seems equally applicable to any other constitutional prerequisite. Media defendants sometimes claim that they are entitled to independent review of all constitutional defamation issues.[32] Some courts have extrapolated the even broader principle that independent review is required not only in libel cases but in any case in which a restriction on speech is held constitutional.[33] The scope of independent review remains unclear, in part because courts sometimes reverse judgments without making clear whether they are exercising the kind of independent review described in *New York Times v. Sullivan* or the more conventional power to set aside findings they deem "clearly erroneous" or unsupported by evidence.[34]

Whatever its proper scope, independent review is available only to defendants.[35] Its purpose is to assure "that the judgment does not constitute a forbidden intrusion on the field of free expression"[36]— not to assure that the judgment does not unnecessarily sacrifice reputation.

Summary Judgment

The Court has transferred power from juries to judges in yet another way by encouraging trial judges to grant defendants' motions for summary judgment. The Court has never endorsed the view of some lower courts that summary judgment should be a preferred remedy in defamation cases to protect the press from the chilling effect of extended litigation.[37] At one point the Court suggested the contrary: that summary judgment might be the exception rather than the rule in libel cases because the actual-malice issue, involving the defendant's state of mind, does not lend itself readily to summary disposition.[38] Once judges were invited to decide the actual-malice issue for themselves *after* trial, however, it was inevitable that they would be inclined to do so before trial as well. In practice, the defendant's ostensible summary judgment burden of negating the existence of any genuine issue of material fact became a burden on plaintiffs to show affirmatively a basis on which a finding of actual malice might be made.[39] As a result, media defendants' motions for summary judgment enjoy unusually high success rates.[40]

When the Court eventually decided an issue of summary judgment procedure, it held that under the Federal Rules of Civil Procedure, the clear-and-convincing-proof standard controls at the summary judgment stage as well as at trial.[41] To survive the defendant's Rule 56 motion for summary judgment in a libel case controlled by *Sullivan*, a plaintiff must produce not merely some evidence to create a genuine issue as to the existence of actual malice, but evidence from which actual malice could be found by clear and convincing proof.[42] The enhanced standard of proof also controls when a defendant claiming the protections of *Sullivan* moves for a directed verdict.[43] The Court's earlier suggestion that summary judgment might be inappropriate on the actual-malice issue was dismissed as "simply an acknowledgment of our general reluctance 'to grant special procedural protections to defendants in libel and defamation actions.' "[44] Because the new rule was applicable to any type of case in which a party faced an enhanced evidentiary standard, it did not amount to such a special protection.[45] The consequence is that judges are encouraged to take the actual-malice issue away from the jury before trial, both informally, by the logic of independent judicial review, and formally, by the application of the convincing-clarity standard even in the preliminary stages of litigation. As a result, only a small proportion of libel suits governed by *New York Times v. Sullivan* ever reach a jury.[46]

Public Figures

These constitutional rules applied only to libel suits by public officials originally, but they now govern most libel cases. The Court extended the requirements of *Sullivan* to candidates for public office[47] and appointed officials, reaching down "at the very least to those among the hierarchy of government employees who have, or appear to the public to have, substantial responsibility for or control over the conduct of governmental affairs."[48] The same requirements were also extend ed to plaintiffs who hold no official position but "are nevertheless intimately involved in the resolution of important public questions or, by reason of their fame, shape events in areas of concern to society at large."[49] The lower courts have tended to view both the public-official and public-figure categories expansively. Police officers, for example, are almost invariably classified as public officials, no matter how low their rank.[50] The public-figure category includes not only those who seek to influence public affairs,[51] but also those who attract media attention by success in their career[52] or avocation[53] or by their relationships with celebrities.[54] The plaintiff's fame or influence need not be widespread; notoriety within a particular circle is sufficient to make a person a public figure for purposes of defamation within that circle.[55]

The upshot is that the vast majority of those whose activities are likely to attract media attention—and who therefore are at risk of being defamed in the media—are subject to the actual-malice rule and the phalanx of other rules that surround it.

The classification of plaintiffs might seem to be primarily factual, depending on the nature of the person's position and responsibilities (if the person is alleged to be a public official) or the scope of the person's fame or involvement in public issues (if the person is alleged to be a public figure). But the lower courts almost universally treat the question as one of law, to be decided by judges not juries.[56]

Private Plaintiffs

Plaintiffs who avoid the public-official and public-figure classifications find their defamation claims only slightly less restricted by constitutional rules. Private persons who are defamed in discussions about matters of public concern may recover for their actual injury without meeting the requirements described above, provided they show that the defendant acted with some degree of fault (e.g., negligence).[57] Only if they seek something more than compensation for actual injury, namely, presumed damages or punitive damages, must they meet the actual-malice test[58] (and perhaps the other requirements of *Sullivan*). Actual injury includes "impairment of reputation and standing in the community, personal humiliation, and mental anguish and suffering."[60] Unlike the tort concept of special damage, actual injury is not limited to out-of-pocket loss: "[A]ll awards must be supported by competent evidence concerning the injury, although there need be no evidence which assigns an actual dollar value to the injury."[61] Surprisingly, perhaps, actual injury need not include any harm to reputation; if a state chooses to allow a defamation action for mental anguish alone, unaccompanied by any claim for harm to reputation, the actual-injury requirement is not offended.[62]

Yet another set of rules governs some private-plaintiff cases. The scheme described in the preceding paragraph applies to private persons defamed in connection with matters of public concern. Because "speech on matters of purely private concern is of less First Amendment concern,"[63] private plaintiffs defamed in speech of that kind may recover presumed and punitive damages without showing actual malice.[64] Whether such plaintiffs are also relieve from meeting the fault requirement of *Gertz* has not been decided.[65]

In practice, few suits proceed under the negligence standard[66] because plaintiffs rarely sue for actual injury only. This may be because they are unable to prove actual injury and thus must seek presumed damages, or because they wish to punish the defendant and thus seek punitive damages. Even if they have a modest amount of provable actual injury and no desire to further punish the defendant, the economics of litigation are likely to steer them away from the negligence–actual-injury system and into the actual-malice scheme. Since the law provides no other method by which a plaintiff of modest means can finance the litigation, the plaintiff's ability to pursue the claim depends on a lawyer's willingness to take the case on a contingent-fee basis.[67] Most lawyers see media defendants as tenacious, well-represented litigants whose insurers generally will honor the defendant's reluctance to settle. The prospective recovery must be large enough to justify the lawyer's investment of time in a protracted and expensive lawsuit that may produce no recovery at all. In most cases, only the prospect of presumed and/or punitive damages makes the stakes high enough. Even prospective plaintiffs who are able to

pay lawyers on a fee-for-time basis must make some similar calculation unless they are liberated by wealth or irrationality from considering the financial consequences of suit. As a result of these pragmatic
concerns, suits under the negligence formula of *Gertz* have turned out
to be rare. Thus, the full panoply of constitutional rules developed
for public-plaintiff cases controls the great majority of libel cases,
including those brought by private plaintiffs.

Neutral Reportage

Another constitutional rule, yet to receive either specific approval or
condemnation from the Supreme Court, is the neutral-reportage
privilege.[68] It creates an absolute privilege for accurate and dis-
interested reporting of defamatory accusations made by responsible
organizations. Where recognized, this privilege protects the media
even when they know the charges they are reporting are false or they
seriously doubt their truth. As first articulated, the neutral-reportage
privilege applied only to accusations against public figures, but some
jurisdictions have allowed it to be invoked against private plaintiffs as
well.[69]

The neutral-reportage defense has not been widely embraced,
and several important jurisdictions have declined to adopt it.[70] Nevertheless, most jurisdictions probably would apply it in the right case. If
the president of the United States baselessly accused the vice president of plotting to assassinate him, for example, most courts surely
would hold that the media could safely report the president's accusation even if they seriously doubted its truth.

Falsity

Finally, and perhaps most important, the Court has switched the
burden of proof on falsity. The universal common law rule that truth
was a defense is unconstitutional, and both public and private plaintiffs must now prove the falsity of the defamation.[71] This is a relatively recent development, the importance of which has yet to be fully
appreciated. Much of the Court's dissatisfaction with the common law
of libel in *Sullivan* was, in fact, dissatisfaction with the treatment of
truth as a defensive matter:

> Allowance of the defense of truth, with the burden of proving it on the
> defendant, does not mean that only false speech will be deterred. Even
> courts accepting this defense as an adequate safeguard have recognized
> the difficulties of adducing legal proofs that the alleged libel was true in

all its factual particulars. Under such a rule, would-be critics of official conduct may be deterred from voicing their criticism, even though it is believed to be true and even though it is in fact true, because of doubt whether it can be proved in court or fear of the expense of having to do so. . . . The rule thus dampens the vigor and limits the variety of public debate.[72]

The unconstitutionality of treating truth as a defense, at least in public official cases, was implied in *Garrison v. Louisiana*,[73] where the Court said that a public official may recover for libel "only if he establishes that the utterance was false and that it was made with knowledge of its falsity or in reckless disregard of whether it was false or true."[74] Even then, many seemed reluctant to believe that the Court meant what it said. The (second) *Restatement of Torts*, for example, expressed no opinion as to whether the burden of proof had been changed by constitutional law.[75] Finally, in 1986, the Court put the matter to rest, squarely holding that the Constitution requires that plaintiffs bear the burden of proving falsity in both private-plaintiff and public-plaintiff cases.[76]

In public-plaintiff cases, courts generally have held that plaintiffs must prove falsity by clear and convincing proof.[77] In *Philadelphia Newspapers, Inc. v. Hepps*, the Court found "no occasion to consider the quantity of proof of falsity that a private-figure plaintiff must present."[78]

Nonfactual Expressions

For a time, the lower courts were developing a doctrine so malleable and expansive that it seemed destined to become the most important constitutional restriction on libel law. The doctrine was that expressions of opinion were absolutely protected, and it evolved from the following passage in *Gertz:* "Under the First Amendment there is no such thing as a false idea. However pernicious an opinion may seem, we depend for its correction not on the conscience of judges and juries but on the competition of other ideas."[79]

Many courts saw in this passage an implication that opinion is constitutionally protected.[80] Opinion is protected at common law by the privilege of fair comment, but that privilege attaches only if the statement does not imply the existence of undisclosed defamatory facts,[81] and defamatory statements of opinion often contain such implications. Moreover, the common law privilege is destroyed by proof that the speaker did not honestly hold the opinion stated or spoke for the purpose of harming the plaintiff.[82] The courts imposed no such limitations on the constitutional protection of opinion. They read *Gertz* as creating an absolute protection for opinion, so that the defendant's motive and the honesty with which the belief was held were irrelevant.[83]

The most widely used method for distinguishing fact from opinion called for the analysis of four factors to determine whether "the totality of circumstances in which the statements are made" indicated that the average reader would understand them as opinion rather than fact.[84] The factors were (1) the common meaning of the language used, (2) the verifiability of the statement, (3) the journalistic context in which the statement was made (e.g., editorial column vs. news article), and (4) the setting in which the statement occurred (e.g., political controversy vs. private business dispute).[85] The result was to give absolute constitutional protection to many highly defamatory statements. Examples include the following: a broadcast characterizing plaintiff as a member of "an 'international network of medical quackery' " whose patients were victims of 'cancer con artists' ";[86] a published assertion that plaintiff "is the Al Capone of the City";[87] and a review of a television documentary on sex education in which the reviewer stated, "My impression is that the executive producer [plaintiff] . . . told his writer/producer. . . . 'We've got a hot potato here— let's pour on titillating innuendo and as much bare flesh as we can get away with. Viewers will eat it up!' "[88]

Though some courts construed the doctrine more narrowly, virtually none refused to read *Gertz* as creating constitutional protection for opinion, and the Supreme Court initially passed up numerous opportunities to review cases applying the constitutional immunity for opinion.[89] As a result, the doctrine was the fastest-growing body of defamation law in the 1980s. Unlike all the other rules that flow from *Sullivan,* the opinion rule worked at the beginning of litigation. Whether the defamatory statement was opinion often could be determined from the publication itself or with a minimum of discovery. It therefore could be invoked by a motion to dismiss for failure to state a cause of action or by an early summary judgment motion. Of all the constitutional defamation rules, therefore, the opinion rule best served as an early screening device by which judges could dispose of cases they considered unmeritorious. Perhaps for that reason, it was used to resolve many cases that at common law would not have been thought to involve opinion.

The opinion doctrine died, however, in *Milkovich v. Lorain Journal Co.*[90] The Supreme Court explicitly refused to adopt the theory that a "separate constitutional privilege for 'opinion' is required to ensure the freedom of expression guaranteed by the First Amendment."[91] The much-quoted sentences from *Gertz* were not intended "to create a wholesale defamation exemption for anything that might be labeled 'opinion.' "[92] The Court explained that statements of opinion often convey implications that can cause as much damage to reputation as explicit statements of fact.[93] It concluded that the other constitutional protections adequately protect the free and uninhibited discussion of public issues, and that any benefits resulting from the proposed privilege for opinion did not outweigh society's " 'pervasive and strong interest in preventing and redressing attacks upon reputation.' "[94]

Nonetheless, the Court recognized that there are "constitutional limits on the *type* of speech which may be the subject of state defamation actions."[95] The Court cited cases in which it had examined the language used and determined that it was constitutionally incapable of a defamatory meaning. In *Greenbelt Cooperative Publishing Association v. Bresler*,[96] the Court reversed the libel judgment won by a developer whose position in negotiations with the city had been characterized as "blackmail." The state courts, analyzing the problem in accordance with established common law tort rules, had held that the word was capable of conveying a defamatory meaning; whether it was so understood therefore was a question for the jury.[97] But the Supreme Court decided that issue itself, holding that a reasonable reader would not have thought the plaintiff was being charged with the crime of blackmail but would have understood that the word was "no more than rhetorical hyperbole, a vigorous epithet used by those who considered Bresler's negotiating position extremely unreasonable."[98] The decision established two principles: (1) interpretation of language can be a constitutional issue;[99] and (2) the reviewing court ultimately does the interpreting, without much regard for traditional judge–jury roles.

The Court employed the Bresler analysis by analogy in *Old Dominion Branch No. 496, National Association of Letter Carriers v. Austin*.[100] The publication in question quoted Jack London's famous definition of a "scab" as a "traitor to his God, his country, his family and his class,"[101] and implied that the plaintiffs fit the definition.[102] The Court held that this implication could not reasonably be understood as defamatory.[103]

The Court employed the first principle of *Bresler in Hustler Magazine, Inc. v. Falwell*[104] and held that an action for intentional infliction of emotional distress was constitutionally precluded where the publication in question was satirical and could not be understood as describing actual facts about the plaintiff. Because the jury had so found in the plaintiff's companion suit for libel,[105] it was not necessary to invoke the second Bresler principle of independent review.

In *Milkovich*, the Court interpreted these three cases as providing constitutional protection for "statements that cannot 'reasonably [be] interpreted as stating actual facts' about an individual,"[106] and asserted that "[t]his provides assurance that public debate will not suffer for lack of 'imaginative expression' or the 'rhetorical hyperbole' which has traditionally added much to the discourse of our Nation."[107] The Court held that these protections, together with the *Hepps* requirement that "a statement on matters of public concern must be provable as false before there can be liability," provide sufficient protection for opinion.[108]

The remaining question, of course, is, "How broad is the exception for statements that do not state actual facts?" The argument for protecting opinion was, in part, that it did not state "actual facts." Dissenting in *Milkovich*, Justice Brennan labeled as "conjecture" the statements that the lower courts had called opinion and argued that conjecture is as important to robust discourse as rhetorical hyperbole.[109] The majority's rejection of that argument makes clear that the exception is not broad enough to swallow up all that previously was protected as opinion. But hyperbole and satire are not the only modes of expression that communicate without stating actual facts, and it seems certain that there will now be pressure to extend the Bresler rationale to many other types of speech.

What Remains Is Not a General Remedy for Defamation

Very few victims of defamation have any hope of remedy under this system. Most have no chance unless, in addition to proving publication of a defamatory statement, (1) they can produce before trial clear and convincing proof that the defendant seriously doubted the truth of the defamation; (2) the trial judge, jury, and all reviewing courts independently agree that such proof is clear and convincing; (3) the accusation is not hyperbolic, rhetorical, satirical, or otherwise incapable of sufficiently precise factual content; (4) the plaintiff is able to prove its falsity, perhaps by the clear-and-convincing standard; and (5) the defendant is not neutrally repeating the defamatory accusation of a responsible organization about a matter of public concern.

The plaintiff who survives this gauntlet may still fall victim to common law rules about special damages, state law privileges, retraction statutes, unusually short statutes of limitations, and other peculiar state limitations. What libel law provides today is not a general remedy with exceptions but a general scheme of nonliability that permits a remedy only in exceptional cases.

THE RESIDUAL REMEDY

The problem *Sullivan* sought to solve was that the common law of libel produced too much self-censorship, deterring critics of official conduct from voicing criticism they believed to be true, "thus dampen-[ing] the vigor and limit[ing] the variety of public debate."[110] The complex rules the Court created to solve the problem have not proved to be a happy solution for reasons that have to do with the way the rules operate in litigation.

Protracted Litigation

The actual-malice requirement introduces into every public-plaintiff case[111] a difficult issue that does not lend itself to preliminary disposition. Indeed, the issue does not readily lend itself to disposition at all. Cases that turn on actual malice sometimes continue for ten or fifteen years.[112]

The actual-malice rule makes constitutional protection dependent on the defendant's state of mind. The decisive question is whether "the defendant in fact entertained serious doubts as to the truth of his publication."[113] This is a complex factual issue that normally cannot be resolved without discovery, sometimes in prodigious quantities. In the most notorious example, a deposition of a television producer "continued intermittently for over a year and filled twenty-six volumes containing nearly 3,000 pages and 240 exhibits."[114] After thirteen years of discovery and discovery-related litigation (including two district court decisions, two appeals to the court of appeals, and one Supreme Court decision), the case was dismissed on the ground that there was not sufficient evidence of actual malice to require trial.[115]

Although the actual-malice rule is frequently invoked on motion for summary judgment,[116] it is not a test that lends itself to summary disposition. Want of actual malice will rarely be apparent from the pleadings alone; thus, it does not provide a ground for a motion to dismiss. If the admonition that a summary judgment movant bears the burden of establishing the absence of any genuine issue of material fact is taken seriously, a defendant seeking disposition on this ground has a classic problem of proving a negative: that he did not entertain serious doubts about the truth of the publication. The Supreme Court has said that the defendant cannot "automatically insure a favorable verdict by testifying that he published with a belief that the statements were true."[117] A fortiori, similar testimony in a self-serving affidavit cannot suffice on motion for summary judgment.[118]

Actual malice, like other state-of-mind determinations, is normally inferred from circumstantial evidence. By way of example, the Supreme Court has said malice might be inferred

> where a story is fabricated by the defendant, is the product of his imagination, or is based wholly on an unverified anonymous telephone call[, or] . . . when the publisher's allegations are so inherently improbable that only a reckless man would have put them in circulation[, or] . . . where there are obvious reasons to doubt the veracity of the informant or the accuracy of his reports.[119]

One difficulty in attempting to decide such an issue on summary judgment is that appraising the relevant circumstances requires development and review of a large amount of factual evidence. A second and more fundamental difficulty is that deciding what inferences to draw from circumstances is peculiarly a jury function.

To make the actual-malice test effective in preventing the chill that would result from fully litigating claims that eventually turn out to be constitutionally barred, the courts have had to bend the rules of summary judgment procedure. Occasionally this is done explicitly. Some of the U.S. courts of appeal, for example, have stated that judges should give such motions special consideration because of the First Amendment interest in preventing the chilling effect on speech that might result from protracted litigation.[120] More often, the courts achieve the same result *sub silentio* simply by rigorously scrutinizing the evidence of actual malice offered by the plaintiff in response to the motion.[121] Summary judgment motions based on want of actual malice tend to be preferred even by courts that do not acknowledge such a preference explicitly.[122] The empirical evidence tends to corroborate this: One study suggests that about 80 percent of all media libel cases are disposed of by summary judgment.[123]

The Supreme Court has never endorsed the notion that summary judgment is a favored remedy in public-figure libel cases, but it has made it easier for such motions to succeed. Without according any special protection to libel defendants as such, the Court held, in *Anderson v. Liberty Lobby, Inc.*,[124] that elevated standards of proof, of which the clear-and-convincing standard is a prominent example, must be applied under the federal summary judgment rule. The result is that a judge hearing a summary judgment motion in a public-figure libel case must make this mind-bending determination: Has the defendant established that there is no genuine issue of material fact as to whether the plaintiff could prove actual malice by clear and convincing proof? In practice, this means that a defendant who supports his or her summary judgment motion with affidavits or other evidence indicating lack of actual malice will win unless the plaintiff can prove actual malice with convincing clarity at that preliminary stage. This creates a formidable early barrier to public-plaintiff libel claims, but only by shifting the difficult matter of proving actual malice from the trial to the discovery stage of litigation. If the plaintiff must prove actual malice with convincing clarity to survive a motion for summary judgment, he or she must be given full opportunity to discover any evidence from which such proof might be inferred. The *Anderson* Court acknowledged as much: "[T]he plaintiff must present affirmative evidence in order to defeat a properly supported motion for summary judgment. This is true even where the evidence is likely to be within the possession of the defendant, as long as the plaintiff has had a full opportunity to conduct discovery."[125] The actual-malice test is thereby made more effective as a device for summary disposition, but only by requiring that a key factual issue in the case be resolved through discovery.

Uncontrolled Damages

At least part of the chilling effect of libel suits results from the possibility of huge damage awards, and the present constitutional law of libel does little to reduce this chill. Public-figure libel litigation usually involves high stakes. In most torts, where plaintiffs must prove the amount of their damage, the facts of the case impose some finite ceiling on potential damages. But in public-figure defamation, where damages are presumed, there is no such ceiling. As Justice Powell observed: "Juries may award substantial sums as compensation for supposed damage to reputation without any proof that such harm actually occurred."[126] The amount is limited only by "the sound discretion of the jury."[127]

Punitive damages, although available for all torts in most jurisdictions, are especially likely to be claimed and awarded in these defamation cases. This is not surprising because a plaintiff who is able to prove knowing or reckless falsity to establish liability is already closer to qualifying for punitive damages than one who need only prove negligence to establish liability. Most states require a showing of ill will or some other species of common law malice in addition to the constitutionally required showing of actual malice as a prerequisite for punitive damages,[128] but the former often can be inferred from the same evidence as the latter.[129]

Because of the availability of presumed and punitive damages, public-figure defamation claimants often seek millions of dollars in damages. Defendants must take such claims seriously because juries sometimes do. Juries have returned verdicts exceeding $15 million in a number of public-figure defamation cases against the media.[130] The *average* verdict in such cases in 1989 and 1990 exceeded $4 million;[131] one study found average libel verdicts to be three times as high as average verdicts in medical malpractice and product liability litigation.[132] Such enormous verdicts rarely survive appeal: The largest affirmed to date in a media case is $3,050,000.[133] Nonetheless, the size of potential recoveries escalates the chilling effect in several ways.

First, large verdicts exact a financial penalty even when they are later reversed. Until they are overturned, they are contingent liabilities on the defendant's balance sheet, threatening the defendant's ability to secure financing or acquire orbe acquired by other entities. The appeal itself often exacts a substantial price. In a jurisdiction that requires a *supersedeas* bond commensurate with the size of the judgment, a large verdict pressures the defendant to settle even when an appeal would be likely to succeed.[134]

Second, even a remote possibility of suffering a catastrophic loss is sobering. Even if the defendant's counsel believes such a loss is highly unlikely, he or she cannot assure the client that it will not happen. The apparent high stakes, therefore, probably have a stronger effect *in terrorem* than the actual loss experience of the media would dictate.

Third, the high stakes make it all but inevitable that litigating the claim will be expensive and time-consuming. If the maximum loss were, say, $200,000, there would be an effective limit on the amount of time and money that could be rationally devoted to either the prosecution or the defense of the claim. When the potential loss is unpredictable, however, it is more difficult for either side to know how much effort is justified. The result is that both sides are likely to spend more in litigation costs than the actual chances of recovery would indicate. This is probably one reason why legal fees account for about 80 percent of the total cost of libel suits against the press.[135] For many potential defendants, the most relevant source of the chilling effect is not the danger of losing a judgment but the prospect of having to pay the costs of defending.[136] To the extent that *Sullivan* discourages plaintiffs from suing, it reduces this source of self-censorship. But against this benefit must be weighed the possibility that the actual-malice rule tends to increase potential verdicts and/or defense costs.

Intrusion into Editorial Processes

In other contexts, the Supreme Court is sensitive to the dangers of judicial intrusion into editorial matters. For example, it invalidated

Florida's right-of-reply statute, partly on the ground that the remedy would involve the courts too deeply in the editorial process.[137] Yet it is hard to conceive of any legal rule that would involve the courts more deeply in that process than the actual-malice rule does.

Under that rule, constitutional protection turns not on what is published, or on the objective truth or falsity of what is published, but on defendants' knowledge or doubts with respect to falsity. Courts are required to determine what defendants thought, and because only defendants know the answer to that, it would hardly do to accept their self-serving testimony as conclusive. So defendants' thoughts are usually inferred from what they did or said.[138]

Inferring state of mind from circumstantial evidence invites the following kinds of inquiries:

1. *What a reporter said to an editor, or vice versa.*[139] Did either express doubts as to the truth of the defamatory matter? Mention contradictory evidence? Question credibility of sources? Express skepticism about the accusations? Suggest further investigation? A defendant who admits having engaged in these journalistically desirable discussions risks weakening the defense by giving the plaintiff a basis for inferring the existence of serious doubts. Moreover, the plaintiff need not accept the defendant's conclusory answers on questions of this sort; under general principles of discovery, plaintiffs are entitled to probe all that was said and make their own decision as to whether the conversation suggested skepticism, reservations, or incredulity.

2. *Information that defendant possessed or considered but did not include in the article.*[140] Evidence that the defendant had information conclusively refuting the defamatory allegation would be proof of knowing falsehood. Evidence that the defendant had information contradicting the allegation may support an inference of serious doubts.[141] The plaintiff therefore is entitled to discover pertinent information in the defendant's possession to determine what inferences might be drawn from it. Reporters' notes, tape recordings, investigative files, correspondence, clippings, and outtakes thus become targets of discovery.[142]

3. *Defendant's attitudes toward plaintiff, toward the subject discussed in the defamatory article, and toward journalism.* A showing that the defendant harbored ill will toward the plaintiff, the sort of common law malice that might support an award of punitive damages, is *not* evidence of actual malice.[143] Such evidence is admissible, however, to show why the defendant might have published despite serious doubts.[144] A history of conflict between the defendant and plaintiff

may be admissible for the same reason.[145] Evidence that the defendant espoused a particular journalistic philosophy or objective (e.g., "sophisticated muckraking") may be admissible to permit an adverse inference to be drawn from the defendant's failure to adequately investigate.[146]

4. *The competitive and journalistic pressures under which the defamatory material was prepared and published.* Courts sometimes suggest that reckless disregard might be inferred from failure to investigate when the matter is not "hot news."[147] This proposition is controversial,[148] but the converse—that the urgency of publication or the immediacy of deadlines is a circumstance preventing the drawing of adverse inferences from failure to investigate—is generally accepted.[149] How the publisher viewed the urgency of the story and why are therefore legitimate matters for inquiry.

5. *The sufficiency of the defendant's journalistic efforts.* Although it is clear that failure to investigate is not in itself evidence of reckless disregard,[150] it is equally clear that other circumstantial evidence may make such a failure relevant.[151] Inherently improbable charges[152] or affirmative evidence of falsity,[153] for example, may permit an inference of reckless disregard to be drawn from the defendant's failure to investigate. Whether such additional circumstances exist is not normally known at the beginning of litigation; the nature, scope, and results of the defendant's journalistic investigation are therefore usually discoverable on the theory that they may become part of the total corpus of circumstantial evidence from which the defendant's state of mind may be adduced.

6. *Defendant's behavior after publication.* The time of publication is the moment at which the defendant's knowledge or doubt is to be determined.[154] Postpublication activities, however, may shed retrospective light on the defendant's state of mind at the time of publication and thus may be discoverable. On the one hand, prompt publication of a retraction is evidence tending to negate a finding of actual malice or an award of punitive damages.[155] On the other hand, destruction of documents pending litigation supports an inference that the documents contained evidence tending to show reckless disregard of the truth.[156]

7. *Credibility of defendant's informants.* The Court has said that "recklessness may be found where there are obvious reasons to doubt the veracity of the informant or the accuracy of his reports."[157] It follows that the plaintiff must be allowed to learn who the informant is, at least as long as the informant is not a confidential source. The plaintiff may be entitled to probe the defendant's relationship with the informant as a possible way of showing that the defendant may

have doubted the source's credibility. This authorizes considerable intrusion into the defendant's relationship with sources. It invites the plaintiff to discover the informant's motivations for cooperating with the defendant, the defendant's previous dealings with the informant, and the defendant's policies regarding such relationships.

8. *Confidential sources.* The greatest intrusion into editorial processes comes when the defendant claims the defamatory material is based on information from a confidential source. For the reasons stated above, the plaintiff is entitled to show that the defendant had reason to doubt the source's credibility. In addition, "professions of good faith" are unlikely to prevail "where a story is fabricated by the defendant, is the product of his imagination, or is based wholly on an unverified anonymous telephone call."[158] The plaintiff is therefore entitled to challenge the very existence of a source, confidential or otherwise. The plaintiff is entitled to pursue the suspicion that the claim of a confidential source conceals the absence of any independent basis for the defamatory accusation.[159] This creates a conundrum: Compelling disclosure of the source has the potential to chill an important newsgathering method,[160] but refusing to do so may deprive the plaintiff of the opportunity to prove that the defamation was indeed a fabrication.

In all these ways, the actual-malice standard requires intrusions, through discovery and at trial, into journalistic matters that are usually not called into question by the other issues in a libel case. Even if the standard were otherwise thought to be highly desirable, its intrusiveness into the relationships between reporters, editors, and sources would still cast doubts on its appropriateness.

Diverting the Inquiry Away from Truth

A plaintiff who files a libel suit against a media entity says, in effect, "That's a lie." In cases to which the actual-malice standard applies, the alleged lie is, by hypothesis, about something in which the public has an interest. Often the "lie" is about matters in which the public has an interest of the highest order: the honesty of a public official, the fitness of a candidate for office, the conduct of a public figure. By filing the suit, the plaintiff publicly challenges the truth of the defendant's statements about a public matter.

The defendant's general denial puts truth at issue. Often, however, the truth or falsity of the statement gets little more attention for the remainder of the litigation. One explanation may be that "[t]ruth is little used as a defense, though it would enable a decisive confrontation, because it may be very expensive to establish."[161] There are at least two other reasons, however, why defendants do not often contest falsity. One is that sometimes it is futile to do so: Plaintiffs probably do not normally sue over statements that are true, or they are at least more likely to sue over falsehoods. The second is that it is easier and less risky to invoke the actual-malice standard. Falsity is a classic fact issue on which the defendant is unlikely to win summary judgment. Actual malice is nominally a fact issue also, but as explained above, the courts have largely taken it away from the jury and made it a basis for summary judgment.

Defending accusations of libel by contesting falsity is, therefore, more likely to require a full-blown trial. Although not necessarily more expensive or time-consuming than a defense on the actual-malice ground, the defense of truth is risky. In England, the jury may treat an unsuccessful defense of truth as a factor aggravating damages.[162] No such instruction is permitted in the United States, but libel defense lawyers know that a similar danger exists. Jurors will not be oblivious to the additional travail suffered by the plaintiff as a result of the defendant's continued assertion of the truth of a statement the jury finds to be false.

By choosing to fight on the ground of actual malice rather than falsity, the defendant gets the best of both worlds. The defendant can formally deny the plaintiff's charge of falsity and maintain a "we-stand-by-our-story" posture without actually standing by the story. Even if it knows the story is false, the defendant can continue to proclaim the truth of the story while in fact building a defense around the actual-malice standard.[163] The availability of the actual-malice defense not only deprives the plaintiff and the public of a judicial determination of the falsity issue but can also deprive the plaintiff and public of an admission of falsity even in those cases where falsity is not seriously contested.

The public has a substantial interest in learning whether the statement published by the defendant and challenged by the plaintiff is true or false. It has very little interest in knowing whether the defendant entertained serious doubts about the truth of the statement. The actual-malice standard, however, almost assures that the latter rather than the former will be the focus of the litigation.

Prejudicing Defendants

Because the actual-malice standard turns the focus of the trial from the plaintiff's conduct to the defendant's, it may increase rather than decrease the threat to speech interests. Before *Sullivan*, the libel trial was often an ordeal for the plaintiff. The plaintiff's conduct and reputation were subjected to scrutiny on the issues of truth and mitigation of damages, respectively, and many victorious plaintiffs came away bloodied.[164] In cases in which actual malice is the decisive issue, however, the blood is often the defendant's. There is little scrutiny of the plaintiff's conduct or reputation if falsity and damage are not seriously at issue. Instead, the focus is on the *defendant's* conduct. The kinds of evidence from which actual malice may be inferred invite searching inquiry into the defendant's practices, motives, and views.[165] Trial lawyers love to paint disputes as contests between good and evil, and a trial in which actual malice is the controlling issue gives the skillful plaintiff's lawyer an unusual opportunity to portray the defendant as journalistic evil incarnate.

After a trial in which much of the time is spent dissecting evidence that the defendant knowingly lied or ignored its own serious doubts, one is not surprised at the jury's inclination to punish the defendant. It is not a trial in which the jury sees both parties as mortals with imperfections. It is one in which little attention is paid to the plaintiff, while the jury decides whether the defendant is a liar or merely incompetent.

In such a trial, if the jury finds actual malice, an award of punitive damages is almost a foregone conclusion. A jury could deny them on the ground that common law malice is not shown though actual malice is, but usually evidence of the latter makes it easy for the jury to find whatever additional level of culpability the state requires for an award of punitive damages.[166] These dynamics create potent threats of punishment for unpopular journalism. The evidentiary focus created by the actual-malice test gives the jury the motive to punish, and a finding that the test is met gives the jury the means. It is not surprising that jury awards are high in cases where actual malice is found.[167]

The purpose of the actual-malice standard was to protect robust public discussion by reducing the extent to which the press censors itself due to the threat of litigation. It undoubtedly serves that purpose in various irrational ways—for example, by creating an exaggerated impression in the minds of some potential plaintiffs and lawyers that the press is impervious to public-plaintiff libel suits. The rule's actual effect on litigation, however, gives the press more cause for anxiety than for comfort.

THE REPUTATIONAL AND SOCIAL COSTS

Even if the actual-malice standard were an efficient and effective way of protecting the press and other speakers, it could not be pronounced a success without taking into account the price it exacts from other values. One of those, the cost to personal reputation, is obvious. The very purpose of the standard is to deny a remedy to some whose reputation has been harmed by defamatory falsehoods. There are at least two other exactions, less obvious but perhaps even more costly to society. One is the effect on the political process; the other is the effect on public discourse generally.

Reputational Costs

By design, the actual-malice standard deprives public figures and public officials of any legal remedy for most defamatory falsehoods. As explained previously,[168] public officials are not limited to elected officials, or even to those we would normally think of as officials, but include ordinary governmental employees such as police officers. The public-figure category includes celebrities, persons who seek to influence the outcome of public controversies, and some who are involuntarily caught up in public events or issues. The category is not restricted to national celebrities or national controversies.[169] As a result, millions of Americans are likely to be classified as public officials or public figures when they are defamed.

The actual-malice standard also denies any remedy to many who are neither public officials nor public figures. Anyone who is defamed in connection with a matter of public concern must prove actual malice if he or she cannot prove actual injury. This limitation rarely bars suit because actual injury can be established by proof of emotional distress, which few defamation plaintiffs lack.[170] But it often denies any remedy as a practical matter because the plaintiff's provable actual injury is not large enough to induce a lawyer to take the case on a contingency-fee basis.[171] Many, if not most, private plaintiffs cannot afford to litigate unless they can recover presumed damages, and those damages are unavailable unless actual malice is shown.

The actual-malice rule, therefore, leaves vast numbers of people—perhaps most of the victims of media defamation—with no legal remedy for damage to reputation. The cost to the victims, in terms of anguish and reputational harm, is incalculable. There is room, of course, for much disagreement about the law's ability to identify and quantify injuries of this sort. Because of these doubts, the law no longer provides a remedy for some of the wrongs that produce these injuries, such as seduction and breach of promise to marry.[172] But for many centuries and in most of the civilizations of the world, the injuries caused by defamation were thought to be harms for which the law can and should provide remedies. Eloquent reasons for this virtually universal protection of reputation have been advanced throughout history,[173] but the contemporary consensus is captured in Justice Stewart's classic explanation: "The right of a man to the protection of his own reputation from unjustified invasion and wrongful hurt reflects no more than our basic concept of the essential dignity and worth of every human being—a concept at the root of any decent system of ordered liberty."[174] It is probably safe to say that no major legal system in the world provides as little protection for reputation as the United States now provides.

The Supreme Court has never candidly faced up to the reputational costs exacted by the actual-malice rule. Instead, the Court has tried to minimize the sacrifice of reputations by unconvincing rationalizations, the two most prominent being the self-help and waiver rationalizations.[175]

The self-help rationalization contends that public plaintiffs are less vulnerable to reputational harm than are private persons because they usually have more access to media and therefore more opportunity to protect their reputation through self-help. Justice Brennan demolished this argument in a passage in *Rosenbloom v. Metromedia, Inc.*[176] that deserves full quotation:

> While the argument that public figures need less protection because they can command media attention to counter criticism may be true for some very prominent people, even then it is the rare case where the denial overtakes the original charge. Denials, retractions, and corrections are not "hot" news, and rarely receive the prominence of the original story. When the public official or public figure is a minor functionary, or has left the position that put him in the public eye . . . the argument loses all of its force. In the vast majority of libels involving public officials or public figures, the ability to respond through the media will depend on the same complex factor on which the ability of a private individual depends: the unpredictable event of the media's continuing interest in the story. Thus the unproved, and highly improbable, generalization that an as yet undefined class of "public figures" involved in matters of public concern will be better able to respond through the media than private individuals also involved in such matters seems too insubstantial a reed on which to rest a constitutional distinction.[177]

The waiver argument as articulated by Justice Powell is as unpersuasive as the self-help argument:

> [T]here is a compelling normative consideration underlying the distinction between public and private defamation plaintiffs. An individual who decides to seek governmental office must accept certain necessary

146, 405

consequences of that involvement in public affairs. He runs the risk of closer public scrutiny than might otherwise be the case. . . . Those classed as public figures stand in a similar position. Hypothetically, it may be possible for someone to become a public figure through no purposeful action of his own, but the instances of truly involuntary public figures must be exceedingly rare. For the most part those who attain this status have assumed roles of especial prominence in the affairs of society. Some occupy positions of such persuasive power and influence that they are deemed public figures for all purposes. More commonly, those classed as public figures have thrust themselves to the forefront of particular public controversies in order to influence the resolution of the issues involved. In either event, they invite attention and comment.[178]

This argument is riddled with fallacies. First, the idea that a public official "runs the risk of closer public scrutiny" hardly compels the conclusion that he or she must be left without remedy when the scrutiny is actually defamatory falsehood. Logic supports the opposite conclusion equally well: Because the risk of close public scrutiny—and therefore defamation—is greater, the law should be more protective of the reputational interest.[179]

Second, the public-official classification is by no means limited to those who "seek governmental office" in the usual understanding of that phrase. For example, police officers are almost invariably classed as public officials, no matter how low their rank.[180] Whatever validity the waiver argument might have for those who seek elective office, it has little for the individual who is a "public official" simply because he or she holds a position of some responsibility in some unit of government.

Third, many public figures are not people who have thrust themselves to the forefront of public controversies. Rather, they are people who have been unusually successful in their career—whether in business, the arts, sports, entertainment, or some other profession. Johnny Carson is a public figure because he is a popular television entertainer, not because he seeks to influence public affairs.[181] His wife is a public figure simply because she is married to him.[182] A professional football player can become a public figure by being involved in a highly publicized player trade.[183] A belly dancer may be a public figure because she welcomed publicity about her performances.[184] These people have made no choice to sacrifice reputation in exchange for power and influence; indeed, those attributes sometimes seem to accrue in largest measure to those who seek them least. Power and influence, along with fame and wealth, simply tend to follow success.[185]

Fourth, and most important, the waiver argument is circular. If those who seek public office or seek to influence the outcome of public controversies waive some portion of reputational protection by doing so, it is only because the law says so. It cannot explain *why* the law says so. Public figures do not choose to forego remedies for defamation. True, they may know that they are more likely to be discussed and hence to be defamed, but as suggested above, that need not weaken their claim to the law's protection.

Although the Court's rationalizations for minimizing the reputational costs of the actual-malice rule are unconvincing, the disregard of these costs has not been widely criticized. Perhaps this reflects a sense that the Court is right even if its reasons are unpersuasive. If one believes that reputational costs are in fact negligible, the lack of satisfactory reasons for ignoring them is less troublesome.

The unarticulated reason may be a belief that public plaintiffs are intrinsically less worthy of protection than others. Perhaps the real "compelling normative consideration underlying the distinction between public and private defamation plaintiffs"[186] is a perception that public officials and public figures *deserve* to be defamed. Perhaps some people believe that public officials and candidates, as a class, are more venal than the rest of us, or that they care less about their reputation. Maybe it is thought that they deserve to "die by the sword" because they live by it—that they probably destroyed or damaged the reputation of others in their own climb to prominence and therefore deserve little sympathy when they fall prey to similar tactics.[187] There may be a feeling that a license to defame those who achieve prominence in public life is a fair price to exact as a cost of success: Just as the wealthy should pay more in taxes, the famous should give up more in the way of reputation.[188] Maybe the idea is more explicitly political: that denying the prominent some measure of the usual protection for reputation is a useful counterweight to the power—social, political, and economic—they otherwise enjoy.

Some of these perceptions would be applicable to public figures as well as to public officials. A steady diet of disclosures about the personal, moral, and financial peccadillos of entertainment stars, business leaders, evangelists, sports heroes, and other celebrities may persuade some that these people too are more venal than the rest of us or less concerned about reputation. One may think that the adulation they receive is often undeserved and that undeserved condemnation therefore is no great injustice. Because public figures enjoy a great deal of power as a result of the favorable attention of the press and public, fairness might require a counterbalance to this heightened power by allowing the press and public the right to scrutinize and criticize them.[189]

Each of these views undoubtedly has some subscribers. On balance, however, I reject the proposition that public plaintiffs deserve less protection than others. I doubt that as a class, public plaintiffs are more venal. Even if they are, their venality can be taken into account more fairly by evaluating their transgressions in individual cases.

The rationale that public plaintiffs should have to suffer adverse publicity because they have benefited from good publicity, or because they have harmed reputations on their way to the top, is inapplicable to many public plaintiffs. Many lesser public figures and lower-level public officials have done neither. Even among the most prominent elected officials and celebrities, not all have lived by the sword of defamation.

The view that defamation is a just counterbalance to power should at least be critically examined. Those holding this view should be required to explain why other limitations on power are inadequate. If we accept that argument, we should decide openly how much reputational protection must be sacrificed to effectively control the power, instead of pretending that the powerful have waived their right to reputational protection.

The courts have never espoused the idea that the falsehoods protected by the actual-malice rule cause no harm, or that those harmed are unworthy of a remedy.[190] But neither have the courts forthrightly acknowledged that the rule exacts a serious sacrifice in the form of uncompensated injury to reputation.

Social Costs

The reputational costs described above are primarily private costs borne by the individuals who are left without a remedy for their reputational injuries. In addition to those costs, the actual-malice rule also exacts a price from society at large. It imposes costs on public life, by which I mean not only politics but also cultural, religious, educational, and business life.

The actual-malice rule obviously deters participation in public life.[191] No rational person can fail to take into account the reputational consequences of this rule when deciding whether to run for public office. Although the full effect of the rule and all its accoutrements is probably understood by very few lawyers, let alone nonlawyers, virtually all potential candidates must have some awareness that it is difficult for a public official or political candidate to recover for defamation.[192]

Some of this deterrence may be salutary. To the extent that those deterred fear disclosure of their future (or past) misdeeds in office, the rule is beneficial. But it undoubtedly deters others who do not fear disclosure of misdeeds but do fear false accusations about matters in which they are blameless.[193] Even those so confident of their reputation that they fear no harm from falsehoods may be deterred from public life simply because they have no stomach for a life in which they know they and their families will have to endure scurrilous aspersions. Defending a state law precursor of the actual-malice rule in 1908, the Kansas Supreme Court said, "Here at least men of unimpeachable character from all political parties continually present themselves as candidates in sufficient numbers to fill the public offices and manage the public institutions, and the conduct of the press is as honest, clean, and free from abuse as it is in states where the narrow view of privilege obtains."[194] It is difficult to be so sanguine today about the quality of people who present themselves for public office.

The constitutional rules also create risks for other forms of citizen participation in public matters—from the local PTA to religious controversies to the abortion controversy and other great issues of the day. Although not everyone may realize that the actual-malice rule also applies to public figures, here, too, any observant person can see that those who participate in public matters seem to receive little protection from the law of defamation.

The rule's deterrent effect on participation in public life has a corollary: Those who choose to participate despite the risk are likely to be *different* from those who are deterred from participation. Vulnerability to certain types of defamation often depends on the victim's generation, life experiences, profession, or ethnic background. A false accusation may seem plausible because it fits a stereotype: an accusation of drug use directed at someone who grew up in the ghetto, a charge of sexual promiscuity against someone who was a college student in the late 1960s, a rumor of organized crime connections directed at a person with an Italian surname, or an implication of dishonesty directed at someone employed in the legal gambling industry. Some people may avoid public life simply because they fit a high-risk stereotype. Those who take the risks of participation may be people who care less about their reputation than others do—people who might say, "I don't care what they say about me as long as they spell my name right." Personality types who relish the combat of personal attack and counterattack may be attracted to public life while other types are repelled.[195]

These corollary effects are most pronounced in politics—both electoral and issue politics—but they are also felt in other fields of public life. In some aspects of show business, for example, a thick skin is a virtual necessity and a willingnes s to endure or even cultivate the most scurrilous publicity can be an asset. A talented actor or popular musician who lacks a tolerance for scandal may be at a competitive disadvantage. A person who is deeply disturbed by defamatory false-hoods may find it hard to survive at the highest and most visible levels of sports, business, religion, or education.

These effects are all speculative, but so is the "chilling effect" on speech that the actual-malice rule exists to prevent. The constitutional law of libel rests on the unproven assumption that failure to protect those who report on public life will tend to deter news reporting and commentary. This proposition has never been demonstrated empir-ically, but it is an intuition no one seriously challenges.[196] It is no more compelling intuitively, however, than the assumption that failure to protect those who participate in public life will deter some persons from participating. Most of the important choices in law, as in life, have to be made on the basis of unprovable assumptions about human behavior. I do not doubt the existence of the "chilling effect" or deprecate its importance merely because it has not been empirically confirmed. Neither can we afford to ignore the deterrent effects of the actual malice rule for want of empirical proof.

The actual-malice rule has an effect not only on participation in, but also on discussion about, public life. The journalistic commitment to substantive coverage of issues is always in some competition with market pressures to serve the public appetite for scandal. One of the challenges of journalism is to engage the public's attention in sub-stantive matters against the competition of the titillating.[197] Though scandal may be difficult to uncover, it is comparatively easy to pre-sent. A world that can be explained by mendacity, perfidy, or venality is easier to understand than one that is a product of historical, eco-nomic, demographic, social, and scientific forces, as well as human failings. The former view tends to be self-reinforcing; the more scandal we see, the more plausible it seems that scandal explains our situation.[198] The latter view, on the other hand, tends to be confusing and inconsistent; there is always disagreement as to what the forces are, let alone what their significance may be. Evaluating these forces requires more mental effort from the reader or viewer. For the journalist, uncovering scandal is likely to seem a surer route to recognition and advancement than the tedious and incremental pro-cess of identifying and explaining the other forces that shape the world.[199]

The journalism of scandal therefore enjoys a considerable advan-tage over its alternatives, even without help from the law. The actual-malice rule reinforces that advantage by eliminating most of the risks associated with the journalism of scandal, at least when it is directed at public officials or public figures. It thus throws the weight of the law on the side of the public appetite for scandal. This tilt encourages even those in the press who would prefer another direction to gravitate toward scandal.

These two effects—skewing the personality profile of those who are willing to participate in public life and encouraging journalistic preoccupation with scandal—exalt a politics of scandal. In election campaigns, voting records and positions on issues cannot successfully compete for voter attention against accusations of adultery, larceny, and corruption. The experience and qualifications of nominees to high judicial or executive office are hard to keep in focus when the nominee's enemies are free to offer more lurid images without much need to worry about whether they are true or false.[200] The result is a dynamic that debases politics and public life.[201] As Justice Stewart observed, "[T]he poisonous atmosphere of the easy lie can infect and degrade a whole society."[202]

The other major social cost of the actual-malice rule is its deprecation of truth in public discourse. The rule's very purpose is to protect the dissemination of falsehoods. As a consequence, "the stream of information about public officials and public affairs is polluted and often remains polluted by false information."[203] I do not doubt that at times falsehood must be protected, even defamatory falsehood. Indeed, I fully subscribe to the Court's determination that defamatory falsehoods must be protected unless they can be proved false. But we must not forget that these concessions are made to facilitate the pursuit of truth. The utility of protecting some falsehood in the course of that pursuit must always be carefully weighed against the ultimate cost to the truth-seeking enterprise.[204]

To the extent that the actual-malice rule protects falsehood, it also undermines the credibility of the press. If the public knows the press is legally accountable for defamatory falsehoods, it may infer that the press must have some evidence that a defamatory accusation is true. A reader or viewer who understands the actual-malice rule can only infer that the press believes the victim will not be able to prove with convincing clarity that the publisher had serious doubts as to the truth of the accusation. Few readers and viewers are that sophisticated, of course, but surely many sense in a general way that the law imposes only rather loose constraints of truth on the press's discussion of public people. To that extent, the press is as much a victim as a beneficiary of the actual-malice rule. The rule devalues the currency of public information, and the strength of that currency is ultimately more important to the press than to anyone else.[205]

How can the actual malice-rule be underprotective of *both* speech and reputation? At least part of the answer lies in an information gap arising from the nature of the actual-malice requirement.[206] Actual malice is a subjective state-of-mind test: whether the defendant had serious doubts about the truth of the accusation. When the victim is deciding whether to sue, he or she usually has little information about this issue. Moreover, the victim cannot gain this information quickly once litigation begins. Defendants' pleadings normally deny the existence of actual malice in some conclusory fashion, and defendants' answers to interrogatories are unlikely to contain any more on this issue than self-serving declarations that the defendant believed the publication to be true. Only after more thorough discovery, with the certainty of expense and the potential for intrusion into editorial processes, is the plaintiff likely to be able to make any informed judgment as to the likelihood of proving actual malice.

In cases in which actual malice is an issue, plaintiffs often have no way of knowing whether they have any chance of succeeding until discovery is completed. They must therefore put themselves and defendants to considerable expense and inconvenience *before* they have the information needed to make rational litigation decisions. It is not surprising, then, if they tend to overestimate their chances of succeeding;[207] given a choice between an uninformed decision to sue and an equally uninformed decision to desist, plaintiffs understandably might choose to err on the side of seeking redress.[208]

To the extent that the actual-malice rule forces plaintiffs to make their litigation decisions without adequate information about the decisive issue in the case, it almost guarantees that hopeless cases will be filed and litigated at least through discovery. This result burdens speech without any commensurate benefit to reputation and helps explain why the actual-malice rule does not add to the field of free speech all that it subtracts from the protection of individual reputation.[209]

OPPORTUNITIES FOR REFORM

Reconsidering the Constitutional Law

Media discontent with the existing system of libel law could be alleviated by changes consistent with existing constitutional rules—for example, by abolishing the tort altogether or by further restricting the cause of action to eliminate large recoveries or reduce litigation costs. The need to reduce burdens on speech, though, is only one side of the case for libel law reform; the present system's evisceration of remedies for victims of defamation is equally unsatisfactory. Victims' discontent with the system can be addressed only by changing some of the constitutional rules or by finding better remedies consistent with the existing rules. A reform agenda should not foreclose either possibility.

First, we should assume that if the remedies are less burdensome on speech, the constitutional limitations can be less burdensome on plaintiffs. Media partisans sometimes declaim as if they believe no scheme of libel law can be constitutional unless it retains all the rules that have evolved from *New York Times v. Sullivan.*[210] Neither the logic nor the history of the rules supports that proposition, however. The rules represent the Court's "continuing effort to define the proper accommodation" between "the need for a vigorous and uninhibited press and the legitimate interest in redressing wrongful injury."[211] The logic of balancing implies that when the weight on one side changes, an adjustment on the other side may be appropriate. The Court made just such an adjustment in private-plaintiff cases, holding that actual malice need not be required when recovery is confined to actual injury, though it must be shown if punitive or presumed damages are sought.[212]

Sullivan was a response to libel law as it existed in 1964, when the press enjoyed far less protection than it has today. One of the rationales for the actual-malice rule was the belief that under then-existing law, speech would be chilled "even though it is believed to be true and even though it is in fact true, because of doubt whether it can be proved in court or fear of the expense of having to do so."[213] Now that plaintiffs must prove falsity, this concern is alleviated. Moreover, when *Sullivan* was decided, there were no constitutional rules protecting nonfactual expressions or neutral reportage and no authorization of judicial activism on the issues of defamatory meaning, substantial truth, and colloquium.[214] Quite apart from the actual-malice rule, the press today enjoys far more protection than it did in 1964. It is nonsense to insist that *Sullivan*, the Court's first effort to protect the press, must continue to be read as if the Court has done nothing to preserve freedom of the press since then.

Second, we should recognize that the present constitutional restrictions are not all mutually dependent. The rules on nonfactual expression, neutral reportage, and falsity can stand quite independently of the actual-malice rule (and of each other). The relationships among independent review and clear and convincing proof, on the one hand, and actual malice, substantial truth, colloquium, and defamatory meaning, on the other, are intertwined, but perhaps not inextricably so. Aggressive judicial review developed largely in the context of actual malice, but now that the practice is established, judges could continue to employ it in connection with other issues even if the actual-malice rule were abolished. Likewise, even though convincing clarity originated as the standard of proof for actual malice, it could easily be applied to other issues.

Third, the actual-malice rule itself should be reconsidered. Although it was originally the centerpiece of constitutional libel law, there are now many other sources of protection. Moreover, it is now clear that however useful that rule may be, the costs it imposes on reputation, on public life, and on the press are substantial. The Court has shown remarkable fealty to the rule and is probably unlikely to abolish it outright. But its applicability to celebrities (and perhaps other public figures who cannot be analogized to public officials) may well be ripe for reconsideration.

Fourth, the Court should encourage judges to decide certain crucial issues before trial. Defamatory meaning, colloquium, and substantial truth are normally treated as jury issues requiring trial, but the Court has already subordinated the jury's role by allowing independent review of those issues after trial. If the jury's finding is not to be respected anyway, it is more sensible to allow judges to make the determination at the beginning of litigation than to require the parties to engage in years of discovery, litigation, and appeals, only to have an appellate court eventually dispose of the case on an issue that could have been decided on the pleadings or with minimal discovery.

Early decision should also be encouraged when the statement sued upon is claimed to be nonfactual. Although the Court was right to stop the unprincipled growth of the opinion defense, it was equally correct in recognizing that there are some statements that, though capable of defamatory interpretation, are not sufficiently factual to provide the basis for a libel claim. The Court should make it clear that judges have wide latitude to decide that matter—and other issues relating to defamatory meaning, colloquium, and substantial truth—on a motion to dismiss or an early summary judgment motion.

Finally, the Court should rethink the roles of judge and jury. The constitutional libel law reforms of the past quarter century have been effective in protecting speech primarily because they have transferred a great deal of power from juries to judges. The actual-malice rule, by itself, would have effected comparatively little change in the law of defamation; it would have merely created another issue for the jury. Actual malice has become an effective obstacle to recovery only because of the ancillary rules of clear and convincing proof and independent review that enable judges to take matters out of the jury's hands altogether. Allowing judges to decide who is a public figure and what types of speech may be actionable has further diminished the jury's role. Since independent review occurs only when the jury finds for the plaintiff, this shift of power is a one-way movement that benefits defendants exclusively.

Historically, this denial of jury power in the name of the First Amendment is ironic, to say the least. Libel law reformers of the eighteenth century believed that the salvation of free speech lay in the transfer of power to juries. They saw the state and its judges as the principal threat to free speech, so they fought to give juries power to determine the defamatory tendencies of words, exonerate defendants upon proof of truth, and judge the law as well as the facts by giving general verdicts.[215] It is understandable that the Court has chosen not to announce that it is rejecting the assumptions of the framers of the First Amendment. That it is doing so must be understood, however, if we are to appreciate fully what is occurring in the law of defamation.

Ironic as it may be, the shift of power away from juries is unquestionably necessary. Today it is the prejudice and profligacy of juries that threaten free speech, not the criminal law of libel. For whatever reasons, the media today are so out of favor with the general populace that reliance on juries as reliable protectors of freedom of the press would be nostalgic nonsense. On the whole, judges are more sympathetic to speech interests than jurors and more sensitive to subtle threats against those interests. We may as well be candid: Constitutional protection of speech against the chilling effects of libel consists primarily of rules encouraging judges to decide factual matters that previously were left to juries. Judges now hold the ultimate power to deny recovery for want of clear and convincing proof of actual malice, because the statement is not sufficiently factual, false, or defamatory or because it does not sufficiently identify the plaintiff.

Having abandoned the fact of jury hegemony in libel, we should now abandon the fiction of it. Allowing judges to make these determinations early in the litigation avoids the expense and delay of unnecessary jury trials. These benefits are lost when judges make their decisive judgments only *after* a jury has made its own determination of the matter. We cling to the notion that the judge's role, though "independent" of the jury, is still one of "review." In some cases, judges convert the power of independent review into a power of preliminary disposition by fudging on the usual summary judgment standards.[216] In most cases, however, to preserve an illusion of deference to the jury, judges exercise their power only at the end of litigation. Even though the eventual holding is that no liability can be constitutionally imposed whatever the jury may find, that judgment is not made until after jury trial.

When the determination depends on full development of facts, there can be no preliminary disposition no matter who makes the decision. Many cases, though, are ultimately disposed of on the basis of judicial analysis of the publication itself. Cases are litigated for years, only to have an appellate court eventually decide that the statement itself is constitutionally incapable of supporting a libel judgment.[217]

Devising a way to obtain these crucial determinations without full trial of all issues is an obvious avenue of reform. What is needed is a mechanism for identifying issues that (1) are likely to be decisive, (2) can be decided independently of other issues in the case, and (3) are suitable for resolution by judges rather than juries. Procedures would have to be created to secure the trial judge's decision on these matters in advance of trial. It might or might not be desirable to provide for interlocutory appeals; to avoid expanding litigation in the attempt to simplify it, the process would have to be kept lean and restricted to truly decisive issues.

These are not easy matters to resolve, but the most perilous step has already been taken in the decision to transfer the ultimate decision from juries to judges. Defendants, who now enjoy two chances of prevailing on any independently reviewable issue, may argue that taking away one of those chances denies their right to jury trial, but the argument is untenable. If plaintiffs' rights are not violated by allowing judges to ignore jury findings after the fact, defendants' right to jury trial cannot be violated by making the same findings before trial.

Litigation Costs

The impact of litigation costs on media is well recognized. The chilling effect of which the media complain obviously does not come solely from the judgments they ultimately pay, since the media enjoy success rates that most other classes of tort defendants would envy. Rather, the chill comes primarily from the cost of litigating. Some of these costs, such as the loss of credibility and interference with editorial and business functions, are intangible. The major cost, however, is the expense of litigating in an area where even the most ordinary case is likely to involve complex constitutional issues. Controlling these costs must be a target of any reform.

Less well recognized are the effects of litigation costs on defamation plaintiffs. Plaintiffs probably do not match media defendants' expenditures dollar for dollar, but a plaintiff must incur substantial expense to compete against a defendant who is willing to spend six- or seven-figure amounts. For high-profile public-figure plaintiffs, litigation expenses in excess of $1 million are not unusual.[218]

Informed lawyers considering taking libel cases on a contingent-fee basis must look for even larger recoveries than they would require in other tort cases because they know that libel cases, at least against media defendants, tend to be expensive and protracted, defendants are not likely to settle, and judgments are likely to be reversed on appeal. Unless their litigation decisions are utterly unconstrained by financial considerations, those few plaintiffs who pay their lawyers on an hourly basis must make some similar calculation.[219]

For most plaintiffs, libel litigation is economically feasible only because of the possibility of recovering presumed or punitive damages. Very few libel plaintiffs suffer enough provable pecuniary loss to justify litigating for that element of damages alone. In the physical torts, the expansiveness of damages for pain and suffering often makes it possible for plaintiffs to seek recovery for the medical expenses and lost earnings that otherwise would not be worth suing for. Damages for emotional distress do not fully serve that role in defamation because juries normally do not award them as generously as they award damages for pain and suffering.

Reforms that deny recovery for presumed and punitive damages therefore create a substantial risk of abolishing the libel action de facto. Liability can be abolished almost as effectively by making it uneconomical for plaintiffs to sue as by adopting rules denying liability. Retaining the present liability rules but restricting recovery to actual injury would have that effect because it would reduce the economic incentive to sue without reducing the expense of litigating. Reforms that reduce potential recovery (or replace monetary recovery with some other remedy such as declaratory judgment) must also scale down litigation costs so plaintiffs can afford to pursue the remedy.

One cannot assume that reducing the stakes will necessarily reduce litigation costs because financial constraints do not operate symmetrically on defamation plaintiffs and media defendants. The latter are potential repeat players in the libel arena. Most are committed to a policy of aggressively contesting all libel claims.[220] Their litigation decisions in a particular case may be influenced by the effects of those decisions on other potential libel plaintiffs. Spending $100,000 successfully defending a case that could have been settled for $50,000 may be perfectly sound economically if it deters others from suing. Likewise, a manifest willingness to spend $100,000 to defend a suit for $50,000 in actual injury makes sense if it persuades the plaintiff that winning will cost too much to be economically rewarding.

Even the declaratory judgment action is subject to this repeat-player influence. Media might decide that their long-term interests require that they contest such actions with a vigor totally out of proportion to the stakes in the particular case, with the aim of discouraging future declaratory judgment plaintiffs.[221] The solution is to either (1) make it possible for both sides to spend enough to be competitive or (2) control litigation costs so neither plaintiffs nor defendants are priced out of the libel litigation market. Either is exceedingly difficult to achieve.

Providing a mechanism to shift litigation costs may create more problems than it solves. A rule awarding attorneys' fees to the prevailing party is not a satisfactory solution. Such a rule increases the stakes for both sides when the objective should be to reduce them. If both sides have perfect information about their chances of winning and act rationally on that information, a fee-shifting rule should have no effect on total litigation costs. But if either side overestimates its chances, it is likely to overspend, unjustifiably increasing the total cost of litigation to the detriment of the party that eventually pays the costs. The available data suggest that on the plaintiff's side, at least, lawyers' expectations of success tend to be "wildly overoptimistic."[222] And defendants, for the reasons described above, may overspend in particular cases to achieve long-term benefits in other cases.

A two-way fee-shifting rule is unsatisfactory for the additional reason that in practice it will tend to be a one-way rule. Media defendants, as a class, are more likely to be able to pay a judgment, including a judgment for attorneys' fees, than defamation plaintiffs. Thus, prevailing plaintiffs would get a reliable source of recompense for litigation costs, while prevailing defendants would often get only an uncollectable judgment. Attempting to require the parties to give some advance assurance of ability to pay might create as many problems as it solved. For example, a rule requiring plaintiffs to post substantial bonds to assure payment of attorneys' fees might make it easier than ever for defendants to price plaintiffs out of the contest. A one-way rule, awarding attorneys' fees to prevailing plaintiffs, would make it easier for deserving plaintiffs to obtain a remedy. It would create a plaintiff's libel bar, which would make the level of expertise more nearly equal on each side and thus make the system work more esthetically and perhaps more justly. But it might also foster an unacceptable level of harassment of the media.

Limiting litigation costs is also problematic. The usual assumption is that simplifying the issues—for example, omitting any fault requirement from the declaratory judgment action—will reduce litigation costs enough to make the remedy economically feasible. No matter how streamlined the proceeding, however, it is sure to leave the determined litigator many opportunities to make the litigation costly to the opponent. Determinations of truth or falsity, which seem to be the irreducible minimum in all the reform proposals, can sometimes be expensive undertakings. Most of the evidence in the *Westmoreland* case, on which both parties are said to have spent at least $7 million,[223] went to the issue of falsity. Many of the proposals impose threshold requirements, such as demands for retraction. The adequacy of the plaintiff's demand and effectiveness of the defendant's response are sure to present issues that can quickly multiply the cost of the proceeding. Moreover, no reform can assure that there will not be expensive quarrels over jurisdictional, procedural, and evidentiary points.

The reformers' dilemma is that anything that makes it financially feasible for plaintiffs to litigate elevates the stakes. This induces both sides to litigate more vigorously and expensively, diminishing the effectiveness of the remedy while increasing the chill on speech. The root of the problem is that media defendants, as a class, have the means and the incentive to spend what it takes to make sure libel does not become an effective remedy. I have little confidence that fee shifting can solve this problem. The professional zeal and economic interest of lawyers conspire to escalate fees on both sides. A better solution is to devise remedies that cannot be thwarted by a willingness to outlitigate the opponent—a challenge that our legal system is rarely able to meet. Proposals to substitute a vindicatory remedy for monetary awards are an attempt to do this, but they cannot succeed unless they can solve the problem of financing litigation without escalating costs.

The dilemma could be solved by a system that gave defamation victims relatively easy recoveries of modest amounts of money. The liability rules would have to be simple and clear enough to make it futile for defendants to spend large sums trying to defeat them, and courts would have to police the size of awards vigilantly. Here, too, the natural proclivities of the bar would press for escalation: Plaintiffs' lawyers would press for higher awards and defendants' lawyers would seek new liability limitations that would create additional litigable issues. Sustained efforts to substitute modest but accessible remedies for full-blown tort litigation have been reasonably successful, however, in other areas (such as worker's compensation), and a similar determination might succeed in libel.

Politics of Reform

The principal interest groups affected by libel law are the media and their lawyers and insurers. Nonmedia defendants[224] and plaintiffs are too randomly distributed to have a collective voice, and there is no organized plaintiffs' libel bar. Libel law reform therefore has no political constituency unless the media and their allies support it. So far they have not done so.

For all the rhetoric about the adverse effects of libel law on speech, it is entirely possible that media fear the chill of expensive litigation less than they fear the chill of more frequent accountability. The former is a known evil, while the perils of the latter can only be guessed. A declaratory judgment remedy, for example, might enmesh the media, or particular media outlets, in many minor-league lawsuits over inaccuracies that today go unchallenged. There are media antagonists, both national and local, who would happily avail themselves of new opportunities to bedevil the media they dislike. The courts might eventually find ways to deny a remedy to those who would use it to harass without withdrawing it from those who have been injured, but it is impossible to assure the media in advance that new remedies cannot be misused.

Any reform that must be accomplished one state at a time offers little comfort to the national media or even to local media whose broadcasts or publications cross state lines. Their risk assessments must take into account the least protective state law to which they may be subject. The flexibility of modern jurisdictional, venue, and choice-of-law rules often allows a plaintiff to choose a state whose law is congenial.[225] The benefits of statutory reform would be fully available to the media only if adopted federally or by all the states uniformly. Constitutional protections have the considerable advantage of being applicable instantly and uniformly throughout the United States.

Moreover, media may feel they have less to gain from reform than the reformers suppose. What the reform proposals offer the media are various devices for avoiding full-scale litigation and disastrously large judgments. But the media already have some control over these risks. Many proposed reforms would allow the media to avoid all or most liability by promptly retracting.[226] Although under current law retraction does not bar liability altogether, it goes a long way toward minimizing risks. Retraction will dissuade some, and perhaps most, plaintiffs from suing.[227] Some states have statutes limiting recovery to pecuniary losses if the defendant retracts. These statutes give the prospective defendant the power to virtually eliminate any risk of a "megaverdict," and often make it uneconomical for the victim to sue at all. In other states, retraction is admissible in mitigation of damages, and frequently it defuses the threat of punitive damages.

Another common feature of many reform proposals is an attempt to limit damage awards, usually by denying punitive or presumed damages. But the media already have some opportunity to control losses through settlement. A cap on damages is better than the settlement option, from the media's point of view, because it also (1) controls losses in cases in which the plaintiff refuses to settle and (2) tends to lower the cost of settling by reducing the stakes. But the gain is the difference between a sure method of controlling losses and an imperfect one, not the difference between a sure method and no control at all. Offering the media a de jure or de facto limit on damages is therefore less enticing than it would be if the media had no present method of controlling losses.

An invisible but important force behind all these considerations is the fact that the risks of libel, including litigation costs, are insurable. For the most part, the risk posed by a megaverdict is not that a newspaper will be put out of business—it is a risk that next year's insurance premiums will increase. A libel suit is no greater threat to the defendant's survival than a suit by a pedestrian run over by one of the newspaper's delivery trucks, and the risk is equally insurable. Libel insurance policies, unlike the policies available to many other classes of defendants, typically allow the insured to be represented by its own lawyers rather than lawyers chosen by the insurance company, and libel insurers often honor their media customers' choice to fight rather than retract or settle. Thus, media often are insured against their own tactical miscalculations as well as the unavoidable risks of litigation.

Although much of the discussion about the free speech implications of libel focuses on the impact of particular cases, the more relevant focus is on aggregate costs. However threatening multi-million-dollar libel judgments may seem, the industry against which they are assessed is one of the largest and most lucrative in the country.[228] To the extent that libel risks are insurable, they do not threaten free speech interests unless the aggregate costs are so great that insurance becomes unavailable or too costly for some media outlets. The insurance system is imperfect, of course; some media fail to secure coverage, some are underinsured, and a few perhaps cannot obtain coverage. But insurance is available far more often than not, and its existence diminishes media zeal for libel law reform.

The libel insurers themselves are not a constituency for reform. Several of the companies are closely allied with the media industries and are therefore unlikely to support proposals their clients oppose. For independent insurers, any program to reduce risks, and therefore premiums, works against the insurer's ultimate interest in maximizing the volume of premium revenues available for investment.

It is easy to overestimate the benefit to media of reforms that substitute declaratory relief for monetary judgments. Losing a libel case costs a media defendant more than money. An image of credibility is to a news organization what an image of fiscal responsibility is to a financial institution. Losing a libel case, even when no damages are awarded, tarnishes that image. Understandably, media will assign some value to this consideration in deciding how much they gain from the substitution of remedies. They should also take into account, however, the extent to which their credibility is undermined—and the public's goodwill eroded—when they prevail under the present system on an issue like want of actual malice. Such a victory may not strike the public as a "fair" win on the merits.

The present law, for all its shortcomings, gives media considerable control over the risks they fear most: high litigation costs and windfall verdicts. Reform offers uncertain benefits and guaranteed uncertainty. One indisputable lesson of the past twenty-five years is that changes in libel law rarely have the effect they were expected to have. Dean Prosser thought *Sullivan* was a death knell for the libel cause of action.[229] Justice White thought the fault requirement of *Gertz* would render defamation victims "powerless to protect themselves."[230] In hindsight, both obviously misjudged the impact of those cases. Media skepticism of reform proposals is understandable. They are being asked to trade risks that are generally known, sometimes controllable, and nearly always insurable for changes whose effects are at least as unpredictable now as the effects of *Sullivan* and *Gertz* were when those cases were decided.

In short, there is no political constituency for reform. The media are largely uninterested, their lawyers are hostile, and plaintiffs are too diffuse to have an effective political voice. Independent law reform entities such as the American Law Institute and the National Conference of Commissioners on Uniform State Laws have continuity and credibility, but whether legislators will embrace their recommendations in the absence of any political impetus is questionable.

State courts, the usual source of change in tort law, are dissuaded from reforming the law of libel by the Supreme Court's de facto preemption of the subject. Theoretically, of course, the scheme devised by the Supreme Court to protect speech from the threat of libel actions is not preemptive; states are free to enforce any other scheme sufficiently protective of speech. The statement that "private plaintiffs may recover for actual injury without showing actual malice" does not state a rule of law but merely the scope of the constitutional limitation.[231] States may (and some do) require private plaintiffs to show actual malice.[232] Likewise, they may (and sometimes do) deny punitive damages even to plaintiffs who do show actual malice[233] or impose the limitations of *Gertz* on all private plaintiffs, including those defamed in purely private speech.[234] State law still controls a great many issues, including what is defamatory, what effect retraction has, what injuries are compensable, and what privileges are applicable. The states therefore retain considerable power to change the law of libel. But the dynamics of litigation do not facilitate innovation, at least when the Supreme Court does not encourage it. Once the Supreme Court prescribes a route that will survive constitutional scrutiny, litigants do not pursue other paths. And when the litigants do not advance alternatives, state courts do not embrace them.

Without some help from the Supreme Court, the reform movement is doomed. The National Conference of Commissioners on Uniform State Laws and other reformers are trapped between constitutional constraints on one side and lack of a political constituency on the other. Both of these obstacles make it unrealistic to look to legislators for the thorough rethinking that libel law needs.

CONCLUSION

The present law of libel is a failure. It denies most defamation victims any remedy and at the same time chills speech by encouraging high litigation costs and occasional large judgments. The route to reform is obvious: Provide a remedy that will simplify litigation and reduce the threat of windfall verdicts. That route, however, is a perilous one, fraught with political difficulty, empirical uncertainties, and dangers for freedom of speech. Deciding whether libel law is worth reforming requires a collective decision about the value we want to place on reputation as we enter the twenty-first century.

As a social value, reputation has been one of the casualties of the twentieth century. In 1942, at the dawn of his brilliant career, David Riesman identified reputation as an essentially precapitalist value more suited to Europe than to the United States. "[W]here tradition is capitalistic rather than feudalistic, reputation is only an asset, 'good will,' not an attribute to be sought after for its intrinsic value. And in the United States these business attitudes have colored social relations. The law of libel is consequently unimportant."[235] That may or may not have been true fifty years ago, but it is certainly a fair description of the law's treatment of reputation today.

A world in which reputation is not a legally protected interest is no longer inconceivable. Recent experience demonstrates that victims of defamation survive and sometimes even prosper without benefit of legal remedy. The public has learned to adjust its perceptions of the media to take into account the extremely complex relationship between truth and defamation that the present law creates; a system in which the law exerted no influence on these matters would be far easier to take into account. Political life and public discourse have adapted to the virtual abandonment of libel and would no doubt survive its actual demise.

Abolishing libel law is the only step that will eliminate the chill it imposes on speech. No reform can provide a remedy for defamation that imposes no burden on speech. Reformers must admit they are willing to burden speech, and media partisans who argue that any chilling effect is unconstitutional must admit they are urging the abolition of libel. The very purpose of libel, and this includes any remedy for harm to reputation, is to chill speech. If there is no speech that deserves to be chilled, there should be no law of libel. Reasonable people can and do hold that view. Others believe damage to reputation is too elusive or evanescent to justify the chill that libel law produces. Still others believe the marketplace should indeed be the only arbiter of truth.

Although I appreciate the force of those views, I do not share them. A world without libel law is not unthinkable, but it would be a less civil world, a less just world for victims of defamation, a world less anchored to truth and reason. The civilizing influence of libel law is valuable enough to justify the price it exacts from speech. Libel law *is* worth reforming, but only if the result offers real protection for the values of truth and reputation commensurate with its inevitable burdens on speech.

Only the Supreme Court can instigate this reform. The system of libel law the Court has created so permeates the field that other agencies of reform are effectively disabled. The system protects media imperfectly, but enough to keep them from espousing serious reforms. It allows a plaintiff to recover occasionally, forestalling the public clamor that might arise if recovery were barred altogether. There is no political constituency for statutory reform and little room within present constitutional constraints for innovation by state courts. The Court must undertake libel law reform itself, at least to the extent of reempowering other instigators of change.

Prescribing the reforms is beyond the compass of this chapter, but the principal strategic options are obvious. One is retrenchment. The Court might simply give up some of the territory it has occupied—by abandoning the actual malice rule, for example. Just as the Court's intervention has driven other players out of the process of revising libel law, so might its retrenchment draw them back. A drastic retrenchment would no doubt make the media more receptive to legislative reforms. That would impose high (though perhaps temporary) costs on speech, however, and the Court is unlikely to abdicate its historic First Amendment role on no more than the hope that other players will step forward to provide satisfactory substitutes.

A second strategy might be to invite proposals for reform. Without abandoning the present constitutional scheme, the Court could announce its willingness to consider alternative accommodations between speech and reputational interests. Such an invitation would free the proponents of legislative reform from the constitutional straitjacket in which they now operate. The uncertainty it would create might make the media more tractable participants in reform discussions. Such an invitation might also stimulate advocates, trial judges, and state appellate courts to propose their own alternatives, thereby restoring the state courts to their traditional role as the principal innovators in the law of defamation. State courts are not oblivious to the interests of the media, and today many are at least as sensitive as the present Supreme Court to free speech concerns. In recent years, some state courts have been creative in their solutions to other types of free speech problems.[236]

This strategy has the advantage of leaving the Court in its familiar reactive role, acting as final arbiter rather than an innovator. But that is also its disadvantage. The strategy assumes that legislators, litigants, and judges will be willing to devise solutions they know the Supreme Court may disapprove. It may be difficult for advocates to persuade their clients to advance, and trial judges to espouse, untried and as yet unapproved theories as long as tried and approved routes are still available. The invitation strategy is better suited to a field the Court has only begun to occupy than to one it dominates.

More important, even if this strategy were to succeed in generating acceptable alternatives to the present constitutional law of libel, its result after many years of effort would probably be a patchwork of differing liability schemes. Eventually a single scheme might evolve, either because the states all agreed on its superiority or, more plausibly, because only one received Supreme Court approval. But unless and until that happened, media and other potential defendants would be subject to even more variations in libel law than they are now. Libel is a field that cries out for some uniformity. Today intrastate speech is even rarer than intrastate commerce. Defamers are rarely subject to only one state's law, and unless they are, they must tailor their speech to the least protective state law to which they may be subject. We should not forget that it was Alabama's eagerness to punish the *New York Times* and other out-of-state media that drew the Supreme Court into libel law in the first place.[237] A system in which an interstate speaker might face declaratory judgment actions without fault defenses in one jurisdiction, negligence-based actions for limited damages in another, and unlimited damages upon a showing of actual malice in another would multiply the already considerable difficulty in assessing risks. Nonuniformity exacerbates the chill of libel law, and a strategy that encourages it is unsatisfactory.

A third strategy—more radical but also more effective—would make the Supreme Court itself the principal reformer of libel law. The Court would prescribe new accommodations of speech and reputational interests as a matter of constitutional law. It might decree, for example, that the Constitution requires no showing of fault if the remedy sought is only a declaration of falsity. It might announce new limitations on damages, with corresponding reductions in plaintiffs' burdens. The Court might devise a more sophisticated accommodation, one that addresses the dynamics and costs of libel litigation as well as questions of fault and remedies. It might explicitly authorize trial judges to decide at the outset whether the challenged statement was sufficiently factual, harmful, and remote from truth to be justifiably burdened by further litigation. Acknowledging that effective protection of speech requires a diminished role for juries, it might authorize even more aggressive use of summary judgment and judicial review. The Court might even take the assessment of damages out of the jury's hands.

Comprehensive law reform is not a familiar task for the Supreme Court. It is not accustomed to reviewing systems of law rather than specific rules. Case-by-case adjudication of specific constitutional issues does not invite advocacy on the redesign of an entire branch of tort law. Those are weighty objections, but they come too late. Over the past quarter century, case by case and bit by bit, the Court has thoroughly revised the common law of libel. It has created not merely a few constitutional limitations on state tort rules but a matrix of substantive principles, evidentiary rules, and de facto innovations in judge–jury roles and other procedural matters. These are all constitutionally based and can only be changed by those who have the power to change constitutional rules. Having created the system that is the source of so much dissatisfaction, the Court cannot now demur on the ground that law reform is not its business.

ACKNOWLEDGMENT

Earlier versions of this chapter were read by my colleagues, L.A. Powe, Jr. and Cynthia Estlund; Prof. Marc A. Franklin of Stanford; and three knowledgeable libel lawyers, P. Cameron DeVore, Marshall Nelson, and Bruce Johnson. With varying degrees of violence, all disagreed with some of the ideas and none should be thought to have endorsed my conclusions. Nonetheless, I benefited greatly from the suggestions of each. I am indebted to Ellen Williams and Howard Lidsky for their research assistance.

NOTES

1. 376 U.S. 254 (1964).

2. The Supreme Court has decided twenty-seven libel cases since *New York Times v. Sullivan*. They are cited here chronologically: Garrison v. Louisiana, 379 U.S. 64 (1964); Henry v. Collins, 380 U.S. 356 (1965); Linn v. United Plant Guard Workers, 383 U.S. 53 (1966) ; Rosenblatt v. Baer, 383 U.S. 75 (1966); Curtis Publishing Co. v. Butts, 388 U.S. 130 (1967); Beckley Newspapers Corp. v. Hanks, 389 U.S. 81 (1967); St. Amant v. Thompson, 390 U.S. 727 (1968); Greenbelt Coop. Publishing Ass'n v. Bresler, 398 U.S. 6 (1970); Monitor Patriot Co. v. Roy, 401 U.S. 265 (1971); Time, Inc. v. Pape, 401 U.S. 279 (1971); Ocala Star-Banner Co. v. Damron, 401 U.S. 295 (1971); Rosenbloom v. Metromedia, Inc., 403 U.S. 29 (1971); Old Dominion Branch No. 496, National Ass'n of Letter C arriers v. Austin, 418 U.S. 264 (1974); Gertz v. Robert Welch, Inc., 418 U.S. 323 (1974); Time, Inc. v. Firestone, 424 U.S. 448 (1976); Herbert v. Lando, 441 U.S. 153 (1979); Hutchinson v. Proxmire, 443 U.S. 111 (1979); Wolston v. Reader's Digest Ass'n, Inc., 443 U.S. 157 (1979); Keeton v. Hustler Magazine, Inc., 465 U.S. 770 (1984); Calder v. Jones, 465 U.S. 783 (1984); Bose Corp. v. Consumers Union, 466 U.S. 485 (1984); Dun & Bradstreet, Inc. v. Greenmoss Builders, Inc., 472 U.S. 749 (1985); Philadelphia Newspapers, Inc., v. Hepps, 475 U.S. 767 (1986); Anderson v. Liberty Lobby, Inc., 477 U.S. 242 (1986); Harte-Hanks Communications v. Connaughton, 491 U.S. 657 (1989); Milkovich v. Lorain Journal Co., 110 S. Ct. 2695 (1990); Masson v. New Yorker Magazine, Inc., 111 S. Ct. 2419 (1991).

3. Scholarly and popular criticism of libel law is voluminous. *See* R. BEZANSON, G. CRANBERG, & J. SOLOSKI, LIBEL LAW AND THE PRESS: MYTH AND REALITY (1987) [hereinafter LIBEL LAW AND THE PRESS]; LOIS G. FORER, A CHILLING EFFECT: THE MOUNTING THREAT OF LIBEL AND INVASION OF PRIVACY ACTIONS TO THE FIRST AMENDMENT (1987); W. WAT HOPKINS, ACTUAL MALICE: TWENTY-FIVE YEARS AFTER *TIMES V. SULLIVAN* (1989); ANTHONY LEWIS, MAKE NO LAW: THE SULLIVAN CASE AND THE FIRST AMENDMENT (1991) [hereinafter MAKE NO LAW]; LUCAS A. POWE,

JR., THE FOURTH ESTATE AND THE CONSTITUTION: FREEDOM
OF THE PRESS IN AMERICA (1991); RODNEY A. SMOLLA, SUING
THE PRESS (1986) [hereinafter SMOLLA, SUING]; WILLIAM
TAVOULAREAS, FIGHTING BACK (1985). The most important articles
include Barron, *The Search for Media Accountability,* 19 SUFFOLK U. L. REV.
789 (1985); Bezanson, *The Libel Tort Today,* 45 WASH. & LEE L. REV. 535
(1988) [hereinafter *Libel Tort Today];* Bezanson & Murchison, *The Three Voices
of Libel,* 47 WASH. & LEE L. REV. 213 (1990) [hereinafter *Three Voices];*
Elder, *Defamation, Public Officialdom and the* Rosenblatt v. Baer *Criteria—A
Proposal for Revivification: Two Decades After* New York Times Co. v. Sullivan,
33 BUFFALO L. REV. 579 (1985); Entin, *Privacy, Emotional Distress, and the
Limits of Libel Law Reform,* 38 MERCER L. REV. 835 (1987); Epstein, *Was* New
York Times v. Sullivan *Wrong?,* 53 U. CHI. L. REV. 782 (1986); Franklin,
Good Names and Bad Law: A Critique of Libel Law and a Proposal, 18 U.S.F. L.
REV. 1 (1983); Franklin & Bussel, *The Plaintiff's Burden in Defamation: Aware-
ness and Falsity,* 25 WM. & MARY L. REV. 825 (1984); Halpern, *Values and
Value: An Essay on Libel Reform,* 47 WASH. & LEE L. REV. 227 (1990); Ingber,
Defamation: A Conflict Between Reason and Decency, 65 VA. L. REV. 785 (1979);
Lewis, New York Times v. Sullivan *Reconsidered: Time to Return to "The Central
Meaning of the First Amendment,"* 83 COLUM. L. REV. 603 (1983) [hereinafter
Lewis, New York Times v. Sullivan *Reconsidered];* Massing, *The Libel Chill: How
Cold Is It Out There?,* COLUM. JOURNALISM REV., May/June 1985, at 31;
Post, *The Social Foundations of Defamation Law: Reputation and the Constitution,*
74 CALIF. L. REV. 691 (1986); Schauer, *Public Figures,* 25 WM. & MARY L.
REV. 905 (1984); Schneider, *A Model for Relating Defamatory "Opinions" to First
Amendment Protected "Ideas,"* 43 ARK. L. REV. 57 (1990); Smolla, Dun &
Bradstreet, Hepps and Liberty Lobby: *A New Analytic Primer on the Future
Course of Defamation,* 75 GEO. L.J. 1519 (1987); Smolla, *Let the Author Beware:
The Rejuvenation of the American Law of Libel,* 132 U. PA. L. REV. 1 (1983) [here
inafter Smolla, *Let the Author Beware];* Smolla & Gaertner, *The Annenberg Libel
Reform Proposal: The Case for Enactment,* 31 WM. & MARY L. REV. 25 (1989);
Van Alstyne, *First Amendment Limitations on Recovery from the Press—An Ex-
tended Comment on "The Anderson Solution,"* 25 WM. & MARY L. REV. 793
(1984); Zimmerman, *Curbing the High Price of Loose Talk,* 18 U.C. DAVIS L.
REV. 359 (1985); *see also* Anderson, *Reputation, Compensation, and Proof,* 25
WM. & MARY L. REV. 747 (1984); Abrams, *Why We Should Change the Libel
Law,* N.Y. TIMES, Sept. 29, 1985, § 6 (Magazine), at 34.

The articles cited *infra* note 5, proposing various reforms, also contain
much criticism of existing libel law.

4. *See* Sweeney v. Patterson, 128 F.2d 457, 458, *cert. denied,* 317 U.S. 678
(1942) ("Whatever is added to the field of libel is taken from the field of free
debate."). Indeed, I argue that the present law takes even more from speech
than it contributes to protecting reputation. *See infra* notes 206–09 and
accompanying text.

5. For the most widely discussed proposals, see H.R. 2846, 99th Cong.,
1st Sess. (1985) (proposal by Rep. Charles E. Schumer); THE ANNENBERG
WASHINGTON PROGRAM, PROPOSAL FOR THE REFORM OF LIBEL

LAW (1988) [hereinafter ANNENBERG PROPOSAL]; Policy Guide of the American Civil Liberties Union 11-13 (June 1989) (on file with author) (policy no. 6, Libel and Invasions of Privacy Through Speech).

For other reform proposals, some comprehensive and some aimed at limited areas of libel law, see Barrett, *Declaratory Judgments for Libel: A Better Alternative*, 74 CALIF. L. REV. 847 (1986); Cendali, *Of Things to Come—The Actual Impact of* Herbert v. Lando *and a Proposed National Correction Statute*, 22 HARV. J. ON LEGIS. 441 (1985); Cook, *Reconciling the First Amendment with the Individual's Reputation: The Declaratory Judgment as an Option for Libel Suits*, 93 DICK. L. REV. 265 (1989); Dienes, *Libel Reform: An Appraisal*, 23 U. MICH. J.L. REF. 1 (1989); Franklin, *A Declaratory Judgment Alternative to Current Libel Law*, 74 CALIF. L. REV. 809 (1986); Halpern, *Of Libel, Language, and Law:* New York Times v. Sullivan *at Twenty-Five*, 68 N.C. L. REV. 273 (1990); Hulme, *Vindicating Reputation: An Alternative to Damages as a Remedy for Defamation*, 30 AM. U. L. REV. 375 (1981); Ingber, *Rethinking Intangible Injuries: A Focus on Remedy*, 73 CALIF. L. REV. 772 (1985); LeBel, *Reforming the Tort of Defamation: An Accommodation of the Competing Interests Within the Current Constitutional Framework*, 66 NEB. L. REV. 249 (1987); Leval, *The No-Money, No-Fault Libel Suit: Keeping Sullivan in Its Proper Place*, 101 HARV. L. REV. 1287 (1988).

6. *See, e.g.,* Dienes, *supra* note 5, at 2 (noting that all libel reforms have faced a hostile media response); Johnston & Kaufman, *Annenberg*, Sullivan at Twenty-Five, and the Question of Libel Reform, 7 COMM. LAW. 4 (1989) (criticizing the proposals set forth in the Libel Reform Act, which include a broadened remedy of retraction and reply, declaratory judgments on the issue of truth or judgments on the issue of truth or falsity, and prior consent of both parties to authorize a suit for monetary damages).

7. *See* UNIFORM DEFAMATION ACT (Prop. Off. Draft Oct. 10, 1991) [hereinafter PROPOSED DEFAMATION ACT].

The PROPOSED DEFAMATION ACT is intricate and must be read in full for a complete appreciation of its effects. It is subject to change before final adoption. As of this writing, however, its major reform provisions may be summarized as follows:

1. A defendant who makes a sufficient retraction within forty-five days of plaintiff's request (or service of process) is liable only for plaintiff's pecuniary losses to the time of retraction. *See Act* §§ 13, 12(b), 15.

2. Anytime up to trial, a defendant may avoid liability for all except pecuniary losses by offering to make a sufficient retraction and pay plaintiff's litigation expenses. *See Act* § 9.

3. A plaintiff who elects to sue for vindication rather than damages need not prove fault or overcome conditional privileges to obtain a judicial declaration of falsity and an order requiring defendant to publish the declaration or pay plaintiff to do so, and may be awarded attorneys' fees if defendant unreasonably refused to retract. *See Act* §§ 2, 5, 7.

4. A defendant may be awarded attorneys' fees from a plaintiff who brings a vindication action without basis. *See Act* § 7(a)(ii).

5. A plaintiff may recover only for pecuniary loss or proved harm to

reputation and emotional distress resulting therefrom, and may not recover presumed damages. *See Act* § 10.

6. A plaintiff who prevails in a damage action may recover attorneys' fees by proving that defendant refused plaintiff's timely request for retraction, caused plaintiff pecuniary harm, and published with knowledge of falsity or reckless disregard for the truth. *See Act* § 14.

7. Punitive damages may be recovered only upon clear and convincing proof that defendant published with knowledge of falsity and ill will toward plaintiff. *See Act* § 11.

The proposal contains many less fundamental changes in existing libel law. Some of them are unquestionably salutary, such as a requirement that plaintiffs specifically identify in their requests for retractions and pleading the language or implication claimed to be defamatory, *see Act* § 4(a), and provisions consolidating and rationalizing the many absolute and conditional privileges, *see Act* §§ 16-18.

This chapter is not intended as a critique of the proposed uniform act. I single it out only because it is the current, and perhaps most credible, embodiment of the reform movement.

8. 376 U.S. 254 (1964).

9. *Id.* at 279-80.

10. *See id.* at 286-88.

11. *See* Garrison v. Louisiana, 379 U.S. 64, 78-79 (1964).

12. *See* St. Amant v. Thompson, 390 U.S. 727, 732-33 (1968).

13. *Id.* at 731.

14. *See* Masson v. New Yorker Magazine, Inc., 111 S. Ct. 2419, 2433 (1991).

15. *Sullivan,* 376 U.S. at 285-86.

16. *See* Harte-Hanks Communications, Inc. v. Connaughton, 491 U.S. 657, 661 n.2 (1989).

17. *Id.* at 659.

18. It was not clear in the *Sullivan* decision itself that these were distinct rules. The Court merely asserted that "considerations of effective judicial administration require us to review the evidence in the present record to determine whether it could constitutionally support a judgment for respondent." *Sullivan,* 376 U.S. at 284-85. After engaging in that review, the Court concluded that "the proof presented to show actual malice lacks the convincing clarity which the constitutional standard demands." *Id.* at 285-86. It did not explain why the Constitution required either a judicial review of evidence or a heightened standard of proof. These soon emerged, however, as important rules in their own right. *See* Rosenbloom v. Metromedia, Inc., 403 U.S. 29, 55 (1971); Greenbelt Coop. Publishing Ass'n v. Bresler, 398 U.S. 6, 11 (1970).

19. *See infra* notes 41–43 and accompanying text.

20. Bose Corp. v. Consumers Union, Inc., 466 U.S. 485, 511 (1984).

21. *See, e.g.,* Bose Corp. v. Consumers Union, Inc., 692 F.2d 189, 195 (1st Cir. 1982), *aff'd,* 466 U.S. 485 (1984).

22. Libel defendants have tried to convert the independent-review rule

into a requirement of de novo review, that is, one that disregards the jury's findings altogether. The Court, however, has refused to take that step. *See* Harte-Hanks Communications, Inc. v. Connaughton, 491 U.S. 657, 688-89 (1989). In *Connaughton*, the Court held that the jury's credibility determinations must be accepted unless they are clearly erroneous. *See id.* Whether the clearly erroneous standard also governs review of other subsidiary fact findings from which the jury infers actual malice has not been decided. *See id.* at 689-90.

23. *See Bose Corp.*, 466 U.S. at 514 n.31.

24. *See, e.g.*, Bindrim v. Mitchell, 155 Cal. Rptr. 29 (holding that readers could reasonably identify a purportedly fictional character as the plaintiff), *cert. denied*, 444 U.S. 984 (1979).

25. *Sullivan*, 376 U.S. at 292. This was the primary basis of the *Times*'s appeal. The actual-malice standard was an alternative argument advanced by the *Times*. It reportedly was embraced by Justice Brennan after the Court in conference had agreed to reverse on the ground that the Constitution required the common law elements of defamation to be proven with convincing clarity in a suit by a public official against a critic of his official conduct. According to this report, the independent review requirement evolved from extended negotiations among Justices Clark, Harlan, Black, and Brennan over appropriate means of preventing retrial. *See* MAKE NO LAW, *supra* note 3, at 120-21, 172-81; *see also* BERNARD SCHWARTZ, SUPER CHIEF 532-34 (1983).

26. *Sullivan*, 376 U.S. at 288. This review is probably not applicable to the identification-of-plaintiff issue generally, but only when identification is sought to be established by an inference that smacks of seditious libel. The Court has not reviewed evidence on this issue in any case since *New York Times v. Sullivan*. Nevertheless, review of the issue even in that limited context suggests that the Court's power to engage in extraordinary review of jury findings arises not from something peculiar to the actual-malice issue but from a more general concern for the impact of particular fact findings on speech issues in defamation cases.

27. *Id.* at 289.

28. 401 U.S. 279 (1971).

29. *See id.* at 289.

30. *See, e.g.*, Gomba v. McLaughlin, 504 P.2d 337, 339 (Colo. 1972) (holding that error is not actionable unless it "produces a different effect upon the reader than that which would be produced by the literal truth of the matter").

31. These cases are discussed below; *see infra* notes 79-109 and accompanying text.

32. In Newton v. NBC, 930 F.2d 662 (9th Cir. 1990), *cert. denied*, 112 S. Ct. 192 (1991), the defendants demanded independent review not only of jury findings on constitutional issues but also of the jury's finding of hatred or ill will to meet the state law standard for punitive damages. *See* Brief of Appellants at 48 n.44, Newton V. NBC (Nos. 89-55220, 89-55285). (The author was of counsel to the plaintiff in *Newton*.) *But see* McCoy v. Hearst

Corp., 727 P.2d 711, 715-16 (Cal. 1986) ("Thus, this court must make an independent assessment of the entire record, but only as it pertains to actual malice. Issues apart from this constitutional question need not be reviewed de novo and are subject to the usual rules of appellate review."), *cert. denied*, 481 U.S. 1041 (1987).

33. *See* Daily Herald Co. v. Munro, 838 F.2d 380, 383 (9th Cir. 1988).

34. *See, e.g.,* Smith v. Suburban Restaurants, Inc., 373 N.E.2d 215, 218 (Mass. 1978) (finding that summary judgment was improper on the ground that a jury might reasonably have viewed the letter in question as defamatory).

35. *See, e.g.,* Brown v. K.N.D. Corp., 529 A.2d 1292, 1294-95 (Conn. 1987) (holding that the appellate court should use the "clearly erroneous" standard of review when, at the trial level, there is a finding for the defendant).

36. *Sullivan,* 376 U.S. at 285.

37. *See, e.g.,* Bon Air Hotel v. Time, Inc., 426 F.2d 858, 865 (5th Cir. 1970) (noting that summary judgment assures the press freedom from legal harassment and, thus, self-censorship).

38. *See* Hutchinson v. Proxmire, 443 U.S. 111, 120 n.9 (1979).

39. *See, e.g.,* Liberty Lobby, Inc. v. Dow Jones & Co., 838 F.2d 1287, 1293 (D.C. Cir.) (stating that the "plaintiff must demonstrate that the defendant himself entertained a 'high degree of awareness of . . . probable falsity' [and that] [t]his requirement, too, is applicable when considering a motion for summary judgment" (quoting Garrison v. Louisiana, 379 U.S. 64, 74 (1964))), *cert. denied,* 488 U.S. 825 (1988).

40. In one study of 110 summary judgment motions by media defendants in 1980-81, 74 percent of the motions were granted in cases involving public figure or public official plaintiffs. *See Summary Judgment in Libel Litigation: Assessing the Impact of* Hutchinson v. Proxmire, LIBEL DEFENSE RESOURCE CENTER, BULLETIN NO. 4 (LDRC, New York, N.Y.), Oct. 15, 1982, at 2 [hereinafter LDRC BULL. No. 4].

41. *See* Anderson v. Liberty Lobby, Inc., 477 U.S. 242, 254-55 (1986).

42. *See id.* at 244. For an analysis of the effect of this rule on litigation strategy, see Issacharoff & Loewenstein, *Second Thoughts About Summary Judgment,* 100 YALE L.J. 73 (1990).

43. *See Anderson,* 477 U.S. at 251-52.

44. *Id.* at 256 n.7 (quoting Calder v. Jones, 465 U.S. 783, 790-91 (1984)).

45. *See id.* at 257 n.1 (Brennan, J., dissenting).

46. *See* Franklin, *Winners and Losers and Why: A Study of Defamation Litigation,* 1980 AM. B. FOUND. RES. J. 455, 492 (noting that media defendants won before trial in 68 percent of cases involving the *Sullivan* rule).

47. *See* Ocala Star-Banner Co. v. Damron, 401 U.S. 295 (1971); Monitor Patriot Co. v. Roy, 401 U.S. 265 (1971).

48. Rosenblatt v. Baer, 383 U.S. 75, 85 (1966).

49. Curtis Publishing Co. v. Butts, 388 U.S. 130, 164 (1967) (Warren, C.J., concurring in the result).

50. *See, e.g.,* Roche v. Egan, 433 A.2d 757, 762 (Me. 1981) ("Our re-

search has disclosed that every court that has faced the issue has decided that an officer of law enforcement, from ordinary patrolman to Chief of Police, is a 'public official' within the meaning of federal constitutional law.").

51. *See, e.g.,* Associated Press v. Walker, 388 U.S. 130, 154 (1967) (finding a politically prominent man who was active in college campus riot a "public figure").

52. *See, e.g.,* Chuy v. Philadelphia Eagles Football Club, 595 F.2d 1265, 1280 (3d Cir. 1979) (en banc) (professional football player); James v. Gannett Co., 353 N.E.2d 834, 839 (N.Y. 1976) (belly dancer).

53. *See, e.g.,* Holt v. Cox Enters., 590 F. Supp. 408, 412 (N.D. Ga. 1984) (college football player).

54. *See, e.g.,* Brewer v. Memphis Publishing Co., 626 F.2d 1238, 1255 (5th Cir. 1980) (former girl friend of Elvis Presley, wife of retired football star), *cert. denied,* 452 U.S. 962 (1981).

55. *See, e.g.,* Waldbaum v. Fairchild Publications, Inc., 627 F.2d 1287, 1300 (D.C. Cir.) (innovator in grocery business was public figure for limited purpose of comment on his own business), *cert. denied,* 449 U.S. 898 (1980); Williams v. Pasma, 656 P.2d 212, 216 (Mont. 1982) (former candidate for U.S. Senate who was well-known in state was public figure), *cert. denied,* 461 U.S. 945 (1983).

56. *See, e.g.,* Kassel v. Gannett Co., 875 F.2d 935, 940 (1st Cir. 1989) (holding that under federal law, the public-official and public-figure questions are for the court); White v. Mobile Press Register, Inc., 514 So. 2d 902, 904 (Ala. 1987) (affirming summary judgment against EPA administrator who the lower court found to be a public figure). The Supreme Court has said only that "as is the case with questions of privilege generally, it is for the trial judge in the first instance to determine whether the proofs show respondent to be a 'public official.'" Rosenblatt v. Baer, 383 U.S. 75, 88 (1966).

57. *See* Gertz v. Robert Welch, Inc., 418 U.S. 323, 347 (1974).

58. *See id.* at 349.

59. *Cf.* Meadows v. Taft Broadcasting Co., 40 N.Y.S.2d 205 (App. Div. 1983) (private plaintiff seeking punitive damages must prove actual malice with convincing clarity) with Pirre v. Printing Devs., Inc., 468 F. Supp. 1028 (S.D.N.Y.) (private plaintiff seeking punitive damages need only prove actual malice by preponderance of evidence), *aff'd mem.,* 614 F.2d 1290 (2d Cir. 1979). Cases on both sides are discussed in Marcone v. Penthouse Int'l, Ltd., 577 F. Supp. 318, 326-28 (E.D. Pa. 1983), *rev'd on other grounds,* 754 F.2d 1072 (3d Cir. 1985).

60. *Gertz,* 418 U.S. at 350.

61. *Id.*

62. *See* Time, Inc., v. Firestone, 424 U.S. 448, 460 (1976).

63. Dun & Bradstreet, Inc. v. Greenmoss Builders, Inc., 472 U.S. 749, 759 (1985).

64. *See id.* at 761.

65. *See id.* at 773-74 (White, J., concurring in the judgment) ("[I]t must be that the Gertz requirement of some kind of fault on the part of the defendant is also inapplicable in cases such as this.") There is also some

uncertainty about the applicability of the *Sullivan* requirements when the defamation occurs in advertising. *See* United States Healthcare, Inc. v. Blue Cross, 898 F.2d 914, 924 (3d Cir.) (distinguishing between defamation and commercial disparagement), *cert. denied,* 111 S. Ct. 58 (1990).

66. One study of appellate cases found seveny-five cases in which *Sullivan* supplied the controlling constitutional principles and only twenty-four in which *Gertz* was controlling. *See* Franklin, *Suing Media for Libel: A Litigation Study,* 1981 AM. B. FOUND. RES. J. 795, 824.

67. Over 80 percent of the plaintiffs in the Iowa Libel Research Project engaged their lawyers on a contingent-fee basis. *See* LIBEL LAW AND THE PRESS, *supra* note 3, at 148.

68. The privilege was first recognized in Edwards v. National Audubon Soc'y, 556 F.2d 113, 120 (2d Cir.), *cert. denied,* 434 U.S. 1002 (1977).

69. *See* April v. Reflector-Herald, Inc., 546 N.E.2d 466, 469 (Ohio Ct. App. 1988) (holding the privilege equally applicable whether plaintiff is public figure or private person).

70. Among the cases rejecting the privilege are Dickey v. CBS, 583 F.2d 1221 (3d Cir. 1978); McCall v. Courier-Journal, 623 S.W.2d 882 (Ky. 1981), *cert. denied,* 456 U.S. 975 (1982); Postill v. Booth Newspapers, 325 N.W.2d 511 (Mich. Ct. App. 1982); Hogan v. The Herald Co., 444 N.E.2d 1002 (N.Y. 1982); Janklow v. Viking Press, 378 N.W.2d 875 (S.D. 1985).

71. *See* Philadelphia Newspapers, Inc. v. Hepps, 475 U.S. 767, 775-76 (1986).

72. *Sullivan,* 376 U.S. at 279 (footnote and citations omitted).

73. 379 U.S. 64 (1964).

74. *Id.* at 74.

75. *See* RESTATEMENT (SECOND) OF TORTS § 613 caveat (ALI 1977) [hereinafter RESTATEMENT] ("The Institute expresses no opinion on the extent to which the common law rule placing on the defendant the burden of proof to show the truth of the defamatory communication has been changed. . . .").

76. *See* Philadelphia Newspapers, Inc. v. Hepps, 475 U.S. 767, 775-76 (1986). The Court did not decide whether the burden must be shifted to plaintiffs in nonmedia cases, cases not involving matters of public concern, or cases seeking a declaration of falsity rather than damages. *See id.* at 779 n.4.

77. *See, e.g.,* Buckley v. Littell, 539 F.2d 882, 889 (2d Cir. 1976) (stating that a public figure must demonstrate "with convincing clarity" the falsity of defendant's statements), *cert. denied,* 429 U.S. 1062 (1977); Firestone v. Time, Inc., 460 F.2d 712, 723 (5th Cir.) (Bell, J., concurring) (extending the clear-and-convincing-proof standard to plaintiff's burden of "proving that the statement was false in the first instance"), *cert. denied,* 409 U.S. 875 (1972).

78. *Hepps,* 475 U.S. at 779 n.4.

79. Gertz v. Robert Welch, Inc., 418 U.S. 323, 339-40 (1974) (footnote omitted).

80. Numerous cases holding that opinion is constitutionally protected are cited in McCrory, Bernins, Jones, and Grygiel, *Constitutional Privilege in Libel Law,* in 1 COMMUNICATIONS LAW 403, 420 (Practising Law Institute ed. 1989).

81. *See, e.g.,* RESTATEMENT, *Supra* note 75, § 566.

82. *See id.* § 556, comment a.

83. *See, e.g.,* Carr v. Brasher, 776 S.W.2d 567, 570 (Tex. 1989) (interpreting Gertz as elevating "to a constitutional principle the distinction between [statements of] fact and opinion," with only the former being actionable).

84. *See* Ollman v. Evans, 750 F.2d 970, 979 (D.C. Cir. 1984) (en banc), *cert. denied,* 471 U.S. 1127 (1985).

85. *See id.* Other courts considered additional factors. *See, e.g.,* Information Control Corp. v. Genesis One Computer Corp., 611 F.2d 781, 784 (9th Cir. 1980) (use of cautionary terms and the nature of the audience); Marchiondo v. Brown, 649 P.2d 462, 469 (N.M. 1982) (the likely understanding of reasonably prudent readers).

86. Kirk v. CBS, 14 Media L. Rep. (BNA) 1263, 1264 (N.D. Ill. 1987).

87. Rowland v. Fayed, 14 Media L. Rep. (BNA) 1257, 1257 (D.C. 1987).

88. Baker v. Los Angeles Herald Examiner, 721 P.2d 87, 89 (Cal. 1986), *cert. denied,* 479 U.S. 1032 (1987).

89. *See* Ault v. Hustler Magazine, 860 F.2d 877 (9th Cir. 1988), *cert. denied,* 489 U.S. 1080 (1989); Ollman v. Evans, 750 F.2d 970 (D.C. Cir. 1984) (en banc), *cert. denied,* 471 U.S. 1127 (1985); Baker v. Los Angeles Herald Examiner, 721 P.2d 87 (Cal. 1986), *cert. denied,* 479 U.S. 1032 (1987); Miskovsky v. Tulsa Tribune, 678 P.2d 242 (Okla. 1983), *cert. denied,* 465 U.S. 1006 (1984).

90. 110 S. Ct. 2695 (1990).

91. *Id.* at 2707.

92. *Id.* at 2705.

93. *See id.* at 2705-06.

94. *Id.* at 2707 (quoting Rosenblatt v. Baer, 383 U.S. 75, 86 (1966)).

95. *Id.* at 2704.

96. 398 U.S. 6 (1970).

97. *See* Greenbelt Coop. Publishing Ass'n v. Bresler, 252 A.2d 755, 770 (Md. Ct. App. 1969), rev'd, 398 U.S. 6 (1970).

98. *Bresler,* 398 U.S. at 14.

99. If the original decision left any doubt, the Court recently confirmed that whether a statement is reasonably capable of a defamatory meaning is a constitutional issue. *See Milkovich,* 110 S. Ct. at 2704-05. Although Justice Brennan dissented in *Milkovich,* he agreed with the majority on this point. *Id.* at 2708-09 (Brennan, J., dissenting).

100. 418 U.S. 264 (1974).

101. *Id.* at 268.

102. *See id.* at 267-68.

103. *See id.* at 285-86. The underlying cause of action was based on federal labor law rather than state tort law, so the Court's decision might be seen as an interpretation of federal labor law rather than constitutional law, but the Court relied on *Bresler* as precedent and indicated that it was engaging in the same kind of review that is required in First Amendment cases. *See id.* at 280-82.

104. 485 U.S. 46 (1988).

105. *See id.* at 57.
106. *Milkovich,* 110 S. Ct. at 2706 (citation omitted) (quoting *Falwell,* 485 U.S. at 50).
107. *Id.*
108. *See id.*
109. *See id.* at 2714 (Brennan, J., dissenting).
110. *Sullivan,* 376 U.S. at 279.
111. And because of the limitations on damages that apply if it is not proved, into almost every other case. *See supra* notes 57-67 and accompanying text.
112. *See, e.g.,* Milkovich v. Lorain Journal Co., 110 S. Ct. 2695 (1990) (fifteen years); Herbert v. Lando, 781 F.2d 298 (2d Cir.), *cert. denied,* 476 U.S. 1182 (1986) (twelve years); Gertz v. Robert Welch, Inc., 680 F.2d 527 (7th Cir. 1982), *cert. denied,* 459 U.S. 1226 (1983) (fourteen years); Sprague v. Philadelphia Newspapers, Inc., No. 3644, (Pa. C.P., Philadelphia County, May 3, 1990), reported in News Notes, 17 Media L. Rep. (BNA) No. 23, May 15, 1990 (seventeen years). The *Milkovich* and *Sprague* decisions cited did not resolve the cases; *Milkovich* was remanded and *Sprague* was merely the trial court verdict.
113. St. Amant v. Thompson, 390 U.S. 727, 731 (1968).
114. Herbert v. Lando, 441 U.S. 153, 176 n.25 (1979).
115. *See* Herbert v. Lando, 781 F.2d 298 (2d Cir.), cert. denied, 476 U.S. 1182 (1986).
116. Media defendants' success rate is even higher in summary judgment motions based on the actual-malice issue (81 percent) than in summary judgment motions generally (75 percent). *See* LDRC BULL. No. 4, *supra note* 40, at 2.
117. *St. Amant,* 390 U.S. at 732.
118. *See* Anderson v. Liberty Lobby, Inc., 477 U.S. 242, 255 (1986) ("Our holding . . . by no means authorizes trial on affidavits."). For a case interpreting a state summary judgment rule to allow a defendant to prevail solely on the basis of an affidavit that he believed his statement to be true, see Casso v. Brand, 776 S.W.2d 551 (Tex. 1989).
119. *St. Amant,* 390 U.S. at 732.
120. *See* Guam Fed'n of Teachers, Local 1581 v. Ysrael, 492 F.2d 438, 441 (9th Cir.), *cert. denied,* 419 U.S. 872 (1974); Washington Post Co. v. Keogh, 365 F.2d 965, 968 (D.C. Cir. 1966), *cert. denied,* 385 U.S. 1011 (1967).
121. *See* Steaks Unlimited, Inc. v. Deaner, 623 F.2d 264 (3d Cir. 1980); Yiamouyiannis v. Consumers Union of the United States, Inc., 619 F.2d 932 (2d Cir.), *cert. denied,* 449 U.S. 839 (1980); Tucci v. Gannett Publishing Co., 464 A.2d 161 (Me. 1983).
122. *See* ROBERT D. SACK, LIBEL, SLANDER, AND RELATED PROBLEMS 542-44 (1980).
123. *See* LDRC BULL. No. 4, *supra* note 40, at 2.
124. 477 U.S. 242 (1986).
125. *Id.* at 257.
126. Gertz v. Robert Welch, Inc., 418 U.S. 323, 349 (1974).

127. 4 J.G. SUTHERLAND, A TREATISE ON THE LAW OF DAMAGES § 1206 (4th ed. 1916).

128. *See, e.g.,* Burnett v. National Enquirer, 144 Cal. App. 3d 991, 193 Cal. Rptr. 206, 222 (1983) (holding that "malice in fact" or ill will is required in addition to "malice in law" to permit punitive damages in libel actions), *appeal dismissed,* 465 U.S. 1014 (1984); Gannett Co. v. Re, 496 A.2d 553, 559 (Del. 1985) (holding that states are not bound by the actual-malice standard and may impose additional burdens on plaintiffs seeking punitive damages in libel actions); Mahoney v. Adirondack Publishing Co., 509 N.Y.S.2d 193, 200 (1986) (holding that the imposition of punitive damages in libel actions requires proof of common law malice in addition to proof of malice in its constitutional sense), *rev'd on other grounds,* 517 N.E.2d 1365 (N.Y. 1987).

129. *See, e.g.,* Sharon v. Time, Inc., 599 F. Supp. 538, 587 (S.D.N.Y. 1984) (holding that common law malice or ill will can be inferred from evidence proving "constitutional" malice for the purpose of allowing punitive damages in a libel action).

130. *See* Newton v. NBC, 930 F.2d 662 (9th Cir. 1990) ($19.3 million verdict), *cert. denied,* 112 S. Ct. 192 (1991); Lerman v. Flynt Distrib. Co., 745 F.2d 123 (2d Cir. 1984) ($40 million verdict), *cert. denied,* 471 U.S. 1054 (1985); Pring v. Penthouse Int'l, Ltd. 695 F.2d 438 (10th Cir. 1982) ($26.5 million verdict), *cert. denied,* 462 U.S. 1132 (1983); Guccione v. Hustler Magazine, Inc., 7 Media L. Rep. (BNA) 2077 (Ohio Ct. App. 1981) ($40.3 million verdict); Sprague v. Philadelphia Newspapers, Inc., No. 3644 (Pa. C.P., Philadelphia County, May 3, 1990), *reported in* News Notes, 17 Media L. Rep. (BNA) No. 23, May 15, 1990) ($34 million); Feazell v. Belo Broadcasting Corp. (Tex. Dist. Ct., McLennan County, June 7, 1991), *reported in* Wall St. J., June 28, 1991, at B4 ($58 million); Srivastava v. Harte-Hanks Television Inc., No. 85-CI-15150 (Tex. Dist. Ct., Apr. 15, 1990), *reported in* News Notes, 17 Media L. Rep. (BNA) No. 25, May 29, 1990 ($29 million).

131. *See* Jones, *News Media's Libel Costs Rising, Study Says,* N.Y. TIMES, Sept. 26, 1991, at A28. The average verdict for the decade 1981–90 was $1.8 million. *See* News Notes, *LDRC Finds Increase in Media Damage Awards,* 19 Media L. Rep. (BNA) No. 9, Oct. 8, 1991.

132. *See Juries and Damages: Comparing the Media's Libel Experience to Other Civil Litigants,* LIBEL DEFENSE RESOURCE CENTER, BULLETIN NO. 9 (LDRC, New York, N.Y.), Jan. 31, 1984, at 28.

133. *See* Brown & Williamson Tobacco Corp. v. Jacobson, 827 F.2d 1119 (7th Cir. 1987), *cert. denied,* 485 U.S. 933 (1988).

134. The cost of a *supersedeas* bond, which prevents the plaintiff from collecting the judgment pending appeal, is usually a percentage of the amount of the verdict. A television company that would have been required to post a $58 million bond to appeal a libel judgment in that amount settled for an undisclosed sum rather than pursue the appeal. *See A.H. Belo Broadcast Unit Settles Libel Suit in Texas,* WALL ST. J., June 28, 1991, at B4.

135. *See* SMOLLA, SUING, supra note 3, at 75.

136. *See id.* at 74.

137. *See* Miami Herald Publishing Co. v. Tornillo, 418 U.S. 241, 261 (1974) (White, J., concurring).

138. *See, e.g.,* Herbert v. Lando, 441 U.S. 153, 160 (1979) ("[P]roof of the [defendant's] necessary state of mind could be in the form of objective circumstances from which the ultimate fact could be inferred. . . . "); Tavoulareas v. Piro, 817 F.2d 762, 789(D.C. Cir.) (en banc) ("[A] plaintiff may prove the defendant's subjective state of mind through the cumulation of circumstantial evidence. . . ."), *cert. denied,* 484 U.S. 870 (1987).

139. *See Herbert,* 441 U.S. at 174.

140. *See, e.g.,* Robertson v. McCloskey, 666 F. Supp. 241, 250-51 (D.D.C. 1987) (holding that evidence in defendant's possession contradicting the allegedly defamatory statements is relevant in determining defendant's state of mind).

141. *See* Hunt v. Liberty Lobby, 720 F.2d 631, 645 (11th Cir. 1983); Montandon v. Triangle Publications, Inc., 120 Cal. Rptr. 186, *cert. denied,* 423 U.S. 893 (1975).

142. Of course, discovery of these materials may be thwarted by claims of privilege or other limitations on discovery. *See, e.g.,* Contemporary Mission, Inc. v. New York Times, 665 F. Supp. 248, 268-69 (S.D.N.Y. 1987) (denying additional discovery where evidence would be cumulative), *aff'd,* 842 F.2d 612 (2d Cir.), *cert. denied,* 488 U.S. 856 (1988); Lal v. CBS, Inc., 551 F. Supp. 356, 363-62 (E.D. Pa. 1982) (noting that a television reporter's notes, scripts, and outtakes were privileged under state statute), *aff'd,* 726 F.2d 97 (3d Cir. 1984).

143. *See* Greenbelt Coop. Publishing Ass'n v. Bresler, 398 U.S. 6, 10-11 (1970); Garrison v. Louisiana, 379 U.S. 64, 71-73 (1964).

144. *See* Sharon v. Time, Inc., 599 F. Supp. 538, 584 (S.D.N.Y. 1984) (stating that although evidence of bias could not establish actual malice, such evidence could provide a motive for defamation or explain unsupported conclusions in the published material); Cochran v. Indianapolis Newspapers, Inc., 372 N.E.2d 1211, 1220 (Ind. Ct. App. 1978) (stating that ill will is "relevant and admissible *as evidence* in the determination of whether defendant possessed a state of mind highly conducive to reckless disregard of falsity," even though ill will is not itself an element of actual malice).

145. *See* Indianapolis Newspapers, Inc. v. Fields, 259 N.E.2d 651, 663-64 (Ind.), *cert. denied,* 400 U.S. 930 (1970).

146. *See* Curtis Publishing Co. v. Butts, 388 U.S. 130, 158 (1967).

147. *See id.* at 157; Carson v. Allied News Co., 529 F.2d 206, 211 (7th Cir. 1976); Vandenburg v. Newsweek, Inc., 507 F.2d 1024, 1026 (5th Cir. 1975); Goldwater v. Ginzburg, 414 F.2d 324, 339 (2d Cir. 1969), *cert. denied,* 396 U.S. 1049 (1970); Widener v. Pacific Gas & Elec. Corp., 142 Cal. Rptr. 304, 314 (1977), *cert. denied,* 436 U.S. 918 (1978); Fopay v. Noveroske, 334 N.E.2d 79, 88 (Ill. App. 1975).

148. *See* Tavoulareas v. Piro, 817 F.2d 762, 797 (D.C. Cir.) (en banc) (stating that where there is overwhelming evidence that an article was published in good faith, "the absence of deadline pressure is probative of nothing"), *cert. denied,* 484 U.S. 870 (1987).

149. *See* Simonson v. United Press Int'l, Inc., 500 F. Supp. 1261, 1269 (E.D. Wis. 1980), aff'd, 654 F.2d 478 (7th Cir. 1981); Times Publishing Co. v. Huffstetler, 409 So. 2d 112, 113 n.1 (Fla. Dist. Ct. App. 1982).

150. *See* McCoy v. Hearst Corp., 727 P.2d 711, 728 (Cal. 1986) (holding that investigatory failures will not deprive a defamatory falsehood of its privileged status), *cert. denied*, 481 U.S. 1041 (1987); Wanless v. Rothballer, 503 N.E.2d 316, 322 (Ill. 1986) (stating that the failure to investigate "does not constitute actual malice if the defendants did not seriously doubt the truth of their assertions, and the failure to solicit plaintiff's reaction was nothing more than a failure to follow a course of investigation and verification"), *cert. denied*, 482 U.S. 929 (1987).

151. *See, e.g.,* Akins v. Altus Newspapers, Inc., 609 P.2d 1263, 1266-67 (Okla. 1977) (stating that reporter's failure to verify news story was part of "evidence of heedless conduct to show wanton indifference to [the] consequences" of publishing the story), *cert. denied*, 449 U.S. 1010 (1980).

152. *See* St. Amant v. Thompson, 390 U.S. 727, 732 (1968) (stating that professions of good faith are unlikely to prevail "when the publisher's allegations are so inherently improbable that only a reckless man would have put them in circulation").

153. *See* Nash v. Keene Publishing Corp., 498 A.2d 348, 355 (N.H. 1985) (stating that a failure to verify in the face of affirmative evidence of falsehood and inaccuracy could be sufficient evidence for a jury to find reckless disregard of the truth).

154. *See* Dupler v. Mansfield Journal, 413 N.E.2d 1187, 1193 (Ohio 1980), *cert. denied*, 452 U.S. 962 (1981); Taylor v. Miskovsky, 640 P.2d 959, 962 (Okla. 1981).

155. *See* Kerwick v. Orange County Publications, 420 N.E.2d 970, 970 (N.Y. 1981) (stating that a promptly published retraction "might be considered evidence of lack of malice in certain instances"); *see also* Cape Publications, Inc. v. Teri's Health Studio, Inc., 385 So. 2d 188, 190 (Fla. Dist. Ct. App. 1980) (reversing an award of punitive damages where newspaper printed a full and fair retraction).

156. *See* Brown & Williamson Tobacco Corp. v. Jacobson, 827 F.2d 1119, 1134 (7th Cir. 1987) (holding that selective destruction of documents is "strong evidence of actual malice," and that a "court and a jury are entitled to presume that documents destroyed in bad faith while litigation is pending would be unfavorable to the party that has destroyed the documents"), *cert. denied*, 485 U.S. 993 (1988).

157. St. Amant v. Thompson, 390 U.S. 727, 732 (1968).

158. *Id.*

159. *See, e.g.,* Winegard v. Oxberger, 258 N.W.2d 847, 852 (Iowa 1977) (holding that where information sought by discovery is necessary or crucial to a cause of action, where other reasonable means of obtaining the information have been exhausted, and where the actions are not patently frivolous, a newsgatherer's privilege to withhold confidential information may be subordinated by the compelling state interest in the fair administration of justice), *cert. denied*, 436 U.S. 905 (1978).

160. *See* Blasi, *The Newsman's Privilege: An Empirical Study,* 70 MICH. L. REV. 229, 265-74 (1971). In its only consideration of this issue, the Court declined to recognize a privilege against compelled disclosure in the cases before it, but a majority recognized the potential chill. *See* Branzburg v. Hayes, 408 U.S. 665, 710 (1972) (Powell, J., concurring) (arguing that the privilege should be judged by balancing vital constitutional and societal interests on a case-by-case basis). In dissent, Justice Douglas wrote that "[f]ear of disclosure will cause dissidents to communicate less openly to reporters," and that "fear of accountability will cause editors and critics to write with more restrained pens." *Id.* at 721 (Douglas, J., dissenting). In a separate dissent joined by Justices Brennan and Marshall, Justice Stewart wrote that the Court's holding would "needlessly discourage" First Amendment activity. *See id.* at 741 (Stewart, J., dissenting).

161. MARC A. FRANKLIN, CASES AND MATERIALS ON MASS MEDIA LAW 137 (3d ed. 1987).

162. *See* GATLEY ON LIBEL AND SLANDER § 330 (Phillip Lewis ed., 8th ed. 1981).

163. The only risk is the possibility that the defendant will have to pay the costs incurred by the plaintiff in proving falsity as a sanction for having failed to make a proper admission on that issue. *See* FED. R. CIV. P. 37(c).

164. A famous example is Reynolds v. Pegler, 223 F.2d 429 (2d Cir.), *cert. denied,* 350 U.S. 846 (1955). The plaintiff, writer Quentin Reynolds, won $175,000 in punitive damages but only $1 in compensatory damages for a scurrilously defamatory attack; the defendants' trial strategy was to smear Reynolds with suggestions that he had associations with Communists. *See id.* at 435.

165. *See supra* notes 137-60 and accompanying text.

166. "While the required showing of common law malice has not been eliminated as an additional obstacle to punitive damage recovery if a state's underlying common law requires it, even in such cases proof of actual malice will almost always, as a practical matter, satisfy the common law standard of malice as well." *Libel Tort Today, supra* note 3, at 546.

167. *See Defamation Trials, Damage Awards and Appeals III: Two-Year Update (1984–1986),* LIBEL DEFENSE RESOURCE CENTER BULLETIN NO. 21 (LDRC, New York, N.Y.), Fall 1987, at 20, tbl. 13-e.

168. *See supra* notes 47-48 and accompanying text.

169. *See supra* notes 49-55 and accompanying text.

170. *See* Time, Inc. v. Firestone, 424 U.S. 448, 460 (1976) (stating that states may base defamation awards on elements other than injury to reputation, including "'personal humiliation and mental anguish and suffering'" (quoting Gertz v. Robert Welch, Inc., 418 U.S. 323, 350 (1974))). State law sometimes requires plaintiffs to show more than emotional distress. *See, e.g.,* Gobin v. Globe Publishing Co., 649 P.2d 1239, 1244 (Kan. 1982) (agreeing with New York rule requiring harm to reputation before claim of mental anguish can be compensable). Generally, however, no such requirement exists. In Hearst Corp. v. Hughes, 466 A.2d 486, 489 (Md. 1983), for example, the court declined to require harm to reputation before compensatory

damages could be awarded. The court stated that if victims of defamation "can convince a trier of fact that their emotional distress is genuine and can prove the other common law and constitutionally required elements of a negligent defamation case, we see no social purpose to be served by requiring the plaintiff additionally to prove actual impairment of reputation." *Id.* at 495.

171. The available data indicate that most plaintiffs engage their lawyers on a contingency-fee basis. *See* LIBEL LAW AND THE PRESS, *supra* note 3, at 69.

172. The demise of remedies for these kinds of injuries is described in W. P. KEETON, D. DOBBS, R. KEETON, & D. OWEN, PROSSER AND KEETON ON THE LAW OF TORTS § 124, at 930 (5th ed. 1984). Some courts have recognized actions for negligent infliction of emotional distress under various circumstances, but there is no general principle authorizing recovery for negligently inflicted distress. *See* Scott, Note, *Proving Beyond a Reasonable Doubt: The Negligent Infliction of Emotional Distress,* 11 CARDOZO L. REV 235, 237-44 (1989) (discussing various types of actions recognized in different jurisdictions).

173. Some of the more famous bits of rhetoric are quoted—and perceptively examined—in Smolla, *Let the Author Beware, supra* note 3, at 14-15 & n.84.

174. Rosenblatt v. Baer, 383 U.S. 75, 92 (1966) (Stewart, J., concurring).

175. In the course of explaining why the Court declined to impose on private plaintiffs the same burdens it had imposed on public officials and public figures, Justice Powell described these rationales and asserted reasons why they were not applicable to private persons. *See* Gertz v. Robert Welch, Inc., 418 U.S. 323, 344-45 (1974). The Court had not previously relied on these arguments as reasons for imposing greater burdens on public plaintiffs, however.

176. 403 U.S. 29 (1971).

177. *Id.* at 46-47 (plurality opinion by Brennan, J.) (citation omitted). Adopting the self-help argument in *Gertz,* despite Justice Brennan's criticism, Justice Powell responded rather lamely that "the fact that the self-help remedy of rebuttal, standing alone, is inadequate to its task does not mean that it is irrelevant to our inquiry." 418 U.S. at 344 n.9.

178. *Gertz,* 418 U.S. at 344-45.

179. In many states, the murder of a law enforcement officer is a more serious offense than the murder of a private citizen. This is not because officers' lives are more valuable but because they are exposed to more risk. In view of this increased risk, the criminal law attempts to provide more protection by increasing the legal deterrent. I am not arguing that this comparison proves that public plaintiffs should receive more protection in libel than private plaintiffs; only that logic does not require that public plaintiffs receive less.

180. Cases examining what groups of people are classified as public officials are collected in McCrory, *supra* note 80, at 516-27.

181. *See* Carson v. Allied News Co., 529 F.2d 206, 209-10 (7th Cir. 1976).

182. *Id.* at 210.

183. *See* Chuy v. Philadelphia Eagles Football Club, 595 F.2d 1265, 1280 (3d Cir. 1979) (en banc).

184. *See* James v. Gannett Co., 353 N.E.2d 834, 840 (N.Y. 1976).

185. *See* Schauer, *supra* note 3, at 914-21 (arguing that the Supreme Court's reasons for extending the actual-malice rule from public officials to public figures have little application to many of those now swept within the category of public figures).

186. Gertz v. Robert Welch, Inc., 418 U.S. 323, 344 (1974).

187. *See* Smolla, *Let the Author Beware*, *supra* note 3, at 2 (noting that many defamation plaintiffs, including public officials, have used media attention to their benefit in the past).

188. This view apparently is not shared by the general public, however. According to one survey, three fourths of the public believe libel laws ought to be the same for public officials as for private citizens, and two thirds believe public officials should be able to recover for defamation even if defendants believed the report was true at the time of publication. *See* TIMES-MIRROR CENTER FOR THE PEOPLE AND THE PRESS, THE PEOPLE AND THE PRESS—PART I: ATTITUDES TOWARD THE NEWS MEDIA 35-36 (Gallup poll conducted in January 1986), *reported in* LARRY J. SABATO, FEEDING FRENZY: HOW ATTACK JOURNALISM HAS TRANSFORMED AMERICAN POLITICS 202 (1991).

189. One version of this idea is discussed in Gabler, *The Gossip of Mount Olympus*, N.Y. TIMES, Apr. 17, 1991, at A23.

All gossip is predicated on the idea that there is a world from which we have been excluded. By collecting gossipy anecdotes, we invade the celebrity's world. By shaping narratives around their pecadilloes [sic], we assert our priority over them. It's the prose version of the strip search.

Of course, gossips receive nothing but opprobrium. . . . [But i]n a democratic society, what may seem like voyeurism may actually be a healthy activity not only because it provides us with a means of framing our values but because it channels our vengeance against the prevailing elites and knocks them down to size.

Id.

190. *See, e.g.*, Dun & Bradstreet, Inc. v. Greenmoss Builders, Inc., 472 U.S. 749, 756 (1985) (noting that the level of constitutional protection for defamation depends on both the strength of the state interests in protecting reputation and the concerns of the First Amendment).

191. "Simply put, the price of power has been raised dramatically, far too high for many outstanding potential officeholders." SABATO, *supra* note 188, at 211 (footnote omitted).

192. The rule is sufficiently recognized in the popular culture to serve as the premise for a movie, *see* ABSENCE OF MALICE (Columbia Pictures Indus. 1981), starring Paul Newman and Sally Field, and the title of a popular book, *see* RENATA ADLER, RECKLESS DISREGARD (1986).

193. Worse, perhaps, is the fear of opportunistic exploitation of the ordinary sins that accumulate in most lives.

194. Coleman v. MacLennan, 98 P. 281, 289 (Kan. 1908).

195. "'If we tell people there's to be absolutely nothing private left to them, then we will attract to public office only those most brazen, least sensitive personalities.'" SABATO, *supra* note 188, at 212 (quoting *New York Times* columnist Anthony Lewis).

196. The best analysis of the assumptions underlying the chilling-effect concept is Schauer, *Fear, Risk and the First Amendment: Unraveling the "Chilling Effect,"* 58 B.U. L. REV. 685 (1978).

197. The inequality of the contest is illustrated in a journalism review analysis of the media treatment of two news events in April 1991. A biography appeared containing salacious accusations about Nancy Reagan, and a few days later a former Carter administration official made public allegations that the Reagan campaign had made a deal with Iranian revolutionaries to delay the release of American hostages until after Reagan's inauguration. The allegations about Nancy Reagan were reported in major stories on the evening news programs of ABC, NBC, and CBS, on page one of the *New York Times,* and in cover stories in *Time* and *Newsweek.* The allegations about the presidential campaign appeared on page 10 of the *New York Times,* did not make the evening newscasts of any of the three networks, and appeared in *Time* and *Newsweek* only several weeks later in noncover stories. *See* Cohen, *Who Will Unwrap the October Surprise?,* COLUM. JOURNALISM REV., Sept./Oct. 1991, at 32.

198. In news coverage of charges against public officials and candidates, "the approach usually taken by journalists is clear: a repetitive, disproportionate stress on scandal, a 'more of the same' theme, a 'what can you expect from politicians' tone that deepens, extends, and reinforces the enduring public suspicion of all things political." SABATO, *supra* note 188, at 207 (footnote omitted).

199. *Cf.* Weinberg, *The Kitty Kelley Syndrome,* COLUM. JOURNALISM REV., July/Aug. 1991, at 36, 37 (noting that author of scandalous celebrity biographies enjoyed continuing fame and financial success despite documented history of inaccuracy).

200. For the most recent example of the power of the lurid, compare the attention paid to the first round of Senate Judiciary Committee hearings on the nomination of Justice Thomas, which focused on his executive and judicial record, with that paid to the second round, which focused on an allegation of sexual harassment.

201. *See* Rosenberg, *NBC News: How Mighty Have Fallen,* L.A. TIMES, May 1, 1991, at F1 (concluding that the accusations made against potential presidential candidate Charles Robb in a network news program aired during television ratings sweeps were largely unsubstantiated).

202. Rosenblatt v. Baer, 383 U.S. 75, 94 (1966) (Stewart, J. concurring).

203. Dun & Bradstreet, Inc. v. Greenmoss Builders, Inc., 472 U.S. 749, 769 (1985) (White, J., concurring in the judgment).

204. As Justice White wrote:

> Criticism and assessment of the performance of public officials and of government in general are not subject to penalties imposed by law. But these First Amendment values are not at all served by circulating false statements of fact about public officials. On the contrary, erroneous information frustrates these values.

Id. at 767.

205. As my colleague L.A. Powe, Jr. puts it: "Like the Holy Roman Empire which was neither Holy nor Roman nor an Empire, the constitutional rules of libel protect neither reputation nor the press nor the public's interest in receiving accurate information." *Powe, Mass Communications and the First Amendment: An Overview,* 55 LAW & CONTEMP. PROBS. 53, 60 (1992).

206. This explanation was first suggested to me by my colleague Cynthia Estlund.

207. *See, e.g.,* Priest & Klein, *The Selection of Disputes for Litigation,* 13 J. LEGAL STUD. 1, 4-6 (1984) (contending that imperfect information and unwarranted optimism are litigation stimuli throughout the law).

208. No doubt some plaintiffs err in the other direction—that is, they refrain from suing for defamatory falsehoods because they are unaware of the evidence that would enable them to prove actual malice and do not litigate to discover it because of the perceived difficulties of meeting that standard. In these instances, the standard underprotects reputation and overprotects speech.

209. Other possible explanations might be that (1) victims react to defamation emotionally rather than rationally, suing when they know (or should know) that they have no chance of winning, or (2) defendants react irrationally, incurring costs (and thus burdening speech) in amounts greater than would be necessary to pay for the reputational harm they have caused.

210. *See, e.g.,* Report of the Libel Defense Resource Center on the [Uniform] Defamation Act (June 25, 1990) (unpublished manuscript, on file with author). This report is a critique of the model defamation act proposed to the National Conference of Commissioners on Uniform State Laws on July 13-20, 1990, a predecessor of the PROPOSED DEFAMATION ACT, *supra* note 7.

211. Gertz v. Robert Welch, Inc., 418 U.S. 323, 342 (1974).

212. *See id.* at 348-50.

213. New York Times v. Sullivan, 376 U.S. 254, 279 (1964).

214. *See supra* notes 23-36 & 68-70 and accompanying text.

215. *See, e.g.,* JAMES ALEXANDER, A BRIEF NARRATIVE OF THE CASE AND TRIAL OF JOHN PETER ZENGER 23 (Stanley Katz ed., 1963) (describing Andrew Hamilton's defense of Zenger, in which he argued not only that a libel case was for a jury to decide but also that "truth was a defense against an accusation of libel, and that the jury had the right to return a general verdict where law and fact were intertwined"). *See generally*

LEONARD W. LEVY, EMERGENCE OF A FREE PRESS 128-33 (1985) (discussing the Zenger case and its influence on contemporary understanding of freedom of the press).

216. *See supra* notes 37-46 and accompanying text.

217. *See, e.g.,* Janklow v. Newsweek, Inc., 788 F.2d 1300 (8th Cir.) (holding that defendant's statements were absolutely protected), *cert. denied,* 479 U.S. 883 (1986); Pring v. Penthouse Int'l, Ltd., 695 F.2d 438 (10th Cir. 1982) (holding that a fictional statement incapable of literal interpretation was protected), *cert. denied,* 462 U.S. 1132 (1983).

218. The plaintiff in Tavoulareas v. Piro, 817 F.2d 762 (D.C. Cir.) (en banc), *cert. denied,* 484 U.S. 870 (1987), is reported to have incurred attorneys' fees of $2 million. See ANNENBERG PROPOSAL, *supra* note 5, at 9. An attorney for entertainer Wayne Newton testified that his client had incurred expenses of "well over a million dollars" by the time of trial. See Brief of Plaintiff/Appellee at 76 n.89, Newton v. NBC, 930 F.2d 662 (9th Cir. 1990) (Nos. 89-55220, 89-55285), *cert. denied,* 112 S. Ct. 192 (1991). The foundation that financed Gen. William Westmoreland's suit against CBS is reported to have spent more than $3.5 million in his behalf. *See* BOB BREWIN & SYDNEY SHAW, VIETNAM ON TRIAL: *WESTMORELAND VS. CBS* 365 (1987).

219. *See supra* note 67 and accompanying text.

220. The following excerpt from an article about the success that super- market tabloids enjoy in avoiding libel liability describes such a policy:

> The tabloids' lawyers, employing a defense strategy that is often used by daily newspapers and other publications in libel suits, usually file a barrage of motions in court that tend to delay cases and put pressure on the plaintiffs to settle.
>
> As a result, very few lawsuits ever come to trial. Some end with a settlement that includes a printed retraction or an agreement that the newspaper will not write anything about the celebrity for a specified period.
>
> *   *   *
>
> "Our strategy is to do the best possible job for our client," [a lawyer for the National Enquirer] said. "And that, of course, means litigating with all the resources necessary. We do what we need to do to win the case. We do not engage in over kill. We engage in a thorough defense of the Enquirer."

How the Supermarket Tabloids Stay out of Court, N.Y. TIMES, Jan. 4, 1991, at B14.

221. Media might also decide they can achieve about the same result far more cheaply by simply refusing to contest declaratory judgment actions, thereby depriving the judgments of any significance.

222. *See* LIBEL LAW AND THE PRESS, *supra* note 3, at 72.

223. *See* Tolchin, *Westmoreland Urges News Media to Provide a New Libel Remedy,* N.Y. TIMES, Mar. 16, 1985, at 8. This estimate may be too low; according to one source, CBS spent $5–$10 million and Westmoreland more than $3.5 million. *See* BREWIN & SHAW, *supra* note 218, at 354, 365.

224. Credit reporting agencies, data banks, and other information businesses are potential interest groups, but so far they have not been a significant voice.

225. *See* Keeton v. Hustler Magazine, Inc., 465 U.S. 770, 779 (1984) (holding that the plaintiff, despite having no connection to the forum state, could maintain suit there to take advantage of that state's unique statute of limitations so long as defendant had the requisite minimum contacts).

226. *See, e.g.,* ANNENBERG PROPOSAL, *supra* note 5, § 3(a); PROPOSED DEFAMATION ACT § 6.

227. In the Iowa study, 71 percent of the plaintiffs said they would have been satisfied with a correction or retraction. *See* LIBEL LAW AND THE PRESS, *supra* note 3, at 24.

228. The communications industry is said to account for 6 percent of the gross national product. *See* Harwood, *Multiple Media Inc.,* WASH. POST, Mar. 17, 1991, at D6.

229. *See* WILLIAM L. PROSSER, HANDBOOK OF THE LAW OF TORTS 819 (4th ed. 1971).

230. Gertz v. Robert Welch, Inc., 418 U.S. 323, 370 (1974) (White, J., dissenting).

231. *Id.* at 347.

232. *See, e.g.,* Sisler v. Gannett Co., 516 A.2d 1083, 1095 (N.J. 1986) (holding that a private plaintiff whose activities create risk of publicity must show actual malice); *cf.* Chapadeau v. Utica Observer-Dispatch, Inc., 341 N.E.2d 569, 571 (N.Y. 1975) (holding that private plaintiff must show that the publisher acted in a "grossly irresponsible manner" if the content of the publication was within the sphere of legitimate public concern).

233. *See, e.g.,* Stone v. Essex County Newspapers, 330 N.E.2d 161, 169 (Mass. 1975) (refusing to allow punitive damages in defamation actions); Wheeler v. Green, 593 P.2d 777, 789 (Or. 1979) (holding that the Oregon Constitution prohibits punitive damage awards in defamation cases).

234. *See, e.g.,* New England Tractor-Trailer Training v. Globe Newspaper Co., 480 N.E.2d 1005, 1009 n.4 (Mass. 1985) ("We view the fault requirement of Gertz to be intact regardless whether the private parties are suing on matters of public or private concern.").

235. Riesman, *Democracy and Defamation: Control of Group Libel,* 42 COLUM. L. REV. 727, 730 (1942).

236. *See, e.g.,* Chapadeau v. Utica Observer-Dispatch, Inc., 341 N.E.2d 569, 571 (N.Y. 1975) (creating "gross irresponsibility" fault standard for private-plaintiff libel cases); Renwick v. News & Observer Publishing Co., 312 S.E.2d 405, 411 (N.C. 1984) (rejecting false-light theory of recovery in invasion of privacy action); State v. Henry, 732 P.2d 9, 17 (Or. 1987) (interpreting Oregon Constitution to protect sale of obscenity to consenting adults); An-

derson v. Fisher Broadcasting Cos., 712 P.2d 803, 814 (Or. 1986) (redefining the private-facts branch of invasion of privacy).

237. *See* Lewis, New York Times v. Sullivan *Reconsidered, supra* note 3, at 604-07 (describing the reaction of public officials in Montgomery, Alabama, to the advertisement in the New York Times that became the subject of *New York Times v. Sullivan*).

chapter 2

A Declaratory Judgment Alternative to Current Libel Law*

MARC A. FRANKLIN[†]

The high-visibility libel cases of the last few years have focused public attention on the sensational aspects of defamation law. One by-product has been renewed criticism of the theory and practice of libel law. This chapter presents a statutory scheme based, with minor changes, on a proposal I sketched several years ago.[1] Events since then, primarily the emergence of legislative proposals at the congressional[2] and state levels[3] and recent commentary on my description,[4] warrant this step.

Plaintiffs, defendants, and observers have different perspectives on what is wrong with today's libel law. Some who think current law insufficiently protective of defendants stress the number of "groundless" cases in the courts and the enormous defense costs even in the vast majority of cases in which defendants prevail. Others emphasize the great danger to the survival of the grass-roots press posed by suits brought by powerful plaintiffs against smaller media.[5] On the other hand, some who think that the law is too restrictive to protect plaintiffs point to the paradigm of the ordinary citizen who is hurt by errors in the urban newspaper.[6] Others focus on the citizen who is discouraged from seeking office or serving in government by fear of being libeled without recourse.[7]

---

*This chapter was originally published in 74 CALIF. L. REV. 809 (1986).
[†]Frederick I. Richman Professor of Law, Stanford University. A.B. 1953; LL.B. 1956, Cornell University.

Some plaintiffs seek recourse in terms of monetary damages; others may want only a chance to restore their reputation.[8] Even more so than in other civil actions, pecuniary awards are not the only form of recourse for defamation. A declaratory judgment approach offers a promising remedy for the parties and society.

The motivating force behind this chapter and the draft proposal was my sense that libel law, particularly media libel law, has developed into a high-stakes game that serves the purposes of neither the parties nor the public.[9] I found the problem to be particularly acute for small media.[10] My goal was to frame a proposal that provides an alternative within the boundaries set by the Supreme Court's decisions.

The first step in developing alternatives to current libel law is to decide which goals have top priority and how much importance they deserve. Several are likely to warrant some weight. How important is it to adjudicate the truth or falsity of the defamation? How important is it to deter serious misbehavior at the prepublication stage? How important is it to protect defendants from fear of adverse monetary awards despite their prepublication behavior? How important is it to prevent extended pretrial discovery of editorial practices? How important is it to let plaintiffs seek damages where they can prove no special damages? In what situations can postpublication behavior best undo existing harm?

Ranking these goals is complicated by the fact that neither plaintiffs nor defendants are homogeneous groups. Plaintiffs vary from people who want only to clear their name, to those who feel the need to recover special damages they have suffered, to those who feel that they deserve general damages, to those who care more about intimidating the press than about gaining redress. Among defendants, there are media and nonmedia groups. In the media cluster, there are large and small media, and profitable and unprofitable media. Of course, even among the large and profitable media, some focus on traditional news reporting, others on in-depth magazine stories, and others on sex or gossip. The nonmedia cases involve defendants engaged in political activities, former employers writing reference letters, and competitors fighting over business. It is difficult to develop legislation that takes into account these vast differences.

A second set of issues to be faced in developing alternatives is related to the first but is more technical, involving such questions as whether any changes should be state or federal, legislative or judicial, mandatory or optional. Further, should the legislature (or the courts) mandate a single remedy for a particular situation? If optional remedies are provided, who gets the option?

Addressing the problem of remedies, the role given to the damage action for libel depends on the perceived importance of a variety of factors. Traditionally, tort actions have achieved two basic goals: (1) compensating (usually innocent) plaintiffs who have suffered cognizable harm and (2) imposing costs on defendants to make them aware that their conduct has fallen below the socially acceptable level. When a damage award achieves both goals at the same time, the system works fairly smoothly. There is tension, however, when a damage award achieves only one of the goals, as is often the case in libel law. Although the idea of contributory negligence seems inapplicable to this area,[11] it is common to have two innocent parties in cases in which the defendant's conduct has not been socially unacceptable. In libel law, we are concerned about the dangers of unwarranted liability because of the chilling effect on potential speakers.[12] Fortunately, in libel law, unlike personal-injury law, the injuries suffered by innocent victims often can be redressed in large part by remedies other than damages.

All of the considerations should shape the search for alternatives. Most current dissatisfaction with libel law is due to the failure of state courts and legislatures to appreciate these considerations and act within their respective domains to reduce libel law's high stakes. The Supreme Court alone cannot fine-tune a system as complex as libel law. As long as plaintiffs have no alternative to a damage suit, it may not take much to induce them to sue. If they had a more effective way of restoring their reputation, they might not be so quick to trigger this expensive remedy, which is generally unsuccessful for plaintiffs and poses great danger for defendants.

Rather than discuss these competing goals in the abstract or even in the context of libel reform, I think it better to present my proposal, which is framed in a sequence that roughly parallels the Schumer bill,[13] to permit easier comparison. Next, I discuss clarifications and changes from my earlier proposal. I then respond to criticism of the declaratory judgment approach. Finally, I set forth the Schumer bill and compare the two.[14]

THE PROPOSAL

The Plaintiff's Option Libel Reform Act[15]

Section 1. Action for Declaratory Judgment That Statement Is False and Defamatory

(a) *Cause of Action.*

(1) Any person who is the subject of any defamation may bring an action in any court of competent jurisdiction for a dec-

laratory judgment that such publication or broadcast was false and defamatory.

(2) Paragraph (1) shall not be construed to require proof of the state of mind of the defendant.

(3) No damages shall be awarded in such an action.

(b) *Burden of Proof.* The plaintiff seeking a declaratory judgment under subsection (a) shall bear the burden of proving by clear and convincing evidence each element of the cause of action described in subsection (a). In an action under subsection (a), a report of a statement made by an identified source not associated with the defendant shall not be deemed false if it is accurately reported.

(c) *Defenses.* Privileges that already exist at common law or by statute, including but not limited to the privilege of fair and accurate report, shall apply to actions brought under this section.

(d) *Bar to Certain Claims.* A plaintiff who brings an action for a declaratory judgment under subsection (a) shall be forever barred from asserting any other claim or cause of action arising out of a publication or broadcast which is the subject of such action.

Section 2. Limitation on Action

(a) Any action arising out of a publication or broadcast which is alleged to be false and defamatory must be commenced not later than one (1) year after the first date of such publication or broadcast.

(b) It shall be a complete defense to an action brought under Section 1 that the defendant published or broadcast an appropriate retraction before the action was filed.

(c) No pretrial discovery of any sort shall be allowed in any action brought under Section 1.

(d) When setting trial dates, courts shall give actions brought under Section 1 priority over other civil actions.

Section 3. Proof and Recovery in Damage Actions

(a) In any action for damages for libel or slander or false-light invasion of privacy, the plaintiff may recover no damages unless the plaintiff proves both falsity and actual malice by clear and convincing evidence.

(b) Punitive damages may not be awarded in any action for libel or slander or false-light invasion of privacy.

(c) A plaintiff who brings an action for damages for libel or slander or false-light invasion of privacy shall be forever barred from asserting any other claim or cause of action arising out of a publication or broadcast which is the subject of such action.

Section 4. Attorneys' Fees

(a) *General Rule.* Except as provided in subsection (b), in any action arising out of a publication or broadcast which is alleged to be false and defamatory, the court shall award the prevailing party reasonable attorneys' fees.

(b) *Exceptions.*

(1) In an action for damages, a prevailing defendant shall not be awarded attorneys' fees if the plaintiff sustained special damages and the action is found to have been brought and maintained with a reasonable chance of success.

(2) In an action brought under Section 1, a prevailing defendant shall not be awarded attorneys' fees if the plaintiff has brought and maintained the action with a reasonable chance of success and presented, or formally tried to present, to the defendant evidence that the statement was false and defamatory before the action was filed.

(3) In an action brought under Section 1, a prevailing plaintiff shall not be awarded attorneys' fees if the plaintiff has prevailed on the basis of evidence that the plaintiff did not present, or formally try to present, to the defendant before the action was filed.

(4) In any action brought under Section 1 in which the defendant has made an appropriate retraction after the filing of suit, the plaintiff shall be treated as the prevailing party up to that point and the defendant shall be treated as the prevailing party after that point.

Section 5. Effective Date

This Act shall apply to any cause of action that arises on or after the date of the enactment of this Act.

COMMENTARY

My goal has been to put into statutory framework the prose objectives asserted in my original critique.[16] A few changes and clarifications should be noted.

Elimination of the Preaction Conference

This proposal does not contain a provision for a preaction conference as my earlier article suggested. In light of the results of the Iowa study[17] and the criticisms of Prof. David A. Barrett,[18] I now think that although such a conference is desirable, the marginal gain does not justify requiring all plaintiffs to present their evidence of falsity to defendants in advance of a declaratory judgment action.[19] Mandating such conferences may also be unnecessary. First, since most plaintiffs seek corrections immediately after the appearance of the claimed error[20] and state that they would be satisfied with a correction,[21] they probably will present evidence of falsity to defendants voluntarily prior to suing. Second, the proposal uses fee incentives to encourage plaintiffs to present their evidence of falsity at an early stage.[22] Some plaintiffs who currently harass defendants with damage actions may also try to use the declaratory judgment action for harassment. Plaintiffs using the declaratory judgment action may hope for a default, which could make the defendant look even worse than he now looks after a successful but expensive defense. Awarding fees to the prevailing party discourages this possibility and encourages early good-faith discussions.

Extension to All Defendants

My earlier critique addressed the problem of media defendants only, although it was clear then[23] and is still now[24] that nonmedia defendants, particularly those involved in political disputes, are at serious risk of being sued for libel. Nonmedia defendants, such as persons who write letters to the editor[25] and persons who circulate petitions,[26] need the protection of this proposal as much as, if not more than, media defendants. First, these targets are particularly vulnerable to suits when the plaintiffs are motivated more by the desire to squelch criticism than to restore their reputations. Second, even the small media, as "chilled" as they may be by the current situation, have insurance, lawyers, professional editors, and reporters who know at least a few ground rules of libel. Nonmedia defendants, on the other hand, usually lack insurance and sophistication in the area of libel law, and their frequent lack of a corporate structure makes them extremely vulnerable to the threat of damage liability.[27]

There is also no reason why a plaintiff who claims to have been defamed by a nonmedia defendant should be denied access to the declaratory judgment alternative. Some plaintiffs may find that the declaratory judgment action is less attractive against nonmedia defendants because plaintiffs may not be able to bargain for a retraction that will reach the same audience that received the initial statement. Nevertheless, even nonmedia defendants may be able to reach their original audience fairly effectively in some cases, as where the claim arises from a mass mailing. In any event, retraction, although often an important private remedy in libel cases, is not a central feature of the declaratory judgment approach. This approach relies instead on the potential force and effect of an authoritative determination. The goal of a quick determination of falsity, thus, might appeal to both sides. Not allowing a plaintiff to pursue a declaratory judgment action against a nonmedia defendant serves no apparent social policy.[28]

Accordingly, this proposal benefits media and nonmedia defendants. First, the proposal makes damage actions less threatening to defendants by reducing available damages and increasing the likelihood that defendants can recover fees. Second, the public will probably know of the existence of the nonmonetary alternative to big damage actions and question the motives of powerful plaintiffs who choose to sue for absurd amounts of money. The availability of a low-stakes alternative uniquely suited to resolving disputes over falsity quickly will undercut claims of simply setting the record straight and expose nuisance suits as such.

The Role of Retraction

Although a judicial declaration of falsity is valuable, an appropriate retraction is preferable to a judicial declaration issued after a disputed hearing.[29] A plaintiff who would be satisfied by a declaratory judgment should be at least as satisfied with an appropriate retraction. An appropriate retraction not only establishes the falsity of the challenged statement but also constitutes an admission and publication of the correct facts.[30] My proposal therefore provides that an appropriate retraction forecloses a declaratory judgment action but not a damage action.[31] If the defendant publishes an appropriate retraction once the plaintiff begins the declaratory judgment action, the retraction is not a complete defense. Instead, the defendant is treated as the prevailing party after the retraction and may recover attorneys' fees. This provision thus encourages the plaintiff to settle once the defendant issues the retraction.[32]

The Questions of Existing Privileges

The state rules for absolute and qualified privileges have developed over the years to protect defendants from the strict-liability standard of the common law. The privileges deny relief to some plaintiffs who are the objects of false and defamatory statements in order to encourage certain speech. It is important to consider whether these privileges are necessary under my proposal since it would encourage speech by reducing fears of damage awards.

The courts accord most absolute privileges only to government officials. These absolute privileges are intended to permit government officials to carry out their duties free from the burden of defending libel cases.[33] The need for such privileges would continue, and perhaps be even greater, if a new action were added to the plaintiff's arsenal. There seems to be little reason to delete the absolute privileges in these cases.

Closely related to these privileges, and of great importance to the media, is the privilege of fair and accurate report, which facilitates wide-open public debate.[34] This privilege allows defendants being sued for repeating statements made by another to escape liability since they never vouched for their truth in the first place. It would be perverse to use the declaratory judgment action to put the defendant in the position of having to defend the truth of another's statement. In this situation, the plaintiff should pursue whatever remedies may be available against the originator of the statement.[35]

Thus, the privileges for government officials and for fair and accurate report should remain effective. It is true that the goal of a declaratory judgment action is to increase the number of libel cases that reach the question of truth and falsity. Nevertheless, the goal is not to reach 100 percent of all challenged statements. Such a goal would burden defendants by creating substantially more cases that need defending. More important, the loss of state privileges would counteract the overall goal of the new remedy—to reduce the current reticence of some defendants to speak freely about persons who they think are likely to sue.

The Federal–State Question

In my original critique, I did not resolve the question whether the state or federal government should consider libel reform. I have concluded for two reasons that the introduction of my proposed declaratory judgment remedy in libel cases might best occur at the state level. First, the libel suit has long been a state law action. Any proposed action must be meshed with existing law. States vary in attitudes toward litigation in general, toward libel law in particular, and toward the role of media. Probably as a result, journalists appear to differ in their sensitivity to the pressures of libel law. The presence or absence of such legal devices as retraction statutes probably influences media perceptions of the need for reforms. The state legislature is in the best position to account for these variances and make reforms consistent with current law.

Second, this area is ideal for state experimentation. Despite First Amendment limits on state power in libel law, the states still have room to experiment with ways to create greater satisfaction for all concerned. The current law is seriously deficient and statutory reform is worth attempting, but the implications are not yet clear enough to warrant a national approach.[36]

Fees

Although my statutory proposal contains some fee provisions that were not explicit in my original critique, these provisions are better discussed in connection with the fee provisions of the Schumer bill.[37]

DEFENDING THE DECLARATORY JUDGMENT APPROACH

In this section, I address criticisms of the declaratory judgment approach in general and my proposal in particular. Criticisms that center on comparisons with the Schumer bill are discussed in the next section.

Is the Proposal Unconstitutional?

Two constitutional questions might be raised about the proposal.[38] The first concerns the permissibility of entering a declaratory judgment against a media defendant without any showing of fault. The second relates to the permissibility of fee shifting without a showing of fault. The argument underlying both questions is that even if damages are not involved, First Amendment doctrine forbids entry of any judgment against media defendants without a showing of fault.[39] This exception to strict liability at common law for media defendants derives from *Gertz v. Robert Welch, Inc.*[40] and is still viable after *Dun & Bradstreet, Inc. v. Greenmoss Builders, Inc.,*[41] which seems unlikely to affect many mass media cases.[42]

Considering the underlying rationale of the doctrine and the Court's attempts to diminish the chill on media defendants while preserving the state's interest in protecting reputation,[43] the declaratory judgment provision should not be adjudged unconstitutional. First, the chilling effect has been produced by fear of large damage awards, which induce large and unrecoverable defense costs. The declaratory judgment action eliminates this fear of damages by reducing incentive to sue and allowing for awards of fees.

Second, even if the declaratory judgment action increases media defense costs by increasing the number of libel suits brought,[44] the defendant still can default and avoid those costs. While default is not an attractive alternative for any responsible defendant,[45] especially a media defendant that values its reputation for truth and accuracy, the proposal contemplates situations in which a defendant may feel justified in defaulting. For example, if the costs of defending a factually complex case would deplete the resources of a small newspaper, the publisher might decide to default and explain that behavior to the readership. That scenario is roughly analogous to the choice many newspapers face today when they assert the defense of actual malice in an effort to avoid litigating falsity. On the other hand, plaintiffs who do not view a default judgment as an admission might instead bring damage actions against defendants with a proclivity to default.[46] In these cases, the plaintiff must still show actual malice.[47]

Despite its viability as an alternative, default probably will not occur often enough to deprive plaintiffs of a remedy. Because the fear of liability is gone and defense costs will probably be lower and possibly recoverable, I would expect defaults by responsible publishers to be few and far between. Accordingly, the proposal will reduce chill by reducing media defendants' fear of large damage awards and giving them an opportunity to default in any event.

Finally, the Court's willingness to delete the actual-malice requirement for punitive damages in *Greenmoss*[48] suggests that the Court is less concerned about chill (at least in private-plaintiff cases) than it was previously. Considering the significant decrease in chill with the declaratory judgment action and the Court's lessened emphasis on chill, the Court probably would uphold a no-fault declaratory judgment.

The second, related constitutional question concerns fee shifting in the declaratory judgment action absent a finding of fault. The above explanation of how my proposal will reduce chill[49] applies here as well, and the Court should not be compelled by prior holdings to invalidate the fee-shifting provision. The possibility of recovering fees may be important in encouraging use of the declaratory action and therefore decreasing chill on media defendants. Even if the Court were to disallow that portion of the fee-shifting provision that allows the plaintiff to recover fees without a showing of fault, many plaintiffs might still be willing to spend their own funds to get a quick adjudication of falsity in a declaratory judgment action. Nevertheless, a plaintiff's inability to recover costs may cause serious problems for those who cannot afford an unreimbursable fee. These plaintiffs might find it easier to get a lawyer on a contingency basis and bring a damage action, even with a small chance of success. Although that might expose a losing plaintiff to liability for fees because that portion of the fee-shifting provision might be severable, how likely is the successful defendant to press for fees in a case in which the plaintiff could not afford a lawyer for a declaratory action?

Even if the Court held that the defendant must be found at fault to shift fees, a statute allowing the plaintiff to show fault by proving that the defendant's refusal to offer or make a proper retraction was unreasonable may be a solution. For example, a refusal might be unreasonable if the plaintiff showed the defendant strong evidence of falsity and the defendant had nothing substantial to rebut it. The liability for attorneys' fees would be based on conduct after the publication. *Gertz* need not be read as requiring that the "fault" here be found in behavior that preceded the publication. Indeed, using postpublication fault is more protective of the media because it provides the defendant with another chance to correct its mistake and avoid financial liability, often with the information provided by the plaintiff.[50] Therefore, the constitutional arguments against the declaratory judgment action and fee-shifting provision of my proposal can be answered.

Rejection of All Adjudication

Those who flatly reject the libel damage action will likely also reject a declaratory judgment approach. They favor absolute privilege, arguing that a judicial declaration of truth or falsity is not the way to air or resolve fact disputes.[51] This "marketplace" view instead assumes that the public can become informed about both sides of a dispute and can reach a judgment on the merits.

As long as the fact dispute involves major issues of governance and policy, even an admittedly flawed marketplace, with its unequal voices and unequal spending, is acceptable.[52] When false statements by the media injure an individual, however, leaving correction to the general marketplace of ideas is less attractive. The injured person's ideal remedy is likely to be a speedy retraction or correction that reaches the same audience as the original charges, as well as possibly damages. But government power to order the retraction or correction, even if constitutional,[53] is too dangerous to accept. Short of such coercion, which the supporters of absolute privilege would probably also reject, some opportunity for adjudication is necessary.

Since judicial determinations are necessary in some cases, it is desirable to offer a remedy that lowers the stakes of those determinations. Although these determinations are not always correct, the risk of judicial error is worth taking if the decision does not result in a monetary award or other serious penalty. Those who think that judicial adjudications of truth and falsity are too fragile to support the large monetary sanctions that often follow are aiming at the wrong target. They should not be concerned with the adjudication, which the parties may dispute afterward,[54] but with the remedies. A declaratory judgment of falsity that carries with it no monetary award presents a very different risk from those involved under the current libel regime.

Concern for Private Plaintiffs

My proposal bars negligence as a basis for damage liability. This surely makes it more difficult for "private" plaintiffs to use state law under *Gertz* to recover actual damages.[55] I have concluded earlier, however, that *Gertz* unsoundly draws a line between public and private plaintiffs. In addition, its negligence standard brings strict liability back into the libel area through the back door because it is simply too easy for plaintiffs to prove.[56] It is a small jump from finding an error to concluding that someone in the operation behaved unreasonably—either by failing to check with still another source or by failing to wait another day until the plaintiff could be reached.[57] Furthermore, the availability of negligence liability disproportionately hurts small media.[58] Professor Bloom,[59] who believes that the negligence system is functioning effectively, concludes that a media defendant's "[v]erification" of the disputed facts is the "key issue in most negligence litigation."[60] Since fewer than fifty cases have discussed the sufficiency of negligence,[61] he concludes that there is no reason why "reasonably clear standards will not eventually develop" in this area.[62] However, "reasonably clear standards" of negligence have not emerged in decades of personal-injury or property-damage tort actions—unless the standard is that plaintiffs win. If no other standards developed in negligence libel cases, a judge would probably accept a jury's findings on negligence liability. The jury could always find that the media defendant should have sought "verification" from still another source. This would lead to denials of summary judgment, trials at which juries find negligence, and appeals in which courts refuse to upset verdicts solely on the sufficiency point.[63]

The trade-off of smaller verdicts for negligence that was envisioned in *Gertz* is not likely to be of much solace to defendants because of the ruling that actual injuries included emotional distress.[64] The actual-injury category also includes special damages. Since business plaintiffs may have special damages,[65] media defendants face the possibility of very large damage judgments even under negligence. Even if *Gertz* is sound constitutional law,[66] a state could properly protect speech that is not reckless from damage liability, particularly if the plaintiff was offered an opportunity to obtain a no-fault decision on truth and falsity.[67]

Accordingly, it is not at all clear that the passage of time will make the situation more tolerable: Negligence simply flows too readily from error in libel cases. The elimination of a damage action for negligence is a valuable reform.

Will Eligible Plaintiffs Make the Election?

A critical question in any reform is how it will work in practice. This proposal seeks to encourage those who cannot obtain quick retractions from the publisher to choose the declaratory judgment route rather than the damage route. The proposal makes the damage remedy less attractive because it eliminates punitive damages, introduces a fee-shifting provision, and increases the burden of proof for private plaintiffs. The proposal also enhances the attractiveness of the declaratory judgment action by using fee-shifting provisions.[68] Will these reforms deter enough prospective plaintiffs from bringing damage actions to help relieve the chill on free speech under current libel law? This proposal may achieve that goal since legal expenses, even if not diminishing, may become more predictable in total and more uniform in each case. If insurance continues to use the deductible or retention clauses in declaratory judgment cases,[69] enough fee reimbursements may be granted to successful defendants to reduce the chill on editors and publishers.

Some organizations and individuals who are mainly interested in harassing defendants may hesitate to bring damage actions lest they become liable for the legal expenses of both sides under this proposal. The many public officials and others who now sue under a contingency-fee arrangement[70] would incur a new financial risk because of fee shifting. Nonetheless, other organizations that file nuisance suits are unlikely to use attorneys on a contingency-fee basis.[71] These organizations are already prepared to pay their own attorneys to maintain cases that by definition they cannot realistically win.[72] The fee-shifting provision would render such plaintiffs liable for defense fees that may run double or triple their own legal costs.[73] Nevertheless, groups that are powerful enough to harass effectively are probably sufficiently solvent to comply with any fee shift. Therefore, whether these groups would change their strategy is not clear. I suspect that many would not because one of their purposes is to cost the media defendant its deductible and perhaps lead to an increase in insurance premiums. Under the fee-shifting provision, the defendant would come out of a successful defense in the same position as it went in—except for the interruption of daily operations.[74]

Might harassing plaintiffs use declaratory judgments as opposed to damage actions? This also seems unlikely. First, in a declaratory judgment action, the falsity question lends itself to quicker resolution with accompanying embarrassment if the suit is not well grounded. Second, the simpler nature of the action means that the goal of costing defendants time and money would not be achieved nearly as effectively as with a damage action which would last longer and cost more.

Even if harassing plaintiffs may not change their habits, other plaintiffs will find the declaratory judgment action attractive. The available evidence indicates that many plaintiffs, particularly public officials, state that their primary goal is to correct the record and that they need not obtain damages if they can get a quick nonmonetary remedy.[75] Although one must examine carefully such self-serving statements, that position makes sense given the few cases in which plaintiffs can demonstrate clearly that they have sustained financial harm. Furthermore, those who cannot prove "actual malice" but who wish to restore their name will have the incentive to use the declaratory judgment action. They will be able to restore their reputation without putting the defendants at risk for large sums.

A great many subtle factors will control which plaintiffs will elect the declaratory judgment. Reform should be gradual to uproot as little tort law as possible in order to monitor how proposed reforms work. If states experiment with different versions, we can begin to identify the most important variables. The libel crisis warrants moving ahead with reforms, but the uncertainties indicate the wisdom of moving ahead slowly and acting at the state level.

Is Failure to Require Publication of an Adverse Judgment a Fatal Flaw?

My proposal has been criticized because of the absence of a mechanism to require retractions.[76] It is undesirable and unnecessary to mandate retractions under the declaratory judgment alternative. A timely retraction is crucial so that those who learned of the first statement will receive word of the correction. In the declaratory judgment situation, however, the judgment comes at a minimum several months after the initial statement. In addition, the declaratory judgment performs a different function than retraction. It resolves cases in which the statements do not lend themselves to retraction because the facts are uncertain. A case involving unclear facts is the least compelling one for mandatory publication of the judgment because it allows government coercion of speech in a doubtful situation. If a clear error emerges in the course of litigation, the fee-shifting arrangements probably would induce a voluntary retraction along the way.

Even absent a mandatory retraction provision, my proposal improves the plaintiffs' ability to restore their reputation. Since the act of initiating a damage suit itself may help restore the plaintiff's reputation,[77] initiating a declaratory judgment action should have the same effect. The declaratory judgment action also is more likely to reach the falsity question than is the damage action and to reach it sooner. At worst, a plaintiff emerges from the process with a judgment of falsity that can be used effectively with employers, creditors, acquaintances, and others who, in the plaintiff's estimation, may have been distant since the original statements. Beyond that, some judgments will surely be reported by the other local, regional, or national media as news, even if the defendant chooses not to publish them. The defendant may also find it newsworthy that a court has found its statements defamatory and false under the clear-and-convincing standard.

On balance, the overall danger of governmental coercion of the press involved in mandating retraction outweighs the marginal benefits lost by not requiring publication of the result of a declaratory judgment action.[78] Thus, I remain opposed to mandatory retraction proposals.

Should the Declaratory Judgment Action Include Discovery?

My decision to prohibit the use of discovery in the declaratory judgment action has also drawn fire. The objections stem from concern that the plaintiff will not have access to everything needed to prove falsity and, therefore, will be dissuaded from using the remedy.[79] Providing for discovery in the declaratory judgment action is unwarranted. First, most discovery by libel plaintiffs relates to actual malice; they usually do not use it to get information on falsity.[80] Second, in cases of the defendant's clear error, discovery is unnecessary to clarify facts. Therefore, the lack of discovery will speed restoration of the plaintiff's reputation rather than hinder the process in these cases. Even if the falsity issue is arguable, the plaintiff presumably already knows enough to render discovery unnecessary. The plaintiff may be curious about how the defendant made its mistake, but that is irrelevant if the plaintiff is confident of the facts. Of course, each party can do further investigation without the aid of discovery.

The foregoing argument is complicated, however, by my provision that winning plaintiffs cannot obtain fees if they have not disclosed their essential evidence of falsity to the defendant before seeking the declaratory judgment.[81] It is possible that a plaintiff who wants to recover fees will be disadvantaged by the defendant's prior knowledge of the plaintiff's case where the plaintiff has no advance knowledge of the defendant's case. This does not present a serious problem. The plaintiff may not know what the defense will be, but since the plaintiff usually starts with ample proof of falsity, this disparity is not serious.[82] Moreover, although the proposal may not require the defendant to submit its evidence to the plaintiff, the defendant may find it desirable to do so. If the defendant has powerful evidence of truth, disclosure will allow it to claim that, should it win, its legal fees incurred after that point should be reimbursable.[83] Full discovery is not essential to assure that a court's subsequent adjudication of the issues is accorded legitimacy[84] because plaintiffs know much about the facts necessary to litigate falsity.

Although I still reject discovery, my proposal should not fail on this point alone because allowing discovery will probably not cause fatal difficulties. Even defendants who care deeply about their credibility are managed by practical people who recognize that moderation may be appropriate when the stake no longer includes potentially enormous damage awards. Of course, some cases may become fierce battlegrounds over falsity. Even there, the cost of discovery would probably be far lower than the cost incurred in the same case today because fewer issues would be in contention.

Will My Proposal Delay Settlements?

In order to preserve the opportunity to recover fees under this proposal, the plaintiff will probably present or try to present evidence of falsity to the defendant before electing which route, if any, to follow.[85] In such situations, one commentator suggested that the defendant may delay settling until the plaintiff chooses a route and thus establishes the litigation's stakes.[86] This delay is unlikely, however, for several reasons. First, defendants probably realize that many plaintiffs are eager for quick corrections[87] and, where the case warrants it, will try to prevent litigation by admitting error or by granting the plaintiff the opportunity to reply.[88] Moreover, the plaintiff probably will complain very soon after the statement appears,[89] providing the defendant with the opportunity to avoid suits.

Second, under my proposal, the plaintiff could obtain a judgment of falsity more cheaply, rapidly, and effectively than is possible in a traditional damage suit. Accordingly, media defendants in particular would have to consider the likely increase in plaintiffs' willingness to sue and in the concomitant negative publicity for media. Such circumstances would encourage the defendant to settle unless it was confident of its version of the facts.

Finally, the fee-shifting provision, which encourages the parties to meet, may result in early settlement. Currently, many plaintiffs state that newspaper defendants antagonize them when they complain and that this propels them to sue.[90] This antagonism sometimes occurs at the hands of the embarrassed or angry reporter.[91] A more formal meeting with the potential defendant's top management or lawyer might focus discussion on hard evidence of falsity rather than on emotion. The organization may be happy to have the chance to correct without suit—a chance they might not have without the meeting.[92] Therefore, providing the plaintiff the option to pursue a nondamage action would reduce the likelihood of litigation.

THE SCHUMER BILL

Although legislation affecting libel is being introduced in state legislatures,[93] primary attention has focused on H.R. 2846, introduced in 1985 by Rep. Charles E. Schumer (D-N.Y.).[94] The House has already held hearings.[95] I have included the text of that bill to facilitate easy comparison with my proposal.

99TH Congress, 1st Session
H.R. 2846

To protect the constitutional right to freedom of speech by establishing a new cause of action for defamation, and for other purposes.

In the House of Representatives
June 24, 1985

Mr. Schumer introduced the following bill; which was referred to the Committee on the Judiciary

A Bill

To protect the constitutional right to freedom of speech by establishing a new cause of action for defamation, and for other purposes.

Be it enacted by the Senate and House of Representatives of the United States of America in Congress assembled,

Section 1. Action for Declaratory Judgment That Statement Is False and Defamatory

(a) *Cause of Action.*

(1) A public official or public figure who is the subject of a publication or broadcast which is published or broadcast in the print or electronic media may bring an action in any court of competent jurisdiction for a declaratory judgment that such publication or broadcast was false and defamatory.

(2) Paragraph (1) shall not be construed to require proof of the state of mind of the defendant.

(3) No damages shall be awarded in such an action.

(b) *Burden of Proof.* The plaintiff seeking a declaratory judgment under subsection (a) shall bear the burden of proving by clear and convincing evidence each element of the cause of action described in subsection (a).

(c) *Bar to Certain Claims.* A plaintiff who brings an action for a declaratory judgment under subsection (a) shall be forever barred from asserting any other claim or cause of action arising out of a publication or broadcast which is the subject of such action.

(d) *Election by Defendant.*

(1) A defendant in an action brought by a public official or public figure arising out of a publication or broadcast in the print or electronic media which is alleged to be false and defamatory shall have the right, at the time of filing its answer or within ninety (90) days from the commencement of the action, whichever comes first, to designate the action as an action for a declaratory judgment pursuant to subsection (a).

(2) Any action designated as an action for a declaratory judgment pursuant to Paragraph (1) shall be treated for all purposes as if it had been filed originally as an action for a declaratory judgment under subsection (a), and the plaintiff shall be forever barred from asserting or recovering for any other claim or cause of action arising out of a publication or broadcast which is the subject of such action.

Section 2. Limitation on Action

Any action arising out of a publication or broadcast which is alleged to be false and defamatory must be commenced not later than one year after the first date of such publication or broadcast.

Section 3. Punitive Damages Prohibited

Punitive damages may not be awarded in any action arising out of a publication or broadcast which is alleged to be false and defamatory.

Section 4. Attorney's Fees

In any action arising out of a publication or broadcast which is alleged to be false and defamatory, the court shall award the prevailing party reasonably attorney's fees, except that—

(1) The court may reduce or disallow the award of attorney's fees if it determines that there is an overriding reason to do so; and

(2) The court shall not award attorney's fees against a defendant which proves that it exercised reasonable efforts to ascertain that the publication or broadcast was not false and defamatory or that it published or broadcast a retraction not later than ten (10) days after the action was filed.

Section 5. Effective Date

This Act shall apply to any cause of action which arises on or after the date of the enactment of this Act.

The Schumer bill and my proposal agree on several features, including the initial plaintiff's option to elect a declaratory judgment action,[96] the burden of proof in that action,[97] the abolition of punitive damages in libel actions,[98] the effect of the election on the damage action,[99] and a one-year statute of limitations.[100] Both also recognize the need for some fee shifting.[101] On the other hand, several major differences exist as well, two of which have already been addressed.[102] I now turn to others.

The Defendant's Election

My central disagreement with the Schumer bill is that it gives the defendant rather than the plaintiff control over election of remedies. Although the plaintiff has the first chance to elect, the defendant may override the plaintiff's choice of damages and convert the action into one for declaratory judgment.[103] The result is that any eligible defendant[104] may unilaterally avoid exposure to damage liability without regard to its prepublication behavior and without regard to ensuing harm. (Moreover, a defendant can even avoid liability for any attorneys' fees simply by retracting within ten days of the plaintiff's filing.[105]) This provision of the Schumer bill is objectionable because it (1) is unfair to all plaintiffs, especially those with special damages; (2) shows premature willingness to concede society's inability to handle intentional defamatory falsehoods; (3) destroys a long-standing tort remedy without a showing that less drastic alternatives are not available; and (4) is politically unattractive.

First, the defendant's election is unfair to plaintiffs since plaintiffs who have suffered harm will be effectively barred from suing for damages by the likelihood that these damage cases will be converted into declaratory judgment actions by the defendant. I suspect also that damage cases involving public plaintiffs[106] will virtually disappear. Public plaintiffs who think they can show falsity but not actual malice will elect the declaratory judgment route. Those who think they can prove actual malice and who feel the need for damages will bring the tort action, yet those "strong" cases are the ones that the media defendants will convert to declaratory judgment actions. The only plausible situation in which media defendants might willingly expose themselves to damage liability and extensive defense costs is when the defendant perceives only a minimal risk of liability and would rather accept that chance than either admit error or have falsity adjudged in the declaratory action. Yet, even in that situation and even if the defendant can recoup its legal costs if it prevails, the time and interruption cannot be recouped and the damage action will remain costly. In short, the damage action will rarely be used.[107]

The self-serving assertion of many plaintiffs that they sue for nonmonetary relief[108] does not support a conclusion that no plaintiff should be permitted a nontrumpable election to seek damages. Even the press itself appears concerned about the fairness of this approach.[109] Unless one denies the existence of harm in libel cases, something that most journalists are unwilling to do,[110] it is hard to justify the de facto elimination of damage awards in virtually all cases.

Second, the defendant's election represents an unwise capitulation to irresponsible publishers who intentionally defame others. My approach and that underlying the Schumer bill differ about how effective the availability of a libel damage action is as a deterrent to defamation. The 5 percent chance of suffering an unpredictable damage judgment[111] and the higher chance of incurring unrecoupable costs in damage actions clearly do chill the aggressiveness of responsible journalists.[112] Barrett argues that giving defendants the option to avoid damages in exchange for a declaratory judgment action that is harder to defend will reduce the chill, thus producing benefits that exceed the cost of increasing the propensity of irresponsible publishers to lie.[113] This conclusion reflects an incorrect assessment of the costs and benefits. I have already shown that my proposal can reduce some chilling of responsible publishers without functionally eliminating the damage action.[114]

The defendant's election is also premised on a misunderstanding of the ability of damage actions to deter irresponsible publishers. The traditional results of a 5 percent success rate[115] probably do not apply to an irresponsible publisher who is determined to build audiences with defamatory lies. This figure was derived mainly from cases involving traditional publishers and broadcasters.[116] Now that Carol Burnett, for example, has broken the ice,[117] we are seeing an increasing amount of litigation against organizations like the *National Enquirer* and *Globe International*.[118] It is unlikely that deliberate defamers will be held liable at a rate as low as 5 percent in the coming years. Under my proposal, plaintiffs in such cases would be able to control the remedy. In contrast, under the Schumer bill, the defendant may convert the damage action into a declaratory judgment and defend, risking exposure to nothing more than fee shifting. The defendant's election removes any deterrent effect of libel law by allowing irresponsible publishers to choose either to retract and escape liability for attorneys' fees or to default and face only minimal fee shifting.[119]

Moreover, the scandal press is not the only group that can be called "irresponsible" and which would no longer be subject to the deterrent force of libel damage actions under the Schumer bill. Another candidate for that category is the narrow-spectrum publisher or broadcaster whose message is pitched to a faithful political or religious following and who may be tempted to play fast and loose with the truth.[120] Also, the small publisher or broadcaster who has great local power but lacks ethical standards may be tempted by the defendant's election to defame intentionally. The Schumer bill would free these groups from restraint. I do not argue that the actual-malice rule is generally necessary to provide responsible publishers with incentives to be careful. Most already have professional and social incentives to be honest and careful.[121] But if the group of potentially irresponsible publishers is broader than the "professional criminal"[122] category, as I believe it is, then to release all media from legal control as the Schumer bill does would not only be morally dubious but would produce new instances of irresponsibility.[123]

Barrett justifies this loss of checks against intentional defamation in part by asserting that it "is a fair and necessary trade-off for the parties in light of societal interests, particularly the First Amendment interest in robust debate."[124] The Schumer bill, however, draws no distinction between public officials and public figures and is not limited to statements that implicate self-governance or any other subject matter. As a result, it deprives low-level public officials[125] and involuntary public figures[126] of their actions in the name of improving the quality of public debate. Does "debate on public issues" include anything that titillates any segment of the public? If the defendant's election were limited to stories concerning self-governance,[127] with all the line drawing that would entail, one might be able to understand and maybe even agree with the point. Now, however, the bill sweeps so broadly that it protects everything in print about "public" persons.

Although critics agree that large transaction costs play a role in the current libel law problem, the amount saved by any proposal will depend on the attractiveness and simplicity of its low-stakes alternatives. The Schumer bill appears to conclude that the current situation is so bad that there is no time to try measures that are less protective of the press. Many who deplore the current situation probably empathize with plaintiffs and would find the Schumer bill a giant step in the wrong direction. My proposal is based on a perception of problems on both sides.

Third, the defendant's election is undesirable because enough uncertainties exist over the effects of libel law reform to warrant rejection of the Schumer bill's immediate and uniform imposition of a defendant's option. The results of my proposal are sufficiently unpredictable that it is far too early to conclude that it or some variation of it will not encourage enough plaintiffs to use the declaratory judgment action to reduce transaction costs while preserving existing legal techniques to protect citizens from being defamed at will without effective recourse. The Schumer bill, without any evidence that an approach based on the plaintiff's election will not do the job, would permit any defendant to avoid the compensatory and deterrent functions of tort law.

Fourth, the Schumer bill is politically unattractive. Barrett has suggested that POLRA is unlikely to command public support.[128] Its major political drawback seems to be the increase in proof requirements for private plaintiffs.[129] As I earlier responded,[130] giving all such plaintiffs an election to seek a declaratory judgment warrants the increase in proof requirements.[131] Despite my treatment of private plaintiffs, I believe that my proposal is more likely to have widespread support than is the Schumer bill. I would not relish having to convince a legislature or the electorate to adopt a statute that allows "irresponsible publishers" to escape all liability for whatever harm they may impose by their use of deliberate falsehoods.[132]

The Shifting of Fees

Although both my proposal and the Schumer bill place heavy emphasis on fee shifting in both damage actions and declaratory judgment
actions, they approach the matter differently. For a damage action,
the Schumer bill allows a court to alter the rule that the prevailing
party gets reasonable attorneys' fees when "there is an overriding
reason to do so."[133] Under my proposal, the general fee shift will
occur in damage actions except when a losing plaintiff has in fact
sustained special damages and had a reasonable chance of proving
falsity and actual malice with convincing clarity.[134] My fee-shifting
provision is preferable because it will encourage a move away from
damage actions. The Schumer bill's open-ended, overriding-reason
provision probably would not be used because of judicial reluctance to
prejudice further any plaintiff, with or without special damages, who
could clearly show falsity, even if the plaintiff's evidence of actual
malice was truly weak.

In the declaratory judgment situation, also, we agree that fees
play a central role but disagree over that role. The Schumer bill's
general rule that the winner gets reasonable fees is again subject to
the overriding-reason exception.[135] In the Schumer bill, the plaintiff
need not be able to predict the outcome in order to elect remedies
because the defendant can, and is likely to, override the plaintiff's
election of a damage action. Since in my proposal the plaintiff's
election controls, the plaintiff must be given some reasonable expectation about when he can recover fees. It is important that the fee rules
be fairly predictable because there will be no other money changing
hands in a declaratory judgment action.

In addition to the overriding-reason exception, the Schumer bill
would deny a successful plaintiff fees in two other situations. First, the
successful plaintiff in either a damage or a declaratory judgment
action would be denied fees if the defendant could prove that it made
reasonable efforts to avoid the publication of the false and defamatory statement.[136] This would greatly discourage the use of the
declaratory judgment action—if the election were with the plaintiff. If
fees were crucial, the plaintiff would have to become concerned with
the defendant's prepublication behavior. Rather than focus only on
falsity, the plaintiff would have to consider how difficult it would be to
show falsity and then guess about what the defense would be able to
show on the question of its due care in order to determine the size of
the fees in the case. This uncertainty may well deter plaintiffs who
otherwise would be inclined to seek a declaratory judgment from
doing so.[137]

The second situation in which the Schumer bill would deny the successful plaintiff fees occurs when the defendant has retracted within ten days after suit was filed, whether it is a suit for damages or for declaratory relief.[138] In damage actions, I would leave the role of retractions to state law.[139] I see no reason why a plaintiff who shows actual malice and recovers compensatory damages should be unable to recover attorneys' fees simply because a retraction was published as much as a year after the original defamation.[140]

In contrast to these two provisions of the Schumer bill, my fee-shifting provisions are designed to lead the plaintiff to elect the declaratory judgment action, in part by emphasizing postpublication conduct. The proposal provides that losing plaintiffs will not owe fees unless they brought or maintained the action without reasonable chance for success or failed to present their evidence to the defendant in advance of the action.[141] Plaintiffs who put their cards on the table early either will get a quick correction or reply or will have falsity adjudicated. In addition, if they prevail, they will recover fees. If plaintiffs lose the action, they will not owe fees unless they are found to have acted unreasonably in bringing or maintaining the action. I consider that a reasonable package to encourage resort to the action.

My proposal thus tries to encourage quick resolution of cases. The goal is to encourage a plaintiff to try to get a correction or an opportunity to reply without resort to the legal process. A plaintiff who is not seeking damages or trying to burden the defendant should not hesitate to present that evidence.[142]

In order to encourage settlements, the proposal states that an appropriate retraction made before the action is filed is a complete defense to an action for declaratory judgment.[143] If an appropriate retraction is made after the declaratory action is filed, the question instead becomes one of fees rather than one of absolute defense as under the Schumer bill. Until the retraction, the defendant has forced the plaintiff to incur legal costs and the defendant should become the prevailing party only after that point. The result is that the proposal treats the plaintiff as the prevailing party on the publication of an appropriate retraction but exposes the plaintiff to liability for the defendant's fees after that point if the plaintiff does not accept the retraction and dismiss the action.

CONCLUSION

In this chapter, I have provided a statutory version of a proposal that I had previously only described. I have sought to defend the declaratory judgment approach in general and the specifics of my proposal from a variety of claims. Finally, I have responded to assertions that the Schumer bill is preferable to my proposal.

On this last point, we would do well to recall the Supreme Court's admonition about the dangers of absolute privilege for falsehood:

> [T]he use of the known lie as a tool is at once at odds with the premises of democratic government and with the orderly manner in which economic, social, or political change is to be effected. Calculated falsehood falls into that class of utterances which "are no essential part of any exposition of ideas, and are of such slight social value as a step to truth that any benefit that may be derived from them is clearly outweighed by the social interest in order and morality. . . ." [citation omitted] Hence the knowingly false statement and the false statement made with reckless disregard of the truth, do not enjoy constitutional protection.[144]

The Schumer bill, with the defendant's election, puts the power to publish intentionally false and defamatory statements with practical impunity into the hands of all media. Furthermore, this power would likely be used by the most irresponsible publishers. The state of libel law today has not reached the point of needing such a dramatic and traumatic overhaul. We would do better by moving toward state experimentation with an intermediate solution such as my proposal.

NOTES

1. Franklin, *Good Names and Bad Law: A Critique of Libel Law and a Proposal,* 18 U.S.F. L. REV. 1 (1983).

2. *See* H.R. 2846, 99th Cong., 1st Sess. 1985 (introduced by Rep. Charles E. Schumer (D-N.Y.)).

3. *E.g.,* S. 1979, 1985-86 Cal. Leg., Reg. Sess. (1986) (introduced by Sen. Bill Lockyer).

4. *E.g.,* Cendali, *Of Things to Come—The Actual Impact of* Herbert v. Lando *and a Proposed National Correction Statute,* 22 HARV. J. ON LEGIS. 441, 478-79 (1985).

5. This concern also applies to suits brought by powerful plaintiffs against nonmedia defendants, such as political and tenant groups. *E.g.,* E. PELL, THE BIG CHILL 159-88 (1984).

6. *E.g.,* Gertz v. Robert Welch, Inc., 418 U.S. 323, 392 (1974) (White, J., concurring) (focus on the "ordinary citizens" and "defenseless individual" hurt by "the owners of the press" who, along with "stockholders," can better bear the burdens of libel).

7. B. FEIN, NEW YORK TIMES V. SULLIVAN: AN OBSTACLE TO ENLIGHTENED PUBLIC DISCOURSE AND GOVERNMENT RESPONSIVENESS TO THE PEOPLE 9-11 (1984).

8. *See* Soloski, *The Study and the Libel Plaintiff: Who Sues for Libel?*, 71 IOWA L. REV. 217, 220 (1985) (summarizing results of Iowa study, based on interviews of 164 libel plaintiffs).

9. Franklin, *supra* note 1, at 2-22.

10. *Id.* at 14-22; *see also* Nagel, *How to Stop Libel Suits and Still Protect Individual Reputation*, WASH. MONTHLY, Nov. 1985, at 12, 18 (proposing special rules for a "news organization that is too poor to afford even legal fees").

11. *But see* Note, *In Defense of Fault in Defamation Law*, 88 YALE L.J. 1735, 1747-49 (1979) (proposing to exclude evidence "that a plaintiff refused to disclose to the defendant in response to detailed defamatory charges and that was not otherwise reasonablyavailable at the time of publication").

12. Franklin, *supra note 1*, at 13-22; Barrett, *Declaratory Judgments for Libel: A Better Alternative*, 74 CALIF. L. REV. 847 (1986). *See generally* Schauer, *Fear, Risk, and the First Amendment: Unraveling the "Chilling Effect,"* 58 B.U.L. REV. 685 (1978) (discussing the role of the chilling-effect doctrine in First Amendment jurisprudence, including libel law). Although I think the phrase "steering wide" captures better the concern of the Court in this area, *see* New York Times Co. v. Sullivan, 376 U.S. 254, 279 (1963) (quoting Speiser v. Randall, 357 U.S. 513, 526 (1957)), the phrase "chilling effect" for better or worse has become the dominant phrase.

13. *Supra* note 2.

14. Barrett comments at length on my proposal and on the Schumer bill, *supra* note 12. For a comparison of the financial impact of these proposals on publishers, *see* Franklin, *The Financial Impact of Libel Reform on Repeat Players*, in THE COST OF LIBEL: ECONOMIC AND POLICY IMPLICA- TIONS (E. Dennis & E. Noam eds.).

15. Hereinafter POLRA.

16. *See* Franklin, *supra* note 1, at 35-49.

17. Bezanson, Cranberg, & Soloski, *Libel Law and the Press: Setting the Record Straight*, 71 IOWA L. REV. 215-33 (1985).

18. Barrett, *supra* note 12, at 877-78.

19. In my earlier article, *supra* note 1, I referred to the nonmonetary action as a "restoration" action. Contrary to Barrett's hunch, *supra* note 12, at 848-49, I did not choose the name to suggest that plaintiffs are made whole by this remedy—any more than other tort plaintiffs are made whole by "dam- ages." The word "restoration" is more accurate than the word "vindication," which has been used in this context, *see* Hulme, *Vindicating Reputation: An Alternative to Damages as a Remedy for Defamation*, 30 AM. U.L. REV. 375 (1981); Note, *Vindication of the Reputation of a Public Official*, 80 HARV. L. REV. 1730 (1967), but here "declaratory judgment" is used because that is the procedural device employed and is consistent with the Schumer bill's ter- minology. *See infra* notes 95-96 and accompanying text.

20. Half of the plaintiffs in the Iowa study went to the media before they spoke to an attorney. Soloski, *supra* note 8, at 217, 219-20. The study further found that "nearly three-quarters of the plaintiffs on their own, through their attorney or with their attorney, contacted the media prior to filing their libel suit. Nearly all of the contacts with the media occurred within

two days of publication or broadcast of the alleged libel." Statement of John Soloski at Joint ABA-ANPA Task Force National Symposium on Libel, tape 2, at 9 (Mar. 21, 1986) (on file with author) [hereinafter Soloski statement].

21. Soloski, *supra* note 8, at 220; Soloski statement, *supra* note 20, tape 2, at 8-9.

22. POLRA §§ 4(b)(2)-(b)(3). This does not limit the evidence that the plaintiff would be able to introduce at the trial, though it does affect the question of shifting fees. Although POLRA does not go so far, I think it might be appropriate to permit the trial judge to award fees to a losing defendant where it appears that the plaintiff deliberately withheld evidence of falsity until trial. This would suggest that the plaintiff's goal was not to demonstrate falsity as soon as possible but rather to engage the defendant in a legal proceeding that could have been avoided. The related question of the role of discovery in the declaratory judgment action is discussed *infra* notes 79-84 and accompanying text.

23. *See* PELL, *supra* note 5, at 159-88.

24. *E.g.,* Greenhouse, *Outspoken Private Critics Increasingly Face Slander Lawsuits,* N.Y. TIMES, Feb. 14, 1985, at B11, col. 1 (nat'l ed.); Pring, *Intimidation Suits Against Citizens: A Risk for Public-Policy Advocates,* NAT'L L.J., July 22, 1985, at 16.

25. *E.g.,* Karnell v. Campbell, 206 N.J. Super, 81, 501 A.2d 1029 (1985).

26. *E.g.,* Good Government Group of Seal Beach, Inc. v. Superior Court, 22 Cal. 3d 672, 586 P.2d 572, 150 Cal. Rptr. 258 (1978), *cert. denied,* 441 U.S. 961 (1979).

27. If the defendant's election under the Schumer bill, *supra* note 2, can ever be justified, which I doubt, *see infra* notes 103-32 and accompanying text, and the worthiest recipient might well be certain nonmedia defendants. However, the bill excludes this group of potential libel defendants from coverage because of its focus on media defendants, Schumer bill, *supra* note 2, §1(a)(1). Note that a few states may permit successful libel defendants to recover their costs. CAL. CIV. PROC. CODE §1021.7 (Deering 1972).

28. The only plausible one, that nonmedia defendants might be further chilled by not being able to defend on actual-malice grounds, seems not to be borne out because of the impact damage suits are having on such groups under current law. *See supra* note 24.

29. The word "appropriate" is always to be implied when retractions are discussed. It is simply not the case that any correction will suffice. *See infra* note 30 (discussing judicial handling of retraction). A private agreement may also be appropriate. Apart from a payment of money, this might include an agreement by a media defendant to publish a reply or a letter to the editor to resolve the dispute. Even if such an undertaking does not involve a formal settlement of the dispute, it may satisfy the needs of the plaintiff to such an extent that further legal action is unnecessary.

30. The issue is the adequacy of the retraction and not plaintiff's sense of that adequacy. The adequacy of a retraction is a question within the traditional purview of courts. *See, e.g.,* Boswell v. Superior Court, 125 Ariz. 307, 609 P.2d 577 (1980); *see also* Annotation, *Libel and Slander: Who Is*

Protected by Statute Restricting Recovery Unless Retraction Is Demanded, 84 A.L.R. 3d 1249 (1978) (discussing who is eligible to take advantage of a retraction statute). The introduction of constitutional fault rules has removed much of the value from retraction statutes and they no longer play a major role in litigation. Eaton, *The American Law of Defamation Through* Gertz v. Robert Welch, Inc. *and Beyond: An Analytical Primer*, 61 VA. L. REV. 1349, 1439-43 (1975).

It is unlikely that the creation of a declaratory judgment action will sharply increase the number of retractions made by libel defendants. To the extent legal questions arise—what parties are covered, the placement of the retraction, and the language used—they are much more easily resolved than the average substantive libel question. It might also be noted that a defendant who has decided that a retraction is appropriate can avoid virtually all questions of adequacy by generously admitting the error rather than by trying to say as little as a lawyer thinks permissible.

31. POLRA § 2(b). *But see* Cendali, *supra* note 4, at 500 (proposing that an appropriate "correction" will bar a damage action except for special damages). Barrett asserts that my 1983 article provided that a reasonable retraction barred a damage action. Barrett, *supra* note 12, at 873. His efforts to enlist me as a past supporter of a defendant's option can only be achieved by taking my words out of context and by adding two sets of ellipses to a crucial sentence. The first sentence on which he relies appears in a section devoted to discussion of the action for restoration. Franklin, *supra* note 1, at 40. The immediate context involves encouraging the parties to negotiate before going into court. *Id.* at 41-42. The entire sentence reads: "In such a case [one in which the plaintiff has already sued for restoration] the plaintiff will lose the right to a restoration judgment and also the right to bring a damage action [since they are mutually exclusive and plaintiff has already elected restoration] upon defendant's publication of the disputed, now approved, retraction." *Id.* at 42. Little of the 1983 proposal and article would have made sense if the plaintiff could be deprived of a damage action at any time by an unrequested retraction. *Id.* at 37-47. It would make no more sense to say that the plaintiff's act of demanding a retraction, as part of general negotiations and before deciding on an election, waived the right to bring a damage action. That is no way to encourage negotiations.

Barrett also misreads my statement that a retraction would "foreclose" either action. *Id.* at 43-44. This sentence refers to a situation in which a publisher is "convinced it had made an error but that it was not liable for damages. . . ." *Id.* at 43. In that situation, the parties would focus on the restoration action—in which the plaintiff had to demand a retraction before suing for restoration. If the publisher retracted, the plaintiff would be unable to pursue the restoration action because retraction preempts the action—and the plaintiff would be unable to win a damage action because, by hypothesis, it would not lie on the merits. This is the only plausible reading, given the next paragraph with its emphasis on negotiations preceding election and the recognition that the demand for retraction must precede a restoration action. *Id.* at 44. Again, it is inconceivable that serious negotiations before election that included the plaintiff's demand for a retraction could amount to waiver. Finally, Barrett's reading is inconsistent with several other passages in the article. *Id.* at 36, 43, 45, 46.

32. POLRA § 4(b)(4). Because the test is the appropriateness of the retraction and not the reasonableness of the plaintiff's belief, plaintiff's reasonable but erroneous rejection of an appropriate retraction will not prevent fee shifting.

33. *E.g.,* Barr v. Matteo, 360 U.S. 564, 571 (1959). An extended explanation of the doctrine appears in Gregoire v. Biddle, 177 F.2d 579 (2d Cir. 1949), *cert. denied,* 339 U.S. 949 (1950), in which Judge Learned Hand stated:

[I]t is impossible to know whether the claim is well founded until the case has been tried, and . . . to submit all officials, the innocent as well as the guilty, to the burden of a trial and to the inevitable danger of its outcome, would dampen the ardor of all but the most resolute, or the most irresponsible, in the unflinching discharge of their duties. Again and again the public interest calls for action which may turn out to be founded on a mistake, in the face of which an official may later find himself hard put to it to satisfy a jury of his good faith. . . . In this instance it has been thought in the end better to leave unredressed the wrongs done by dishonest officers than to subject those who try to do their duty to the constant dread of retaliation. *Id.* at 581.

34. *See* R. SACK, LIBEL, SLANDER, AND RELATED PROBLEMS 144-51, 316-25 (1980); B. SANFORD, LIBEL AND PRIVACY 179-84, 370-93 (1985).

35. The other qualified privileges, such as common interest or the protection of one's or another's interest, *see* W.P. KEETON, D. DOBBS, R. KEETON, & D. OWEN, PROSSER AND KEETON ON THE LAW OF TORTS §115, at 824-36 (5th ed. 1984), do not seem to present serious problems today. They seem to be fairly far from the concern that generates proposals of reform—the encouragement of more wide-open public debate. My inclination is to leave these in place as well.

It seems increasingly clear that fair comment and opinion privileges are not privileges but part of the plaintiff's case on falsity. *See* Philadelphia Newspapers, Inc. v. Hepps, 475 U.S. 767 (1986); Franklin & Bussel, *The Plaintiff's Burden in Defamation: Awareness and Falsity,* 25 WM. & MARY L. REV. 825 (1984). But *see* Barrett, *supra* note 12, at 863 n.100 (discussing the role of fair comment and opinion privileges in declaratory judgment actions). My proposal's requirement that damage actions be based on actual malice, *see infra* notes 55-67 and accompanying text, has the incidental benefit of eliminating the vexing state law questions of when defendants lose the current qualified privileges. *See* Smolla, *Let the Author Beware: The Rejuvenation of the American Law of Libel,* 132 U. PA. L. REV. 1, 78-81 (1983).

36. To the extent that problems common to several states can be resolved uniformly, as perhaps with differing statutes of limitations, congressional action might well be appropriate. *See* Schumer bill § 2 (providing for a one-year statute of limitations in both damage and declaratory judgment actions). *See generally* Levine, *Preliminary Procedural Protection for the Press from*

Jurisdiction in Distant Forums after Calder *and* Keeton, 1984 ARIZ. ST. L.J. 459 (discussing court-created procedural protections for small-media defendants sued in distant jurisdictions where their circulation is limited). Perhaps questions involving the availability and pricing of libel insurance also are appropriate for national attention.

37. *See infra* notes 133-43 and accompanying text.

38. Cendali, *supra* note 4, at 479.

39. Gertz v. Robert Welch, Inc., 418 U.S. 323, 347 (1973) (in order to recover general compensatory and punitive damages for defamation of a private plaintiff by a media defendant, plaintiff must show actual malice); New York Times Co. v. Sullivan, 376 U.S. 254, 279-80 (1963) (in order to recover damages for defamation, public official must show that the media defendant acted with actual malice).

40. 418 U.S. 323 (1973).

41. 472 U.S. 749 (1985). In *Greenmoss*, the Court held that *Gertz* did not apply to a case between a company and a credit reporting agency. The agency falsely reported to five subscribers that plaintiff had filed for bankruptcy. *Id.* at 751. The Court held that the private plaintiff did not have to show actual malice in order to recover presumed or punitive damages since the false report was not a matter of public concern.

42. The Court's focus in *Greenmoss* on content, context, and form makes it unlikely that many media stories about private persons will fall within it. It is doubtful, for example, that the Court would have ruled the same way had the identical story with the same error caused in the same manner appeared in a traditional newspaper. The focus on the narrow audience and their obligation to keep the information confidential seemed central to the plurality's approach.

43. *Gertz,* 418 U.S. at 340-41; *Greenmoss,* 472 U.S. at 757-61.

44. Although the number of libel suits may increase because plaintiffs no longer need to prove fault, aggregate costs of libel defense should decline. Expenses probably would fall because declaratory judgment actions will not involve litigation over fault, which is the focus of the present extensive discovery. *See* Barrett, *supra* note 12, at 855-57. Shifting defense costs would also reduce the aggregate expenditures of media.

45. Most plaintiffs are not likely to gain much from a defendant's default. A plaintiff fearing that the defendant is likely to default might seek a guarantee from the defendant that it will not default if the plaintiff chooses the declaratory judgment path. The likelihood of default, the impact of that default on the plaintiff, and the plaintiff's expectation of success in a damage action are likely to affect the plaintiff's choices and negotiations. *See infra* note 119 and accompanying text.

46. The deterrence from the threat of damage actions is lost under the Schumer bill's defendant's option. *See infra* note 119. Barrett nowhere discusses the implications of default on the Schumer bill. With the plaintiff controlling the option, the plaintiff may be able to bargain against default by conditioning his election of the declaratory path.

47. POLRA § 3(a).

48. 472 U.S. at 760-61

49. *See supra* notes 43-48 and accompanying text.

50. *See* Franklin, *supra* note 1, at 47-49; *see also* Barrett, *supra* note 12, at 858-59 (treating fees as costs).

51. *See* Franklin, *supra* note 1, at 23 n.105 (citing commentators who suggest this approach and discussing the ACLU's decision to support absolute privilege for some speech on matters of public concern).

52. M. FRANKLIN, CASES AND MATERIALS ON MASS MEDIA LAW 14-20 (2d ed. 1982). For recent criticism of the marketplace view, *see* Ingber, *The Marketplace of Ideas: A Legitimizing Myth*, 1984 DUKE L.J. 1, 16-49 (arguing that current First Amendment doctrine conceptualizing a marketplace of ideas masks its bias toward preserving the status quo).

53. Justice Brennan has suggested the possibility of permitting a court to order a press defendant to publish a determination that the defendant has been found to have defamed a plaintiff. *See* Miami Herald Publishing Co. v. Tornillo, 418 U.S. 241, 258 (1974) (concurring opinion); Rosenbloom v. Metromedia, Inc., 403 U.S. 29, 47 (1971) (plurality opinion). I have previously elaborated on the constitutional and other more fundamental reasons for not requiring media to report that a government agency has found that their defamatory statements were false. Franklin, *supra* note 1, at 34; *see also* Barrett, *supra* note 12, at 870 n.138 (discussing reasons for not requiring publication of judgment).

54. Recent examples might include such murky situations as the disputes over the counting of enemy troop strength, at the core of Westmoreland v. CBS Inc., 596 F. Supp. 1166 (S.D.N.Y. 1984), and the events occurring before the attack on the refugee camps, at issue in Sharon v. Time, Inc., 599 F. Supp. 538 (S.D.N.Y. 1984).

55. Barrett suggests that on the merits the elimination of liability based on negligence may be sound. Barrett, *supra* note 12, at 879-80.

56. Franklin, *What Does "Negligence" Mean in Defamation Cases?*, 6 COMM./ENT. L.J. 259, 264-81 (1984).

57. *See* Remarks of Charles Nutt, Jr., Executive Editor of the *Bridgewater Courier News,* at the Joint ABA-ANPA Task Force National Symposium on Libel, tape 5, at 17 (Mar. 21, 1986) (on file with author) [hereinafter Remarks of Charles Nutt, Jr.] (arguing that juries have interpreted negligence standards in "a predictable way": "If something in the article was wrong, then clearly the newspaper must have been negligent. 20/20 hindsight says that there must have been some other step somewhere that the newspaper could have taken.").

Barrett objects that this provision will make my proposal politically unattractive. Barrett, *supra* note 12, at 879-80. The question of political attractiveness is addressed *infra* notes 128-32 and accompanying text.

58. Nutt, whose paper has a circulation of 54,000, has observed that courts have tended to find the sorts of persons his paper writes about—local bankers and important persons in town—to be private persons, because a person who may be important in one part of the area served may be relatively unknown in another community served. Remarks of Charles Nutt, Jr., *supra*

note 57, tape 5, at 12, 16. He also observed that his paper was larger than most, with 85 percent of all dailies having circulations under 50,000, and half being under 25,000. *Id.* This tendency of the courts to designate local people as "private" exposes the local, small-community newspaper to greater liability than might be incurred by media that cover the national or state scene.

59. Bloom, *Proof of Fault in Media Defamation Litigation*, 38 VAND. L. REV. 247 (1985).

60. *Id.* at 389.

61. *See id.* at 386 nn.511 & 512, 387 n.513 (listing cases). Several of these cases were decided on multiple grounds. Plaintiffs who lose at the trial level are much less likely to appeal than are losing media defendants because plaintiffs have their best chance at the trial level. Also, media defendants are often repeat players who wish to undo losses and thus will appeal adverse verdicts.

62. *Id.* at 390.

63. *Cf.* LIBEL DEFENSE RESOURCE CENTER, BULLETIN NO. 6, (LDRC, New York, N.Y.), (Mar. 15, 1983) at 35, 42 (reporting finding that no negligence cases were reversed on appeal exclusively because of an inadequate showing of negligence).

64. *See* Time, Inc. v. Firestone, 424 U.S. 448, 460-61 (1976).

65. *See infra* note 67.

66. For writers who have expressed doubts on this, *see* L. TRIBE, AMERICAN CONSTITUTIONAL LAW 631-51 (1978); Christie, *Underlying Contradictions in the Supreme Court's Classification of Defamation*, 1981 DUKE L.J. 811; Franklin, *supra* note 56, at 280-81.

67. Cendali asserts that although I designed my proposal "in part to provide a remedy for those plaintiffs who cannot afford to bring a full-fledged action . . . a plaintiff who has suffered actual damages will not be made whole by a purely nonmonetary remedy." Cendali, *supra* note 4, at 478. It is true that those who feel that they must have damages have little choice. Under her proposal, private plaintiffs would have a negligence action only for special damages (out-of-pocket losses) unless the defendant has failed to retract after a sufficient request. *Id.* at 490. These plaintiffs might be better off with this negligence damage action than with the choice under my proposal of a declaratory judgment or actual-malice damage action. On the other hand, all plaintiffs who had suffered nonspecial damages at the hands of a defendant who later retracts would be worse off under her proposal than under mine.

Moreover, very few plaintiffs can establish special damages. Statement of Charles Morgan, attorney for libel plaintiffs, at the Conference on Protection of Reputation in a Democratic Society: The News Makers vs. the News Media, University of California, Berkeley 201 (Nov. 1, 2, 1985) (on file with author). The only significant plaintiffs likely to have such damages are business owners and managers, whom the Iowa study found to be a "distinct minority" of plaintiffs. Soloski, *supra* note 8, at 219.

Some states have rejected the *Gertz* approach even in the absence of an alternative remedy. *See, e.g.,* Gaeta v. New York News, Inc., 62 N.Y.2d 340,

465 N.E.2d 802, 477 N.Y.S.2d 82 (1984) (requiring a showing of gross irresponsibility rather than simple negligence to establish liability in areas of legitimate public concern warranting public exposition).

68. Barrett argues that I have done little to make my declaratory judgment action politically attractive. Barrett, *supra* note 12, at 877-80. For private plaintiffs, the attractiveness of the proposal depends on the impact of my rejection of the damage action based on negligence, and for all plaintiffs on the impact of the fee-shifting provisions and the elimination of punitive damages. Whatever the impact of these changes, my proposal offers an opportunity to remove some cases from the damage route and reduce the current pressure toward costly damage actions. It displaces relatively little of the tort action but may encourage enough lower-stake actions to produce substantial social gains.

Barrett also argues that I have done things to make the declaratory judgment action distinctly unattractive. *Id.* at 877-80. Some of these points are discussed *infra* notes 78 & 83 and accompanying text.

69. Libel insurance is written so that exposure to the initial cost of any claim is retained by the insured. This is analogous to a deductible. Then the insurer enters and covers legal expenses and any liability up to the limits of the policy. *See* Franklin, *supra* note 1, at 18-22. More recently, a major insurer has added a coinsurance provision under which the insured must share 20 percent of all legal fees and expenses whatever the outcome of the case. Massing, *Libel Insurance: Scrambling for Coverage,* COLUM. JOURNALISM REV., Jan./Feb. 1986, at 35, 36.

70. Bezanson, *Libel Law and the Realities of Litigation: Setting the Record Straight,* 71 IOWA L. REV. 226 (1985).

71. Plaintiffs' lawyers are more likely to make a more realistic assessment of their prospects and may be discouraged from accepting libel cases on a contingency-fee basis—especially in light of Sharon v. Time, Inc., 599 F. Supp. 538 (S.D.N.Y. 1984), and Westmoreland v. CBS, Inc., 596 F. Supp. 1166 (S.D.N.Y. 1984).

72. Thus, the elimination of punitive damages probably would not significantly change their current practices.

73. The plaintiff's financial liability under fee shifting will depend on the actual and reasonable defense costs. In some cases, these may well exceed twice the plaintiff's expenses, given (1) the frequent disparity in wealth between libel plaintiffs and large media defendants, (2) the fact that many of these cases proceed on a contingency-fee basis, and (3) the fact that defendants are often motivated by a remote, but real, risk of being held liable for vast damages.

74. This assumes that the judge finds that the defense costs were reasonable. Because groups bringing nuisance suits probably would sue for large amounts and conduct extensive pretrial discovery, a rigorous defense would be justified, and full reimbursement is likely. Moreover, these are precisely the groups that are wealthy enough to feel the sting of fee shifting.

75. Soloski, *supra* note 8, at 219-20.

76. *See, e.g.,* Cendali, *supra* note 4, at 478-79.

77. Bezanson, *supra* note 70, at 228 ("[P]laintiffs see the act of initiating suit, independent of its result, as an effective and public form of reply or response. By invoking the formal judicial system, the plaintiffs legitimize their claim of falsity. Reputational repair follows without the assistance of—indeed in spite of—the judicial system.").

78. Franklin, *supra* note 1, at 33-34, 42-43 (rejecting mandatory publication of adverse judgment).

79. *See* Barrett, *supra* note 12, at 877-78.

80. Conversation with Chad Milton, assistant vice president of Media/Professional Insurance, Inc. (Mar. 19, 1986).

81. POLRA § 4(b)(2); *see infra* note 82.

82. Although the provision suggests that a plaintiff who finds new and important evidence of falsity just before the trial cannot recover fees even if he prevails, this could be changed to provide that fees after that point cannot be recovered unless that new information is shown to the defendant reasonably soon after it is acquired. This situation is likely to be rare since most plaintiffs will not begin without good evidence of falsity. The plaintiff might present evidence to the publisher but be told that the newspaper would like to see more. The plaintiff has up to a year to collect evidence of falsity and make subsequent presentations. It is not likely that the plaintiff will acquire a critical piece of evidence after that.

83. POLRA allows the plaintiff to recover attorneys' fees if the plaintiff did not have a reasonable chance of prevailing in the action. POLRA §§ 4(a)-(b)(2). One way to show that the plaintiff did not have a reasonable chance of success would be for the defendant to present its powerful evidence of the truth to the plaintiff prior to the litigation. This may answer Barrett's concern that under my proposal, a defendant might sit back and then trounce the unsuspecting plaintiff with a devastating showing of truth. Barrett, *supra* note 12, at 878. One could also meet this concern by requiring the parties to exchange witness lists or summaries of evidence to be offered before trial. In addition, defendants might find summary judgment appropriate in cases in which the "defamatory" element is missing, such as the case of a libel-proof plaintiff. *See* note, *The Libel-Proof Plaintiff Doctrine,* 98 HARV. L. REV. 1909, 1916 (1985). However, depending on the costs of moving for summary judgment, the likelihood of appeals from the granting or denial of the motion, and the fee-shifting provisions, the defendant may find it cheaper and simpler to wait for the hearing.

84. *But see* Barrett, *supra* note 12, at 879 (a court judgment on truth should be "reached with the benefit of the full panoply of procedural devices developed by the courts to ascertain the truth"). On the other hand, although discovery is little used in the criminal justice system, that system's legitimacy is not questioned on that basis.

85. The irrevocability of the plaintiff's election between damages and declaratory judgment makes this timing likely. *See* POLRA § 1(d).

86. Cendali, *supra* note 4, at 479. Although Cendali's comments are

addressed to the plan described in the original critique, which included the mandatory preaction meeting, *see supra* notes 17-22 and accompanying text, her concerns would still be valid under the new approach.

87. *See* Soloski, *supra* note 8, at 219-20.

88. *But see id.* at 220 (reporting that the media reject most requests for corrections).

89. Most complain within two days. *See supra* note 20.

90. Cranberg, *Fanning the Fire: The Media's Role in Libel Litigation,* 71 IOWA L. REV. 231, 221 (1985) ("An overwhelming number of plaintiffs told us that their postpublication experiences with the press influenced their decisions to bring suit.").

91. *Id.* at 223-24.

92. The newspaper business, which accounts for almost two thirds of all suits against media defendants, Franklin, *Suing Media for Libel,* 1981 AM. B. FOUND. RES. J. 795, 810, by nature focuses on the future. *See* Cranberg, *supra* note 90, at 222 (arguing that newspapers are geared to the next day, not yesterday's "fallout"). It is thus unlikely that the top management of most newspapers will learn of their errors prior to a lawsuit without such a meeting.

93. *E.g.,* S. 1979, 1985-86 Cal. Leg., Reg. Sess. (1986) (introduced by Sen. Bill Lockyer).

94. *See supra* note 2.

95. Hearings on libel law and possible reforms were held on July 18, 1985, and on February 26, 1986.

96. Compare POLRA § 1(a) *with* Schumer bill § 1(a).

97. Compare POLRA § 1(b) *with* Schumer bill § 1(b).

98. Compare POLRA § 3(b) *with* Schumer bill § 3.

99. Compare POLRA § 1(d) *with* Schumer bill § 1(c).

100. Compare POLRA § 2(a) *with* Schumer bill § 2.

101. Compare POLRA § 4 *with* Schumer bill § 4. Nonetheless, the philosophy and details of each proposal differ.

102. *See supra* notes 79-84 and accompanying text (discovery), and *supra* notes 29-32 and accompanying text (role of retraction). For criticism of the Schumer bill's approach to retractions, *see infra* notes 139-40 and accompanying text.

103. Schumer bill § 1(d).

104. Sections 1(a) and 1(d) of the Schumer bill speak in terms of defamation claims that arise out of mass media situations but do not explicitly state that the cases must involve media defendants. It is possible to read the bill to cover claims made by plaintiffs against nonmedia individuals who have uttered the alleged defamations through mass media. On the other hand, the retraction provision in section 4(2) of the Schumer bill suggests that the drafters focused on suits against mass media defendants.

     I have made my proposal applicable to all defamation defendants. *See* POLRA § 1(a)(1); *see also supra* notes 23-28 and accompanying text.

105. Schumer bill § 4(2).

106. *See* Schumer bill § 1(a)(1) (limiting declaratory judgment action to

public officials and public figures). This means that actions by private plaintiffs are unaffected by section 1 of the Schumer bill. The other provisions of the bill are not so limited.

107. Barrett suggests that defendants are more likely to defend damage actions brought by public plaintiffs than I believe they are. He states that "prominent and profitable national media organizations, may well conclude in some cases that the potential reputational injury of losing a libel suit justifies risking the slight chance of a damage award in return for the actual malice defense." Barrett, *supra* note 12, at 870. If a media organization truly prizes its reputation for accuracy, it might be expected to defend the accuracy of the particular story in the declaratory judgment action rather than to assert an actual-malice defense, which only obscures the accuracy point.

In fact, one of the major purposes of Barrett's comment is to identify problems with the damage action and to give reasons why its virtual, if not total, demise is something to applaud. *See, e.g., id.* at 856 (juries are likely to misunderstand their function); *id.* at 856-57 (jury verdicts are unpredictable); *id.* at 871-73 (lengthy discussion on the significance of damages). He further suggests that the public-plaintiff damage action seriously threatens "responsible" journalism. *See id.* at 872. Most of his criticisms, however, also apply to actions brought by private plaintiffs.

Barrett argues that the "most important justification" for the defendant's election is that "eliminating the actual-malice defense is . . . an enormous concession to [public figure] plaintiffs." *Id.* at 871. The enormity of that concession depends in part on how quick and inexpensive the declaratory judgment rack turns out to be.

108. *See* Soloski, *supra* note 8, at 219-20.

109. The press has doubts about bills that take no account of pre-publication behavior or of harm actually suffered. *See, e.g.,* Denniston, *A Bill That's on the Money,* WASH. JOURNALISM REV., Jan. 1986, at 50 (suggesting that the defendant's election is the "shakiest part" of the Schumer bill and that "whatever else Congress may be able to do about libel, there is the deepest doubt that it could get away with doing that"); *Public Affairs, the Media, and the Democratic Process,* CENTER MAG., May/June 1985, at 10, 35 (reporting dialogue of a meeting at which William Thomas, editor, *L.A. Times,* said: "A law that says, if you retract as prominently as you injured, there shall be no damages, would be quite a law. I don't know whether that would be fair to the plaintiff at all.").

The specifics of the Schumer bill aside, much of the press has general doubts about absolute privilege. *See* Franklin, *supra* note 1, at 26-28.

110. *See, e.g.,* Remarks of Robert Maynard, publisher, *Oakland Tribune,* at the Conference on Protection of Reputation in a Democratic Society: The News Makers vs. the News Media, University of California, Berkeley 190 (Nov. 1, 2, 1985) (on file with author).

111. For support of the 5 percent success rate, *see* Franklin, *supra* note 92, at 803; *see also* Bezanson, *supra* note 70, at 228 ("less than 10 percent of media libel cases are won in court. . . .").

112. *See supra* note 12 and accompanying text.

113. *See* Barrett, *supra* note 12, at 871-73.

114. *See supra* notes 23-28 & 55-74 and accompanying text.

115. *See supra* note 111.

116. Franklin, *supra* note 92, at 810. The published studies deal with libel cases litigated to conclusion. It is clear, however, that settlements do occur with some frequency and may occur more often now that insureds must bear a percentage of defense costs. *See supra* note 69. For a discussion of an unpublished study of settled libel cases, *see* Franklin, *supra* note 92, at 800 n.12. The Iowa study expects to publish data on settlements. *See* Remarks of Randall Bezanson at the Joint ABA-APNA Task Force National Symposium on Libel, tape 2, at 22, 24 (Mar. 21, 1986) (on file with author) [hereinafter Remarks of Randall Bezanson]. A defendant's option will eliminate virtually all of these settlements.

117. Burnett v. National Equirer, Inc., 144 Cal. App. 3d 991, 193 Cal. Rptr. 206 (1983), *appeal dismissed*, 465 U.S. 1014 (1984).

118. For example, television producer Arthur Fellows has sued the *National Enquirer*. Fellows v. National Enquirer, Inc., 42 Cal. 3d 234, 721 P.2d 97, 228 Cal. Rptr. 215 (1986). The father of actor Tom Selleck has sued the *Globe* for libel, alleging that he neither granted an interview to the *Globe* nor made the statements attributed to him. Selleck v. Globe Int'l, Inc., 166 Cal. App. 3d 1123, 212 Cal. Rptr. 838 (1985) (reversing dismissal of libel action); *see* Eisler, *Tabloid Will Seek Supreme Court Review of Ruling Allowing Suit by Actor's Father*, L.A. DAILY J., Apr. 19, 1985, Pt. II, at 1, col. 1. The California Supreme Court, on a vote of 4–3, denied a hearing on August 1, 1985. Tom Selleck has settled a claim against the *National Enquirer*, which printed a retraction. *The Enquirer Settles with Tom Selleck*, SAN FRANCISCO CHRON., Oct. 7, 1985, at 59, col. 3. Dionne Warwick settled a libel suit against the *Globe* in which she originally sought $30 million in damages. *Singer Withdraws Tabloid Suit*, SAN JOSE MERCURY NEWS, May 8, 1986, at 4A.

119. This type of publisher probably will not be embarrassed by regular defaults. For example, assuming the allegations by Tom Selleck's father are true, a publisher willing to print a fabricated, defamatory "interview," *see supra* note 118, despite likely liability for damages, probably would view the option to default with monetary impunity as a windfall. The defendant's option could only encourage such conduct.

It is not clear whether the same consideration applies to the narrow-spectrum magazine, *see infra* note 120 and accompanying text, which may be more sensitive to this problem because regular defaults may hurt its credibility with its adherents. One wonders, though, how the defendant in Gertz v. Robert Welch, Inc., 418 U.S. 323 (1974), the publisher of a John Birch Society magazine, would have responded if it could have elected between a damage action and a declaratory action.

On the other hand, there can be little doubt that in most media organizations, a default would hurt the morale of the staff at least as badly as a settlement does under current law.

120. For an example of a case involving a narrow-spectrum publisher, *see* Gertz v. Robert Welch, Inc., 680 F.2d 527 (7th Cir. 1982), *cert. denied*, 459 U.S. 1226 (1983); *see also supra* note 119.

121. *See* Franklin, *supra* note 1, at 27-28. In addition to concern about the attitudes of the general public, responsible journalists may be influenced by the appraisals of peers in academic publications such as the *Columbia Journalism Review* or the *Washington Journalism Review,* and professional publications such as the *Bulletin of the American Society of Newspaper Editors.*

122. *See* Barrett, *supra* note 12, at 872.

123. Barrett asserts that "expansion in the scope of libel defenses would lead to greater press irresponsibility." *Id.* at 872. It seems odd for Barrett to assert that my proposal may encourage these defendants when he supports the Schumer bill, which allows these defendants the option to avoid damage actions for libel.

One answer is that if "irresponsible" publishers develop a history of defaulting in declaratory judgment actions, it is unlikely that plaintiffs will take that route. Both the higher success rate against these defendants and increasing willingness of individuals to sue them, *see supra* notes 111-18 and accompanying text, will probably further induce those with claims against these defendants to use the damage route. Thus, those hurt by these defendants probably will be the least likely to be satisfied with a default judgment and will opt for a damage action. To the extent plaintiffs tend to use the declaratory judgment action against responsible publishers and the damage action against irresponsible defendants (or those media members guilty of serious breakdowns), my proposal has a real chance to succeed without eviscerating libel law.

124. Barrett, *supra* note 12, at 882.

125. Barrett does express concern about, but no solution for, the low-level public officials who may be deprived of their damage actions under the Schumer bill. *Id.* at 868 n. 133.

126. For a case involving an involuntary public figure, *see* Dameron v. Washington Magazine, Inc., 779 F.2d 736 (D.C. Cir. 1985) (holding that a federal air controller was an involuntary public figure in connection with a story about an air crash eight years earlier), *cert. denied,* 476 U.S. 1141 (1986).

127. The focus of a defendant's election would then be on the subject matter of the alleged defamation rather than on the status of the plaintiff. Even if the Supreme Court's rejection of that approach for constitutional purposes in *Gertz* was sound, Gertz v. Robert Welch, Inc., 418 U.S. 323, 345-46 (1973), that rejection casts no doubt on a legislative approach that seeks to protect certain kinds of speech.

128. Barrett, *supra* note 12, at 880.

129. *Id.* at 879-80.

130. *See supra* notes 55-67 and accompanying text.

131. If protecting public debate is important to the Schumer bill, it is odd for it to perpetuate the current law's focus on the plaintiff's status. Schumer bill § 1(d)(1). The result is to handle a case based on the facts of *Gertz* under state law—negligence and a preponderance of the evidence—but to permit a defendant's election in a case based on the facts of Burnett v. National Enquirer, Inc., 144 Cal. App. 3d 991, 193 Cal. Rptr. 206 (1983), *appeal dismissed,* 465 U.S. 1014 (1984), so that the plaintiff must prove falsity by clear and convincing evidence even to get a declaratory judgment.

Denying any election to private plaintiffs forces them to take the damage route. Given the ease with which negligence can be shown to flow from error, *see supra* notes 56-57 and accompanying text, many media defendants will be subject to too great a risk of monetary liability. Smaller defendants who could benefit greatly from the avowed goals of the Schumer bill may be least able to take advantage of it. *See supra* note 58 and accompanying text.

132. *See supra* note 109 (media questioning the fairness of the defendant's election). If any jurisdiction should nonetheless be attracted to the Schumer approach, it should at least include a provision preserving the right to sue for damages of those who have suffered special damages.

133. Schumer bill § 4(1). Barrett defends this provision because it permits judges to take into account "such factors as extreme disparity in the wealth of the parties" or the existence of noncompensable special damages. Barrett, *supra* note 12, at 875 n.160. Considerations of overriding reason in general or comparative wealth in particular may make prediction of fee shifting uncertain. A plaintiff sure of falsity but uncertain about fees and actual malice may elect the damage action—though the defendant can override that and then win on fees no matter what the outcome. Predictability of fee shifting is crucial in an approach based on a plaintiff's election.

Barrett's example of a situation in which a person who suffered special damages and then lost the damage action, *see id.* at 874 n.158, is precisely the situation covered in section 4(b)(1) of my proposal without creating the uncertain set of fee rules that the Schumer bill would.

134. POLRA § 4(b)(1). Note that the test is objective and not based on what an attorney might advise. According to the Iowa study, plaintiffs report that their attorneys were far more encouraging than the law or the facts warranted. Remarks of Randall Bezanson, *supra* note 116, tape 2, at 24-25. Barrett misreads this test when he asserts that the attorney's advice is relevant. Barrett, *supra* note 12, at 874 n.157.

135. Schumer bill § 4(1).

136. Schumer bill § 4(2).

137. Of course, this does not matter under the Schumer bill since the defendant can convert the suit to a declaratory judgment action anyway.

138. Schumer bill § 4(2).

139. A majority of states have such statutes. SANFORD, *supra* note 34, at 663-700 (collecting and quoting thirty-three statutes).

140. If the plaintiff takes close to a year to investigate before deciding to sue for damages, the defendant would still have ten days in which to retract and escape all fees, whether or not the defendant decided to convert the action into one for declaratory judgment.

The Schumer bill's retraction provision is much more acceptable in the declaratory judgment context because the plaintiff has already signaled willingness to forgo damages by filing that action. Since the defendant's admission of error will be at least as valuable a remedy as the court's later adjudication of that error, an appropriate retraction should obviate the need for adjudication. This should be true at least if the plaintiff has not already expended substantial legal fees.

141. POLRA § 4(b)(2).

142. For discussion and rejection of concerns that this provision will place the plaintiff at a serious disadvantage, *see supra* notes 81-83 and accompanying text.

143. POLRA § 2(b). This section assumes that the defendant will have a reasonable time in which to consider the evidence and decide whether to retract. This should not cause a problem because, as noted in the text, a retraction made shortly after suit will diminish the defendant's liability for attorneys' fees.

144. Garrison v. Louisiana, 379 U.S. 64, 75 (1964) (quoting Chaplinsky v. New Hampshire, 315 U.S. 568, 572 (1942)).

chapter 3

Declaratory Judgments for Libel: A Better Alternative*

DAVID A BARRETT[†]

This chapter originally appeared as a comment responding to criticism by Professor Marc Franklin of the "Schumer bill," which was introduced in Congress in 1985. Franklin's piece appears as Chapter 2 of this volume; his "Plaintiff's Option Libel Reform Act" and the Schumer bill are both reprinted there. Although the focus of these two chapters is on the Schumer and Franklin proposals, many of the points of contention (and agreement) also apply to the other proposals discussed in this book. In particular, the debate over the Schumer bill's novel "defendant's option," which would allow a defendant to convert a libel damage claim into a declaratory judgment action over the plaintiff's objection, is crucial to evaluations of current reform efforts.

Written by a practicing litigator, this chapter reflects the perception that a litigation-oriented perspective is an essential element in evaluating any libel reform proposal. In addition, the practicalities of the legislative process require that a proposal not only be sound in theory but be balanced and appealing to various political constituencies if it is to be enacted. This chapter addresses libel reform from these perspectives.

Although nonlitigation alternatives to libel lawsuits are now being widely discussed, the effectiveness of any reform proposal (short of

---

*This chapter was originally published in 74 CALIF. L. REV. 847 (1986).

[†]Senior partner, Duker & Barrett, New York, N.Y. A.B. 1971, Harvard; J.D. 1974 Columbia. The author assisted Rep. Charles E. Schumer in drafting H.R. 2846, the bill discussed in this chapter.

outlawing libel altogether or subjecting libel claims to mandatory arbitration) still must be judged by how it will work in the litigation process. Even if the parties to a dispute want to settle without court intervention, the parameters of their negotiations will be dictated by their perceptions of what will happen if they do not settle—that is, by the likely outcome of court proceedings. Although relatively few disputes may actually be litigated, the outcome of many negotiations is shaped by the parties' views of what is likely to happen in litigation.

For this reason, even a proposal that seeks to encourage primarily nonjudicial resolution of libel claims must be analyzed in terms of how the nonsettling cases will play out in court. For example, if litigation occurs, will the proposal's procedural regime tend to favor plaintiffs or defendants? Will its substantive rules tip the scales to one side or the other? How costly will litigation be in terms of legal fees and expenditures of time and energy by the principals?

In addition to these issues, which primarily affect the actions of the individual parties to a dispute, analysis of reform proposals must consider the overall costs and benefits to society as a whole of both the present system of libel law and the proposed changes. Because defamation is a peculiarly social offense—indeed, it occurs only upon publication of an offending statement to a third person—this aspect of the analysis is most important. It is in the evaluation of these social costs and benefits that Professor Franklin and I differ most sharply. Again, although the two chapters focus on the Schumer and Franklin proposals, the analytical framework can be readily applied to subsequent proposals as well.

*   *   *

Empirical studies of the operation of libel law, most notably the pioneering work of Prof. Marc A. Franklin[1] and the Iowa Libel Research Project,[2] have demonstrated that we face a libel crisis. As Franklin concludes, "[L]ibel law, particularly media libel law, has developed into a high-stakes game that serves the purposes of neither the parties nor the public."[3] Yet, having made the case for "radical surgery" in his prior studies,[4] Franklin now backs away from the operating table.

Although Franklin believes, as I do, that the most promising solution to the libel crisis is legislative creation of a declaratory judgment remedy, he is unwilling to make that remedy truly effective. This chapter argues that libel defendants—as well as plaintiffs—should be given the option to choose declaratory relief in suits by public officials and public figures and thereby avoid the chilling impact of limitless damage awards.

I advocate an approach embodied in H.R. 2846, a federal libel reform proposal introduced by Rep. Charles E. Schumer (D-N.Y.) in 1985 as a "study bill" to stimulate discussion of alternatives to libel damage actions.[5] While the use of the declaratory judgment as a libel remedy had been suggested before,[6] Franklin gave the idea timely impetus in a 1983 lecture.[7] His 1983 proposal described a declaratory judgment remedy in some detail, although it did not suggest actual language for a statute. Franklin now presents a proposal in legislative form which adopts the framework and much of the substance of the Schumer bill.[8] Franklin's new proposal also modifies and clarifies his 1983 proposal in several significant ways, most notably with respect to restrictions on discovery and proof at trial which I had criticized in an earlier draft of this chapter.[9]

This chapter briefly describes the Schumer and Franklin proposals for resolving the libel crisis. It then suggests an analytical framework that relates the empirically identified defects of the present libel system to the underlying structure of libel law and demonstrates that the declaratory judgment is the most promising alternative remedy. After establishing an analytical basis for reform, this chapter addresses Franklin's criticism of the defendant's option and assesses the differences in the way that the Schumer bill and Franklin's proposal would actually operate. In addition, several suggestions for improving the Schumer bill are made.

PROPOSED LEGISLATIVE SOLUTIONS TO THE LIBEL CRISIS

In many ways, the similarities between the Schumer bill and Franklin's proposal are more significant than the differences. Franklin has said that "legislation is the best hope to develop a workable and fair system of libel law.[10]" Although he had called his 1983 proposal a "restoration action,"[11] it was, in substance, a no-fault declaratory judgment remedy.[12] By now employing the language and format of the Schumer bill, Franklin acknowledges that the most promising new remedy under current constitutional law[13] is a declaratory judgment in which the defendant's state of mind is not at issue.[14]

Franklin also recognizes that effective and balanced libel reform would incorporate a number of additional changes. Franklin's new legislative proposal substantially incorporates two reforms proposed in the Schumer bill. First, with some modification, Franklin adopts Section 3 of the Schumer bill, which would abolish punitive damages in all libel actions.[15] Franklin also adopts *in haec verba* Section 2 of the

Schumer bill, which would establish a uniform national one-year statute of limitations for all libel claims.[16]

In addition to these areas of almost complete agreement, both the Schumer bill and the Franklin proposal adopt some version of the English rule, which would require the losing party to pay the winner's attorneys' fees.[17] Although substantial differences exist on the fee-shifting aspects of the proposals,[18] the acceptance of the English rule ultimately may be more significant. Fee shifting provides the dual benefits of making deserving plaintiffs whole and discouraging frivolous suits. It is essential, moreover, to make the declaratory judgment a feasible remedy for plaintiffs who are not wealthy.

In important respects, the declaratory judgment remedies that would be created under both the Schumer bill and Franklin's new proposal are also similar. Section 1 of the Schumer bill would create a new cause of action permitting a public official or public figure[19] to bring an action for a declaratory judgment against a media defendant that allegedly published a false and defamatory statement concerning the plaintiff.[20] Franklin's proposal would do the same.[21] With respect to other aspects of the new cause of action, Franklin's legislative proposal adopts the language of the Schumer bill. No proof of the defendant's state of mind would be required, effectively making the action one of strict liability.[22] Thus, a public figure could obtain a libel judgment without the burden of proving actual malice as required under current law.[23] In return for this major expansion in the scope of liability, recovery of damages would be precluded in the declaratory judgment action,[24] and its filing would automatically bar the plaintiff from ever asserting any other claim, including a claim for damages, arising out of the same statement.[25] Finally, the plaintiff would have to prove all elements of the cause of action by clear and convincing evidence.[26]

There are, however, crucial differences between the declaratory judgment remedies proposed in the Schumer bill and by Franklin. While Franklin proposes the same new cause of action, he would not limit its use either to public-figure plaintiffs or to media defendants.[27] Although there seems little reason to limit the new action to media defendants,[28] applying it to all plaintiffs is more problematic.[29]

The Schumer bill also diverges from Franklin's proposal in its most novel aspect—the defendant's conversion option. Franklin would allow only libel plaintiffs to choose the declaratory judgment remedy. The Schumer bill, on the other hand, would grant media defendants sued by public figures the right to convert the damage action into a new action for declaratory judgment.[30] Upon a defendant's election, the plaintiff would be barred from recovering any damages caused by publication of the statement at issue.[31] Absent such an election by the defendant, the case would proceed as a damage action under the actual-malice standard.

Franklin attacks the Schumer bill for giving defendants the power to override a plaintiff's choice of the damage remedy.[32] This criticism is not surprising in light of the common law's traditional insistence that the plaintiff is master of his or her claim. In this instance, however, tradition must give way to practical necessity. Libel cases are no longer governed by common law principles alone. Current libel law is an incompatible marriage between common law doctrine and First Amendment imperatives.[33] The defendant's option offers the best hope of saving the marriage while effectively protecting reputation and preserving constitutional principles.

SOURCES OF THE LIBEL CRISIS

The State-of-Mind Problem

The root of the present libel crisis lies in the fact that reputation can be injured by words, but the common law offers redress only in the form of money damages.[34] Indeed, Frederick Pollock remarked a century ago that libel law "has gone wrong from the beginning in making the damage and not the insult the cause of action."[35] Although similar sentiments have prompted suggestions for nondamage remedies, such as injunctive and declaratory relief proposals[36] and retraction and reply statutes,[37] the common law damage action still represents the primary means of vindicating injury to reputation.

When the inflationary increase in tort verdicts produced a libel judgment of $500,000, the Supreme Court in *New York Times Co. v. Sullivan*[38] responded by imposing constitutional constraints on the damage action. The *Sullivan* decision rested on concern that truthful, socially desirable speech would be deterred by the threat of "libel judgments virtually unlimited in amount."[39] Such judgments would cause publishers to doubt whether truth "can be proved in court" and to fear "the expense of having to do so."[40] Rather than reduce this chilling effect by directly limiting the damage amounts recoverable in libel actions, however, the Court chose instead an indirect means: It engrafted a new substantive element onto the existing common law elements of the plaintiff's case, holding that plaintiffs could recover damages only if they proved that the defendant acted with a culpable state of mind.[41]

In the case of public-figure plaintiffs, the requisite state of mind was "actual malice"—publication of a statement with knowledge of its falsity or in reckless disregard of the truth.[42] With respect to private plaintiffs, the Court in *Gertz v. Robert Welch, Inc.*[43] held that a greater state interest in protecting the plaintiff's reputation permitted states to reduce the substantive standard to negligence.[44] In contrast to *Sullivan, Gertz* addressed the problem of excessive damages directly, albeit incompletely, by limiting recovery under the negligence standard to compensation for "actual injury." Yet even the negligence standard requires some proof of state of mind, and damages for "actual injury" can be enormous. Further, if plaintiffs can prove actual malice as well as negligence, they can recover presumed and punitive damages.[45]

Experience with the *Sullivan* and *Gertz* rules demonstrate that the Court correctly anticipated that fault-based rules would reduce the incidence of damage recoveries. Damage awards are generally upheld in only 5 to 10 percent of all libel suits.[46] Although this undoubtedly has reduced the chilling effect on the press, a substantial number of plaintiffs who are in fact injured by defamatory falsehoods nevertheless fail to obtain legal redress solely because they are unable to prove fault.[47] Because *Sullivan* added a new substantive element to the plaintiff's case, this effect on plaintiffs was foreseeable.

More difficult to anticipate was a profound metamorphosis in the character of libel actions. By requiring plaintiffs to prove fault, the *Sullivan* and *Gertz* rules shifted the focus of libel suits away from the question of falsehood and to the constitutionally mandated question of the defendant's state of mind. As the Iowa Libel Research Project has demonstrated, the libel action, theoretically intended to vindicate the plaintiff's reputation, has become an "action for enforcement of press responsibility."[48]

With seven out of eight libel suits decided on constitutional privilege grounds—that is, the defendant's state of mind—"[a]s a practical matter, the truth or falsity of the challenged statement is no longer pertinent."[49] The current irrelevance of the falsehood determination is demonstrated by Justice Stevens's dissent, joined by three other members of the Court, in *Philadelphia Newspapers, Inc. v. Hepps.*[50] The Court held in *Hepps* that the First Amendment compels a private plaintiff to prove that an alleged defamation is false. Justice Stevens's dissent argued, however, that burdening plaintiffs with proof of falsity was unfair because the "*antecedent* fault determination" would limit the cases in which truth is even considered to those where the defendant has published with some degree of culpability.[51]

Justice Stevens thus acknowledged the practical irrelevance of truth, even in constitutional adjudication, in all but the small fraction of cases in which the shift in burden of proof would affect the outcome.

The post-*Sullivan* focus on state of mind has raised the stakes in libel actions so high that the chilling effect—the original target of *Sullivan's* state-of-mind defense—has remained a serious problem, notwithstanding defendants' impressive success rate.[52] Even if a defendant avoids damage liability, it must incur the enormous expense of litigating state of mind and may find that the exposure of its questionable reporting practices stings almost as much as an adverse judgment.[53]

In addition, state-of-mind defenses have other deleterious effects. From the viewpoint of the plaintiff, whose primary aim is to set the record straight, state of mind is at best an irrelevancy and at worst an insurmountable barrier. The plaintiff suffers the same ill effects and has the same need for redress whether a falsehood was a calculated lie or merely resulted from sloppy typesetting.[54] Yet the present system forces a plaintiff to undertake discovery and trial of the state-of-mind issues of negligence or actual malice and to expend money and energy to prove facts concerning the defendant's state of mind that are wholly tangential to the primary goal of vindication.[55] If a plaintiff cannot prove the requisite state of mind, he or she has no remedy whatsoever. Even if a plaintiff does win, the damage award will not include the costs of litigating this irrelevant issue.

The High-Stakes Problem

Since *New York Times v. Sullivan* was decided, the costs of both prosecuting and defending libel suits have spiraled upward. These increases·are not solely attributable to the expense of litigating the state-of-mind issues. The trend to higher judgments in libel cases no doubt reflects a general movement toward broader tort liability and higher damages,[56] but it also involves factors unique to libel cases, including the focus on state of mind issues. Juries may well perceive, as the Iowa project suggests, that they are charged with judging the media's responsibility.[57] As a result, juries in libel cases are not awarding damages only to compensate injury to the plaintiff's reputation, but are effectively imposing punishment for the defendant's irresponsible conduct as well.

The media's own instinct to sensationalize news reports of libel claims also contributes to increased verdicts. A prospective juror cannot help but be influenced by repeated media descriptions of absurdly high *ad damnum* clauses, such as references to "Westmoreland's $120 million damage suit against CBS."[58] Constant repetition of these fanciful figures suggests to the public that they have some meaningful relation to damages deserving recompense.[59] It is no wonder that seven-figure libel verdicts are almost the norm, and eight-figure verdicts are not uncommon.[60]

Rising litigation costs have paralleled the increase in jury verdict amounts. In part, the rising costs reflect the increasing sophistication of the plaintiffs' bar. In the years immediately following *Sullivan,* defense lawyers quickly ended public-figure libel cases with motions for summary judgment on actual-malice grounds. Such motions typically were based on affidavits submitted by the reporter and editor which described the process of investigating, writing, and editing the story and asserted that the responsible persons had no knowledge of the falsehood claimed by plaintiff. If, as often occurred, the plaintiff opposed this factual showing merely by repeating in an affidavit the actual-malice allegations of the complaint, unsupported by additional facts, the defendant was entitled to summary judgment. The defendant's unrebutted affidavits as to state of mind were conclusive.[61] This led some members of the defense bar to the unwarranted assumption that the First Amendment virtually mandated summary judgment on malice. It does not.

Plaintiffs' lawyers eventually learned that they could avoid summary judgment by taking discovery on the state-of-mind issue. In *Herbert v. Lando,*[62] the Supreme Court expressly authorized inquiry into the editorial process to prove "actual malice." Thus, if the defendant pleads lack of malice as a constitutional defense, the plaintiff is entitled to probe the facts behind it, just as any other defense. If issues of fact relating to the malice defense are raised, as they frequently are in depositions or document discovery of defendants, a court may well find summary judgment inappropriate.[63]

With summary judgment more difficult to obtain, the costs of defending libel suits have risen substantially. Lawyers' fees and expenses, together with indirect expenditures of personnel time, have escalated to the point that winning a suit may be as costly as losing. The time and energy expended by management and news staff in defending a suit can be enormous.[64] Reporters and editors often have been effectively transferred to the publisher's legal staff, forced to work full time on their own legal defenses.[65]

The insulating effect of libel insurance has also diminished sharply. When Franklin made his original proposal in 1983, he estimated that about three quarters of all newspapers and broadcasters carried libel insurance.[66] Although 75 to 80 percent of premium costs were attributable to defense expenses rather than to payment of damages, those premiums were relatively low.[67] By the mid-1980's, libel insurance had become unavailable at any cost or, if available, beyond the means of many small publishers.[68] Insurers raised deductibles and lowered coverage maximums. At least one insurer required 20 percent copayment of defense costs after the deductible had been exceeded.[69] One major libel insurance carrier dropped out of the field entirely and others ceased writing new policies.[70]

Plaintiffs have faced comparable cost increases. Whether the plaintiff is a public figure or a private individual, hiring a lawyer to sue is costly. The magnitude of these costs is suggested by reports that Mobil Corporation provided its top executives with an "insurance" policy of up to $10 million to cover the costs of bringing a libel suit[71] after its president, William Tavoulareas, sued the *Washington Post*.[72] Even in a simple suit, a plaintiff cannot expect to try a case for less than $25,000 to $100,000. The alternative is a contingency-fee arrangement, but many lawyers may be increasingly reluctant to accept such arrangements, particularly if the suit involves a potentially strong actual-malice defense.

Unlike defendants, libel plaintiffs may compensate for costs by excessively inflating their damage claims. Like a sweepstakes jackpot, the prospect of a multi-million-dollar payoff may induce a contingency-fee lawyer or the plaintiff him- or herself to finance the suit. A plaintiff may also find a backer willing to underwrite legal fees for personal or political reasons.[73] None of the plaintiffs in three celebrated cases in the early 1980s paid their own fees, which undoubtedly exceeded $1 million in each case. In *Tavoulareas v. Piro*,[74] the plaintiff's employer paid;[75] in *Sharon v. Time, Inc.*,[76] services were contributed by counsel;[77] and in *Westmoreland v. CBS*,[78] the Capital Legal Foundation, a conservative legal action organization supported by contributions, served as counsel with law firm volunteers. Carol Burnett complained that even a $200,000 damage award was not enough to offset her legal fees.[80] These experiences and others suggest that serious libel litigation under the present legal rules is beyond the means of even wealthy individuals.[81]

The perceived need of plaintiffs to make enormous damage claims creates a vicious cycle. Even if a defendant believes the possibility of losing an action is remote, the size of the claim forces the defendant to defend itself vigorously. Such full-scale defense, often conducted by a top law firm in the manner of a major securities or antitrust action,[82] in turn compels a serious plaintiff to litigate with equal fervor and to claim still greater damages.

A defendant that knows it cannot afford to mount such a large-scale libel defense has few choices. It may be forced to settle, admitting error where none existed, thus damaging its own reputation. It may litigate less aggressively and risk an adverse verdict that could lead to bankruptcy.[83] The most probable response, however, is for the defendant to try to minimize the risk of libel suits altogether. To the extent that this entails publishers taking greater care in gathering information, writing, and editing, libel law is performing an appropriate deterrent function. But mounting evidence indicates that apart from certain "large and profitable" media defendants that deny any impact on their editorial practices, many publishers and broadcasters are feeling a significant chilling effect.[84] Important news, responsible commentary and political advocacy may not be reaching the public. For example, apparently out of fear of libel suits, some twenty scientific journals declined to publish a study by scientists at the National Institutes of Health which criticized the methodology of other prominent researchers.[85] Newspaper and magazine publishers acknowledge having decided not to run controversial stories that they believed to be true but could not economically afford to stand behind.[86] Fear of libel suits has also silenced citizens' criticism of powerful community figures.[87]

Social Costs of the Present Libel System

The enormous costs that libel suits impose on the rest of society are no less significant a reason justifying reform of the present libel system. Like the high-stakes problem, these social costs flow primarily from state-of-mind defenses, but they have an impact far beyond the parties themselves.

The most obvious social cost of libel damage awards is their chilling effect on the press, which leads to reduced investigative reporting and reduced coverage of controversial issues and personalities.[88] Less apparent social costs include not only the largely wasted transaction costs of administering the damage system, but also the price paid under the current system in the form of public cynicism regarding press accuracy and the integrity of public figures and officials.

The high transaction costs associated with libel damage actions include the costs of providing judges, courtrooms, jurors, and court personnel to hear complex cases generated primarily by the state-of-mind defense.[89] Although lawyers' time is generally assumed to be infinitely expandable, some distortions must arise as time and resources are diverted from other tasks to libel suits. The Iowa Libel Research Project indicates the extent of these transaction costs in its findings that pretrial motions involving privilege issues "are made in

virtually every" libel case, and that in about half the cases, an interlocutory appeal is taken from the trial court's decision on these
issues.[90] Moreover, privilege claims are presumably at issue in every
one of the 20 to 25 percent of libel cases that reach trial, and virtually
all cases are appealed after trial.[91] Ultimately, state-of-mind defenses
determine the outcome in 88 percent of all media libel cases.[92]

In addition to direct transaction costs, libel suits today generate
large social costs in the form of increased public cynicism. Because
truth has become almost irrelevant in libel actions, the press has lost
credibility; political leaders and public figures have lost respect; and
the legal system is viewed as having elevated technicality over principle. The public has no way of discerning whether news stories that
become subjects of libel suits are true or false.

Since seven of eight libel suits turn on state-of-mind issues,[93] a
plaintiff who is the subject of a highly damaging but essentially truthful report can effectively persuade the public that the report is false,
without risking exposure of the truth, merely by filing a libel suit.
According to the Iowa project, public figures believe that the very act
of bringing suit is a powerful form of reply and vindication.[94] The
general public, already distrustful of the institutional press, is likely to
believe the plaintiff's allegations of false reporting in the complaint.
The "guilty plaintiff"—perhaps an organized crime figure or a cor-
rupt politician—can be confident that pretrial proceedings will be
lengthy, averaging more than four years, because of issues injected by
state-of-mind defenses.[95] Even if the challenged statement is eventually found to be true, that finding will come too long after the
publicity to be of consequence. And if, as is far more common, the
plaintiff loses not on truth but on a privilege claim, the plaintiff
remains free to maintain the pose of innocent victim by arguing that
the defendant was saved by a technicality.[96]

Current libel law thus encourages the least worthy plaintiffs to
sue by virtually eliminating any risk that they will suffer a judgment
confirming the truth of the charges against them. At the same time,
the present law and social climate offer undeserving plaintiffs substantial vindication by the mere act of suing the media.[97] Merely by
filing complaints, undeserving plaintiffs can mislead the public into
assuming that their claims have merit and immediately undermine
the defendants' credibility. Even if a defendant ultimately wins on a
malice defense, its credibility may not be fully restored because malice
may be perceived as a legal "technicality." Nor is the inference of
falsity that was created in the public's mind by the complaint ever
rebutted.

The distortions created by the focus of libel law on state of mind also make the current damage action almost worthless to an honest victim of a defamatory falsehood. Such a plaintiff faces less than a 10 percent chance of ever seeing the falsity claim adjudicated, while spending years in expensive litigation over state of mind. Only rare individuals will take on such daunting odds. In most cases, the false statement is never corrected or adjudicated, so that not only is the plaintiff's reputation besmirched, but future public discussion is distorted by the uncorrected falsehood.

THE DECLARATORY JUDGMENT SOLUTION

Advantages of Declaratory Judgments in Libel Actions

The creation of a declaratory judgment remedy is a particularly appropriate solution for the libel crisis because it is precisely targeted at the sources of the crisis identified above. Declaratory judgment actions focus primarily on the accuracy of the challenged statements. Irrelevant inquiry into why or how an error was made would no longer be necessary.

Denying plaintiffs the right to damages is a fair price to exact in return for the creation of a far more efficient method of vindication.[98] In contrast to their currently dismal 5 to 10 percent success rate,[99] plaintiffs may well win most declaratory judgment actions. With such a swift and sure remedy, plaintiffs who sue are likely to be quite confident of their claims, and suits by "guilty plaintiffs" should decline.

From the defendants' perspective, the threat of bankrupting damage judgments will be reduced under the Franklin proposal and eliminated by the Schumer bill. With millions of dollars in potential liability no longer at stake, litigation costs will plummet, hastened by the attorneys' fee-shifting provisions included in both proposals. The chilling effect of potential liability on the press should therefore diminish considerably.[100] Finally, declaratory judgments will serve the public interest by allowing courts to make prompt determinations of accuracy. Transaction costs will be reduced, and false statements concerning matters of public interest—whether made by a defendant's challenged report or by a plaintiff's complaint of falsity—will quickly stand exposed. Accurate information will strengthen the quality of public debate and will discourage unfounded suits by guilty plaintiffs.

The Defendant's Option Versus Franklin's Proposal

Criticism of the Schumer bill has focused on its most important and innovative aspect: the defendant's option to convert a damage action to a declaratory judgment over the plaintiff's objection. Although this provision is novel, the notion that some libel plaintiffs must forego monetary compensation for reputational injury in the interest of implementing broader social goals is not new. The common law of libel has always recognized privilege defenses as a means of implementing other social goals.[101] Traditionally, absolute privileges bar recovery altogether, no matter how deserving the plaintiff.[102] Absent a showing of the defendant's bad faith, qualified privileges prevent recovery in many cases where the plaintiff has undoubtedly suffered serious reputational injury, including provable special damages.[103] Unlike these common law privileges, which preclude all relief, a declaratory judgment action will enable public figures to obtain a judgment of falsity where appropriate even though damages would not be recoverable.[104]

The justifications for a declaratory judgment remedy warrant implementing it broadly. Franklin acknowledges this goal when he asks whether plaintiffs will in fact choose the declaratory judgment option and when he discusses ways in which to make damage suits less attractive and declaratory judgments more appealing.[105] The Schumer bill does more than merely recognize this goal. By giving defendants, as well as plaintiffs, the option to choose a declaratory judgment, the bill creates a remedy that forcefully implements the goal.

Franklin's objection to the defendant's option partly stems from his assessments of the sources of the libel crisis described earlier. For example, Franklin acknowledges the problems of high stakes and chilling effect[106] but apparently feels we can live with them during years of experimentation with limited new remedies. Many small publishers may not last that long, however, and large media outlets are daily becoming more bland and timid.[107] Franklin also recognizes the social costs of damage actions,[108] but because he fears "irresponsible publishers,"[109] he stops short of reducing those costs as much as possible. Finally, Franklin refuses to move forcefully to eliminate state-of-mind issues from libel actions. He focuses instead on the importance of preserving a public figure's absolute right to seek damages from a publisher who engages in "intentional defamation."[110]

Franklin overrates the importance of damages as a remedy to public figures and as a deterrent to irresponsible publishers. He underestimates the social costs of libel actions and the dangers of high stakes and chilling effect. Allowing defendants the option to convert damage actions to declaratory judgments will reduce these costs and dangers far more effectively. Although a few potential public-figure plaintiffs may be deprived of damages that reflect actual harm, the overall benefits to society of giving defendants the conversion option will greatly outweigh the hardship to these few plaintiffs. Furthermore, the First Amendment strikes a balance in favor of truthful communication that would otherwise be chilled. As the Supreme Court has noted, "where the scales are in . . . an uncertain balance . . . the Constitution requires us to tip them in favor of protecting true speech."[111]

Fairness to Plaintiffs

Franklin argues that the defendant's option is "unfair" because plaintiffs "who have suffered harm will be effectively barred from suing for damages by the likelihood that these damage cases will be converted into declaratory judgment actions."[112] This concern for "fairness" is greatly exaggerated. First, as Franklin elsewhere acknowledges, a serious problem is posed by "organizations and individuals who are mainly interested in harassing defendants" by maintaining cases "they cannot realistically win."[113] Only the defendant's option will effectively deter suits by these plaintiffs.

If Franklin is worried that plaintiffs who have suffered special damages will be denied recovery, as suggested by his proposal to bar shifting attorneys' fees to losing plaintiffs who "sustained special damages,"[114] his concern is misplaced. The reality of litigation under current libel law demonstrates that plaintiffs "who have suffered harm" in the form of actual pecuniary loss are not necessarily those with good "damage cases," which require proof of actual malice. Where the malice defense applies, deserving plaintiffs do not actually recover appropriate damages with significant frequency because of the difficulty of proving malice.

Conversely, not all plaintiffs who happen to be able to prove actual malice will have suffered significant "harm." The actual reputational impact of a lie may be small, but given the vagaries of jury verdicts, the potential recovery may be enormous.[115] Yet Franklin would allow these plaintiffs to sue for general damages of unlimited amount,[116] thereby perpetuating a significant chilling effect. Given the recognized potential for abuse of general damages,[117] Franklin's failure to consider their abolition, much less to justify maintaining them, seriously weakens his proposal.[118]

A further empirical consideration in evaluating the defendant's option is that, at present, libel plaintiffs have virtually no chance of obtaining meaningful monetary recompense for "harm" they may have suffered. Libel complaints regularly allege astronomical damages.[119] While verdicts averaged from $2 million to $3 million between 1980 and 1984,[120] after completion of the appellate process, only 5 to 10 percent of plaintiffs retain damage awards.[121] A comprehensive survey of libel decisions between 1982 and 1984 showed that only two verdicts under the malice standard were ultimately affirmed, for damages totaling just $42,500.[122] These statistics indicate that few public-figure plaintiffs would lose significant actual recoveries if damage suits were largely eliminated through the defendant's option.[123]

The Iowa Libel Research Project supports this conclusion in its findings that the "dominant interest of most libel plaintiffs is correction of falsity,"[124] and that "money seems rarely to be the reason for suing."[125] Large damage claims appear to serve two purposes in plaintiffs' minds. First, plaintiffs may wish to punish the publisher or "to get even."[126] To the extent this means that plaintiffs are trying to silence annoying critics rather than to recover for actual injury or correct the record, it is an illegitimate purpose that the law should not facilitate. In any event, the chilling effect of massive damage claims and occasional verdicts on all publishers, not just on the libel defendant, is a very high price for society to pay for a victim's dubious satisfaction in "getting even."

A multi-million-dollar damage claim may also serve the victim's interest by securing publicity and providing a sense of vindication. The Iowa study indicates that "[m]ost plaintiffs win by suing. . . . The very act of [filing] suit, itself, represents the only non-self-serving form of response through which plaintiffs' claims of falsity can be legitimized. . . ."[127] A declaratory judgment action, however, would serve exactly this purpose at far less cost to all of the directly involved parties, as well as to society.

Franklin's criticism of the defendant's option also downplays the fact that the Schumer bill limits availability of the defendant's option to suits brought by public figures.[128] The unique role of public figures in modern society justifies the bill's departure from the usual pattern of allowing the plaintiff to control the form of action. The Supreme Court in *Gertz* recognized that public figures "invite attention and comment."[129] Although publicity about a public figure occasionally may cause reputational injury, far more often a public figure needs and wants publicity and will go to great lengths to obtain it. Publicity wins votes and persuades followers. It sells movies, automobiles, and baseball tickets. It gives the subject a sense of power, importance, and satisfaction. Publicity is the lifeblood of public figures.

In exchange for the benefits of publicity, public figures "accept certain necessary consequences of that involvement . . . [including] the risk of closer public scrutiny than might otherwise be the case."[130] Public figures almost invariably are in the public eye precisely because they have chosen to "assume . . . roles of especial prominence in the affairs of society."[131] By seeking publicity, they "have voluntarily exposed themselves to increased risk of injury from defamatory falsehood."[132] Because they have sought the spotlight and benefited greatly from it, it is eminently fair and reasonable to compel public figures to give up damages in return for effective protection from defamatory falsehoods.[133]

In addition to this normative consideration, the Iowa study indicates that public figures are less likely than private plaintiffs to suffer special damages.[134] A "substantial majority" of public-figure plaintiffs believe that their damage suits "achieved reputation-related objectives, even though they lost."[135] Moreover, public-figure plaintiffs have repeatedly asserted that their primary interest is in vindication, not money damages.[136] Accordingly, the Schumer bill, by making it much easier for these plaintiffs to correct the public record, but less likely to recover damages that they rarely suffer in any event, does not seriously harm the interest of public figures in protecting their reputations.

Thus, Franklin's concern that "damage cases involving public plaintiffs will virtually disappear" if the defendant's option were enacted[137] is beside the point. Little actual loss will go uncompensated and reputational objectives will be better served. Moreover, defendants, particularly prominent and profitable national media organizations, may well conclude in some cases that the potential reputational injury of losing a libel suit justifies risking the slight chance of a damage award in return for the protection of the actual-malice defense. Under the Schumer bill, if both parties wish to take this course, it remains open. Given the obvious driving force of pride in all libel litigation, defendants may not so readily accept the high risk of losing a strict-liability truth action as Franklin assumes.

In any event, a declaratory judgment remains a tremendously useful remedy to a public figure. It represents a formal judicial vindication of the plaintiff's reputation. Adding dollars to the declaration does not make it any more "useful," except perhaps to attract publicity for the fact of vindication—which is hardly an appropriate function for damages.[138] By limiting the defendant's option to cases brought by public-figure plaintiffs, the defendant's option would impact upon only those plaintiffs who least frequently win damages and who least need or deserve monetary recompense. The Schumer bill does not, as Franklin implies, "den[y] the existence of harm in libel cases."[139] Rather, the bill realistically seeks to combat that harm by ensuring that truth is ascertained as promptly and efficiently as possible.

Fairness to Defendants

Franklin repeatedly suggests that the defendant's option is tantamount to an "absolute privilege for falsehood"[140] that would allow "citizens" to be "defamed at will without effective recourse,"[141] and that irresponsible publishers could "escape all liability for whatever harm they may impose by their use of deliberate falsehoods."[142] Franklin is wrong. The Schumer bill would foster just the opposite result by imposing a system of strict liability on defendants. Under the Schumer bill, as under Franklin's proposal, defendants will lose a substantial number of declaratory judgment actions and frequently will lose even when they are not at fault. Since plaintiffs can evaluate the strength of truth claims prior to filing suit far more accurately than they can evaluate malice claims, plaintiffs' success rate in declaratory judgment actions will far exceed their current 5 percent success rate in damage actions.[143] Eliminating the malice defense is thus an enormous concession to plaintiffs.

Successful declaratory judgments will also exact a large price on the reputations of defendants for accuracy. Franklin essentially ignores the important normative and economic role that reputation for accuracy plays in keeping the press honest. Although he admits that libel damages are not "necessary to provide responsible publishers with incentives to be careful,"[144] Franklin apparently believes that only the threat of damages will keep "irresponsible publishers" in line. That conclusion, like his argument that the "defendant's election removes any deterrent effect of libel law,"[145] is overstated and untenable.

Libel law, like other legal constraints, is not effective purely because of the threat of punishment. Common sense suggests that, as in other situations where unlawful conduct may be expedient in the short term, the vast majority of people are persuaded to act lawfully not by the deterrent effect of remote and uncertain legal punishment but by a sincere desire to do what is right—the force of moral suasion.

Franklin has recognized that " '[t]here is nothing more important to journalists and journalism than credibility. . . .' "[146] Part of the attractiveness of the declaratory remedy is its reliance on the defendant's self-interest in reputation. A defendant that knows its reputation for accuracy will be tainted without regard to fault every time it makes an error is likely to be more careful than a publisher that knows it is shielded by the actual-malice defense 95 percent of the time. A responsible publisher, believing that its reputation for accuracy attracts customers, measures the total "cost" of any judgment against it not just by the out-of-pocket expense but also by the costs resulting from injured reputation and future lost sales.[147] These "costs" are likely to reach a greater total under the more certain punishment of the declaratory remedy than under the erratic liability determinations of traditional damage actions.

Franklin focuses on the necessity of damage remedies to deter "irresponsible publishers"[148] and points to Burnett v. National Enquirer, Inc.[149] as a paradigm. But an irresponsible publisher, like a professional criminal, is unlikely to be deterred by a legal system with a 5 percent conviction rate and sentences that are little more than a slap on the wrist administered years after the offense.[150] Presumably, a social deviant has calculated that the incremental benefits of misconduct are greater than the marginal risk of punishment.

Moreover, if Franklin's theory were correct, one would expect that expansion in the scope of libel defenses would lead to greater press irresponsibility. Yet there is no evidence to suggest that incidents of culpable press behavior have increased since Sullivan expanded the media's shelter from damages. Nor does the Enquirer seem any less prone to scandal mongering since Burnett. The threat of large legal fees and unpredictable damage judgments that will injure a carefully nurtured reputation chills the law-abiding publisher, not the irresponsible deviant who has already calculated that the distant costs of potential libel losses are outweighed by present circulation increases.[151]

Since the prospect of paying damages has a relatively minor deterrent effect on irresponsible press behavior, Franklin's proposal making declaratory judgments available at the plaintiff's sole option would not substantially diminish the social costs of the present system. Responsible publishers would continue to face the risk of virtually unlimited damage judgments, direct monetary costs for defense, and loss of customers and reputation.[152] Under the Franklin proposal, there is a significant likelihood that others—perhaps plaintiffs tempted by jackpot damages or "guilty plaintiffs" whose real goal is a long and harassing suit—will choose the damage option. In 5 to 10 percent of these cases, it is likely that these plaintiffs will continue to win. Thus, the specter of large damage judgments and legal fees, albeit somewhat smaller than the risk today, would remain under Franklin's proposal. A prudent publisher would have to consider that risk, which would, as a result, continue to exert a substantial chilling effect.

Franklin's 1983 proposal also undercuts the concern he expresses here that irresponsible publishers will cause unrecompensed injury. In 1983, Franklin suggested that a defendant should be able to avoid all liability for damages, including special damages, simply by publishing a "reasonable retraction" at the plaintiff's request.[153] This provision was consistent with the theory of the defendant's option, because it would allow publishers to pretermit damage actions and avoid paying for the "harm" they had allegedly caused, even through intentional falsehood. In return, the plaintiff would receive a public correction of the record—the same outcome as in a successful declaratory judgment action after exercise of the defendant's option. Franklin expressed no concern in 1983 that irresponsible publishers would abuse the retraction option that he offered. His concerns here that irresponsible publishers will abuse the defendant's option— which in practical effect differs little from a retraction—accordingly ring hollow.[154]

Franklin does take some account of this problem by proposing adoption of the English rule with respect to attorneys' fees both in damage actions and in his declaratory judgment proposals.[155] Although the English rule would tend to discourage guilty plaintiffs from pursuing libel actions, a serious chilling effect would persist because Franklin would allow an unsuccessful plaintiff to escape paying the defendant's legal fees if the plaintiff had a "reasonable chance for success" in bringing a declaratory judgment suit or a damage action where the plaintiff "sustained special damages."[156]

This "reasonable chance" standard, however, is so broad that it will not change the risk calculated by prudent publishers. A careful defendant, or a publisher's reasonable insurance company, will have to assume that every losing plaintiff will claim a "reasonable chance of success." These claims will then have to be litigated, with the plaintiff's state of mind in bringing suit at issue and even his attorney's advice presumably subject to discovery.[157] A "reasonable chance of success" is not a very difficult standard for a plaintiff to meet, particularly if his attorney cooperates in recalling advice given prior to suit. American judges, reluctant to award fees against an unsuccessful plaintiff, are likely to allow very few defendants to recover fees under Franklin's proposal.[158] The only suits likely to be weeded out are the patently frivolous. Enough nonfrivolous suits will remain to exert a chilling effect.

Yet Franklin criticizes the Schumer bill's attorneys' fees proposal because it contains an "open-ended" provision permitting the court to disallow fee shifting "if there is an overriding reason to do so."[159] This provision, however, is no more "open ended" than Franklin's "reasonable chance of success" proposal. Indeed, the overriding-reason provision, by its language, imposes a higher standard to disallow fee shifting than reasonable chance, and so should be applied less frequently.[160]

Franklin also criticizes the Schumer bill's provision that attorneys' fees may not be awarded against a defendant that has taken reasonable care to avoid the publication of a libel or that published a retraction within ten days after service of the complaint.[161] Although this exception would in a sense reinject the issue of a defendant's state of mind into some declaratory judgment actions,[162] on balance it appears necessary. First, the standard imposed is an objective one: "reasonable efforts to ascertain" accuracy. Second, a defendant might not raise the issue at all if the plaintiff's fee claim were relatively low. Third, there is some question whether, under the First Amendment, a defendant can be forced to pay the plaintiff any money absent a showing of fault.[163] Last, to the extent that discovery into the editorial process is necessary, it need not occur until after there has been a judgment of liability. Bifurcated discovery would avoid inquiry into the editorial process in all cases that defendants win. When plaintiffs win, fees often will not be an issue because they are relatively modest in amount, because the defendant realizes it was at fault or because some compromise can easily be worked out given the relatively modest stakes.

Practicality of Operation and Feasibility of Adoption

The political attractiveness and practicality of implementation may well be crucial elements in the adoption and ultimate success of any libel reform. A proposal that makes use of existing legal and procedural structures is likely to win public acceptance more easily and to work more smoothly than one that requires major realignment of law and procedure. A reform proposal also should give consideration to political realities if it is to become more than a theoretical exercise.

Except for the absence of damages, litigation of declaratory judgment actions under the Schumer bill would follow the same procedures as other statutory tort-type remedies. Suit may be brought "in any court of competent jurisdiction,"[164] which would include both state trial courts of general jurisdiction[165] and federal district courts in diversity cases.[166] Since the Schumer bill makes no provision for special discovery rules or other procedural changes, normal court procedures would apply. The parties would be free to conduct discovery to the extent that each finds it appropriate in light of the value that each attaches to protecting its reputation. The elimination of damages will greatly reduce pressure to obtain or avoid an enormous judgment by means of massive discovery, multiple motions, and other litigation strategies.[167] The prospect of having to pay the winner's attorneys' fees also should tend to limit these practices.

Franklin proposed in 1983 that plaintiffs would have to present their evidence of falsity to the defendant, seeking a retraction or correction.[168] Only if this forced negotiation were unsuccessful could plaintiffs file a declaratory judgment action. Further, plaintiffs would be limited to presenting in court "essentially" the same evidence that had been shown to the publisher earlier.[169] No discovery would be permitted at any stage in the declaratory judgment action that Franklin initially proposed.[170]

Franklin now recognizes that the preaction conference and the limitation on trial proof that he proposed in 1983 were impractical. Instead of mandating them in all actions, he would now use attorneys' fees as incentive to encourage the conference and limit trial proof.[171] While continuing to urge elimination of discovery, he concedes that allowing it "will probably not cause fatal difficulties."[172]

Franklin's 1983 proposal for mandatory preaction conferences was unnecessary and likely counterproductive. Libel victims today frequently contact the media and try to resolve their disputes without lawyers or lawsuits. Many plaintiffs decide to sue only when they are rebuffed.[173] Any declaratory judgment remedy would encourage defendants to listen more carefully to such complaints because the defendant would be threatened with a no-fault finding of liability. Forcing the parties to talk, however, can only increase friction.

The limitations that Franklin proposed in 1983 on discovery and proof at trial would have made the declaratory judgment action too risky and hence virtually unusable. For example, absent discovery, the defendant would not be required to tell the plaintiff what unpublished evidence of truth the publisher has. A publisher could use this loophole to destroy a plaintiff's reputation by surprising the plaintiff with devastating proof of truth at trial.[174] Furthermore, since the plaintiff would have revealed his or her entire case at the preaction conference, the publisher could prepare to meet that evidence at trial; the plaintiff could only speculate as to the evidence he or she would face. Although the publisher could surprise the plaintiff with secret witnesses or documents, the plaintiff would be limited, even in rebuttal, to "essentially the same evidence presented to the defendant [with the retraction demand] and nothing new."[175]

Franklin's current proposal eliminates the ill-advised preaction conference and modifies the absolute limitations on trial evidence. The absence of discovery, however, still places plaintiffs at considerable risk in a trial by surprise. Plaintiffs' lawyers may well advise clients to avoid Franklin's declaratory judgment action altogether, since it would pose too great a risk against a well-counseled defendant.[176] Limiting discovery poses still a further problem for both parties as well as the public. Such a limitation undercuts the fundamental purpose of the declaratory judgment trial: to determine the "truth" and to give the "truth" a judicial imprimatur.[177] If a court judgment is to be rendered on the issue of truth, it should be a judgment reached with the benefit of the full panoply of procedural devices developed by the courts to ascertain the truth.[178]

Another important practical concern is whether national libel reform legislation is appropriate.[179] Congressional action is warranted, at least in dealing with public-figure damage suits, punitive damages, and the statute of limitations.[180] The problems with the present system in these respects are sufficiently serious to warrant prompt improvement; reform is more likely to come from Congress than from the state legislatures. Even though libel is a state-created cause of action, the common law tort has now been so altered and constrained by application of federal constitutional standards that rationalizing the system on a nationwide basis is essential.

Congress also may be less prone to antipress sentiment that could unbalance a reform proposal.[181] With the liability insurance crisis now focusing attention on broad reform of the tort system in Congress and many state legislatures,[182] it is a propitious time to implement libel reform as well. Nor is pursuit of federal legislation inconsistent with reform at the state level. Alleviation of the crisis even in a few states should improve the present situation. The Schumer bill has been used as a model for bills introduced in the California and Maryland legislatures.[183] Further state activity should be encouraged.

The Schumer bill represents a good starting point for libel reform because it deals aggressively with public-figure damage suits where a consensus for change is most likely to develop. The Schumer bill proposes significant changes affecting private-figure suits as well, but it does not—in contrast to Franklin's proposal—seek to raise the private-figure liability standard from negligence to actual malice. While applying the actual-malice standard to all libel actions may be intellectually sound and would bring welcome consistency to the law,[184] it is a change that is unlikely to command much public support. Judicial reaction to Gertz's invitation to fashion state liability rules for private plaintiffs shows that the negligence standard is

widely believed appropriate.[185] Seeking to raise that standard in an
initial libel reform package will generate strong opposition and may
lead to rejection of reform altogether.[186]

CONCLUSION

Franklin condemns the Schumer bill as politically unattractive primarily because he claims that it would allow " 'irresponsible publishers' to escape all liability for whatever harm they may impose by their
use of deliberate falsehoods."[187] If this were what the bill proposed,
criticism might be justified. But the Schumer bill does nothing of the
kind. Although it would give defendants the opportunity to avoid
damages by invoking the conversion option, the Schumer bill would
also subject defendants to strict liability for false statements. This
strict-liability standard means that defendants will lose "libel suits"
frequently, instead of winning 90 to 95 percent or more as they do
today. A defendant that makes an error will risk fairly certain injury
to its reputation for accuracy and a courtroom loss that can be ex-
ploited by competitors.

Far from freeing libel defendants from all restraint, the defendant's option is crucial to the practical effectiveness of any declaratory judgment remedy. At least with respect to public figures,
granting plaintiffs the exclusive choice of the declaratory judgment
route would unfairly tip the balance of interests against the press and
would ultimately diminish robust public debate. Franklin's legislative
proposal would add a powerful new weapon to "the plaintiff's arsenal" against the media,[188] while doing relatively little to ameliorate the
chilling effect of damage actions.[189]

Franklin's criticism focuses too narrowly on the perceived interests of the parties in libel suits. The First Amendment tells us that
the general social interest in the quality of public debate is of para-
mount importance. By undervaluing the social costs of public-figure
damage action—the transaction costs, the chilling effect, and the
interest in the flow of truthful information about the accuracy of the
facts at issue in libel cases—Franklin overstates the case against the
defendant's option.

The primary social interest in a libel action is to correct a proven
falsehood, not to reveal the defendant's state of mind. The stated
desires of most public-figure plaintiffs are consistent with this social
interest. Plaintiffs emphatically assert that they principally want to set
the record straight and have little interest in damages except as a
means to that end. Accordingly, no substantial purpose is served by

spending thousands and even millions of dollars to discover whether the defendant lied, acted carelessly, or was merely unlucky. Allowing public figures an unfettered choice of remedies in libel cases provides too great a temptation to perpetuate the damage action with its possible jackpot of almost limitless general damages. Franklin's proposal may lessen current libel problems somewhat, but the chilling effect and other social costs will remain excessive.

Nor are general damages for libel essential to keep irresponsible publishers in line, as Franklin maintains. A publisher determined to build an audience with titillating falsehoods is only minimally inhibited by the slight prospect of a damage judgment of uncertain amount years later. With defendants such as CBS, *Time,* and the *Washington Post* involved in celebrated cases, it is evident that present law does not target only "irresponsible publishers." The likelihood of liability, or at least of high defense costs, does chill the aggressiveness of responsible journalists. Allowing defendants the option to avoid damages in return for suffering a much higher frequency of liability and a concomitant loss in reputation for accuracy is a fair and necessary trade-off for the parties in light of social interests, particularly the First Amendment interest in robust debate.

NOTES

1. *See* Franklin, *Good Names and Bad Law: A Critique of Libel Law and a Proposal,* 18 U.S.F. L. REV. 1 (1983) [hereinafter Franklin, *Good Names*]; Franklin, *Suing Media for Libel: A Litigation Study,* 1981 AM. B. FOUND. RES. J. 795; Franklin, *Winners and Losers and Why: A Study of Defamation Litigation,* 1980 AM. B. FOUND. RES. J. 455. Like Franklin and other commentators, this chapter uses, the terms "libel," "defamation," and "slander" interchangeably.

2. *See* Bezanson, *The Libel Suit in Retrospect: What Plaintiffs Want and What Plaintiffs Get,* 74 CALIF. L. REV. 789 (1986); Bezanson, *Libel Law and the Realities of Litigation: Setting the Record Straight.* 71 IOWA L. REV. 226 (1985) [hereinafter Bezanson, Libel Law]; Cranberg, *Fanning the Fire: The Media's Role in Libel Litigation,* 71 IOWA L. REV. 221 (1985); Soloski, *The Study and the Libel Plaintiff: Who Sues for Libel?,* 71 IOWA L. REV. 217 (1985).

3. Franklin, *A Declaratory Judgment Alternative to Current Libel Law,* 74 CALIF. L. REV. 809 (1986), or Chapter 2, this volume.

4. Franklin, *Good Names, supra* note 1, at 29.

5. A bill "[t]o protect the constitutional right to freedom of speech by establishing a new action for defamation." H.R. 2846, 99th Cong., 1st Sess. (1985) [hereinafter the Schumer bill]. The complete text of this bill is reprinted in Franklin, *supra* note 3, at 832-35. *See* 131 CONG. REC. E3478 (daily ed. July 24, 1985) (statement of Representative Schumer) ("The legisla-

tion is intended to provoke wide-ranging discussion about American libel law and to encourage exploration of alternatives to it.").

6. *See, e.g.,* Freund, *Political Libel and Obscenity,* reprinted in 42 F.R.D. 437, 491-518 (1966); Hulme, *Vindicating Reputation: An Alternative to Damages as a Remedy for Defamation,* 30 AM. U.L. REV. 375, 402-13 (1981); Ingber, *Defamation: A Conflict Between Reason and Decency,* 65 VA. L. REV. 785, 852-58(1979); RESTATEMENT (SECOND) OF TORTS § 623 (ALI 1977) (special note on remedies for defamation other than damages) [hereinafter RESTATEMENT].

7. Franklin, *Good Names, supra* note 1, at 29-49.

8. *See* Franklin, *supra* note 3, at 812-13.

9. *Id.* at 828-31.

10. Franklin, *Good Names, supra* note 1, at 35; *see also* Franklin, *supra* note 3, at 819 ("statutory reform is worth attempting," preferably at state level), Cendali, *Of Things to Come—The Actual Impact of* Herbert v. Lando *and a Proposed National Correction Statute,* 22 HARV. J. ON LEGIS. 441, 490-92 (1985) (suggesting adoption of national correction statute to reduce litigation); Ingber, supra note 6, at 850, 852 (proposing a "model for future handling of defamation" that "has both judicial and legislative applications").

11. Franklin, *Good Names, supra* note 1, at 40.

12. The name "restoration action" might serve a useful cosmetic purpose by suggesting to libel victims that the action is "a way to restore reputations that [have] been falsely tarnished." *Id.* As Franklin concedes, however, neither money nor a judicial declaration of falsity can restore a good name. *See* Franklin, *supra* note 3, at 814 n.19; *see also* Rosenblatt v. Baer, 383 U.S. 75, 93 (1966) (Stewart, J., concurring) ("The destruction that defamatory falsehood can bring is . . . often beyond the capacity of the law to redeem."); Ingber, supra note 6, at 824-25 ("financial compensation is not really possible"). In short, marketing labels notwithstanding, Franklin, like Schumer, proposed a declaratory judgment remedy, as he now acknowledges.

13. Like Franklin, I assume that current constitutional law will not be modified substantially. *See* Franklin, *supra* note 3, at 810. One must recognize, however, that a significant minority view does not accept the holdings of New York Times Co. v. Sullivan, 376 U.S. 254 (1964), and Gertz v. Robert Welch, Inc., 418 U.S. 323 (1974). Supreme Court justices have criticized *Sullivan* and *Gertz. See, e.g.,* Dun & Bradstreet, Inc. v. Greenmoss Builders, Inc., 472 U.S. 749, 763-64 (1985) (Burger, C.J., concurring) ("*Gertz* should be overruled"); *id.* at 767 (White, J., concurring) ("the Court struck an improvident balance" in *Sullivan*); *see also* B. FEIN, NEW YORK TIMES V. SULLIVAN: AN OBSTACLE TO ENLIGHTENED PUBLIC DISCOURSE AND GOVERNMENT RESPONSIVENESS TO THE PEOPLE (1984) (*Sullivan* should be overruled and a negligence standard applied to public figures).

Some media opponents of libel reform do not object in principle to changes such as the creation of declaratory remedies. But these opponents do fear that legislative consideration of reform proposals will open *Sullivan* to debate and that antimedia forces will push through legislation sharply curtailing present protections of libel defendants. It seems unlikely that the Supreme Court would uphold legislation directly conflicting with *Sullivan* or *Gertz. See, e.g.,* Philadelphia Newspapers, Inc. v. Hepps, 475 U.S. 767 (1986) (reaffirming *Gertz* and holding that First Amendment requires private-figure plaintiff to prove falsity). *But see* Liberty Lobby, Inc. v. Anderson, 746 F.2d 1563 (D.C. Cir. 1984) (Scalia, J.), *vacated,* 106 S. Ct. 2505 (1986); Tavoulareas v. Piro, 759 F.2d 90 (Scalia, J., concurring), *vacated in part,* 763 F.2d 1472 (Scalia, J., concurring), *reh'g en banc granted,* 763 F.2d 1481 (D.C. Cir. 1985). These reform opponents also fear that the relatively balanced reforms suggested by Representative Schumer and Professor Franklin may be modified to disadvantage defendants. Accordingly, in building a consensus for libel reform, one must recognize that some opposition to change stems from a belief that the risk of opening the issue of reform to political debate outweighs the benefits that might be achieved.

14. Other, nonlegislative libel reform proposals have included not only creative nondamage alternatives but also numerous suggestions for improving the damage remedy. *See* Franklin, *Good Names, supra* note 1, at 37-40. Many of the suggested improvements in the damage remedy are entirely consistent with the creation of new, alternative remedies. Libel reform can and should occur on multiple fronts. *See, e.g.,* Anderson, *Reputation, Compensation, and Proof,* 25 WM. & MARY L. REV. 747 (1984) (tightly limiting damage judgments); Ashdown, *Of Public Figures and Public Interest—The Libel Law Conundrum,* 25 WM. & MARY L. REV. 937 (1984) (redefining the public-figure and public-official categories); Schauer, *Public Figures,* 25 WM. & MARY L. REV. 905 (1984) (same); Franklin & Bussel, *The Plaintiff's Burden in Defamation: Awareness and Falsity,* 25 WM. & MARY L. REV. 825 (1984) (changing burden of proof); Sowle, *Defamation and the First Amendment: The Case for a Constitutional Privilege of Fair Report,* 54 N.Y.U. L. REV. 469 (1979) (protecting "neutral reportage"); Zimmerman, *Curbing the High Price of Loose Talk,* 18 U.C. DAVIS L. REV. 359 (1985) (more effectively protecting statements of opinion); Note, *The Fact-Opinion Distinction in First Amendment Libel Law: The Need for a Bright-Line Rule,* 72 GEO. L.J. 1817 (1984) (same).

15. Compare Schumer bill with Plaintiff's Option Libel Reform Act [hereinafter POLRA], both reprinted in Chapter 2, this volume. Franklin's 1983 proposal advocated abolition of punitive damages. Franklin, *Good Names, supra* note 1, at 39 n.172. A number of other commentators have made similar suggestions. *See, e.g.,* Smolla, *Let the Author Beware: The Rejuvenation of the American Law of Libel,* 132 U. PA. L. REV. 1, 91-92 (1983); Van Alstyne, *First Amendment Limitations on Recovery from the Press—An Extended Comment on "The Anderson Solution,"* 25 WM. & MARY L. REV. 793, 803-09 (1984); Abrams, *Why We Should Change the Libel Law,* N.Y. TIMES, Sept. 29, 1985, § 6 (Magazine), at 34, 93.

The Schumer and Franklin proposals differ in that Franklin specifies that punitive damages are barred in actions "for libel or slander or false-light invasion of privacy," while the Schumer bill would apply to "any action arising out of a publication or broadcast which is alleged to be false and defamatory." Franklin's approach clearly abolishes punitive damages in false-light privacy actions. But the Schumer bill indirectly achieves the same result. Although some courts have indicated that a false-light claim need not allege defamatory meaning, the claims are essentially "duplicative." *See* R. SACK, LIBEL, SLANDER, AND RELATED PROBLEMS 393 (1980). The advantage of the Schumer bill's more general language is that it precludes artful pleaders from claiming punitive damages for causes of action not listed by Franklin but which require proof of defamatory falsehood, such as claims for intentional infliction of emotional distress arising from a false and defamatory statement. *See, e.g.,* Tumminello v. Bergen Evening Record, 454 F. Supp. 1156 (D.N.J. 1978).

16. See Schumer bill § 2, reprinted in Franklin, *supra* note 3, at 832-35; POLRA, § 2(a). The statute of limitations issue has not generated much comment, but reform is highly desirable. With many media outlets operating on a regional or national basis, a uniform limitations period eliminates forum shopping and benefits all parties by ensuring prompt correction of the public record.

    If plaintiffs are genuinely interested in vindicating injury to reputation, it makes no sense to allow the wound to fester for years after the offense. The law should give little weight to any interests that plaintiffs might have in seeking belated damage windfalls or punishing defendants at the end of a long limitations period. The majority of states apply a one-year statute of limitations to libel claims. SACK, *supra* note 15, at 587 (twenty-five states and District of Columbia as of 1980). Thus, the New Hampshire legislature responded to Keeton v. Hustler, Inc., 465 U.S. 770, 779 (1984), in which the plaintiff "search[ed] for a state with a lengthy statute of limitations," by reducing its six-year limitations period to three years. N.H. REV. STAT. ANN. § 508:4(II) (1983).

17. Schumer bill § 4, reprinted in Franklin, *supra* note 3, at 832-35; POLRA § 4; *cf.* Ingber, *supra* note 6, at 854-55 (proposing declaratory remedy with no fee shifting).

18. *See infra* notes 155-63 and accompanying text.

19. For convenience, both categories of plaintiffs are referred to hereinafter as "public figures."

20. Schumer bill § 1(a)(1), reprinted in Franklin, *supra* note 3, at 832-35.

21. POLRA, § 1(a)(1).

22. Schumer bill § 1(a)(2), reprinted in Franklin, *supra* note 3, at 832-35; POLRA, § 1(a)(2). A plaintiff could obtain a declaratory judgment whether the defendant published the false and defamatory statement knowingly, recklessly, negligently, or even innocently.

23. *See infra* notes 41-42 and accompanying text.

24. Schumer bill § 1(a)(3), reprinted in Franklin, *supra* note 3, at 832-35, POLRA § 1(a)(3).

25. Schumer bill § 1(c), reprinted in Franklin, *supra* note 3, at 832-35; POLRA § 1(d).

26. Schumer bill § 1(b), reprinted in Franklin, *supra* note 3, at 832-35; POLRA § 1(b). Professor David Anderson has suggested that actual provable harm to reputation should be a required element of the plaintiff's case in all libel actions, on the theory that the only legitimate purpose of such actions is

compensating harm to a plaintiff's reputation. *See* Anderson, supra note 14, at 749. Neither the Schumer bill nor Franklin would require such proof. Since most of Anderson's objections to presuming harm absent proof of reputational injury pertain specifically to damage actions, it is doubtful that they apply to a declaratory remedy. *See id.* at 749-56. In any event, requiring proof of actual injury in a declaratory action is unwise. As Anderson recognizes, proof of such injury would inject new evidentiary issues into libel cases. *Id.* at 764-73. While these complications may be warranted when large damage awards are at stake, they would undermine the simplicity of the declaratory action.

27. *See* Schumer bill § 1(a)(1), reprinted in Franklin, *supra* note 3, at 832-35; POLRA § 1(a)(1).

28. Franklin cogently argues that the declaratory judgment remedy should apply to suits against all defendants. *See* Franklin, *supra* note 3, at 815-16. The problems that nonmedia defendants may face are serious and troubling. To add one example to those Franklin discusses, individual reporters and editors are often named as codefendants with their media employer and it makes sense to give all codefendants the same option. Moreover, the Schumer bill, as now drafted, applies only to "the print or electronic media." The ambiguity of the term "media" invites litigation: How much circulation or how large an audience is required? What regularity of operation? These issues can be avoided by deleting the phrase. The discussion in this chapter of the impact of present libel law on defendants focuses on media defendants. Although some of the arguments presented do not apply to all nonmedia defendants, the fundamental points would. Thus, I would extend the declaratory judgment remedy to all defendants.

29. Giving certain private plaintiffs, such as wealthy and powerful individuals and corporations, the added remedy of a declaratory judgment will generate a strong chilling effect. *See infra* note 152 and accompanying text. A significant advantage of the defendant's option is that it ameliorates this chilling effect, but where less wealthy private plaintiffs are involved, it may be troubling to do so. Many private plaintiffs do not have the media access that characterizes public figures, nor have they sought or benefited from publicity. *See infra* notes 128-33 and accompanying text. Moreover, private plaintiffs are more likely to suffer actual pecuniary loss than public figures, Bezanson, *Libel Law, supra* note 2, at 228, 231, so involuntary elimination of damages may be more unfair as well. Franklin would minimize the threat to robust debate posed by private-figure damage actions by increasing the fault standard from negligence to actual malice. *See* POLRA § 3(a); Franklin, *supra* note 3, at 823-25. That change, however, will be politically difficult to accomplish. *See infra* notes 184-86 and accompanying text. A reasonable first step in libel reform is to adopt the defendant's option declaratory judgment only for public-figure plaintiffs. Expansion to private plaintiffs can be considered later in light of that experience.

30. Schumer bill § 1(d)(1), reprinted in Franklin, *supra* note 3, at 832-35. The bill provides that the defendant's election must be made at the time an answer is filed or within ninety days of commencement of the action,

whichever is earlier. The ninety-day period, which would protect the plaintiff in the event that a motion to dismiss is filed prior to an answer, is somewhat arbitrary. A more direct way to achieve the same result would be to require making the election at the time the defendant answers or otherwise moves against the complaint on a ground which postpones its time to answer. *See* FED. R. CIV. P. 12(b).

31. Schumer bill § 1(d)(2), reprinted in Franklin, *supra* note 3, at 832-35.

32. Franklin, *supra* note 3, at 815 n.27, 836-42.

33. For this reason, Franklin's preference for "moving ahead slowly," *id.* at 827, on proposals, like the declaratory judgment remedy, "to make major changes in any legal system, especially one several hundred years old," Franklin, *Good Names, supra* note 1, at 29, rests on faulty premises. The present legal framework for libel suits is a shotgun marriage, not a "legal system." Nor is it "several hundred years old." Modern libel law dates only from the Supreme Court's 1964 decision in New York Times Co. v. Sullivan, 376 U.S. 254 (1964), which imposed constitutional constraints on the common law action for the first time. Thus, current libel law does not reflect the distilled wisdom of centuries but is rather a contemporary contrivance in need of immediate overhaul.

34. As Justice Stewart lamented, "[I]mperfect though it is, an action for damages is the only hope for vindication or redress the law gives to a man whose reputation has been falsely dishonored." Rosenblatt v. Baer, 383 U.S. 75, 93 (1966) (Stewart, J., concurring).

35. F. POLLOCK, THE LAW OF TORTS 210 (1887).

36. *See, e.g.,* Pound, *Equitable Relief Against Defamation and Injuries to Personality,* 29 HARV. L. REV. 640 (1916) (injunctive relief); Chafee, *Possible New Remedies for Errors in the Press,* 60 HARV. L. REV. 1 (1946) (declaratory relief).

37. *See, e.g.,* Donnelly, *The Right of Reply: An Alternative to an Action for Libel,* 34 VA. L. REV. 867 (1948); Leflar, *Legal Remedies for Defamation,* 6 ARK. L. REV. 423 (1952); Barron, *Access to the Press—A New First Amendment Right,* 80 HARV. L. REV. 1641 (1967). Recent commentators view retraction statutes as ineffective, largely because they offer defendants insufficient incentive to cooperate. *See, e.g.,* SACK, *supra* note 15, at 382; Hulme, *supra* note 6, at 387-88. The remedy of a compulsory right of reply, absent a judicial finding of defamatory falsehood, was held unconstitutional in Miami Herald Publishing Co. v. Tornillo, 418 U.S. 241 (1974). A recent proposal essentially attempts to reinvigorate the retraction model. *See* Cendali, *supra* note 10.

38. 376 U.S. 254 (1964).

39. *Id.* at 279.

40. *Id. See* Schauer, *Fear, Risk and the First Amendment: Unraveling the "Chilling Effect,"* 58 B.U.L. REV. 685, 705-12 (1978).

41. New York Times Co. v. Sullivan, 376 U.S. 254, 279-80 (1964). Common law libel rules generally treated state of mind as irrelevant to the plaintiff's cause of action. If it were relevant at all, it was purely as a defense. *See* RESTATEMENT OF TORTS §§ 558, 599, 600 (1938). In only a few states did the common law require proof of actual malice. *See Sullivan,* 376 U.S. at 280 n.20.

42. 376 U.S. at 279-80; Curtis Publishing Co. v. Butts, 388 U.S. 130 (1967).

43. 418 U.S. 323 (1974).

44. *Id.* at 349-50.

45. *Id.* The *Gertz* "limitation" of recovery under the negligence standard to "actual injury" has proven illusory. The *Gertz* Court defined "actual injury" to include "personal humiliation, and mental anguish and suffering," 418 U.S. at 350; the Court later held that this could mean emotional injury alone. *See* Time, Inc. v. Firestone, 424 U.S. 448, 458-61 (1976). Thus, the Court kept the door open for virtually unlimited awards for "actual" mental suffering. *See* Ashdown, Gertz *and* Firestone: *A Study in Constitutional Policy-Making*, 61 MINN. L. REV. 645, 670-71 (1977).

46. *See infra* note 121.

47. *See* Philadelphia Newspapers, Inc. v. Hepps, 475 U.S. 767, 776 (1986); Schauer, *supra* note 40, at 708.

48. Bezanson, *Libel Law, supra* note 2, at 227.

49. *Id.* at 230, 232 ("Fault, or abuse of the privilege of negligence or [actual] malice, has . . . become the gravamen of the cause of action.").

50. 475 U.S. 767, 780 (1986).

51. *Id.* at 783 (Stevens, J., dissenting) (emphasis added).

52. *See infra* notes 64-70, 84-87 and accompanying text.

53. For example, the jury in Sharon v. Time, Inc., 599 F. Supp. 538 (S.D.N.Y. 1984), found the statements at issue false and defamatory but not published with actual malice. N.Y. TIMES, Jan. 25, 1985, § 1, at 1, col. 2. A great deal of the trial focused on *Time's* editorial practices. *See* Adler, *Annals of Law (Two Trials),* THE NEW YORKER, June 16, 1986, at 42, and June 23, 1986, at 34 (criticizing editorial activities revealed in *Sharon* and *Westmoreland* cases. Westmoreland v. CBS, Inc., 596 F. Supp. 1166 (S.D. N.Y.), *aff'd sub nom.* Westmoreland v. Columbia Broadcasting Sys., Inc., 752 F.2d 16 (2d Cir. 1984), *cert. denied sub nom.* Cable News Network, Inc. v. U.S. District Court, 472 U.S. 1017 (1985)).

54. *See* Gertz v. Robert Welch, Inc., 418 U.S. 323, 395 (1975) (White, J., dissenting).

55. *See infra* notes 71-81 and accompanying text.

56. *See* Smolla, *supra* note 15, at 22-36.

57. *See supra* notes 48-49 and accompanying text.

58. Virtually every press description of a libel suit includes the *ad damnum* amount with no indication that it is virtually meaningless. *See, e.g.,* Taylor, *Cost of Libel Suits Prompts Calls to Alter System,* N.Y. TIMES, Feb. 25, 1985, at A11, col. 1 ("News Analysis" referring to Westmoreland's "$120 million suit" against CBS even after it was discontinued); *CBS Hit with $100-Million Suit over News Story,* BROADCASTING, Mar. 10, 1986, at 73; *Ex-Agent Files $120 Million Libel Suit Against Publisher,* PUBLISHER'S WEEKLY, Nov. 13, 1981, at 11.

59. So ingrained is this practice that even Floyd Abrams, an outstanding libel defense lawyer, has perpetuated it. In a popular magazine article, after describing an actual libel settlement of $1.4 million and defense costs of $5 million in the *Westmoreland* case—numbers that clearly are meaningful—he

referred to *ad damnum* amounts without criticism or explanation: Governor Janklow's "$10 million libel action"; Lakian's suit "for $50 million." Abrams, *supra* note 15, at 90-92. The casual reader will almost certainly infer that the damage claims are equally meaningful.

60. For example, there were eleven verdicts in excess of $1 million between 1982 and 1984. LIBEL DEFENSE RESOURCE CENTER, BULLE-TIN NO. 11 at 15 (LDRC, New York, N.Y.), Nov. 15, 1984 [hereinafter LDRC BULL. NO. 11]; *see also infra* note 120 and accompanying text.

61. *See, e.g.,* Gospel Spreading Church v. Johnson Publishing Co., 454 F.2d 1050 (D.C. Cir. 1971); Medina v. Time, Inc., 319 F. Supp. 398 (D. Mass. 1970); Washington Post Co. v. Keogh, 365 F.2d 965 (D.C. Cir. 1966).

62. 441 U.S. 153, 176-77 (1979).

63. *See* Anderson v. Liberty Lobby, Inc., 477 U.S. 242, 256 (1986) (plaintiff can defeat "defendant's properly supported motion for summary judgment" by "offering . . . concrete evidence from which a reasonable juror could return a verdict in his favor;" evidence sufficient in "caliber" or "quantity to allow a rational finder of fact to find actual malice by clear and convincing evidence"); Hutchinson v. Proxmire, 443 U.S. 111, 120 n.9 (1979) (actual malice "does not readily lend itself to summary disposition").

64. *See, e.g.,* Massing, *The Libel Chill: How Cold Is It Out There,* COLUM. JOURNALISM REV., May-June 1985, at 31.

65. As McClatchy Newspapers editor Frank McCulloch has stated, "The investigative team no longer exists, not because we're afraid to have it, but because its members have become full-time litigants." *Id.* at 37.

66. Franklin, *Good Names, supra* note 1, at 18-20. Franklin noted, however, that the premium structure was likely to discourage investigative reporting and coverage of controversial stories to a significant degree. *Id.* at 20-22.

67. *Id.* at 18-20 (comparing libel premiums and coverage amounts to those for other types of liability insurance).

68. *See* Baer, *Insurers to Libel Defense Counsel: "The Party's Over,"* AM. LAW., Nov. 1985, at 69.

69. *See* Heavner, *Developments in Obtaining Insurance, Changing Terms, and Market Restrictions,* in MEDIA INSURANCE AND RISK MANAGEMENT (J. Lankenau ed., 1985).

70. *Id.*

71. Sanger, *Tension on the Frontiers of Libel,* N.Y. TIMES, Dec. 18, 1983, § 6 (Magazine), at 4, col. 2.

72. *See* Tavoulareas v. Piro, 759 F.2d 90, *vacated in part,* 763 F.2d 1472, *reh'g en banc granted,* 763 F.2d 1481 (D.C. Cir. 1985).

73. *See* Roper, *Who's Behind the Media Libel Suits?,* EDITOR & PUB-LISHER, Mar. 2, 1985, at 9 (discussing conservative nonprofit organizations supporting libel suits); *"Friends" Chip in for Laxalt,* EDITOR & PUBLISHER, Apr. 5, 1986, at 14 (Senator Laxalt's suit against the *Sacramento Bee* alleging $250 million damages financed by contributions of $263,670 during 1985 from "friends" ranging from Senators Kennedy and Inouye to Roy Cohn and T. Boone Pickens).

74. 759 F.2d 90 (D.C. Cir. 1985).

75. Hanson, *What Went Wrong at the Washington Post,* COLUM. JOUR-NALISM REV., Jan.-Feb. 1983, at 31.

76. 599 F. Supp. 538 (S.D.N.Y. 1984).

77. Adler, *supra* note 53, June 16, 1986, at 48.

78. 596 F. Supp. 1166 (S.D.N.Y. 1984).

79. Roper, *supra* note 73. After the *Westmoreland* case ended, there were reports that plaintiff's counsel, who was employed by the Capital Legal Foundation, had urged settlement strongly, without discussing it with West-moreland's private firm counsel, as a result of the foundation's political agenda or financial situation. *See* Bruck, *How Dan Burt Deserted the General,* AM. LAW., Apr. 1985, at 117. This suggests the danger that conflict of interest may pose for a plaintiff who is not paying counsel directly.

80. Franklin, *Good Names, supra* note 1, at 39 n.176; *see* Burnett v. National Enquirer, Inc., 144 Cal. App. 3d 991, 193 Cal. Rptr. 206 (1983), *appeal dismissed,* 465 U.S. 1014 (1984).

81. Former Rep. Andrew Maguire has described his frustration at being financially unable to do more than threaten to sue book publisher William Morrow & Co. for false accusations that Maguire had improperly hindered a congressional investigation of mob corruption in the toxic waste industry. The authors of the book formally acknowledged their errors; the publisher promised not to reprint the accusations; and it reimbursed Maguire's legal fees. Maguire believes, however, that Morrow was unwilling to negotiate a stronger, more public remedy, such as retraction or withdrawal of the book, because Morrow knew that he could not afford to sue. *Hearings on H.R. 2846* [the Schumer bill] *Before the Subcomm. on Civil and Constitutional Rights of the House Comm. on the Judiciary,* 99th Cong., 2d Sess. (1986) (statement of Andrew Maguire) (on file with author) [hereinafter *1986 House Hearings*].

82. *See* Baer, *supra* note 68.

83. *See, e.g.,* Green v. Alton Telegraph Printing Co., 107 Ill. App. 3d 755, 438 N.E.2d 203 (1982); Smolla, *supra* note 15, at 12-13 (commenting on *Alton Telegraph* case).

84. Franklin, *supra* note 3, at 810; Franklin, *Good Names, supra* note 1, at 16.

85. *1986 House Hearings, supra* note 81 (statement of Walter W. Stewart & Ned Feder, M.D.); Boffey, *Major Study Points to Faulty Research at Two Universities, But, Amid Fears of Libel, It Has Not Been Published,* N.Y. TIMES, Apr. 22, 1986, at C1, col. 4; Abrams, *supra* note 15.

86. *See, e.g.,* Massing, *supra* note 64; *Libel—The Intimidation Factor,* THE CENTER MAGAZINE, May/June 1985, at 33 (chilling effect on small media); *id.* at 35 (quoting David Lawrence, *Detroit Free Press* publisher: "[T]he threat of libel . . . is very chilling, intimidating and frightening, . . . more so than it has ever been before . . . even for an aggressive and honest publisher."); Abrams, *supra* note 15, at 92 (quoting Osborn Elliott, dean of Columbia Graduate School of Journalism: "Care and caution are giving way to timidity in newsrooms across the land."); *1986 House Hearings, supra* note 81 (statement of Homer F. Marcum, editor and publisher of the *Martin*

Countian, Inez, Ky.) ("Each time I paste up a story on my front page, or an editorial that is somewhat controversial, I stop to think 'Is it worth it?' My financial resources are . . . such that I cannot say yes too many more times when some burning issue in my community needs the benefit of a strong editorial voice.").

87. *See, e.g.,* Franklin, *supra* note 3, at 809 n.5, 815 n.24; *Hearings on Libel Reform Before the House Judiciary Subcomm. on Courts, Civil Liberties and the Administration of Justice,* 99th Cong., 1st Sess. (1985) (statements of Gene Roberts, executive editor, the *Philadelphia Enquirer,* and Bruce J. Ennis) (on file with author).

88. *See supra* notes 83-86; Franklin, *supra* note 3, at 811; Franklin, *Good Names, supra* note 1, at 13-22.

89. These so-called tertiary costs of administering any system of legal redress for injuries are largely wasted under the present damage rules because little compensation flows to persons who are actually injured by false statements. *See* Ingber, *supra* note 6, at 814.

90. Bezanson, *Libel Law, supra* note 2, at 227 & n.1, 231.

91. *Id.*

92. *Id.* at 230, 232 "[Q]uestions of constitutional privilege are raised in virtually every case and are determinative in 88 percent of the cases."

93. *Id.*

94. *Id.* at 231.

95. *Id.* "Privilege issues ranging from discovery, access to information, legal status of the plaintiff, and negligence and actual malice, exist and must be addressed in every libel case brought against the press."

96. *Id.* at 230.

97. As the Iowa study reports, a "substantial majority of [public figures] believe that the lawsuit achieved reputation-related objectives, even though they lost." *Id.* at 231. Furthermore, public figures remain "virtually unanimous in their determination to sue again if faced with the same situation." *Id.*

98. The declaratory judgment action must bar a damage action based on the same claim, or the potential chilling effect of the new remedy would be enormous. Not only would the defendant face strict liability in the declaratory judgment action, but it would also continue to face the risks of a large damage recovery.

99. *See* Soloski, *supra* note 2, at 218; Bezanson, *Libel Law, supra* note 2, at 228; Franklin, *Good Names, supra* note 1, at 5; *infra* note 121.

100. Indeed, a great advantage of a properly formulated declaratory judgment remedy is that it would be a market solution to the problem of reputational injury. Since there is no possibility of a damage windfall, both parties will commit financial and personal resources to the lawsuit based on their perceptions of the value of restoring or maintaining their own reputations. A plaintiff who is genuinely concerned about his or her reputation will tend to spend more money to protect it than one who is less committed but who, under the present system, might be tempted by the prospect of large, windfall damages to litigate more aggressively. Similarly, a defendant that is strongly committed to protecting its reputation for accuracy will expend

more time and money on defense than one to which reputation is less important. The calculus, however, will be tied directly to the perceived value of the defendant's reputation, not skewed, as it is today, by the risk of enormous damages.

101. *See* SACK, *supra* note 15, at 267-339.

102. *Id.* at 268.

103. *See id.* at 328-38.

104. Franklin concludes that the state statutory and common law absolute privileges should be recognized as defenses to a new declaratory judgment action. Franklin, *supra* note 3, at 817-18. He is inclined "to leave [qualified] privileges in place as well." *Id.* at 818 n.35. One could argue, however, that because qualified privileges do not protect interests as important as the absolute privileges, a plaintiff should have the opportunity to correct the record in a declaratory judgment action.

Franklin relegates the fair comment and opinion privileges, *see, e.g.*, RESTATEMENT OF TORTS § 606 (1938); RESTATEMENT, *supra* note 6, § 566, to a footnote. Franklin, *supra* note 3, at 818 n.35. Whether they are labeled privileges, as most courts still do, or "part of the plaintiff's case," as Franklin urges, fair comment and opinion should be recognized in declaratory actions. They protect speech that is not demonstrably "true" or "false" and are probably constitutionally compelled, at least in damage actions. *See* Ollman v. Evans, 750 F.2d 970 (D.C. Cir. 1984), *cert. denied*, 471 U.S. 1127 (1985). The values thus protected—the speaker's personal autonomy and the impracticability of proving opinions "true"—would be compromised if a declaratory judgment action did not recognize them.

Although Franklin discusses privileges, he does not respond to the main point of the text—that the common law privileges deny damages to some deserving plaintiffs in order to protect other, overriding societal interests. Franklin's endorsement of privileges is thus inconsistent with his criticism of the defendant's option in the Schumer bill, which would have an effect no different in kind from that of the privileges on plaintiffs' ability to obtain relief.

105. Franklin, *supra* note 3, at 825-27.

106. *Id.* at 810, 811, 838.

107. *See supra* note 86.

108. Franklin, *supra* note 3, at 841; Franklin, *Good Names, supra* note 1, at 30.

109. *Id.* at 838-42.

110. *Id.* at 840.

111. Philadelphia Newspapers, Inc. v. Hepps, 475 U.S. 767, 776 (1986).

112. Franklin, *supra* note 3, at 837.

113. *Id.* at 826; *see also* Franklin, *Good Names, supra* note 1, at 5-6 (reporting estimate that half of all libel cases are "nuisance" cases).

114. POLRA § 4(b)(1); *see also* Franklin, *supra* note 3, at 842.

115. Professor Van Alstyne has suggested that the actual-malice defense makes it more likely that the rare plaintiff who gets to trial will win. This is because when a defendant's fault is an issue for a jury to decide, a skillful

plaintiff's lawyer can turn the trial's focus to the defendant's alleged misconduct. The jury may well feel that the misconduct, and not the injury to the
plaintiff, is the gravamen of the tort. Moreover, by forcing the plaintiff's
lawyer to prepare the malice claim more fully, the defense may also in directly
encourage large verdicts. *See* Van Alstyne, *supra* note 15, at 795-98.

116. *See* Franklin, *Good Names, supra* note 1, at 38.

117. *See supra* note 45.

118. Also significant in this regard are the normative considerations
that apply to voluntary public figures. *See infra* notes 128-33 and accompanying text.

119. *See, e.g.,* Smolla, *supra* note 15, at 2-4 (reviewing multi-million-
dollar libel claims).

120. Goodale, *Survey of Recent Media Verdicts, Their Disposition on Appeal,
and Media Defense Costs,* in MEDIA INSURANCE AND RISK MANAGE-
MENT 1985 at 69, 78 (1985); LIBEL DEFENSE RESOURCE CENTER,
BULLETIN NO. 12 (LDRC, New York, N.Y.), Dec. 31, 1984 [hereinafter
LDRC BULL. NO. 12].

121. Bezanson, *Libel Law, supra* note 2, at 228; Franklin, *Good Names,
supra* note 1, at 4-5. Statistics suggest that in the period 1982 to 1984,
plaintiffs' ultimate success rate dropped even lower—to less than 3 percent.
See LDRC BULL. NO. 11, *supra* note 60.

122. LDRC BULL. NO. 12, *supra* note 120. The total number of libel
damage awards affirmed between 1982 and 1984, including actual-malice
and negligence cases, was six, with an average award of about $60,000. These
figures are substantially lower than the fourteen awards affirmed between
1980 and 1982 for an average award of $120,000, suggesting a trend toward
fewer and smaller awards. Between 1980 and 1982, only seven of the fourteen affirmed awards occurred in cases in which the actual-malice standard
was dispositive, so that only nine "malice" awards were finally upheld over a
four-year period. *Id.;* LDRC BULL. NO. 11, *supra* note 60, at 22, 23.

123. Indeed, because Franklin would require all plaintiffs, including
private figures, to prove actual malice in order to recover any damages, few
private plaintiffs would lose much if the defendant's option were applied to
them. *See* POLRA, § 3(a), Franklin, note 3, at 823-25.

124. Bezanson, *Libel Law, supra* note 2, at 233.

125. *Id.* at 227.

126. *Id.*

127. *Id.* at 233. By filing suit, plaintiffs feel that they are transformed
from victim to active fighter for truth and honor: " 'You walk into the halls
and people you've known for years feel sort of sorry for you. . . . But the
moment I sued, the attitude of everybody changed. . . . Suddenly people
started to believe you. My days changed the day I started the suit.' " Brill,
Inside the Jury Room at the Washington Post Libel Trial, AM. LAW., Nov. 1982, at
1, 90 (quoting Mobil Corp. President William P. Tavoulareas).

128. *See supra* note 29 and accompanying text. Although there is considerable debate over the contours of the public-figure doctrine, the Schumer
bill does not attempt to define this elusive term. *See, e.g.,* Ashdown, *supra* note

14; Daniels, *Public Figures Revisited,* 25 WM. & MARY L. REV. 957 (1984); Schauer, *supra* note 14. Instead, the bill accepts the current doctrine as at least minimally fair and workable, although judicial modification of it would change the scope of the bill's applicability. *See infra* note 133.

129. Gertz v. Robert Welch, Inc., 418 U.S. 323, 345 (1974).

130. *Id.* at 344.

131. *Id.* at 345.

132. *Id.*

133. *Gertz* also distinguishes public figures from private persons because the former "usually enjoy significantly greater access to the channels of effective communication and hence have a more realistic opportunity to counteract false statements" without bringing libel suits. *Id.* at 344. This access to the media also reduces the justification for public figures to recover damages in libel actions.

Applying the foregoing arguments to lower-level appointed public officials, such as school teachers, sanitation workers, and government clerks, as well as to private figures, is problematic. Despite indications from many lower courts that all government employees are public officials, this may be too broad a reading of the Supreme Court's decisions. *See* Elder, *Defamation, Public Officialdom and the* Rosenblatt v. Baer *Criteria—A Proposal for Revivification: Two Decades After* New York Times Co. v. Sullivan, 33 BUFFALO L. REV. 579, 678-79 (1984). Although one never becomes a public official at any level involuntarily, lower-level employees cannot generally be described as seeking and benefiting from the spotlight of publicity. On the other hand, the impact that certain persons and corporations, particularly those of great wealth and power, now classified as private figures have on the community could well justify treating them as public figures.

Franklin's expressed concern for "involuntary" public figures is greatly overstated. See Franklin, supra note 3, at 840 n.127. "The instances of truly involuntary public figures must be exceedingly rare." Gertz v. Robert Welch, Inc., 418 U.S. 323, 345 (1974). The decision Franklin cites does not mention a single other case making such a finding. *See* Dameron v. Washington Magazine, Inc., 779 F.2d 736, 740-43 (D.C. Cir. 1985). *cert. denied,* 476 U.S. 1141 (1986). In any event, although the court did not reach the question, 779 F.2d at 743, it seems likely that Dameron, an air traffic controller, was a public official under current law. Moreover, the story of an air crash is plainly a matter of great public concern, as to which Franklin suggests the defendant's option may be appropriate. *See* Franklin, *supra* note 3, at 840-42.

Thus, in criticizing the Schumer bill for depriving "low-level public officials and involuntary public figures" of damages, Franklin, *supra* note 3, at 840, Franklin is aiming at the wrong target. The problems he identifies stem from overly broad definitions of public officials and should be addressed directly. Although statutory redefinition of these terms might unduly complicate a new declaratory judgment statute, redefinition will be far easier to accomplish, either legislatively or judicially, if the stakes in libel litigation are sharply reduced by adopting the defendant's option.

Franklin also criticizes the Schumer bill because the defendant's option is not limited to "statements that implicate self-governance." *Id.* at 840. Particularly where public figures such as movie stars who desperately seek publicity are concerned, "self-governance" is too narrow a standard. If Hollywood sex lives figure too prominently in the supermarket tabloids, as suggested by Franklin's references to the *Enquirer* and *Globe, see id.* at 838-39, the appropriate solution might be to define privacy rights as prohibiting such offensive discussion, whether it is true or not. *But see* Zimmerman, *Requiem for a Heavyweight: A Farewell to Warren and Brandeis's Privacy Tort,* 68 CORNELL L. REV. 291, 364 (1983) (urging reliance on "social evolution" rather than the law of privacy to reduce "our excessive taste for personal details").

Given all of the justifications for the defendant's option, the interests of the small groups of plaintiffs cited by Franklin seem minimal. The fact that the public-figure concept may need some redefinition does not disqualify it from any use in the meantime. Whatever the outcome of this debate, the argument in the text clearly applies to public figures and to all elected officials and high-ranking appointees.

134. Bezanson, *Libel Law, supra* note 2, at 228, 231.

135. *Id.* at 231.

136. *See, e.g.,* S. 1979, 1985-86 Cal. Leg., Reg. Sess. § 1 (legislative finding that the libel plaintiff "is rarely interested in monetary redress, but rather seeks vindication of his or her reputation").

Lawmakers, themselves public figures, are entitled to rely on these assertions, notwithstanding Franklin's characterization of them as "self-serving." Franklin, *supra* note 3, at 827, 837. Apparently, Franklin does not credit admissions against interest. Even police officers suing for libel after allegedly false accusations of brutality commented, " '[We're] not going to get any money out of them. . . . We want our names cleared.'" E. PELL, THE BIG CHILL 186 (1984).

Whether such statements are self-serving or not, in light of so many consistent statements from such a wide range of plaintiffs, it is fair to take them at their word. In any event, damages are sought by public figures today primarily to cover their costs of suing or to punish or intimidate defendants. The former goal is served directly by the attorneys' fee-shifting provision of the declaratory judgment proposals. The latter goals are totally inappropriate justifications for a system with such enormous social costs.

137. Franklin, *supra* note 3, at 837 (footnote omitted).

138. I agree with Franklin that requiring a defendant to publish a declaratory judgment would be an undesirable, though perhaps not unconstitutional, intrusion into the editorial process. *Id.* at 827-28; Franklin, *Good Names, supra* note 1, at 33-34, 42-43; *see* Miami Herald Publishing Co. v. Tornillo, 418 U.S. 241, 258-59 (Brennan, J., concurring). Any attempt to suppress the news of a libel defeat will likely be futile. A defendant's competitors, in the same medium or another, could use the defeat to gain competitive advantage. *See supra* note 100. The *New York Times* and *Daily News* would no doubt relish reporting the libel misfortunes of the rival *New York Post,* and vice versa. If one newspaper dominates a city, television and radio competitors would still benefit from reporting on the paper's libel defeats.

Even in small communities primarily served by a single newspaper or broadcaster, the growth of alternative communications technologies such as cable television and direct satellite broadcasting makes the prospect of suppression increasingly unlikely.

139. Franklin, *supra* note 3, at 838.

140. *Id.* at 844.

141. *Id.* at 841.

142. *Id.* at 841-42.

143. *See supra* note 121 and accompanying text.

144. Franklin, *supra* note 3, at 839-43.

145. *Id.* at 839.

146. Franklin, *Good Names, supra* note 1, at 46 (quoting *Newsweek*, May 4, 1981, at 50).

147. *See id.* at 27-28.

148. Franklin, *supra* note 3, at 838-43. In addition to the "scandal press," Franklin suggests that "irresponsible publishers" may include political or religious zealots and unethical local media outlets. *Id.* He does not, however, indicate his basis for concluding that irresponsible behavior by publishers is sufficiently widespread to justify the costs of preserving plaintiffs' absolute right to seek damages in virtually unlimited amounts. *See supra* notes 116-18 and accompanying text. While the behavior revealed in the *Burnett* case may be deplorable, the plaintiff there needed the $200,000 judgment only to pay her lawyers. The media are not so evidently infected with venality, and the *Enquirer's* behavior is not so typical, as to justify rejection of the defendant's option for all publishers, responsible and irresponsible alike.

Franklin does suggest that the defendant's option could be modified to allow recovery of special damages even where the option is exercised. Franklin, *supra* note 3, at 842, n.133.

149. 144 Cal. App. 3d 991, 193 Cal, Rptr. 206 (1983), *appeal dismissed*, 465 U.S. 1014 (1984).

150. *See supra* note 122 and accompanying text. Franklin has described the ultimate damage awards as "relatively small." Franklin, *Good Names, supra* note 1, at 5 & n.23.

151. Franklin's assertion that after *Burnett*, "we are seeing an increasing amount of litigation against organizations like the *National Enquirer* and *Globe International*," expresses a hope not a fact. Franklin, *supra* note 3, at 839. He suggests that plaintiffs' 5 percent success rate will rise in damage suits against "irresponsible publishers." Any such increase, however, is unlikely to deter misbehavior, which is the essential justification for Franklin's opposition to the defendant's option. The actual-malice defense is simply too high a burden for most plaintiffs to meet.

Nor do Franklin's anecdotal examples, *id.* at 839 n.119, show that the *Enquirer* and *Globe* are significantly deterred by the threat of damages. Two of the cases were settled, and according to the Iowa Libel Research Project, in the 10 to 15 percent of libel suits that are settled, "usually" no money changes hands. Bezanson, *Libel Law, supra* note 2, at 228, 229. The defendants are obviously prolonging the other suits mentioned, while they continue publishing alleged "fabrications" about the lives of movie stars who avidly seek publicity from others and, with equal fervor, seek to control the content of all public discussion to conform to their carefully cultivated "images."

152. Although Franklin's proposal would bar punitive damage awards, general damages, which he would allow, can include virtually unlimited amounts for emotional injury. *See supra* notes 45, 114, 117-18 and accompanying text. Current trends in jury verdicts for intangible injuries in other torts make this prospect no less chilling than the threat of punitive damages.

153. Franklin, *Good Names, supra* note 1, at 42 ("[T]he plaintiff will lose . . . the right to bring a damage action upon defendant's publication of the . . . retraction."); *id.* at 43-44 ("If the defendant responded [to a retraction demand] with a reasonable retraction, the plaintiff would be foreclosed from pursuing either [a damage or declaratory judgment] action.").

154. Franklin's proposed statute would make retraction prior to filing of suit a complete defense only to a declaratory judgment action. POLRA § 2(b); Franklin, *supra* note 3, at 816-17.

Franklin later reinterpreted his 1983 statements in seeking to counter the argument in the text. *See* Franklin, *supra* note 3, at 816 n.31. The record speaks for itself, however. *See supra* note 153. Moreover, Franklin's criticism begins with a misreading of this chapter. I do not say that Franklin is "a past supporter of a defendant's option." Franklin, supra note 3, at 816 n.31. My point is more subtle. In 1983, Franklin indicated that a "reasonable retraction" would foreclose relief even where a plaintiff suffered special damages or a defendant intentionally lied. That is inconsistent with Franklin's present arguments against the defendant's option, which focus on loss of special damages and lying defendants.

Franklin also takes my words out of context in saying that I "assert that 'expansion in the scope of libel defenses would lead to greater press irresponsibility.' " *Id.* at 843 n.123, quoting *supra,* at 872. He omits the essential qualification that precedes the words he quotes: "[I]f Professor Franklin's theory were correct, one would expect that expansion . . .", etc. I go on to say that the facts do not support that expectation, arguing that Franklin's theory is therefore wrong.

155. POLRA § 4; Franklin, *Good Names, supra* note 1, at 38-39, 42, 43; Franklin, *supra* note 3, at 842-44.

156. POLRA §§ 4(b)(1)-(2); Franklin, *supra* note 3, at 843, 842; Franklin, *Good Names, supra* note 1, at 39, 43. The "special damages" limitation is discussed *infra* note 158.

157. Difficult as it now is for plaintiffs to prove whether a defendant published a falsehood with a culpable state of mind, it would be more difficult still for a defendant to prove the plaintiff's state of mind in bringing a libel suit. Some objective evidence, such as a reporter's notes or drafts of a story, is generally available to prove a defendant's state of mind. Other claims concerning a defendant's state of mind may be tested by questioning interviewees and editors about the process of newsgathering and editing. With respect to a plaintiff's basis for bringing suit, however, the only witnesses are likely to be

the plaintiff and the plaintiff's lawyer. Both have a strong incentive to tell the "right" story, and their testimony cannot likely be challenged by objective evidence such as third-party testimony or contemporaneous documents. In any event, a "reasonable chance of success" could be honestly claimed in any nonfrivolous suit.

Although Franklin asserts that "the test is objective and not based on what an attorney might advise," the language of his proposal makes no such distinction. Compare Franklin, supra note 3, at 842 n.135 with POLRA § 4. It hardly seems fair to punish a plaintiff who filed suit based on an attorney's overly optimistic advice. As a practical matter, the attorney's advice will be admitted in the form of argument to the court, if not in testimony.

158. Franklin does limit the escape from fee shifting in damage actions to plaintiffs "who sustained special damages." POLRA § 4(b)(1); see Franklin, Good Names, supra note 1, at 38-39. This limitation, however, does not significantly mitigate the problems described in the text. Presumably, whether a plaintiff "sustained special damages" is decided by looking at the complaint. If special damages were pleaded in good faith, fees should not be awarded. Thus, plaintiffs' lawyers would be invited to plead creatively and to allege as special damages at least some small amount of actual pecuniary loss. The good faith of such a claim would be difficult to test, and challenging it would result in still more undesirable "post-litigation litigation."

Moreover, the distinction that Franklin draws, between plaintiffs who allege special damages and those who allege only presumed or general damages, is unpersuasive as a basis for deciding the fee-shifting issue. The reason that general damages are allowed in libel actions is precisely because proving special damages, as opposed to pleading special damages, is considered extremely difficult. See SACK, supra note 15, at 345-49. It is illogical to require those who may have suffered severe nonpecuniary injury to bear the risk of having to pay defendants' attorneys' fees.

159. See Franklin, supra note 3 at 842; Schumer bill § 4(1), reprinted in Franklin, supra note 3, at 832-35.

160. The "overriding reasons" that would permit a court to disallow fees would be limited to such factors as extreme disparity in the wealth of the parties. For example, if a police officer or other low-level public official were to lose a job because of a false report by a profitable television station but were unable to prove actual malice, it might be unduly harsh to require the plaintiff to pay the defendant's attorneys' fees.

161. See Franklin, supra note 3, at 843-44; Schumer bill § 4(2), reprinted in Franklin, supra note 3, at 832-35. The argument that unnecessary injury would be caused by precluding attorneys' fees upon publication of a retraction after the complaint is filed has considerable force. Moreover, this provision may provoke undue haste in filing suits. Accordingly, it would be preferable if the retraction exception were changed to provide that the time for publishing a retraction runs from the date that plaintiff demanded a retraction or the date of filing suit, whichever is earlier.

To avoid unfairness to the defendant, a retraction demand would have to specify the facts on which it was based. Franklin proposes that the defendant be allowed a reasonable time to consider the demand; this may he more appropriate than a rigid ten-day limit. *See* Franklin, *supra* note 3 at 844 n.143; POLRA § 2(b).

162. In damage actions, to which the fee-shifting provisions of the Schumer bill would also apply, state of mind will continue to be an issue irrespective of the standards governing fee shifting.

163. Franklin has suggested that if some fault must be shown before a libel defendant is forced to pay attorney's fees, it could be implied from an unreasonable refusal to retract. Franklin, *supra* note 3, at 822; Franklin, *Good Names, supra* note 1, at 48. Aside from the practical problems of requiring a plaintiff to demand a retraction before filing a declaratory judgment action, this suggestion opens the unfortunate possibility of a new tort for unreasonable refusal to retract.

A statute making unreasonable refusal to retract the basis for an award of attorneys' fees could be interpreted as establishing a duty to publish reasonable retractions. A court might well imply a common law right of action for damages from violation of the legislatively imposed duty. Although such an action might well be unconstitutional, the prospect is sufficiently disturbing to argue against Professor Franklin's suggestion. *See supra* note 138; Miami Herald Publishing Co. v. Tornillo, 418 U.S. 241 (1974).

164. Schumer bill § 1(a)(1), reprinted in Franklin, *supra* note 3, at 832-35.

165. The Schumer bill's express jurisdictional language would make it mandatory for state courts of competent jurisdiction to hear declaratory judgment defamation claims brought under the federal statute.

166. 28 U.S.C. § 1332 (1982). The Schumer bill might also be read to confer federal court jurisdiction over all declaratory judgment libel suits because the claim "arises under the . . . laws . . . of the United States." 28 U.S.C. § 1331 (1982). The same theory would also allow removal, under 28 U.S.C. § 1441(b) (1982), of declaratory judgment suits commenced in state court. Since common law libel claims arise under state, not federal, law, libel cases currently must be brought in state courts unless federal diversity jurisdiction exists. *See* 28 U.S.C. § 1332. If the Schumer bill is construed as making libel a federal question, however, it could shift the locus of libel litigation, raising the prospect of overburdening the federal courts with claims whose substance will be largely a matter of state law.

The general federal declaratory judgment statute does not give federal courts jurisdiction over declaratory judgment actions unless diversity exists or a federal question appears on the face of a "well-pleaded complaint." 28 U.S.C. § 2201 (1982); Skelly Oil Co. v. Phillips Petroleum Co., 339 U.S. 667 (1950); *see also* Franchise Tax Bd. v. Construction Laborers Vacation Trust, 463 U.S. 1 (1983) (applying *Skelly Oil* to preclude removal of state declaratory judgment action). The Schumer bill's authorization of declaratory judgments might be construed analogously as "procedural only," Aetna Life Ins. Co. v. Haworth, 300 U.S. 227, 240 (1937), but that result is uncertain in light of the bill's avowed purpose of "establishing a new cause of action," *see supra* note 5, and not merely filling a procedural gap. It would be preferable to eliminate any such uncertainty by expressly providing that original and removal federal question jurisdiction is not available for the new cause of action.

167. Since actual malice will not be an issue, that entire area of discovery and proof at trial will be eliminated. Although cases like *Westmoreland* and *Sharon* demonstrate that discovery and trial on truth alone can be extraordinarily complex, they are certainly the exceptions. In most libel cases, truth will be no more complex an issue than malice and may be much simpler. In every case, eliminating malice will necessarily make that case simpler than it otherwise would be. In the discovery that does occur, plaintiffs will presumably seek to learn what evidence of truth the defendant plans to use, and defendants will want to probe for proof of falsity that the plaintiff possesses. Each party also will want to search for exculpatory evidence within the other party's knowledge.

168. Franklin, *Good Names, supra* note 1, at 41-42.

169. *Id.*

170. *Id.* at 44.

171. POLRA §§ 4(b)(2)-(b)(3); Franklin, *supra* note 3, at 814-15.

172. POLRA § 2(c); Franklin, *supra* note 3, at 829.

173. Cranberg, *supra* note 2, at 221.

174. The threat of a damage action would not necessarily induce publishers to reveal evidence prior to filing suit, since the same evidence would probably make out a malice defense.

175. Franklin, *Good Names, supra* note 1, at 42. Apparently, under Franklin's 1983 proposal, even if the plaintiff found a lost witness or uncovered a forgotten document, the defendant could prevent their use at trial.

176. Franklin argues that discovery is unnecessary because plaintiffs "usually do not use it to get information on falsity" and have "ample proof of falsity." Franklin, *supra* note 3, at 828, 829. These assertions, which are apparently based on a private conversation with Franklin, are probably incorrect. In my own experience litigating libel cases, plaintiffs frequently use discovery to obtain evidence of falsity. Perhaps Franklin is confused by the fact that discovery relating to actual malice under current law necessarily subsumes discovery on falsity, since actual malice requires proof of knowing or reckless falsehood. Eliminating malice will eliminate the need to discover the defendant's intent, but defendants will continue to possess information probative of falsity.

In any event, Franklin errs in dismissing the significance of another essential function of discovery in libel cases—to learn what evidence of truth the defendant may have so that the plaintiff can be prepared to rebut it at trial. If the plaintiff's best friend is going to testify against him or her, it may profoundly affect both the plaintiff's decision whether to go to trial and his or her trial preparation. Franklin would deny the plaintiff that knowledge in the hope that defendants would find it in their self-interest to reveal it. *See id.* at 829. But discovery is such an important aspect of the judicial truth-finding function that it seems unwise to experiment with it. By lowering the stakes in libel actions, however, declaratory judgments will reduce parties' inclination to undertake massive discovery. *See supra* note 167 and accompanying text.

177. Discovery is frequently used to learn of evidence helpful to the discovering party's case. *See supra* note 167. Absent discovery, either party could win at trial even though it was aware of evidence that, had it been produced in discovery, would have changed the outcome.

178. If a less formal proceeding is desirable, the outcome should not he labeled as a court judgment. Franklin's assertion that "discovery is little used in the criminal justice system," *id.* at 829 n.84, ignores the existence of grand juries, which are extraordinarily powerful discovery tools for the prosecution, as well as the constitutional and statutory rights of defendants to compel production of potentially favorable evidence. *See, e.g.,* 18 U.S.C. § 3500 (1982); FED. R. CRIM. P. 15, l6, 26.2; Brady v. Maryland, 373 U.S. 83 (1963).

179. *See* Franklin, *supra* note 3, at 818-19.

180. Franklin agrees that congressional action on the statute-of-limitations issue might be appropriate. *Id.* at 819 n.36.

181. *See supra* note 13; Franklin, *Good Names, supra* note 1, at 8-10; Smolla, *"Where Have You Gone, Walter Cronkite?": The First Amendment and the End of Innocence,* 39 ARK. L. REV. 311 (1985).

182. *See, e.g,* Pear, *Administration Submits Plan to Reduce Damage Awards,* N.Y. TIMES, May 1, 1986, at B9, col. 1; *Gov. Cuomo Names Panel to Study Insurance Rises,* N.Y. TIMES, Jan. 14, 1986, at B2, col. 1. *See also* Sugarman, *Doing Away With Tort Law,* 73 CALIF. L. REV. 555 (1985) (advocating state and congressional legislation and administrative action to create a social insurance system); Pierce, *Institutional Aspects of Tort Reform,* 73 CALIF. L. REV. 917 (1985) (attempts at legislative reform face crowded agendas, opposition from powerful vested interests, and the dangers of compromise legislation).

183. S. 1979, 1985-86 Cal. Leg., Reg. Sess. (introduced by Senator Lockyer); H. 1255, Md. Gen. Ass. 1986 Sess. (introduced by Delegate Rosenberg).

184. *Compare* Franklin, *What Does "Negligence" Mean in Defamation Cases?,* 6 COMM./ENT. L.J. 259 (1984) (negligence standard is in practice the equivalent of strict liability), with Bloom, *Proof of Fault in Media Defamation Litigation,* 38 VAND. L. REV. 247 (1985) (negligence standard works reasonably well and adequately protects press).

185. *See* Bloom, *supra* note 184, at 335 ("The great majority of courts that have addressed the issue to date have adopted a negligence standard."); Franklin, *supra* note 184, at 264-65 (1984) (at least twenty-six states, the District of Columbia, and federal courts interpreting the law of three additional states have applied negligence standard); SACK, *supra* note 15, at 250, 255-60 (as of 1980, six states "may have adopted" actual-malice standard for matters of public interest and seven others have indicated that an intermediate standard might apply).

186. Since the Schumer bill would allow defendants to convert damage actions into suits for declaratory judgment, the question might be raised whether it violates the Due Process Clause by depriving plaintiffs of the right to damages. The answer is no. First, the Supreme Court has held that an individual's interest in reputation is not "liberty" or "property" protected by

due process. Paul v. Davis, 424 U.S. 693, 710-12 (1975). Accordingly, prospective deprivation of a right to sue for libel damages does not violate the Due Process Clause. Second, Congress and the state legislatures have broad powers to fashion new remedies to replace common law damage actions, particularly when the new remedy would be more prompt and certain than the damage action in most cases. The classic example is the replacement of common law negligence actions with workers' compensation statutes. *See, e.g.,* Tipton v. Atchison, T.R.S.F. Ry. Co., 298 U.S. 141 (1934); Cudahy Packing Co. v. Parramore, 263 U.S. 418 (1923); New York Central R.R. Co. v. White, 243 U.S. 188 (1917).

Congress has the constitutional power to enact libel reform legislation, even though libel law historically has been left to state control. Congress could act either under the Commerce Clause, at least with respect to news media that affect interstate commerce, or under Section 5 of the Fourteenth Amendment. Since the First Amendment is incorporated into the Fourteenth, Congress has the power to "enforce" the former "by appropriate legislation," such as the Schumer bill.

187. Franklin, *supra* note 3, at 841-42.

188. *Id.* at 817-18.

189. Perhaps the 5 percent success rate of current libel plaintiffs has distorted our perception of the fairness of the system. Because that rate is so low, allowing a declaratory judgment might appear only to give plaintiffs a reasonable opportunity to win cases. But for the reasons discussed in the text, creating a declaratory judgment remedy without a defendant's conversion option would tip the balance much too far in plaintiffs' favor.

chapter 4

Vindicating Reputation: An Alternative to Damages as a Remedy for Defamation[*]

JAMES H. HULME
STEVEN M. SPRENGER[†]

[The law] has gone wrong from the beginning in making the damage and not the insult the cause of action.[1]

Defamation suits frequently result in exorbitant damage awards to a small number of plaintiffs.[2] Many other plaintiffs receive only nominal compensation.[3] Although other remedies for defamatory falsehood have been the subject of debate,[4] damage awards remain the principal remedy recognized by the courts. Criticized as inadequate at common law,[5] the exclusive use of damage awards as the remedy for defamation is even less effective in light of constitutional law developments that create additional barriers to defamation actions.[6] Although constitutional privilege protects, for example, those who speak or write on matters of public concern, it has left many falsely defamed individuals without legal remedy for their injuries.[7]

[*]This chapter is based on an article that appeared in 30 AM. U. L. REV. 375 (1981).
[†]Hulme is a partner, Arent, Fox, Kintner, Plotkin & Kahn, Washington, D.C. A.B., 1976, Middlebury College; J.D., 1979, American University.
Sprenger is an associate, Arent, Fox, Kintner, Plotkin & Kahn, Washington, D.C. B.A., 1985, Grinnell College; J.D., 1988, University of Iowa.

In response to continued criticism of the damage remedy, a reexamination of alternative remedies for defamation is appropriate to protect reputational interests without undermining established constitutional standards.[8] The ultimate goal is to provide those persons who presently are without legal recourse for defamatory falsehood with the ability to protect their reputations from injurious falsehoods. After undertaking a review of the existing goals and remedies in the law of defamation, this chapter proposes a "vindication action."[9] Such an action would constitute an adjunct to current defamation remedies and would be available, on an elective basis, to all plaintiffs.[10]

This chapter first examines existing defamation law and the effect of constitutional privilege on the common law principles. It then analyzes the problems inherent in the damage-oriented approach and compares that approach with other existing defamation remedies. It then examines a number of proposed nondamage remedies including Section 9-107 of the Model Communicative Torts Act,[11] the Franklin Declaratory Judgment Proposal,[12] and the Schumer bill.[13] Next, this chapter examines the proposed vindication remedy in the context of tension between defamation law and the First Amendment. Finally, while balancing protection of First Amendment guarantees against redress for victims of defamation, the parameters of the vindication action are set forth along with guidelines for the practical application of this proposed defamation remedy.

EXISTING DEFAMATION REMEDIES

The Impact of the Constitutional Privilege

Until 1964, the First Amendment did not include defamatory utterances within its protection.[14] In *New York Times Co. v. Sullivan*,[15] however, the Supreme Court extended qualified First Amendment protection to statements impugning the fitness and character of public officials. The Court held in *Sullivan* that damages could not be awarded to a public official for defamatory falsehood relating to official conduct unless it was proved that the defendant acted with "actual malice."[16]

The Court has extended the application of the *Sullivan* standard of actual malice beyond defamation actions. In *Hustler Magazine, Inc. v. Falwell*,[17] the jury ruled against the plaintiff on his libel claim based on an advertisement parody that depicted the plaintiff and his mother as drunk and immoral. The jury concluded that the advertisement parody could not be reasonably understood as describing actual facts or events.[18] The jury ruled in favor of the plaintiff on his claim for intentional infliction of emotional distress based on the advertisement parody, however.[19] The Court found that the "outrageousness" standard embodied in the tort of intentional infliction of emotional distress was inconsistent with First Amendment considerations.[20] Thus, the Court held that a public figure or public official may not recover for intentional infliction of emotional distress based on a publication without showing actual malice.[21]

At common law, defamation cases centered around such issues as falsity, defamatory content, publication, common law privileges, malice, and damages.[22] *Sullivan* and its progeny added constitutional dimensions to defamation litigation without eliminating any of the common law issues.[23] These constitutional considerations include the plaintiff's status,[24] the defendant's status,[25] the public interest in the communication,[26] the degree of culpability,[27] the existence of actual injury,[28] the provability of the alleged falsehood,[29] and the scope of permissible discovery.[30] These constitutional standards are designed to further the accepted social goal of free political commentary and to prevent individuals from being selectively punished for expressing unpopular views.[31] These standards, however, also serve as an insurmountable bar to redress for many victims of defamatory falsehood. In *Milkovich v. Lorain Journal Co.*,[32] the Supreme Court recognized the difficulties these constitutional obstacles have created for defamed plaintiffs. The *Milkovich Court* clearly indicated its reluctance to create additional obstacles when it rejected a constitutional distinction between "defamatory opinion" and "defamatory fact."[33]

Damages

The law of defamation[34] does not differ markedly from other branches of tort law in its attempt to compensate plaintiffs through the award of monetary damages for injury to reputation.[35] Reputational injury, however, is particularly difficult to establish.[36] This dilemma was recognized at common law, and consequently, several doctrines and presumptions were developed to aid in proving injury to a plaintiff's reputation and to guide the jury in awarding damages. Four discrete categories of damages were available: general damages, special damages, punitive damages, and nominal damages.[37]

General Damages

General damages were classified as compensatory, but a plaintiff did not need to prove actual pecuniary loss before recovering general damages.[38] In the traditional defamation case for libel or slander per se,[39] damage to reputation was presumed merely from the publication of the defamatory falsehood.[40] The defendant could offer evidence to rebut this presumption by demonstrating that, because of the plaintiff's existing bad reputation or the inconsequential nature of the defamatory statement, no injury to reputation occurred.[41] In order to rebut such a defense, the plaintiff was entitled to introduce evidence of both pecuniary loss and harm to reputation.[42]

The presumption of general damages also served to narrow the relevant issues in a defamation case, because the plaintiff was not required to prove reputational injury. Unless the defendant chose to contest the presumption of general damages, this element of the case did not become an issue in the litigation. A plaintiff thus could devote attention to other controverted issues, and a defendant would not pursue the damage issue unless the common law presumption could be attacked successfully.[43]

Gertz v. Robert Welch, Inc.[44] restricted the award of general damages to those plaintiffs who were able to prove "knowledge of falsity or reckless disregard for the truth."[45] Thus, while the plaintiff who could meet the *Sullivan* actual-malice standard did not need to prove damages, all other plaintiffs could recover only actual damages.[46]

Special Damages

When defamation was not actionable per se at common law, a plaintiff had to prove special damages in the nature of actual pecuniary loss.[47] Injury to reputation is not an element of special damages, although "it is . . . to be taken into account in assessing the damages. . . ."[48] Special damages are essentially identical to those damages that are awarded in the typical contract or tort action. All elements of proof required in an ordinary tort action—pecuniary loss, defendant's fault, and a causal connection—are necessary to prevail in such a claim.[49]

Proof of special damages could also be introduced to increase a damage award in cases where a cause of action existed without this evidence.[50] A plaintiff alleging defamation per se, for example, could rest on the presumption provided by the general damages rules; however, he could also introduce evidence of special damages to ensure that he would be compensated for at least his actual injury.[51]

To prove special damages, the plaintiff must demonstrate not only the existence of special damages, but also that they were proximately caused by the defamatory statement.[52] In cases in which either the amount or the causation of damage could be challenged by the defendant, the remedy issue occupied a considerable amount of time at trial. This would result in distracting the fact finder from the issues of falsity and defamatory content.[53] Where the plaintiff had been subjected to false and defamatory statements that did not fall within the per se rule but was unable to prove special damages, the action was barred. The plaintiffs in those cases were unable to vindicate their reputation.[54]

When the Supreme Court restricted the use of general damages in *Gertz*,[55] it simultaneously expanded the concept of actual damages beyond mere "out-of-pocket loss."[56] The Court stated that "impairment of reputation and standing in the community, personal humiliation, and mental anguish and suffering" are compensable so long as such awards are "supported by competent evidence concerning the injury, although there need be no evidence which assigns an actual dollar value to the injury."[57] Thus, constitutional "actual damages" include items that the common law treated as general damages. Some plaintiffs, therefore, may be able to recover general damages under the concept of constitutional "actual damages."

Punitive Damages

A maxim of tort law asserts that punitive damages are awarded not to compensate the plaintiff but to punish the defendant.[58] According to the Supreme Court, punitive damages "are private fines levied by civil juries to punish reprehensible conduct and to deter its future occurrence."[59] Thus, they can be seen as criminal penalties imposed in a civil forum.[60]

The standard at common law for awarding punitive damages focused on the defendant's state of mind. If the evidence demonstrated that the defendant was guilty of malicious conduct toward the particular plaintiff, the jury was empowered to award punitive damages.[61] This standard required that the defendant be motivated by ill will toward the plaintiff and that this malicious attitude give rise to the defamatory utterance.[62]

At common law, punitive damages provided a major incentive for filing a defamation suit.[63] When the plaintiff was unable to demonstrate any reputational injury and, therefore, was entitled only to nominal damages,[64] punitive damages could be recovered if it could be shown that the defendant acted with common law malice.[65] Such recoveries, however, are now barred by *Gertz*, in which the Supreme Court ruled that punitive damages may be awarded only if the plaintiff can meet the *Sullivan* standard of malice, knowing falsity, or reckless disregard for the truth.[66]

Punitive damages have come under increasing constitutional

attack since the Court observed in *Gertz* that "juries assess punitive damages in wholly unpredictable amounts bearing no necessary relation to the actual harm caused."[67] In *Browning-Ferris Industries of Vermont, Inc. v. Kelco Disposal, Inc.*,[68] the Court rejected an attack against punitive damages based on the excessive fines clause of the Eighth Amendment. The Court recently revisited the punitive damages issue in *Pacific Mutual Life Insurance Co. v. Haslip.*[69] In *Haslip,* the Court recognized the legitimate concern about punitive damages "run wild."[70] The Court declined, however, to find a violation of the due process clause of the Fourteenth Amendment for three reasons. First, the jury instructions clearly explained the nature and purpose of punitive damages.[71] Second, posttrial procedures were in place at the trial level which allowed objective scrutiny of any punitive damages award.[72] Third, appellate review ensured that the amount of any punitive damages award would not exceed the amount that would accomplish society's goals of punishment and deterrence.[73]

Nominal Damages

Nominal damages are awarded when the plaintiff can prove the false and defamatory nature of the defendant's statement but is unable to demonstrate reputational injury.[74] This failure may be due to the fact that the plaintiff's good reputation was unassailable[75] and thus not subject to injury. Conversely, the plaintiff's reputation may already have been so tainted that the defamatory statement could not impugn it further.[76] The nominal damage award provides the plaintiff with vindication in the form of a judicial determination that the statement was false and defamatory.[77]

All damage remedies for defamation are subject to the full panoply of defenses and privileges that the common law provides.[78] In addition, the constitutional privileges apply;[79] thus, were a new defamation remedy to be built on the foundations of existing damage remedies, the same defenses and privileges arguably would defeat the new remedy. To avoid this result, alternative nondamage remedies must be examined.

Nondamage Remedies

Injunctions

The use of injunctions as a remedy for defamatory falsehood[80] was restricted by the Supreme Court in *Near v. Minnesota,*[81] where a state statute permitting the issuance of injunctions against newspapers was held unconstitutional as a prior restraint on the press.[82] In the present atmosphere of heightened sensitivity to First Amendment concerns, it is unlikely that a court would enjoin a newspaper from publishing an article because of its defamatory content.[83]

Although the use of the injunction against defamatory statements may not be foreclosed completely, it appears to have little vitality today.[84] It is unlikely, therefore, to provide any practical guidance in a search for acceptable alternative defamation remedies.

Retraction Statutes

The common law provides that although retraction of a defamatory statement can mitigate damages,[85] it rarely serves as a complete defense. Because the defamation is deemed to inflict irreversible damage,[86] retraction is exculpatory only if it is immediate and sufficient to negate completely the effect of the defamatory statement.[87]

State legislatures have modified the common law by enacting retraction statutes that limit, in varying degrees, the amount recoverable in cases in which a newspaper inadvertently publishes a defamatory statement.[88] Some early challenges to retraction statutes were successful,[89] but later efforts to overturn similar statutes failed.[90]

Although retraction may provide a quick and efficient remedy, the availability of this remedy depends entirely on the defendant's cooperation;[91] the defendant cannot legally be compelled to issue a retraction.[92] If the defendant refuses to retract the statement, the plaintiff must pursue the traditional remedy of damages. If the defendant believes that a common law or constitutional privilege could preclude an award of damages, the defendant may refuse to issue a retraction, despite the admitted false and defamatory character of the statement. This would result in denying the plaintiff legal recourse for a recognizable attack on the plaintiff's reputation.

Reply Statutes

A reply statute provides for a right of reply to be given to one who is the subject of an article or news story. The failure to honor the right of reply can result in criminal prosecution. Drawing largely from European experience with the compelled publication of replies, some legal commentators favor a right of reply because it places both sides of the dispute before the community, thereby allowing the public to discern the truth.[93] A second rationale for the use of reply statutes is that the First Amendment guarantees of freedom of expression require that the public have a right of access to the news media.[94] The reply is, in effect, a forced sale: A defendant, under the usual statutory scheme, could be compelled to publish the reply or face a criminal penalty.[95]

The Supreme Court's unanimous ruling that the government may not compel a newspaper editor to publish a reply against his will and under threat of criminal punishment undermined whatever potential right of reply a falsely defamed person may have had.[96] The Court adopted the view that a compelled right of reply impermissibly infringed upon editorial decision making, thereby violating the First Amendment.[97] Because the reply statutes envisioned by legal writers relied on the use of criminal penalties,[98] the Court's decision effectively eliminated the right of reply as a viable remedy for defamatory falsehood.[99]

Declaratory Judgments

The Federal Declaratory Judgment Act[100] authorizes federal courts to declare the rights and legal relations of interested parties and to grant appropriate relief. In addition, the courts in states that either have adopted the Uniform Declaratory Judgment Act or enacted state statutes with similar provisions are empowered to issue declaratory judgments. Although the statutory language of the Act does not specifically authorize suits for a declaration of the false and defamatory content of a statement, the language is broad enough to permit that construction.[101] By adopting a liberal interpretation of the Act, the courts could create a new defamation remedy and avoid the need for legislation establishing such a remedy. Their willingness to do so, however, is largely untested; thus, the declaratory judgment remedy remains academic.

The plaintiff's purpose in filing a suit for a declaratory judgment would be purely vindicatory, as no damages would be awarded.[102] Thus, in one sense, the declaratory judgment action parallels a defamation action for nominal damages.[103] A crucial distinction, however, remains between an action for nominal damages and a declaratory judgment. A traditional defamation suit requesting nominal damages is encumbered by all of the doctrines, privileges, and defenses of defamation law.[104] In contrast, because the plaintiff in a declaratory judgment action desires only a determination of the statement's false and defamatory content, most other issues, and their accompanying privileges and defenses, are rendered immaterial.[105]

Summary

The existing remedies frequently do not allow plaintiffs to vindicate their reputation.[106] Thus, new remedies for the protection of personal reputation—the ultimate goal of the law of defamation[107]— must be considered. With the increasingly impersonal character of modern society, the concept of personal identity has assumed greater importance. Personal identity is closely allied with reputation. The law should recognize this reputational interest and forge new remedies to vindicate the reputations of those who are victims of defamatory falsehood who would otherwise be left without a remedy. Such new remedies must be consistent with the First Amendment, by removing the threat of large damage awards and, in addition, the potential for substantial litigation defense costs that are, by themselves, a potential deterrent to the exercise of First Amendment rights.

ALTERNATIVE NONDAMAGE REMEDIES

In the 1980s, scholars and practitioners proposed a variety of alternative nondamage remedies as part of a libel law reform movement. The stated goal of most of these proposals was to allow plaintiffs to vindicate their reputation quickly, effectively, and at minimum expense. The proposals that have received the most attention are modeled after existing declaratory judgment statutes. These proposals include Section 9-107 of the Model Communicative Torts Act (MCTA),[108] the Franklin Declaratory Judgment Proposal,[109] and the Schumer bill.[110]

Section 9-107 of the MCTA allows a plaintiff to seek a declaratory judgment that a communication contained injurious or disparaging false or misleading statements.[111] The issues to be litigated in such an action are whether the communication was false and misleading and caused the relevant injury.[112] On such a finding, the court would be required to order the offending party to publish in a manner and medium reasonably calculated to reach the same audience as the false or misleading statement the contents of the declaratory judgment or a correction satisfactory to the plaintiff.[113] In addition, the prevailing plaintiff would recover reasonable attorneys' fees and costs.[114] Such actions would be granted docket priority and would be set for trial within 120 days in most instances.[115]

The Franklin Declaratory Judgment Proposal would also allow a plaintiff to sue for a declaratory judgment that a publication or broadcast was false and defamatory.[116] The plaintiff would not be required to prove actual malice but would be required to prove falsity with clear and convincing evidence.[117] In addition, the Franklin proposal would allow defendants to assert the common law privileges as a defense.[118]

The Schumer bill, while quite similar to the Franklin proposal, differs in several critical respects.[119] First, it is limited to public-figure plaintiffs and media defendants.[120] Second, it grants media defendants sued by public figures the right to convert a damage action into an action for a declaratory judgment.[121]

Each of the proposals fails to provide a viable supplementary defamation remedy. Although the MTCA eliminates many of the problematic libel issues (e.g., actual malice and common law privileges), it needlessly retains certain issues that are unrelated to truth or falsity and that serve to increase the costs of litigation. For instance, a plaintiff is still required to prove defamatory content and causation of injury.[122] In addition, the MCTA creates new inequities by allowing successful plaintiffs, but not successful defendants, to recover attorneys' fees.[123] Thus, the MCTA may encourage frivolous declaratory judgment actions.

There are shortcomings to the Franklin proposal as well. The retention of the common law privileges is particularly problematic.[124] This would increase the costs of prosecuting and defending an action brought under the Franklin proposal. The Franklin proposal follows the same defects as the MCTA by requiring that the plaintiff prove that the defamatory statement caused the injury. Finally, the reasons for placing a clear and convincing burden on the plaintiff are not evident. If the goal of the action is to ascertain the truth and to have that determination publicized, then it should be sufficient if the truth is determined by the preponderance of the evidence. Imposition of the clear-and-convincing standard is an invitation to litigate yet another issue, thus raising the costs to all parties.

The Schumer bill is the most problematic. While it contains all of the shortcomings of the other proposals, it also suffers from two of its own. First, it limits the action to public figures who sue media defendants. This makes little sense in light of the fact that such plaintiffs are typically better equipped than other plaintiffs to pursue a damage action.[125] Second, the Schumer bill would allow media defendants to convert a strong damage case to a declaratory judgment case thus depriving the plaintiff of the choice of remedy.[126] As described in the next section, the vindication action avoids the pitfalls of these proposed nondamage remedies.

THE VINDICATION REMEDY AND THE
FIRST AMENDMENT

The sole objective of the vindication process is to secure from the defendant public acknowledgment that he has made false statements about the plaintiff. Accordingly, a vindication action could be initiated after the defendant has made a statement about the plaintiff and refuses to retract it publicly. The primary issue before the trier of fact is the truthfulness of the defendant's statement.[127] If the contested statement is found to be false, the plaintiff would receive a judgment that declares the statement false. Inasmuch as judicial proceedings and decisions are rarely the subject of extensive news coverage, however, the mere issuance of a judgment may not be sufficient to vindicate the plaintiff's reputation.[128] In many cases, therefore, a vital adjunct to the proposed vindication action is an order to the defendant to circulate the judgment of falsity as extensively as was the publication of the defamatory statement.

The vindication action, as set forth above, is designed to provide a defamation remedy that can effectively redeem a plaintiff's reputational interest without offending established constitutional principles.[129] The vindication action is strictly a nondamage remedy and, therefore, does not implicate the concern expressed by the Supreme Court in *Sullivan, Gertz,* and *Falwell* that large damage awards produce excessive media self-censorship. *Gertz* clearly indicated that this concern over financially induced self-censorship is a primary reason for protecting some defamatory statements.[130] The Court in *Gertz* emphasized the protection of First Amendment freedoms through limitations on civil damage awards.[131] Accordingly, because the vindication action does not impose a financial penalty on the defendant, arguably there is no constitutional barrier to such a remedy.[132] It is necessary, however, to examine additional factors leading to constitutional limitations placed on the law of defamation. An examination of these concerns underscores the fact that the vindication action does not burden defendants in a manner inconsistent with the First Amendment.

The vindication action also addresses the concern about excessive attorneys' fees. Although the *Sullivan/Gertz* line of cases has served to limit damage awards by placing the defendant's state of mind at issue, it has had the unexpected side effect of producing enormous litigation costs.[133] Without presumed damages and with the need to prove the defendant's state of mind, the costs of litigating a defamation case have skyrocketed. Media defendants, understandably, are reluctant to produce evidence that reflects the editorial process and, hence, state of mind.[134] As a result, attorneys' fees become even more substantial.

Of course, the costs of defending a traditional defamation action are, by themselves, significant. It has been suggested that the threat of high defense costs alone impinge upon First Amendment interests.[135] The vindication action has been designed to minimize all of these costs. By focusing strictly on the issue of truth, the costs of litigation are greatly reduced because there can be no inquiry into the defendant's state of mind, the plaintiff's reputation, the defendant's privilege in making the statement, and the numerous other issues that exist in traditional defamation actions as well as those issues created by the imposition of constitutional standards.

Chilling Effect of a Damage Remedy

Even in cases where reputational injury is minor, defamation suits may produce windfall recoveries for plaintiffs.[136] The existence of substantial damage awards, however, does not automatically impose a chilling effect upon the press. It must first be established that the awards do in fact prevent certain matters from being published.[137] This was the thrust of Justice White's dissent in *Gertz*, in which he emphasized his belief that "the press today is vigorous and robust,"[138] in spite of the imposition of damage awards for defamation.

After analyzing the competing interests at stake, the Court in *Gertz* concluded that the state interest in compensating individuals who are victims of defamatory falsehood does not include awarding damages in excess of their injuries when actual malice does not exist.[139] The traditional rationale behind such a rule is that First Amendment freedoms must be given "breathing space"[140] or "wide latitude."[141] There is a presumption in favor of First Amendment freedoms when there is doubt as to the effects of a potential infringement.

A nondamage remedy, such as a vindication action, is consistent with the deference to First Amendment principles as expressed in the *Sullivan* decision.[142] Through the use of a vindication remedy the defendant could not be punished by a large damage award or intimidated into silence.[143] Justice Brennan agreed in *Gertz* that the absence of a chilling effect on the defendant in a nondamage cause of action made such an action viable, even though fault could not be proven to the satisfaction of the Court.[144] He postulated that a statute allowing a judicial determination of falsity would pass constitutional scrutiny even though fault was not provable.[145] He stated that the rationale underlying *Gertz* should not be read "to imply that a private plaintiff, unable to prove fault, must inevitably be denied the opportunity to secure a judgment upon the truth or falsity of statements published about him."[146]

In contrast, Justice White apparently believed that the majority in *Gertz* ruled out any defamation action not grounded on some degree of fault, regardless of the remedy being sought.[147] This conclusion ignores the purpose behind the constitutional privilege as expressed by the Supreme Court in *Gertz*—the insulation of defendants from large damage awards that infringe upon First Amendment freedoms.[148] Thus, it is likely that, as Justice Brennan recognized, a nondamage remedy such as a vindication action would be judged by different standards.[149]

Issues Eliminated by the Vindication Action

The vindication action, in addition to providing a constitutionally permissible remedy to deserving plaintiffs, also eliminates or modifies many issues that currently burden the parties to a defamation action. These issues include the plaintiff's status, the degree of culpability, the defendant's status, common law privileges, and defamatory content.

Status of the Plaintiff

All persons, whether public figures or private citizens, have an interest in protecting their reputation.[150] Public figures, however, have been distinguished from other defamation plaintiffs because they purportedly thrust themselves into the public arena, thereby increasing both the probability of public attention and the risk of negligent or innocent errors.[151] The Court has stated that public figures must bear this risk so that First Amendment freedoms are not impaired.[152] If the primary threat to the First Amendment, however, is the imposition of large damage awards, then this rationale cannot be used to exclude public figures from a vindication action.[153] Furthermore, even though public figures have greater access to the media to refute defamatory statements, refutation is not as effective as retraction.

The constitutional principles established by the Supreme Court do not conflict with the plaintiff's interest in obtaining vindication of his reputation. In a vindication action, the status of the plaintiff is not at issue, and, therefore, a major factor contributing to the time and expense of defamation actions is removed.[154] Additionally, uncertainty in the outcome is reduced because the status of the plaintiff no longer figures in the final determination.[155]

Degree of Culpability

Under some circumstances, Justice Brennan supported an alternative remedy that removed the issue of the defendant's fault or other culpability.[156] Elimination of this issue, however, does not mean that the vindication remedy rests on a premise of strict liability. The modern theory of strict liability states that between two "innocent" parties, the burden must fall on the one who is better able to absorb the financial loss.[157] In a vindication action, the burden of loss, if any, remains with the injured party; financial liability is not shifted. The defendant's degree of culpability is simply immaterial. As with eliminating consideration of the plaintiff's status, rejecting the concept of fault in vindication actions would streamline the issues, expedite litigation, and lower the ultimate costs.[158]

The Defendant's Status

The defendant's status has not been a significant factor in the majority of defamation cases to reach the Supreme Court since the *Sullivan* decision. Following the position taken by almost all of the state courts that have addressed the issue,[159] the Supreme Court has concluded that during discovery, the First Amendment does not extend greater protection to media than to nonmedia defendants.[160] In a conventional damage action, a resolution of the issue of the defendant's status may be appropriate. A distinction between media and nonmedia defendants is irrelevant, however, in a vindication action. Once the chilling effect on the exercise of First Amendment rights is removed, both media and nonmedia defendants stand on an equal footing.

Common Law Privileges

Different considerations exist in a conventional defamation action where traditional common law privileges can be asserted as a defense. Like constitutional privileges, common law privileges allow a culpable defendant to escape liability under certain circumstances.[161] Two issues arise at trial: whether a privilege does in fact exist and, if it does, whether it was exceeded and is therefore unavailable.[162]

Of the common law privileges,[163] only the immunity for defamatory statements made by legislators in the course of their official functions has been granted constitutional status. In *Hutchinson v. Proxmire*,[164] the Supreme Court limited the scope of this constitutional privilege, holding that congressional newsletters and press releases are not within the ambit of the speech and debate clause. Consequently, it held that a U.S. senator was not protected from liability for defamatory statements included in such publications.[165]

Other common law privileges[166] do not bear the imprimatur of the Constitution. With the threat of damages removed, the question remains whether there are legitimate reasons to retain common law privileges as a complete defense to a vindication action. The defense of privilege, unlike that of truth, does not turn on the content of the words published. Rather, it focuses on the status of the publisher. The defense exists for the protection of certain societal interests that are considered more compelling than the plaintiff's right to judicial redress.[167] The adoption of the vindication action could provide an effective compromise between these societal interests and the goal of compensating plaintiffs.

Absolute Privileges

There are six identifiable categories of absolute privilege. Of these six, three are grants of immunity accorded members of the three separate branches of government.[168] The governmental immunities applied by the courts are premised on the belief that governmental officials must be free from outside influences that could deter or detract from the effective exercise of their duties. It was assumed that these officials would be more apprehensive about carrying out their responsibilities if the threat of civil liability was present; the fear of damages was the major concern of the courts. Thus, the removal of damages as a possible consequence of a civil action would eliminate the principal rationale behind the governmental immunities.

The remaining three immunities are consent of the plaintiff; communications between husband and wife; and legally mandated broadcasts. These immunities are not premised on the need to eliminate the chilling effect of damages and, therefore, do not lend themselves as well to replacement by a vindication action as do the governmental immunities.

The privilege that arises from the consent of the plaintiff is based on the legal maxim *violenti non fit injuria*[170]—when a plaintiff consents to or instigates a defamation, the courts will not hear the complaint. Even if only a vindication remedy was sought, it would still be inherently unfair to allow a plaintiff to consent to a defamation and later force a defendant into court.

The immunity granted to communications between husband and wife is based on a fiction. The early common law refused to recognize publication when a statement was made to one's spouse because husband and wife were considered to be one person.[171] A more progressive rationale for this immunity is a recognition of the confidential nature of the marital relationship.[172] Neither of these rationales would be threatened significantly by a vindication action.

Finally, it has been held that an absolute immunity exists when a defendant is under a legal obligation to publish the defamatory material. In *Farmers Educational & Cooperative Union of America v. WDAY*,[173] the Supreme Court reasoned that to hold an individual liable for publications legally mandated by Congress would be "an obstacle to the accomplishment and execution of the full purposes and objectives of Congress."[174] Clearly, if a defendant cannot legally refuse to publish material, the defendant should not be held accountable in any way for its content.

Qualified Privileges

Qualified privileges extend protection to publications that advance the publisher's legitimate interests[175] or the interests of others[176] and to communications made to persons who may be expected to act in the public interest.[177] These qualified privileges protect communications that are deemed desirable by eliminating the threat of a civil action for damages and its potential for deterrence when the privilege is exercised in a reasonable manner. Thus, for example, the Supreme Court of Massachusetts has stated that "public policy demands that police investigations should not be thwarted by inability to obtain answers from persons who know facts, but fear civil actions."[178] Through the use of the vindication action, however, any chilling effect would be reduced drastically, and the need for these privileges would lessen accordingly.

Defamatory Content

Truth and defamatory content are two entirely distinct concepts. Defamatory statements are not necessarily false.[179] The test for defamation is whether the statement reduces the plaintiff's prestige in his community.[180] At early common law, truth was no defense to a prosecution for criminal libel;[181] today it is recognized that a statement may defame the plaintiff even if it is entirely true.[182]

An action for damages resulting from the publication of a defamatory falsehood is grounded in the belief that plaintiff's reputation in the community has been unjustifiably disparaged.[183] Unless there is an injury to the plaintiff's reputation, there is no ground for

the presumption of general damages.[184] Thus, the issue of defamatory content is relevant in the traditional common law defamation action only because damages are based on the injury to reputation.[185]

   These concerns, however, do not apply when the remedy sought
is a declaration that the defendant's statement about the plaintiff was
false. Rarely would a plaintiff seek a declaration that a given statement was false unless the statement was also defamatory. Few people
would spend the money and time necessary to challenge a statement
that does them no harm. This inherent control built into the vindication action, however, may be insufficient to prevent some plaintiffs
from pursuing an action despite the absence of a defamatory utterance by the defendant. To protect against frivolous actions challenging nondefamatory statements, a retraction element could be added
to the vindication action. Under this approach, the plaintiff, as predicated to filing the action, must first request the issuance of a retraction or correction in a manner comparable to the publication of the
offending statement. Only if the defendant refuses the retraction or
correction can the vindication action be brought.[186] Few if any plaintiffs will request the retraction or correction of statements that are not
defamatory in the traditional sense. This approach avoids the necessity and expense of litigating the issue of defamatory content while
insuring that vindication actions are not brought to correct harmless
or even favorable mistakes. Finally, to lessen the potential of harassment suits, the court could assess the defamatory impact of the challenged statement in apportioning attorneys' fees[187] and thereby effect
some control over the bringing of frivolous suits.

ELEMENTS RETAINED IN A VINDICATION ACTION

The goals of a vindication suit demand that the elements of a cause of
action be limited in order to ensure administrative and judicial econo-
my and to eliminate the arduous proof requirements imposed upon
the plaintiff in a typical defamation action. Consequently, only those
elements of common law defamation that discourage spurious claims
and ensure fairness to the defendant are retained. These include
proof that (1) the defendant made the false statement;[188] (2) the
statement referred to the plaintiff; (3) the statement was published;
and (4) the statement was one of fact, not opinion. Although in some
cases these issues may be controverted, the proof requirements generally would not be extensive.

Statement by Defendant

If the defendant is to bear the stigma that attaches to those who make false statements about others, the defendant must be identified as the publisher, a proof requirement that should not be burdensome to the plaintiff. The anonymous handbills of colonial America that gave rise to this identification requirement[190] are no longer the prevalent means of publication.[191] Media publishers are readily identifiable, as are those who use public communications systems.[192]

Furthermore, anonymity raises an inference of common law, and possibly *Sullivan*, malice. In such a case, a plaintiff would be more likely to pursue an action for damages than for vindication.[193] In informal communications, the third party hearing the defamatory statement would be required to testify about the language used and the identity of the publisher.

Reference to Plaintiff

An essential element in a cause of action for defamation is the requirement that the libelous words refer to the plaintiff.[194] This identification requirement protects defendants from claims by persons who cannot establish that they were the subject of the alleged false statements. Some jurisdictions require only that a third person recognize that the libelous words refer to the plaintiff,[195] while others employ a reasonable-man standard.[196]

In a vindication action, because the primary issue is truth or falsity, the plaintiff must meet this identification requirement.[197] A statement that clearly did not refer to the plaintiff could never be proved false. On the other hand, a specifically named plaintiff would pass the threshold inquiry. In some cases, the plaintiff might be able to prove through extrinsic evidence that he was the subject of the defamatory remarks.[198] Vague or ambiguous identifications, however, generally would not support a vindication action[199] unless it was demonstrated that the statement was false as to all potential plaintiffs.[200]

Publication

In order to ensure that the plaintiff's claim of reputational injury is legitimate, the common law requires the plaintiff to show that the defamatory language was published by the defendant to a third person.[201] Publication does not require that the statement be printed and distributed in the trade sense of the word but merely that it be communicated to someone other than the plaintiff.[202] The publication issue usually is determined from the facts of the case and, thus, would not reduce the judicial and administrative efficiency sought in a vindication remedy.

Questions concerning republication[203] may be resolved in an efficient manner as well. When there is a republication of the libelous statement, the plaintiff may bring a vindication action against all persons responsible for communicating the defamatory remark. Once the statement is determined false, the responsibility for the retraction may be apportioned among the several defendants to ensure the plaintiff an adequate remedy.[204] If republication occurs subsequent to the plaintiff's original vindication action, the court's determination of truth or falsity in the first action will operate as collateral estoppel in the republication action. Thus, when a statement has been found to be true in a prior vindication suit, the action against the republisher must be dismissed; if the statement was adjudged false, the republisher would be required to publish a retraction.[205]

IMPLEMENTATION OF THE VINDICATION ACTION

The Proceeding

A simplified vindication action can be advantageous for the defendant as well as the plaintiff. The major concern of the defendant—a large assessment of damages—will not be present in a vindication action because a defendant will not be assessed any monetary judgment.[206] Because the proceeding focuses on one issue—the truth of the publication—the legal costs to both parties should be minimal. In fact, the printing of a retraction and correction by the defendant could eliminate the need for the vindication action.

Vindication actions could be terminated at any one of several stages. First, a defendant might avoid the vindication procedure by publishing a responsive retraction.[207] Second, the pleadings and the modest discovery required would, in many cases, allow the parties to settle the action at an early stage. Third, summary judgment might conclude the matter if either side could establish that the question of truth or falsity was so clear as to be a question of law for the court.[208]

For those cases that progress to the trial stage, a jury, where requested, would remain the proper body to decide the falsity issue.[209] The jury would render a special verdict stating whether the publication was true or false.[210] Should several statements be contested in the case, a special issue verdict could be formulated for each statement litigated. Notwithstanding the presence of a jury, the trial should not be complex or lengthy. If the statement was found to be false, a judgment that declares the statement false would vindicate the plaintiff; the defendant would not be assessed any monetary penalty.[211]

Because the litigation is limited to the single task of vindicating the plaintiff's reputation, the pleading and discovery stages should not be lengthy, except in those cases where truth or falsity depends on a complex chain of events. Discovery would not involve an investigation into motive or damages but would be confined to the facts discussed in the allegedly false statement.

The defendant would not be aided by contending that he acted reasonably; the issue of reasonableness does not concern the court in a vindication action. A finding that an "innocent" defendant—one who took all possible care—uttered a false statement and, therefore, is liable in a vindication action is consistent with the rationale that the vindication remedy allows plaintiffs to receive a measure of satisfaction through a determination that even innocently published statements about them are false.

On the other hand, defendants would avoid both the threat of damage awards and the costs inherent in defending multi-issue defamation actions. Thus, defendants would surrender some of the constitutional and common law protections that they currently enjoy. In exchange for this concession, however, they would receive the advantages of lower defense costs and the elimination of damage assessments.

Publication of the Judgment

Compulsory publication of a judgment of falsity is essential because news coverage of judicial proceedings is not always thorough.[212] In order to be effective, the publication of a judgment must be as widely circulated as was the original false statement.[213] Furthermore, the content of a judicially compelled publication should be relatively specific. A simple declaration that judgment was rendered for the plaintiff is too limited a publication. Accordingly, judgments and their publication should be drafted to include the trier of fact's findings of falsity.[214]

Not all findings of falsity, however, will result in compelled publication; the decision to issue such an order is within the sound discretion of the trial court. The court must determine whether public dissemination of the judgment would assist in vindicating the plaintiff's reputation.[215] In addition, the scope and form of publication are discretionary decisions for the court.

An order compelling the publication of a judgment must not intrude on the editorial processes protected by the First Amendment.[216] Thus, a court cannot command a defendant newspaper to provide space for the forced publication or cause a defendant to avoid the discussion of controversial issues.[217] Accordingly, the extent of an order compelling publication must be limited, requiring only that a defendant either purchase space or provide a forum for the publication of the judgment. The publication of a judgment through the voluntary sale or donation of space would avoid the constitutional problems that plague a judicially compelled publication by a defendant newspaper.[218] If, however, an organization is not willing either to sell or donate space for the publication, alternative means of publication such as broadcasting or posting must be utilized.

Of course, the media defendant already has the means to publish a court ruling that vindicates its actions. Therefore, there is no reason to require publication of a judgment of truth since the typical media defendant will do this on its own initiative.

Attorneys' Fees

Under common law, the prevailing party generally is denied an award of attorneys' fees in a civil action.[219] Where a statute authorizes a court to award attorneys' fees as part of the judgment, however, such awards have been made.[220]

A vindication action must provide attorneys' fees for the plaintiff who has been the victim of a false statement and for the defendant who is determined to have published the truth. This provision could be implemented by a statutory allowance for the award of attorneys' fees to the prevailing party in a vindication action. Because the prevailing plaintiff receives no damage award by which to pay his attorney, the attorneys' fees provision is an essential part of the action.[221] Similarly, a potential award of attorneys' fees against a plaintiff will discourage frivolous claims.

The simplified vindication action prevents either party from incurring overwhelming expenses.[222] An award of attorneys' fees in a vindication action should not represent a substantial sum. The size of the award may, at the court's discretion, be limited pursuant to traditional motions of equity.[223] Furthermore, the legislature could prescribe a maximum amount,[224] thereby encouraging parties to forego questionable claims, tactics, or procedures.

The courts should consider additional factors in deciding

whether to award attorneys' fees. These considerations include the good faith of the parties, the nature and severity of the false statement, and the parties' relative abilities to bear the costs of the litigation. Partial awards could also be made whenever the equities so dictate.[225] Finally, allowing an award of reasonable attorneys' fee where the defendant has refused to retract or correct an obviously false statement furthers a policy of encouraging peaceful, simple, and efficient settlements.

PROPOSED BILL TO ADOPT THE VINDICATION ACTION

In order to facilitate further discussion and possible implementation of the vindication action, a proposed legislative bill is set forth.

Alternative Defamation Action

Section 1. Cause of Action

1. Any person who is the subject of any false statement may bring an action in any court of competent jurisdiction for a declaration that such statement was false (a "Vindication Action"), but only after a denial of a request for a retraction or correction as set forth in Paragraph 2.

2. Before instituting a Vindication Action a party must make a written request for a retraction or correction within six (6) months after the false statement was first made. The failure to make a timely request shall constitute an absolute bar to relief under this section. The request must specify the statement(s) claimed to be false and the basis for the claim(s). If the party who made the false statement publishes or causes to be published within thirty (30) days of the request a sufficient retraction or correction in a manner and medium reasonably calculated to reach the same audience as the false statement, the party requesting the retraction or correction shall be forever barred from seeking relief under this section.

3. No other claim may be joined with or raised in a Vindication Action, nor may a Vindication Action be filed as part of any other action. The filing of a Vindication Action by the plaintiff shall operate as a bar to the filing or maintenance of any other action by that plaintiff seeking relief for all statements which are the subject of the Vindication Action.

4. In order to establish a Vindication Action, the plaintiff must show by a preponderance of the evidence that:

    i. The defendant made the false statement
    ii. The statement referred to the plaintiff
    iii. The statement was published
    iv. The statement was one of fact

    5. Paragraph 4 shall not be construed to require proof of the state of mind of the defendant.

Section 2. Findings of Fact

    1. The trier of fact shall issue a special verdict indicating whether the challenged statement(s) is true or false.

    2. If the trier of fact determines the challenged statement(s) to be false, then it shall also provide specific findings of fact that support the determination of falsity.

Section 3. Remedies

If the trier of fact determines that the challenged statement(s) is false, the court shall (1) enter a declaration of falsity with sufficient information based on the trier of fact's findings to vindicate the plaintiff's reputation and (2) order the defendant who made the statement to publish or cause to be published, in a manner and medium reasonably calculated to reach the same audience as the false statement, the contents of the declaration.

Section 4. Attorneys' Fees and Costs

    1. The prevailing party shall be entitled to recover reasonable attorneys' fees and costs actually incurred in bringing or defending the action. The court shall determine the amount of attorneys' fees and costs to be awarded within thirty (30) days following the trier of fact's determination.

    2. The court shall take into consideration the following factors:
        i. The good faith and/or bad faith of the parties
        ii. The nature and severity of the false statement including the impact upon the plaintiff's reputation
        iii. The ability of the parties to bear litigation expenses
        iv. Other equitable considerations

Section 5. Docket Priority

Vindication Actions shall be granted docket priority and, absent consent of the parties, shall be adjudicated in a court or court-annexed proceeding not more than one hundred twenty (120) days after the filing of the complaint, unless the court makes a finding on the record that such an expedited trial is impracticable under the circumstances.

Section 6. Limitation on Action

A Vindication Action must be commenced no later than one (1) year after the first date of publication or broadcast.

CONCLUSION

The defamatory statement intrudes on the most personal interests recognized by civilized society—honor, reputation, and self-esteem. Many innocent victims of defamatory falsehood are public officials or public figures who perform valuable services for society. They are inviting targets for defamatory statements because of their position. Society owes a duty to these public figures as well as to others who are the victims of false and defamatory statements but are without a remedy.

A remedy is available whereby the victim may uphold his reputation and the defendant may continue to exercise his First Amendment freedoms. In a vindication action, a judgment of falsity will not infringe upon First Amendment interests in the manner traditionally identified with damage awards. Through the vindication action, the legal system may begin to remedy the wrongs inflicted on defamation victims who in the past have been unable to satisfy exacting constitutional burdens.

NOTES

1. F. POLLOCK, THE LAW OF TORTS 210 (1887). Pollock believed the law of defamation must provide a remedy to vindicate a person's honor regardless of whether harm was proven. "Reputation and honor are no less precious to good men than bodily safety and freedom. In some cases they may be dearer than life itself." *Id.* at 204.

2. In Simon v. Shearson Lehman Bros., Inc., 895 F.2d 1304 (11th Cir. 1990), the plaintiff received $1 million in compensatory damages and $5 million in punitive damages. On appeal, the court reduced the compensatory damages to $250,000 and the punitive damages to $1 million. In Faulk v. Aware, Inc., 35 Misc. 2d 302, 231 N.Y.S.2d 270 (Sup. Ct. 1962), the jury awarded $1 million in compensatory damages and $2.5 million in punitive damages, divided between two defendants. *See generally* Kurtz, *Spate of Libel*

Judgments May Alter News Practices, WASH. POST, Nov. 24, 1990, at 4A, col. 1 (noting five recent multi-million-dollar libel verdicts).

    In some instances, punitive damage awards may be completely out of proportion to the injury suffered. *See, e.g.,* Goldwater v. Ginzburg, 414 F.2d 324 (2d Cir. 1969) ($1 compensatory; $75,000 punitive), *cert. denied,* 350 U.S. 846 (1955); Newton v. National Broadcasting Co., Inc., 677 F. Supp. 1066 (D. Nev. 1987) ($250,00 compensatory; $5 million punitive); Roemer v. Retail Credit Co., 44 Cal. App. 3d 926, 119 Cal. Rptr. 82 (1975) ($40,000 compensatory; $250,000 punitive); Bobenhausen v. Cassat Ave. Mobile Homes, Inc., 344 So.2d 279 (Fla. Dist. Ct. App. 1977) ($30,000 compensatory; $50,000 punitive), *cert. denied,* 363 So. 2d 1067 (Fla. 1978); Harley-Davidson Motorsports, Inc. v. Markley, 279 Or. 361, 568 P.2d 1359 (1977) ($500 compensatory; $25,000 punitive).

    3. *See, e.g.,* Eulo v. DeVal Aerodynamics, Inc., 47 F.R.D. 35 (E.D. Pa. 1969) (plaintiff sued for $300,000; jury awarded 6 cents), *modified on other grounds,* 430 F.2d 325 (3d Cir. 1970), *cert. denied,* 401 U.S. 974 (1971); D.R.W. Corp. v. Cordes, 65 Wis. 2d 303, 222 N.W.2d 671 (1974) (plaintiff sued for $750; jury awarded nothing although 6 cents cited as usual nominal defamation recovery). Perhaps the most celebrated 6-cent defamation recovery of this century was obtained by Henry Ford in Ford v. Chicago Tribune, Co., No. 67,999 (Mich. Cir. Ct., Wayne County, Aug. 15, 1919). *See also* Kurtz, *Spate of Libel Judgments May Alter News Practices,* WASH. POST, Nov. 24, 1990, at 4A, col. 1 (reporting on Israeli Defense Minister Ariel Sharon's libel victory against Time, Inc. which netted him no compensatory or punitive damages).

    4. Other nondamage remedies include: injunctive relief, *see infra* notes 80-84 and accompanying text; retraction, *see infra notes* 85-92 and accompanying text; reply, *see infra* notes 93-99 and accompanying text; and declaratory judgments, *see infra* notes 101-104 and accompanying text.

    5. *See, e.g.,* Leflar, *The Social Utility of the Criminal Law of Defamation,* 34 TEX. L. REV. 984 (1956). The author stated:

> The inescapable fact is that the Anglo-American genius for justice has not yet produced a generally available remedy for defamation that will give aggrieved persons the vindication which they deserve. The substituted relief of damage in tort is usually the only remedy which our law affords, and that often, for social and psychological reasons, is a remedy available only theoretically, not actually.

Id. at 1027.

    6. Justice White has written of the predicament facing the subject of a false and defamatory statement who is barred from recovering damages because of the constitutional privilege:

> [W]hen the plaintiff loses, the jury will likely return a general verdict and there will be no judgment that the publications was false, even though it was without foundation in reality. The public is left to conclude that the

challenged statement was true after all. Their only chance of being accurately informed is measured by the public official's ability himself to counter the lie, unaided by the courts.

Dun & Bradstreet, Inc. v. Greenmoss Builders, Inc., 472 U.S. 749, 768 (1985) (Justice White, concurring in the judgment).

Such plaintiffs, who suffer injury to their reputations from false and defamatory statements, are currently without any meaningful remedy to rescue their wrongly damaged reputation. *See also infra* notes 8, 22-31 and accompanying text.

7. For those individuals who are without a current legal remedy for injurious falsehood, the sole means for rebutting defamatory falsehood lies in the "marketplace of ideas." The marketplace of ideas analogy is derived from the libertarian view of the utility of free debate in society. As John Stuart Mill observed:

> [T]he peculiar evil of silencing the expression of an opinion is, that it is robbing the human race; posterity as well as the existing generation; those who dissent from the opinion, still more than those who hold it. If the opinion is right, they are deprived of the opportunity of exchanging error for truth: if wrong, they lose, what is almost as great a benefit, the clearer perception and livelier impression of truth, produced by its collision with error.

J.S. MILL, ON LIBERTY 76 (1859).

Compare this formulation of the value of free debate, unimpeded by governmental intervention, with the Supreme Court's "fighting words" doctrine. "Fighting words" remain unprotected by the First Amendment because "[they] are no essential part of any exposition of ideas, and are of such slight social value as a step to truth that any benefit that may be derived from them is clearly outweighed by the social interest in order and morality." Chaplinsky v. New Hampshire, 315 U.S. 568, 572 (1942) ("damned racketeer" and "damned fascist" are epithets likely to provoke retaliation causing a breach of the peace). Although the "fighting words" doctrine is still viable, the category of words that falls within the doctrine has been narrowed. *See, e.g.,* Cohen v. California, 403 U.S. 15 (1971) (offensive words on jacket worn in courthouse held not to constitute "fighting words").

The view expressed by John Stuart Mill may be resurfacing under the guise of a rule in defamation cases that "[t]here is no such thing as a false idea." Gertz v. Robert Welch, Inc., 418 U.S. 323, 339 (1974). The Court, again noting the importance of open debate on public issues, reiterated the words of Thomas Jefferson spoken at his first inaugural address: "Error of opinion may be tolerated where reason is left free to combat it." *Id.* at 340 n.8.

8. For a discussion of constitutional standards *see* cases cited *infra* note 23. Although some constitutional issues remain unresolved, the Supreme Court in Gertz v. Robert Welch, Inc., 418 U.S. 323 (1974), indicated the

direction that future decisions would take. In determining whether the plaintiff was a "public figure" for purposes of invoking the actual-malice standard of New York Times Co. v. Sullivan, 376 U.S. 254 (1964), the Court in *Gertz* explained:

> For the most part those who attain this status have assumed roles of especial prominence in the affairs of society. Some occupy positions of such persuasive power and influence that they are deemed public figures for all purposes. More commonly, those classified as public figures have thrust themselves to the forefront of particular public controversies in order to influence the resolution of the issues involved.

418 U.S. at 345.

These guidelines were further refined in Time, Inc. v. Firestone, 424 U.S. 448 (1976), in which the Court refused to equate "public controversy" with "all controversies of interest to the public." The Court held that the dissolution of the Firest one marriage was not within the ambit of "public controversy" referred to in *Gertz. Id.* at 454. The Court also refused to extend automatically the Sullivan privilege to all reports of judicial proceedings, particularly when they are reported erroneously. *Id.* at 455.

9. For a discussion of the elements retained in a vindication action, *see infra* notes 189-203 and accompanying text.

10. The need for an optional alternative defamation remedy is demonstrated by the problems resulting from the use of damage awards. Although the damage remedy serves a valid function when a defamatory falsehood has caused a plaintiff to suffer "actual injury," Gertz v. Robert Welch, Inc., 418 U.S. at 349-50, there are many situations in which a defamed plaintiff cannot collect damages because of a valid privilege or defense or an inability to demonstrate "actual injury." In those cases, the plaintiff is left without a remedy. *See infra* notes 136-187 and accompanying text.

11. *Model Communicative Torts Act,* 47 WASH. & LEE L. REV. 1 (1990).

12. Franklin, *A Declaratory Judgment Alternative to Current Libel Law,* 74 CALIF. L. REV. 809, 812-13 (1986).

13. H.R. 2846, 99th Cong., 1st Sess. (1985) (introduced by Rep. Charles E. Schumer (D-N.Y.)).

14. *E.g.,* Beauharnais v. Illinois, 343 U.S. 250, 256-57 1952). *See also* Garrison v. Louisiana, 379 U.S. 64, 67 (1964); Roth v. United States, 354 U.S. 476, 483 (1957) (dictum).

15. 376 U.S. 254 (1964).

16. *Id.* at 279-80. For commentary on the *Sullivan* decision and its ramifications for state defamation law, *see* Berney, *Libel and the First Amendment—A New Constitutional Privilege,* 51 VA. L. REV. 1, 47 (1965); Brennan, *The Supreme Court and the Meiklejohn Interpretation of the First Amendment,* 79 HARV. L. REV. 1 (1965); Kalven, *The New York Times Case: A Note on "The Central Meaning of the First Amendment,"* 1964 SUP. CT. REV. 191; Merin, *Libel and the Supreme Court,* 11 WM. & MARY L. REV. 371 (1969); Pedrick, *Freedom*

of the Press & the Law of Libel: The Modern Revised Translation, 49 CORNELL
L.Q. 581, 605-08 (1964); Note, *Recent Developments Concerning Constitutional
Limitations on State Defamation Laws,* 18 VAND. L. REV. 1429 (1965).

17. 485 U.S. 46 (1988).

18. *Id.* at 878.

19. *Id.*

20. *Id.* at 881-82.

21. *Id.* at 882.

22. *See infra* notes 137-87 and accompanying text.

23. Those cases in the defamation and privacy area reaching the U.S.
Supreme Court include: Harte-Hanks Communications, Inc. v. Connaughton, 491 U.S. 657 (1989) (appellate court must use independent judgment to
evaluate whether facts support finding of actual malice by clear and convincing evidence); Philadelphia Newspapers, Inc. v. Hepps, 475 U.S. 767 (1986)
(state statute requiring defendant to demonstrate truth of statement unconstitutional); Dun & Bradstreet, Inc. v. Greenmoss Builders, Inc., 472 U.S.
749 (1985) (private-figure plaintiff not required to demonstrate actual malice
when no issue of public concern involved); McDonald v. Smith, 472 U.S. 479
(1985) (petition clause of First Amendment does not provide absolute privilege); Bose Corp. v. Consumers Union, 466 U.S. 485 (1984) (public-figure
plaintiff must show actual malice by clear and convincing evidence; plaintiff's
evidence of actual malice insufficient as a matter of law); Wolston v. Readers
Digest Ass'n, Inc., 443 U.S. 157 (1979) (private individual not made public
figure merely by association with an event that attracts public attention);
Hutchinson v. Proxmire, 443 U.S. 111 (1979) (private individual not public
figure when, solely as a result of the alleged libel, he is thrust into public
attention and given access to the media); Herbert v. Lando, 441 U.S. 153
(1979) (First Amendment does not bar public figure plaintiff from inquiring
into editorial process of media defendant responsible for defamatory publication); Time, Inc. v. Firestone, 424 U.S. 448 (1976) (private individual not
made public figure by seeking judicial vindication of her rights); Cox
Broadcasting Corp. v. Cohn, 420 U.S. 469 (1975) (considerations of freedom
of the press bar liability for invasion of privacy where the media accurately
reports information that it obtained from public records concerning the
commission and prosecution of crime); Cantrell v. Forest City Publishing Co.,
419 U.S. 245 (1974) (common law standard of malice not equivalent to the
Sullivan actual-malice standard); Gertz v. Robert Welch, Inc., 418 U.S. 323
(1974) (states may set own standards of proof as long as there is a finding of
fault); Local 496, National Ass'n of Letter Carriers v. Austin, 418 U.S. 264
(1974) (plaintiffs in libel action involving a labor dispute must prove actual
malice); Ocala Star-Banner Co. v. Damron, 401 U.S. 295 (1971) (charge of
criminal conduct against a candidate for public office calls into play the
actual-malice standard); Time, Inc. v. Pape, 401 U.S. 279 (1971) (public-
figure plaintiff must prove actual malice against author who repeated a
secondhand report about an event of public interest); Monitor Patriot Co. v.
Roy, 401 U.S. 265 (1971) (plaintiff in libel suit involving question of candidate's fitness for public office must prove actual malice); Greenbelt Coop.

Publishing Ass'n, Inc. v. Bresler, 398 U.S. 6 (1970) (public-figure plaintiff in libel suit must prove actual malice); Pickering v. Board of Educ., 391 U.S. 563 (1968) (teacher's erroneous public statements that did not affect his classroom performance or the regular operation of the school may not be the basis for his dismissal absent a finding of actual malice); St. Amant v. Thompson, 390 U.S. 727 (1968) (actual-malice standard applies to defamatory statements concerning a public figure); Beckley Newspaper Corp. v. Hanks, 389 U.S. 81 (1967) (actual malice requires showing that defendant had high degree of certainty that his statement was false); Curtis Publishing Co. v. Butts, 388 U.S. 130 (1967) (*Sullivan* actual-malice standard applicable to public figures); Time, Inc. v. Hill, 385 U.S.@374 (1967) (erroneous statements about matters of public interest that are innocent or merely negligent are not actionable causes of action for invasion of privacy); Rosenblatt v. Baer, 383 U.S. 75 (1966) (public-official plaintiff must prove that publication made specific reference to him and did so with actual malice); Linn v. Plant Guard Workers Local 114, 383 U.S. 53 (1966) (state court has jurisdiction to apply state remedies in a labor dispute if plaintiff proves injury and actual malice); Henry v. Collins, 380 U.S. 356 (1965) (public official must prove actual malice in order to recover for defamatory falsehood); Garrison v. Louisiana, 379 U.S. 64 (1964) (state may impose criminal sanctions for libel of public officers only in cases in which plaintiff can prove actual malice).

24. *E.g.,* Wolston v. Readers Digest Ass'n, Inc., 443 U.S. 157 (1979) (private individual does not become public figure by mere association with event of public interest); Time, Inc. v. Firestone, 424 U.S. 448, 454 n.3 (1976) (attempt to assert rights in judicial proceedings does not make plaintiff a public figure even though she was a well-known socialite who held press conferences during divorce proceedings); Gertz v. Robert Welch, Inc., 418 U.S. 323 (1974) (attorney in well-publicized civil case not a public figure because he did not thrust himself into public controversy to influence its outcome).

See also Tavoulareas v. Washington Post Co., 817 F.2d 762 (D.C. Cir. 1987) (corporate president who served as CEO of large multinational oil corporation was a "limited-purpose public figure" with respect to a public controversy over the need to reform the structure of the private oil industry where he was outspoken in blaming the 1973 oil crisis on government interference with the free market, and where he made speeches, testified before Congress, published articles, and enjoyed access to the media through the corporation's publicity apparatus).

25. *E.g.,* Hutchinson v. Proxmire, 443 U.S. 111 (1979) (speech and debate clause immunity does not apply to congressional press releases).

26. *E.g.,* Time, Inc. v. Firestone, 424 U.S. 448 (1976) (although divorce proceedings are of interest to public, they do not constitute a public controversy); Cox Broadcasting Corp. v. Cohn, 420 U.S. 469 (1975) (the commission and prosecution of crime are of legitimate public interest); Rosenblatt v. Baer, 383 U.S. 75 (1966) (thievery in operation of government is of public interest).

27. *E.g,* Gertz v. Robert Welch, Inc., 418 U.S. 323 (1974) (states may

impose any standard of liability except liability without fault); Beckley News-paper Corp. v. Hanks, 389 U.S. 81 (1967) (actual malice requires a "high degree of awareness of . . . probable falsity"); St. Amant v. Thompson, 390 U.S. 727 (1968) (to prove reckless disregard for truth, sufficient evidence must be presented to show defendant doubted veracity of publication).

28. Gertz v. Robert Welch, Inc., 418 U.S. 323 (1974) (where liability is based on standard other than actual malice, compensation may be awarded only for injury); Linn v. Plant Guard Workers Local 114, 383 U.S. 53 (1966) (damages may include injury to reputation, mental suffering, monetary loss, and other injuries recognized by state tort laws).

29. Philadelphia Newspapers, Inc. v. Hepps, 475 U.S. 767 (1986).

30. Herbert v. Lando, 441 U.S. 153 (1979) (public figure may probe into defendant's editorial processes and state of mind in order to prove actual malice).

31. *See* New York Times Co. v. Sullivan, 376 U.S. 254, 269-72 (1964).

32. 110 S. Ct. 2695 (1990).

33. *Id.* at 2705-07.

34. Historically, defamation has been divided into two distinct torts: libel and slander. *See* W. PROSSER, HANDBOOK OF THE LAW OF TORTS § 112, at 751-54 (4th ed. 1971). *See also* 3 W. BLACKSTONE, COMMENTARIES 123, 126 (1803); F. HARPER & JAMES, THE LAW OF TORTS § 5.9 (1956).

For the purposes of the present discussion, there is no need to distin-guish between libel and slander. The manner in which the insult was com-municated is unimportant. The concern here is with the essence of both torts—the insult. This chapter, therefore, generally refers to a single tort defamation.

35. The personal interest in one's reputation has been recognized for centuries. Indeed, the law of defamation has been characterized as civilized society's substitution for the blood feud:

> What might be called inviolability of the spiritual person is of no less importance, although much more difficult to secure legally. Men will fight in defense of their honor no less than in defense of their physical persons. Hence the most elementary of social interests, the interest in general security, demands that the one individual interest be secured no less than the other and for much the same reasons. The exaggerated importance of individual honor in primitive and in pioneer society illus-trates this. In a condition of feeble law adequate securing of this interest, which is difficult to secure through law under any circumstances, is quite impossible, and the insistence of the individual on protecting and vindicating it for himself becomes a serious menace to the peace and order of society.

Pound, *Interests of Personality,* 28 HARV. L. REV. 445 (1915).

36. The entire concept of personal reputation is based on intangible and unquantifiable personal interest. Elusiveness remains its essential character.

The harm resulting from an injury to reputation is difficult to demonstrate both because it may involve subtle differences in the conduct of the recipients toward the plaintiff and because the recipients, the only witnesses able to establish the necessary causal connection, may be reluctant to testify that the publication affected their relationships with the plaintiff. Thus some presumptions are necessary if the plaintiff is to be adequately compensated.

Note, *Developments in the Law—Defamation*, 69 HARV. L. REV. 875, 891-92 (1956). *See also* PROSSER, *supra* note 34, § 112, at 765; Murnaghan, *From Figment to Fiction to Philosophy—The Requirement of Proof of Damages in Libel Actions*, 22 CATH. U.L. REV. 1 (1972).

    37. *See generally* RESTATEMENT (SECOND) OF TORTS § 620-622A (ALI 1977) [hereinafter RESTATEMENT]. A brief summary concerning the many inadequacies of the damage remedy and possible alternatives is found at *id., Special Note on Remedies for Defamation Other Than Damages* § 623 [hereinafter SPECIAL NOTE].

    38. *See* RESTATEMENT, *supra* note 37, § 621, comment a. "At common law general damages have traditionally been awarded not only for harm to reputation that is proved to have occurred, but also, in the absence of this proof, for harm to reputation that would normally be assumed to flow from a defamatory publication of the nature involved." *Id. See also* HARPER & JAMES, *supra* note 34, § 5.30, at 468. One court has noted:

> The remedy of general damages purports to compensate the plaintiff for a harm to his reputation—a harm which is not measurable in a money loss and which is not mitigated by a money judgment except to the extent that the entry of the judgment communicates the message that the words printed were false.

Holden v. Pioneer Broadcasting Co., 228 Or. 405, 411, 365 P.2d 845, 852 (1961), *appeal dismissed*, 370 U.S. 157 (1967).

    39. At common law, libel was considered actionable per se, while slander had to fall into one of four categories in order to be actionable per se—the imputation of crime, loathsome disease, or unchastity to a woman, or words having an adverse impact on one's trade, business, or calling. RESTATEMENT, *supra* note 37, § 570; PROSSER, *supra* note 34, § 112, at 754-60.

    40. "Actionable per se" under the common law meant actionable without proof of special damages. Redding v. Carlton, 223 Pa. Super. Ct. 136, 137 n.1, 296 A.2d 880, 881 n.1 (1972). Dean Prosser indicated that the distinction between libel and most slander derived from the historical roots of libel; the printed word was revered and had a greater potential for harm than oral communication. PROSSER, *supra* note 34, § 112, at 751-52.

    41. *See* Ashdown, *Gertz and Firestone: A Study in Constitutional Policy-Making*, 61 MINN. L. REV. 645, 671 n.128 (1977).

    42. This rebuttable presumption enables the plaintiff in a defamation

action to couple a claim for general damages with a claim for special damages, thereby allowing recovery for the damage to items having economic or pecuniary value. *See* RESTATEMENT, *supra* note 37, §§ 575, 662.

43. A defendant may avoid the expense and trouble of rebutting the general damage presumption if there is a solid defense relating to another issue or if it is clear that the plaintiff has suffered damages. In this manner, the general damage presumption saves both parties expense in the preparation for and the conduct of trial.

44. Gertz v. Robert Welch, Inc., 418 U.S. 323 (1974).

45. *Id.* at 349.

46. The actual damages award is granted to the private defamation plaintiff who establishes liability under a less demanding standard than that stated by *Sullivan,* ignoring the private fines assessed to punish reprehensible conduct. *Id.* at 350.

47. RESTATEMENT, *supra* note 37, §§ 574, 622 (special harm is defined as loss of something having pecuniary or measurable economic value). *See, e.g.,* Ellsworth v. Martindale-Hubbell Law Directory, Inc., 68 N.D. 425, 426, 280 N.W. 879, 881 (1938) (diminution in "fairly lucrative law practice" allegedly caused by defendant's libelous publication constituted sufficient averment of special damages).

48. RESTATEMENT, *supra* note 37, § 622, comment b.

49. The *Restatement* specifies three elements that must be proven to secure special damages: (1) economic or pecuniary loss; (2) the defendant's fault; and (3) causation. *Id.* § 575. Proof of special damages in defamation differs from other tort actions because the harm "must result from the conduct of a person other than the defamer or the one defamed. . . ." *Id.* comment b.

50. The need for the latter approach may occur in those cases where the relatively innocent nature of the defamation would cause the jury to refuse to award general damages. "At least nominal damages must be awarded. Of course, plaintiff would further be entitled to recover such actual damages as might be shown to be the proximate result of the publication though not damages which would be speculative or remote." Denton Publishing Co. v. Boyd, 448 S.W.2d 145, 147 (Tex. Civ. App.) (newspaper article reporting that plaintiff, a land developer, had declared bankruptcy and failed to pave streets in development held actionable), *aff'd,* 460 S.W.2d (Tex. 1970). *See also* RESTATEMENT, *supra* note 37, § 622, comment a.

51. RESTATEMENT, *supra* note 37, § 622. In Gertz v. Robert Welch, Inc., 418 U.S. 323 (1974), the Supreme Court questioned the wisdom of allowing the jury discretion to award damages on presumed injuries and suggested the application of "the more customary types of actual harm inflicted by falsehood" with damage awards "supported by competent evidence concerning the injury." *Id.* at 349-50.

52. RESTATEMENT, *supra* note 37, § 622A.

53. The common law courts gradually molded the special damages requirement into a pleading and proof hurdle. Plaintiffs had to prove the special damage with "particularity" and such damages were limited to ele-

ments of pecuniary injury. *See, e.g.,* Life Printing & Publishing Co. v. Field, 324 Ill. App. 254, 258, 58 N.E.2d 307, 311 (1944) (general allegations stating that, as result of publication, persons refused to have any business transactions with plaintiff, not sufficiently particular to meet special damage requirement).

The pecuniary injury requirement may be waived by a court in the exercise of its discretion because such injury is so difficult to prove. *See* Snowden v. Pearl River Broadcasting Co., 251 So. 2d 405, 412 (La. App.), *cert. denied,* 253 So. 2d 217 (La. 1971). In *Snowden,* the court avoided the requirement of finding pecuniary injury despite a state statute requiring proof of "actual damages." *Id.*

For a discussion of defamation damages at common law, *see* Dalton v. Meister, 52 Wis. 2d 173, 179, 188 N.W.2d 494, 497 (1971). When a defendant is able to challenge the plaintiff's alleged pecuniary loss, the battle between the parties will intensify on the special damage issue. *See, e.g.,* Danias v. Fakis, 261 A.2d 529 (Del. Super. Ct. 1969) (wages lost by voluntary absence from work do not constitute pecuniary loss); Williams v. Rutherford Freight Lines, 10 N.C. App. 384, 179 S.E.2d 319 (1971) (special damages require actual pecuniary loss, not mere humiliation of plaintiff).

54. Justice Stewart has expressed reservations about the adequacy of the traditional damage remedy: "The destruction that defamatory falsehood can bring is, to be sure, often beyond the capacity of the law to redeem. Yet, imperfect though it is, an action for damages is the only hope for vindication or redress the law gives to a man whose reputation has been falsely dishonored." Rosenblatt v. Baer, 383 U.S. 75, 92-95 (1965) (Stewart, J., concurring).

55. *See supra* notes 44-46 and accompanying text.

56. 418 U.S. 323, 350 (1974). Such damages may, under proper instruction, compensate plaintiff for impairment of reputation and standing in the community, personal humiliation, and mental anguish and suffering. *Id.*

57. *Id.*

58. *See* generally Morris, *Punitive Damages in Tort Cases,* 44 HARV. L. REV. 1173 (1931); C. McCormick, Handbook on the Law of Damages § 77 (1935).

59. Gertz v. Robert Welch, Inc., 418 U.S. 323, 350 (1974). Noting that jury discretion in awarding punitive damages unnecessarily exacerbates the danger of media self-censorship, the Court held that a plaintiff may not recover punitive damages in the absence of a showing of actual malice, defined as knowledge of falsity or reckless disregard for the truth. *Id.* at 349-50.

60. According to Prosser, punitive damages have been criticized as "undue compensation of the plaintiff beyond his just deserts in the form of a criminal fine which should be paid to the state, if anyone." PROSSER, note 34, § 2, at 11. *See* Morris, *supra* note 58, at 1176-83.

61. *See, e.g.,* Kelite Prods, Inc. v. Binzel, 221 F.2d 131 (5th Cir. 1955) (punitive damages require finding of actual malice or conscious disregard of truth); Reynolds v. Pegler, 223 F.2d 429 (2d Cir.) (substantial proof of malice and ill will warrants assessment of punitive damages), *cert. denied,* 350 U.S.

846 (1955). The common law standard for malice is very different from the constitutional actual-malice standard in defamation cases. The former standard concentrates on the party's motivation; the latter centers only on reckless disregard for the truth.

Actual malice means "knowledge of falsity" or "reckless disregard for the truth." New York Times Co. v. Sullivan, 376 U.S. 254, 280 (1964). To have "knowledge of falsity," the defendant must be subjectively aware that the statement is false. Hutchinson v. Proxmire, 431 F. Supp. 1311, 1328 (W.D. Wis. 1977), aff'd, 579 F.2d 1027 (7th Cir. 1978), rev'd on other grounds, 443 U.S. 111 (1979). To constitute "reckless disregard of the truth," the defendant must act with a "high degree of awareness of . . . probable falsity." Beckley Newspapers Corp. v. Hanks, 389 U.S. 81, 84 (1976). In order to carry his evidentiary burden in proving actual malice, the plaintiff may inquire into the editorial process and state of mind of those responsible for the publication because this inquiry could produce material evidence bearing on a critical element of the plaintiff's cause of action. Herbert v. Lando, 441 U.S. 153, 169-75 (1979). For a cogent discussion by the Supreme Court on the elements of actual malice and its difference from the common law standard of malice, see St. Amant v. Thompson, 390 U.S. 727 (1968).

62. "Malice may be inferred from the very violence and vituperation apparent on the face of the libel itself." Reynolds v. Pegler, 223 F.2d 429, 434 (2d Cir.), cert. denied, 350 U.S. 846 (1955). In Reynolds, the individual defendant wrote a scathing article in which he falsely asserted that the plaintiff had been convicted of fraud involving war contracts and that he was a nudist. The plaintiff was awarded $100,000 in punitive damages from the author, $50,000 in punitive damages from the corporate defendant that had distributed the article to newspapers with nationwide circulation, and $25,000 in punitive damages from the corporate newspaper publisher.

The court applied the actual-malice standard of reckless indifference to the truth in assessing punitive damages against the corporate defendants. It ruled that the officers of the corporation had the opportunity, and were under a duty, to exercise editorial supervision but failed to investigate the charge. 223 F.2d at 434.

63. Professor Barron maintains that punitive damages continue to provide an incentive even after Sullivan. Barron views punitive damages as an "equalizer" that allows plaintiffs to cope with the costs and attorneys' fees normally incurred in litigation with media giants. Barron, Punitive Damages in Libel Cases— First Amendment Equalizer, 47 WASH. & LEE L. REV. 105, 122 (1988).

64. See infra notes 74-79 and accompanying text.

65. See, e.g., Buckley v. Littell, 539 F.2d 882 (2d Cir. 1976), cert. denied, 429 U.S. 1062 (1977) (although no proof of special damages, court awarded $1,000 in punitive damages since defendant knowingly published false facts); Goldwater v. Ginzburg, 414 F. 2d 324 (2d Cir. 1969) (evidence of negligence, malice, and intent may be used, and appropriate inferences drawn therefrom, in establishing actual malice), cert. denied, 396 U.S. 1049 (1970). In each of these cases, plaintiffs recovered nominal compensatory damages but were awarded substantial punitive damages.

66. Gertz v. Robert Welch, Inc., 418 U.S. 323, 349 (1974). The haphazard awarding of punitive damages and their existence as punishment for reprehensible conduct exacerbate the dangers of media self-censorship. "In most jurisdictions jury discretion is limited only by the gentle rule that they not be excessive. Consequently, juries assess punitive damages in wholly unpredictable amounts bearing no necessary relationship to the actual harm caused." *Id.* at 350. One author has pointed out that punitive damages are difficult to insure against, that insurance, if available is very costly, and that there are other benefits to be derived from abolishing punitive damages:

> Although the effect of presumed damages may not be major, Gertz does eliminate punitive damages unless the plaintiff proves knowing or reckless falsity. 418 U.S. at 350. The elimination of punitive damages should significantly reduce the number of large recoveries. [It is argued] that Gertz will increase self-censorship because of the subjective effect on publishers of the increased number of libel actions filed and the greater judicial receptivity to libel actions after Gertz.

Robertson, *Defamation and the First Amendment: In Praise of* Gertz v. Robert Welch, Inc., 54 TEX. L. REV. 199, 260 n.381 (1976) (citation omitted). *See also* Anderson, *Libel and Press Self-Censorship*, 53 TEX. L. REV. 422 (1975).

67. Gertz v. Robert Welch, Inc., 418 U.S. 323, 350 (1974).

68. 492 U.S. 257 (1989).

69. 111 S. Ct. 1032 (1991).

70. *Id.* at 1043.

71. *Id.* at 1044.

72. *Id.*

73. *Id.* at 1045.

74. RESTATEMENT, *supra* note 37, § 620, comment a. *See, e.g.*, Buckley v. Littell, 539 F.2d 882 (2d Cir. 1976) (court affirmed award of $1 in compensatory damages noting that plaintiff's reputation had not suffered as result of defamatory falsehood, and actually may have been enhanced by its publication), *cert. denied*, 429 U.S. 1062 (1977); Koehler v. Wales, 16 Wash. App. 304, 556 P.2d 235 (1976) (plaintiff awarded damages of $1 for slander where actual damages were minimal and statements had little prejudicial effect on plaintiff's reputation).

75. *See* Goldwater v. Ginzburg, 414 F.2d 324 (2d Cir. 1969) (Sen. Barry Goldwater's reputation held immune to attacks by publisher Ralph Ginzburg), *cert. denied*, 396 U.S. 1049 (1970).

76. *See* Ashdown, *supra* note 41, at 671 n.128. The issue of plaintiff's prior bad reputation seldom arises as a separate issue in defamation litigation. When it does, *see* Guccione v. Hustler Magazine, Inc., 632 F. Supp. 313 (S.D.N.Y. 1989), *rev'd in part and aff'd in part*, 800 F.2d 298 (2d Cir.), *cert. denied*, 479 U.S. 109 (1990), however, the courts generally allow a defendant to use such evidence. *See, e.g.*, Walker Carpet Corp. v. Klapprodt, 89 S.D. 172, 231 N.W.2d 370 (1975) (evidence of bad reputation admissible to establish

truth or to mitigate damages); Corabi v. Curtis Publishing Co., 441 Pa. 432, 273 A.2d 899 (1971) (evidence of bad reputation admissible to mitigate damages or to show that defendant merely repeated statements made by others); Vojak v. Jensen, 161 N.W.2d 100 (Iowa 1968) (evidence of plaintiff's bad reputation prior to publication of defamatory statement admissible; evidence of specific bad acts not admissible).

77. It has been noted that nominal damages are proper "when they are the only damages claimed, and the action brought for the purpose of vindicating the plaintiff's character by a verdict of a jury that establishes the falsity of the defamatory matter." RESTATEMENT, *supra* note 37, § 620, comment a.

At common law, the usual award of nominal damages for defamation is 6 cents. The nominal award, however, should not be misunderstood as fixing the worth of the plaintiff's reputation at 6 cents. One court characterized the common law rule as follows: "First, the jury was instructed that if it found the statement in the letter to be defamatory it was required to assess at least nominal damages. It is expected that juries, finding libel but no actual damages, will assess nominal damages, traditionally 6 cents' worth." D.R.W. Corp. v. Cordes, 65 Wis. 2d 305, 315-16, 222 N.W.2d 671, 673 (1974). Another court charged the jury that the 6-cent award was proper as a nominal award:

> You have heard, no doubt, of 6-cent verdicts in libel cases. Six cents is the amount of nominal damages which have been awarded by juries who say in substance: "Yes, we vindicate the plaintiff's reputation. The publication was false and defamatory, but we believe it did him no serious injury." They find for the plaintiff and give damages of 6 cents.

Eulo v. DeVal Aerodynamics, Inc., 47 F.R.D. 35, 46 (E.D. Pa. 1969). News articles emphasizing nominal damage awards reinforce the misinterpretation that the plaintiff's reputation was judged worth only 6 cents. This misconception of the purpose of 6-cent verdicts is a result of the importance placed on large verdicts:

> A plaintiff's claim for damages involves an element of narcissism in that it constitutes his own estimation of his importance. A 6-cent verdict implies that the reputation wrecked was worth little before the libel; that the defendant made a mistake but not an important one. Thus a libel impugning the virtue of the village banker's daughter that results in a verdict for 6 cents implies that her reputation for chastity was worth only that much.

Donnelly, *The Right of Replay: An Alternative to an Action for Libel*, 34 VA. L. REV. 867, 873 (1984). *See also* Leflar, *Legal Remedies for Defamation*, 6 ARK. L. REV. 423, 427 (1952).

78. *See* Evans, *Legal Immunity for Defamation*, 24 MINN. L. REV. 607

(1940). The defenses and privileges provided by the common law generally fall into two classes: those affording protection from liability irrespective of the purpose of the publisher or the manner of publication (consent and absolute privileges) and those affording protection from liability only when the publication is made for a proper purpose or when some other condition is met (conditional privileges and reports of certain public proceedings). *See* generally RESTATEMENT, *supra* note 37, §§ 582-598A, 611, 612.

79. The rationale for the constitutional privileges for certain statements is that damage awards impermissibly chill the freedom of the press. *See* Gertz v. Robert Welch, Inc., 418 U.S. 323, 342-44 (1974). When the imposition of damages is removed as a potential remedy, the reasoning for much of the constitutional privileges allows the consideration of a more flexible, nondamage defamation remedy.

80. Dean Roscoe Pound was the preeminent advocate for the use of injunctive relief in defamation cases. *See* Pound, *Equitable Relief Against Defamation and Injuries to Personality*, 29 HARV. L. REV. 640 (1916). *See also* Chafee, *Possible New Remedies for Errors in the Press*, 60 HARV. L. REV. 1 (1946); Leflar, *supra* note 77, at 431.

81. 283 U.S. 697 (1931).

82. *Id.* at 716. The case involved a state public nuisance statute that allowed injunctions against newspapers that regularly contained "malicious, scandalous, and defamatory" matter. *Id.* The comments enjoined by the lower court had been directed toward public officials and their conduct. *Cf.* New York Times Co. v. Sullivan, 376 U.S. 254 (1964). In *Near,* the Court recognized that "exceptional cases" may permit injunctive relief against the press. 283 U.S. at 716. To date, however, no such case has been presented.

83. Cf. New York Times Co. v. United States, 403 U.S. 713 (1971) (per curiam) (Pentagon Papers case—no prior restraint permitted on publication of secret material).

84. Courts have been extremely reluctant to enjoin defamatory statements, and have done so in few reported U.S. cases. In Krebiozan Research Found. v. Beacon Press, Inc., 334 Mass. 86, 134 N.E.2d 1 (1956), *cert. denied,* 352 U.S. 848 (1956), the court declined to issue an injunction against allegedly defamatory statement. The court noted that "the constitutional protection of free speech and public interest in the discussion of many issues greatly limit the areas in which the power to grant injunctive relief may or should be exercised in defamatory cases." *Id.* at 93, 134 N.E.2d at 6. *But see* Black & Yats, Inc. v. Mahogany Ass'n, 129 F.2d 227 (3d Cir.), *cert. denied,* 317 U.S. 672 (1942), in which the court stated that an injunction could issue to prevent a "pure" trade libel, for example, an action for disparagement of title to goods in which personal defamation was not at issue. *Id.* at 236. The court, however, based its decision in part on traditional equitable powers and jurisdiction over property interests, not on the common law of defamation. *Id.* at 233, 235-36.

85. Taylor v. Hearst, 107 Cal. 262, 40 P. 392 (1895). In Taylor, due to a printing error a newspaper inadvertently charged the plaintiff with fraud. A correction was published four days later, but the court held that a retraction

can operate only to mitigate damages. *Id.* at 270, 40 P. at 394. *See also* PROSSER, *supra* 34, § 116, at 799.

86. See Taylor v. Hearst, 107 Cal. 262, 40 P. 392 (1895). As noted by the Supreme Court, "[t]he law of defamation is rooted in our experience that the truth rarely catches up with a lie." Gertz v. Robert Welch, Inc., 418 U.S. 323, 344 n.9 (1974).

87. *See, e.g.,* Linney v. Maton, 13 Tex. 449, 458 (1855) (if retraction is immediate, in the same conversation, and heard by all who heard the slander, original effect may be overcome so that no action can be maintained); PROSSER, *supra* note 34, § 116, at 799.

88. *See, e.g.,* CAL. CIV. CODE § 48a (Deering 1991); FLA. STAT. §§ 770.02, 836.08 (1990); OHIO REV. CODE ANN. § 2739.13 (Baldwin 1991); OR. REV. STAT. §§ 30.160, .165, .170 (1989). *See* generally Morris, *Inadvertent Newspaper Libel and Retraction*, 32 ILL. L. REV. 36, 41-44 (1937); PROSSER, *supra* note 34, § 116, at 800.

There is some question whether these statutes violate state constitutional provisions that guarantee citizens the right to remedies through due process of law. *E.g.,* Fla. Const. of 1885, Decl. of Rights, § 4; Ohio Const. art. I, § 16.

89. *See, e.g,* Hanson v. Krehbiel, 68 Kan. 670, 75 P. 1041 (1904) (statute limited actual damages that can be recovered after retraction to cases involving injury to property or profession but not injured feelings and humiliation); Byers v. Meridian Printing Co., 84 Ohio St. 408, 95 N.E. 917 (1911) (statute construed as compelling plaintiff to waive, in part, right of recovery if defendant's retraction was held to violate state constitutional protection of remedies).

90. See Werner v. Southern Cal. Associated Newspapers, 35 Cal. 2d 121, 216 P.2d 825 (1950) (statute that limited recovery to damages suffered in respect to property or profession unless correction was demanded and not published held constitutional). *See also* Gersten v. Newark Morning Ledger Co., 52 N.J. Super. 152, 145 A.2d 56 (1958) (retraction statute permitted recovery of general and special damages, excluded only punitive damages); Miami Herald Publishing Co. v. Brown, 66 So. 2d 679 (Fla. 1953) (only actual damages recoverable after retraction of inadvertent libel, but actual damages construed to encompass all but punitive damages).

The court in *Holden v. Pioneer Broadcasting Co.* noted:

> Were we to hold that the legislature cannot constitutionally modify the remedies available to a person who contends that he has been defamed we would, in effect, freeze the law of defamation in the form in which it existed at the time our constitution was adopted. And, logically, such a holding would congeal the remedies for all actions, whether arising out of the law of defamation or any other area of the law.

228 Or. 405, 411-12, 365 P.2d 845, 849 (1961). The Oregon statute was held to create, as a condition precedent to recovery of general damages, a require-

ment that plaintiff plead and prove either intent to defame or defendant's failure to retract on demand. *Id.* at 409, 365 P.2d at 847. *See generally* Fleming, *Retraction and Reply: Alternative Remedies for Defamation,* 12 U. BRIT. COLUM. L. REV. 15 (1978).

The Montana Supreme Court struck down that state's retraction statute because it required that the plaintiff demand a retraction as a prerequisite to bringing a libel action. See Madison v. Yunker, 589 P.2d 126 (Mont. 1978). The court found that the state constitution preserved the right to a remedy for injury to character and that the imposition of a condition precedent to the pursuit of that remedy impermissibly restricted access to the courts. *Id.* at 131. According to the court, the condition precedent to commencement of a suit is "in direct derogation of the clear and unambiguous language of . . . [the] Montana Constitution, which mandates that the courts of this state are open to every person, and a remedy afforded for every injury to character." *Id. See generally* MONT. REV. CODE ANN. §§ 7, 16 (1979).

91. *See, e.g.,* Morris, *supra* note 88, at 69. The author states that "[the plaintiff's vindication depends upon the mercy of the press." If a defamation is inadvertent, there appears to be no reason to refuse to retract. If, however, the defamation is intentional—the publisher believes in the truth of the statements—it is likely that he would choose to defend a suit in order to protect his own reputation.

92. *See, e.g.,* Menard v. Haule, 298 Mass. 546, 11 N.E.2d 436 (1937) (court refused to issue a mandatory injunction to compel a newspaper to publish a retraction). *Cf.* Miami Herald Publishing Co. v. Tornillo, 418 U.S. 241 (1974). In *Tornillo,* the defendant newspaper refused to print the plaintiff's replies to editorials critical of the plaintiff's candidacy for office. The Court expressed reluctance to allow the government to compel a newspaper "to print that which it would not otherwise print." *Id.* at 256. *But see* Red Lion Broadcasting Co. v. FCC, 395 U.S. 567 (1969) (upholding Commission's equal time rules).

93. *See, e.g.,* Pedrick, *supra* note 16, at 604. "So long as the thrust of the judicial action is to facilitate the flow of information and not to deter its publication the law ought to be seen as carrying out the philosophy of the First Amendment, aimed at securing the freedom of public discussion." *Id.* Even those authors who strongly advocated a literal interpretation of First Amendment freedoms and argued for constitutional restrictions on libel law were favorably disposed to right-of-reply statutes. *See, e.g.,* T. EMERSON, THE SYSTEM OF FREEDOM OF EXPRESSION 539 (1970); Berney, *supra* note 16, at 47. *See also* Chafee, *supra* note 80, at 28.

94. *See* J. BARRON, FREEDOM OF THE PRESS FOR WHOM? (1973). Barron spearheaded an unsuccessful attempt to have Congress pass a federal law requiring popular access to all newspapers of general circulation. *Id.* at 53-65.

95. *See* Leflar, *supra* note 77, at 441-44. @Nevada and Mississippi were the first states to experiment with reply statutes. These experiments preceded the academic debate over the use of reply statutes as a defamation remedy. NEV. REV. STAT. § 200.570 (repealed 1969); MISS CODE ANN. § 23-3-35

(1972) (limited right to reply for political candidates). Leflar labeled the reply statutes "legally controlled self-help." Leflar, *supra* note 77, at 443. *See* PROSSER, *supra* note 34, § 116, at 801.

96. Miami Herald Publishing Co. v. Tornillo, 418 U.S. 241, 256 (1974).

97. *Id.* at 258. Tornillo involved the Florida statute that provided:

> If any newspaper in its columns assails the personal character of any candidate for nomination or for election in any election, or charges said candidate with malfeasance or misfeasance in office, or otherwise attacks his official record, or gives to another free space for such purpose, such newspaper shall upon request of such candidate immediately publish free of cost any reply he may make thereto in as conspicuous a place and in the same kind of type as the matter that calls for such reply, provided such reply does not take up more space than the matter replied to. Any person or firm failing to comply with the provisions of this section shall be guilty of a misdemeanor of the first degree.

FLA. STAT. § 104.38 (repealed 1975). Although the reply right provided for was limited rather than general, the Court was unequivocal in its view that the statute violated the First Amendment guarantees of freedom of the press. *Tornillo,* 418 U.S. at 256.

98. *See* Donnelly, *supra* note 77, at 867. The French approach would subject the responsible editor to fines from 50 to 500 francs for failing to publish a reply. *Id.* at 885. The Danish approach similarly contemplates sanctioning an uncooperative editor. *Id.* at 891.

99. Aside from the criminal penalties, the Court in *Tornillo* found two factors that "infringed" upon the exercise of First Amendment freedoms. First, newspapers were compelled to expend time, cost, and space against their will. 418 U.S. at 256. Even if no costs were imposed, however, the reply statute served to replace the editor's discretion and judgment with that of the state and thus constituted an impermissible intrusion into editorial affairs. *Id.* at 257.

Second, the overall effect of the statute would be to cause editors or publishers to avoid controversy so as to be able to refuse requests for response space. *Id.* at 257. This argument, focusing on the chilling effect of the statute, is similar to the concern voiced by the Court in setting limitations on defamation damages.

100. 28 U.S.C. §§ 2201-2202 (1975). In addition, declaratory judgments are available in the courts of those states that have adopted the Uniform Declaratory Judgment Act. Thirty-nine states, the Virgin Islands, and Puerto Rico have done so. *See* Uniform Declaratory Judgment Act Annotated 39 [hereinafter UDJAA].

101. The Uniform Declaratory Judgment Act states:

> Courts of record within their respective jurisdictions shall have power to declare rights, status, and other legal relations whether or not further

relief is or could be claimed. No action or proceeding shall be open to objection on the ground that a declaratory judgment or decree is prayed for. The declaration may be either affirmative or negative in form and effect; and such declarations shall have the force and effect of a final judgment or decree.

UDJAA § 1.

102. Costs or attorneys' fees, or both, however, may be awarded as part of the declaratory judgment. UDJAA §§ 1, 10. *But see infra* notes 127, 219-225 and accompanying text.

103. Justice White pointed out that the practical effect of a nominal damage award is "a judicial declaration that the publication was indeed false." Gertz v. Robert Welch, Inc., 418 U.S. 323, 376 (1974) (White, J., dissenting). *See also supra* note 77.

104. Presumably, a suit for nominal damages would be guided by the usual doctrines and defenses. Perhaps, however, the threat of merely nominal damages should not require the full panoply of common law defamation privilege and defenses. *See* SPECIAL NOTE, *supra* note 37. For cases discussing nominal damages, *see supra* notes 93-97.

105. An action seeking purely a declaration of falsity should not be subject to the full range of constitutional and common law defenses because the defendant is not threatened with the assessment of any damage award if the statement is determined to be false. This view is supported by Justice White:

We entrust to juries and the courts the responsibility of decisions affecting the life and liberty of persons. It is perverse indeed to say that these bodies are incompetent to inquire into the truth of a statement of fact in a defamation case. I can therefore discern nothing in the Constitution that forbids a plaintiff to obtain a judicial decree that a statement is false—a decree he can then use in the community to clear his name and to prevent further damage from a defamation already published.

Dun & Bradstreet, Inc. v. Greenmoss Builders, Inc., 472 U.S. 749, 768 n.2 (1985) (White, J., concurring).

106. The circumstances in which existing remedies are inadequate include cases where a plaintiff cannot surmount a defendant's privilege, *e.g.*, Piracci v. Hearst Corp., 263 F. Supp. 511 (D. Md. 1966), *aff'd*, 371 F.2d 1016 (4th Cir. 1967) (newspaper enjoys privilege to publish reported arrests of, and charges against, persons); Watson v. Southwest Messenger Press, Inc., 12 Ill. App. 3d 968, 299 N.E.2d 409 (1973) (in absence of actual malice, newspaper enjoys privilege to publish activities of municipal government and its officers), or where special damages are required but are not proven, Baker v. Oklahoma Tire & Supply Co., 344 F. Supp. 780 (W.D. Ark. 1972) (after alleged defamation, plaintiff had no difficulty in obtaining employment); Danias v. Fakis, 261 A.2d 529 (Del. Super. Ct. 1969) (lost wages because plaintiff voluntarily stayed away from work do not constitute special damages).

107. *See* Green, *Relational Interests*, 31 ILL. L. REV. 35, 36 (1936); Harper & James, *supra* note 34, § 5.1.

108. *Model Communicative Torts Act*, 47 WASH. & LEE L. REV. 1 (1990).

109. Franklin, *A Declaratory Judgment Alternative to Current Libel Law*, 74 CALIF. L. REV. 809, 812-13 (1986) (hereinafter FRANKLIN PROPOSAL).

110. H.R. 2846, 99th Cong., 1st Sess. (1985) (introduced by Rep. Charles E. Schumer (D-N.Y.)).

111. MCTA § 9-107.

112. MCTA comment to § 9-107.

113. MCTA § 9-107(a)(i).

114. MCTA § 9-107(a)(ii).

115. MCTA § 9-107(b).

116. FRANKLIN PROPOSAL *supra* note 109, at 812 (§ 1(a)(1).

117. *Id.* (§ 1(b)).

118. *Id.* (§ 1(c)).

119. Barrett, *Declaratory Judgments for Libel: A Better Alternative*, 74 CALIF. L. REV. 847, 851 (1986).

120. *Id.* at 852.

121. *Id.* at 853.

122. *Supra* notes 179-87 and accompanying text.

123. *Supra* notes 220-25 and accompanying text.

124. *Supra* notes 161-78 and accompanying text.

125. FRANKLIN PROPOSAL *supra* note 109, at 815 n.27, 836-42.

126. *Id.*

127. The limited nature of the judicial inquiry could resemble an action under a fault standard, where fault is equated with publishing a false statement. "Media liability may thus effectively turn on falsity alone, with little weight given to the defendant's efforts to verify a story before publication." Ashdown, *supra* note 41, at 673. *See also* Holzberg, *Bifurcating Defamation Trials Opposed*, 16 LITIGATION NEWS 1 (Feb. 1991) (reporting on proposal of National Conference of Commissioners on Uniform State Laws to require jury determination that statement was false before proceeding to other issues).

By eliminating the surpluses in defamation law, the vindication action allows the fundamental issue of truth or falsity to be determined without the intrusion of peripheral considerations. Issues other than falsity, however, may be relevant in certain vindication actions. These issues include whether the statement is one of fact or opinion, whether the defendant made the statement involved in the litigation, whether the statement refers to the plaintiff, and whether a retraction or correction is sufficient. The award of attorneys' fees may be conditioned upon the plaintiff's good faith in bringing the action and the nature an severity of the statement. The possibility of incurring the defamer's costs and attorneys' fees could discourage superfluous litigation. *See infra* notes 219-25 and accompanying text.

It should be noted that lower legal costs could have the negative effect of encouraging vindication actions in an already overburdened court system. Liberal awards of attorneys' fees, however, may help to deter the filing of nonmeritorious claims. The conclusions about excessive legal expenses in defamation cases emanate from the experiences in full-fledged actions. *See* Anderson, *Libel and Press Self-Censorship*, 53 TEX. L. REV. 422, 431-36 (1975); *infra* note 221 and accompanying text.

128. As one commentator observed:

> [E]xculpation in the eyes of the world is not accomplished by quiet entry of a judgment on the musty rolls of a court. The judgment must be publicized, if those who have read the libel are to know of its adjudged falsity. Unless the community is both small and interested, so that news of the judgment is spread throughout it verbally, the plaintiff's vindication depends upon the mercy of the press. The vanquished defendant may not mention the judgment. Even his competitors—if he has any—may keep silent, out of fear of advertising a weapon which may be used against them when next they boggle.

Morris, *supra* note 88, at 38. *See also supra* note 91.

129. The creation of new remedies is plainly within the prerogative of the state legislatures and Congress: "The Constitution does not forbid the creation of new rights, or the abolition of old ones recognized by the common law, to attain a permissible legislative objective." Silver v. Silver, 280 U.S. 117, 122 (1929). *See also supra* note 90.

SPECIAL NOTE, *supra* note 37, indicates that there are several methods by which a vindication action may be created without resort to the formal legislative process. First, the plaintiff may sue only for nominal damage. Under this approach, however, the plaintiff may be burdened by both common law and constitutional requirements that apply to defamation actions. *See also supra* note 104. Second, the plaintiff may ask for a special verdict on the issue of falsity and defamatory content. The plaintiff would be bound by the traditional common law and constitutional doctrines under this approach as well. In addition, the cause of action must reach the jury before a special verdict can aid the plaintiff. Finally, a plaintiff who is unable to present a prima facie case on all of the elements involved in the traditional defamation action may be susceptible to an adverse summary judgment. *See* Wasserman v. Time, Inc., 424 F.2d 920, 921-22 (D.C. Cir.) (Wright, J., concurring), *cert. denied*, 398 U.S. 940 (1970). In a concurring opinion, Judge Wright set out his view on the use of summary judgment procedure in libel litigation by specifying the difficulties facing the plaintiff in successfully sending the case to the jury. According to Judge Wright, the issue of actual malice should be decided first by the trial judge applying the *Sullivan* test of actual knowledge or reckless disregard of the truth. This is necessary because the plaintiff may be able to prove falsity but unable to establish other essential elements, such as negligence, actual malice, or damages. In this situation, it is likely that the suit would be disposed of by the judge in a summary proceeding before trial. Thus, the jury would never have an opportunity to render a special verdict.

New legislation creating a specific vindication action is preferable to continued judicial construction of existing statutes and remedies. Specific legislation would permit the proposed remedy to be tailored to fit its stated goals without being bound by past practice, ancient doctrines, and unnecessary defenses.

130. Gertz v. Robert Welch, Inc., 418 U.S. 323, 340-41 (1974).

131. The Court framed the issue in *Gertz* as one of "the publisher's constitutional privilege against liability for defamation. . . ." *Id.* at 325 (emphasis added).

132. Unless the remedy involves an impermissible prior restraint on free speech, Near v. Minnesota, 283 U.S. 697 (1931), or a direct infringement of the editor's freedom and discretion to decide what to print, Miami Herald Publishing Co. v. Tornillo, 418 U.S. 241 (1974), it is presumptively valid.

133. Barrett, *supra* note 119, at 859-60.

134. In the *Westmoreland* case, the defendant was reluctant to produce documents that revealed the editorial process. As a result, the plaintiff had to move to compel production three times. *See* Westmoreland v. CBS, Inc., 596 F. Supp. 1166 (S.D.N.Y. 1984) (requiring defendant to produce a report); 9 Med. L. Rptr. 2316 (S.D.N.Y. 1983) (requiring defendant to produce drafts of the report); 10 Med. L. Rptr. 1215 (S.D.N.Y. 1984) (requiring defendant to produce notes concerning the report).

135. *See* Barrett, *supra* note 119, at 860; Franklin, *supra* note 109, at 820.

136. *See* Harley Davidson Motorsports, Inc. v. Markley, 279 Or. 361, 568 P.2d 1359 (1977) (private defamation suit arising from false complaint letter sent to dealership; court awarded $500 in compensatory and $25,000 in punitive damages). For other cases exemplifying windfall recoveries, *see supra* note 2.

137. The Court in *Gertz* expressed its fear that "the prospect of civil liability for injurious falsehood might dissuade a timorous press from the effective exercise of First Amendment freedoms." Gertz v. Robert Welch, Inc., 418 U.S. 323, 341 (1974). Aware of the nexus between defamation law and First Amendment infringement, Justice Douglas noted that "[t]here can be no doubt that a state impinges upon free and open discussion when it sanctions the imposition of damages for such discussion through its civil libel laws." *Id.* at 359.

138. *Id.* at 390.

139. *Id.* at 349.

140. *See* NAACP v. Button, 571 U.S. 415, 433 (1963).

141. *See* Rosenbloom v. Metromedia, Inc., 403 U.S. 29, 43 (1971).

142. New York Times Co. v. Sullivan, 376 U.S. 254, 277-78 (1964).

143. Although a defendant might be afraid of the potential embarrassment caused by an adverse judgment, defamation judgments frequently recede into oblivion through a "conspiracy of silence." Donnelly, *supra* note 77, at 873. Additionally, the new remedy would not be burdened by many of the inadequacies inherent in the damage remedy:

The preoccupation of our law of defamation with damages has been a crippling experience over the centuries. The damages remedy is not only singularly inept for dealing with, but actually exacerbates, the tension between protection of reputation and freedom of expression, both equally important values in a civilized and democratic community. A defamed plaintiff has a legitimate claim to vindicate in order to restore his damaged reputation but a settlement for, or even a court award of, damages is hardly the most efficient way to attain that objective. In either case, the refutation of the libel is not attended with much publicity, if any, and, if listed by the defendant, occurs long after the libel has spread its poison. Plaintiffs sometimes settle on condition that the defendant make an apology in open court, but there is no law that actually requires a defendant to do so even after he has lost a verdict. So far as the plaintiff is concerned, damages offer him a pot of gold which he may not even desire, but since this is all that the law provides him as a token of vindication, it is still widely regarded as necessary for honorable men to demand a large sum of damages lest it be misinterpreted as a tacit admission that one's reputation was not worth more.

Fleming, *supra* note 90, at 15. In England, plaintiffs may sue for a declaration of defamatory falsehood, but the remedy is not used extensively because British plaintiffs are not burdened by the constitutional requirements that exist in the United States. *Id.* at 15 n.1.

  144. 418 U.S. 323 (1974).

  145. *Id.* at 368 n.3 (Brennan, J., dissenting). This proposition is central to the vindication action. One must assess the constitutionally objectionable impact of the existing damage remedies and compare it with the hypothetical impact of the vindication action.

  146. *Id.* Justice Brennan further elaborated:

[M]y Brother White argues that the Court's view and mine will prevent a plaintiff—unable to demonstrate some degree of fault—from vindicating his reputation by securing a judgment that the publication was false. This argument overlooks the possible enactment of statute, not requiring proof of fault, which provide for an action for retraction or for publication of a court's determination of falsity. . . .

Id.

   The assumption that a plaintiff could vindicate his reputation by receiving a judgment of falsity without actually proving fault seems evident from the Court's holding that "so long as they do not impose liability without fault, the State may define for themselves the appropriate standard of liability for a publisher or broadcaster of defamatory falsehood injurious to a private individual." Gertz v. Robert Welch, Inc., 418 U.S. 323, 347 (1974) (citation omitted).

  147. Disagreeing with what he perceived as the majority position, Justice White stated that "[e]ven if the plaintiff should recover no monetary damages, he should be able to prevail and have a judgment that the publica-

tion is false." *Id.* at 393. Indeed, one of Justice White's criticisms was that with the additional burden on the plaintiff of proving negligence or other fault, it would be exceedingly difficult for him to vindicate his reputational interest by securing a judgment for nominal damages. *Id.* at 376. Justice White now apparently sees no constitutional impediment to an action seeking a declaration of falsity. *See infra* note 6.

148. The *Gertz* opinion evinced a belief by the Court that First Amendment rights were violated by the excessive economic sanctions imposed on defendants in defamation actions. The latitude allowed juries in assessing the intangible damage in defamation cases was the impetus for the Court's construction of constitutional limits on that discretion. "The largely uncontrolled discretion of juries to award damages where there is no loss unnecessarily compounds the potential of any system of liability for defamatory falsehood to inhibit the vigorous exercise of First Amendment freedoms." *Id.* at 349. The economic factor, however, is not the only cause for the chilling effect. The mere time and expense of the lawsuit may inhibit publishers as well. *See infra* note 155.

149. Gertz v. Robert Welch, Inc., 418 U.S. 323, 168 n.3 (1974) (Brennan, J., dissenting). Any remedy, however, must be judged by the chilling effect it may inflict on First Amendment freedoms. That level of infringement may depend on the method by which the remedy is created. The simplest manner would be by specified legislative authorization, either by a new and explicit statute or by an amendment to the Uniform Declaratory Judgment Act. The judgment in a vindication action would be required to include only a declaration of the falsity of the challenged statement, perhaps detailing the court's finding of fact. This should create a very minimal level of infringement.

The vindication action could also be judicially created though interpretation of the Uniform Declaratory Judgment Act or through the use of nominal damage awards. With the use of the judicial approach, however, the existing defamation privileges, defenses, and doctrines would complicate the action for nominal damage. As a result, the vindication action would lose its expedient and inexpensive qualities and would retain a potential for inhibiting First Amendment expression. *See generally* SPECIAL NOTE, *supra* note 37.

150. The Supreme Court recognized this interest and also the state's interest in compensating victims of defamation when the Court admitted that the *Sullivan* test stands as a "substantial abridgment of the state law right to compensation for wrongful hurt to one's reputation." Gertz v. Robert Welch, Inc., 418 U.S. 323, 343 (1974).

151. Gertz v. Robert Welch, Inc., 418 U.S. 323, 344 (1974). *See also* PROSSER, *supra* note 34, § 118, at 824.

152. New York Times Co. v. Sullivan, 376 U.S. 254, 269-75 (1964); Gertz v. Robert Welch, Inc., 418 U.S. 323, 334 (1974); Miami Herald Publishing Co. v. Tornillo, 418 U.S. 241, 252 (1974).

153. If a declaration of falsity does not cause an impermissible chill on First Amendment freedoms, the status of the plaintiff is no longer an issue of

constitutional importance. Even if the declaration might cause a slight infringement, by way of self-imposed censorship, the competing interests must be "balanced" using the *Gertz* analysis. *Gertz* interprets *Sullivan* as accommodating the interest of the press and the limited state interest of compensation for wrongful injury present in libel actions. Gertz v. Robert Welch, Inc., 418 U.S. 323, 342-43 (1974).

154. *See* Anderson, *supra* note 127. Eaton, *The American Law of Defamation Through* Gertz v. Robert Welch, Inc. and *Beyond: An Analytical Primer,* 61 VA. L. REV. 1349, 1390-93 (1975); Robertson, *supra* note 66.

155. The propriety and efficacy of trying issues of truth and falsity in a judicial context do not solve all the problems.

> Litigation to determine the truth or falsehood of a statement in a newspaper or periodical poses a dilemma for the publisher. Defense of the action will be costly—not only in terms of legal fees and court costs but in staff time and energy as well. A requirement that the publisher pay the legal fees of the plaintiff if the statement is found to be false would further increase this burden. Yet the failure of the publisher to defend will tend to discredit his publication.

DuVal, *Free Communication of Ideas and the Quest for Truth: Toward a Teleological Approach to First Amendment Adjudication,* 41 GEO. WASH. U.L. REV. 161, 231 (1972).

It should be noted, however, that the judiciary has centuries of experience in litigating claims of truth or falsity. The proposed vindication action should satisfy the many plaintiffs who desire only absolution of their tarnished reputations. One commentator has stated:

> The crude Anglo-Saxon notion of vindication of honor by getting cash has become unsatisfactory to many decent people. They want a less sordid and more convenient procedure, which will focus its attention on what most concerns them, the mistakes in the defendant's statement. It would be desirable for a court to be able to do something tangible to
> * reduce the injurious effect of those mistakes, without having to bother about any of the hard fought questions of damages which now take up so much time in a libel suit. The present libel action will remain for those who want to use it, but it ought not to be the sole remedy.

Chafee, *supra* note 80, at 7. Professor Chafee set forth three possible remedies: a right of reply, compulsory retraction, and optional retraction.

156. *See supra* notes 144-46 and accompanying text.

157. *See generally* PROSSER, *supra* note 34, § 75, at 494-96.

158. *The Restatement* recognizes that strict liability may be permissible for a nondamage remedy. SPECIAL NOTE, *supra* note 37, § 623. This issue, however, has not clearly been resolved.

159. Herbert v. Lando, 441 U.S. 153, 169 (1979). The Court refused to

extend to the press a First Amendment protection concerning pretrial depositions during a libel case. Had the press won this point, the plaintiff's burden
of proving actual malice on the part of media defendants would have been
increased.

160. *See, e.g.,* Johnson Publishing Co. v. Davis, 271 Ala. 474, 124 So. 2d
441 (1960) (editor may be cross-examined on the meaning of a magazine
article); Scott v. Times-Mirror Co., 181 Cal. 345, 184 P. 672 (1919) (all
relevant circumstances surrounding publication are admissible); Freeman v.
Mills, 97 Cal. App. 2d 161, 217 P.2d 687 (1950) (malice may be inferred or
established by direct proof of a person's state of mind).

161. A privilege does not serve to justify the activity but to excuse the
actor from liability for the activity due to other compelling reasons. Privilege,
according to Prosser, "rests upon the same idea, that conduct which otherwise
would be actionable is to escape liability because the defendant is acting in
furtherance of some interest of social importance, which is entitled to protection even at the expense of uncompensated harm to the plaintiff's reputation." PROSSER, *supra* note 34, § 114, at 776.

Prosser lists twelve broad areas of common law privilege, both absolute and qualified. The absolute privileges protect statements made under the
following circumstances: in legislative and judicial proceedings, by members
of the executive branch within the scope of their duties, between husband and
wife, with the consent of the plaintiff, and pursuant to a legal requirement to
make the publication. A qualified privilege may exist where statements are
necessary to protect: the defendant or another unable to protect himself, a
group endeavor, the public interest, and the principle of fair comment.
PROSSER, *supra* note 34, §§ 114-15, at 776-92.

162. *Id.* § 16, at 98-99.

163. For further discussion of the various common law privileges, *see* C.
MORRIS, TORTS 329-32 (2d ed. 1980); PROSSER, *supra* note 34, §§ 114-15,
at 776-96.

164. 443 U.S. 111 (1979). The speech and debate clause protects members of Congress from being questioned outside of Congress regarding
speeches and debates made in Congress. *See* U.S. Const. art. I, § 6; 443 U.S. at
124.

165. *Id.* at 133. The case illustrates the enormous costs of defending
complex damage actions—$124,351 for a case that finally settled for $10,000.
Id.

166. *See generally* PROSSER, *supra* note 34, §§ 114-15, at 776-96.

167. *See generally id.* § 114, at 776.

168. There are absolute immunities available for the judicial, executive,
and legislative branch. Legislative immunity for national legislators has been
raised to the level of constitutional protection through the speech and debate
clause. U.S. Const. art. I, § 6, cl. *See* Killbourn v. Thompson, 103 U.S. 168
(1880); *supra* notes 164-65 and accompanying text. *See also* Bradley v. Fisher,
80 U.S. (13 Wall.) 335 (1871) (judicial immunity); Spalding v. Vilas, 161 U.S.
483 (1895) (executive immunity).

169. The Supreme Court in *Barr v. Matteo* stated:

The reasons for the recognition of the privilege have been often stated. It has been thought important that officials of government should be free to exercise their duties unembarrassed by the fear of damage suits in respect of acts done in the course of those duties—suits which would consume time and energies which would otherwise be devoted to governmental service and the threat of which might appreciably inhibit . . . effective administration of policies of government.

360 U.S. 564, 571 (1959) (extending executive immunity to lower-level employees).

170. The literal translation is: "He who consents cannot receive an injury." See Shinglemeyer v. Wright, 124 Mich. 230, 82 N.W. 887 (1900).

171. See Dyer v. MacDougall, 93 F. Supp. 484 (E.D.N.Y. 1950); Lawler v. Merritt, 182 Misc. 648, 48 N.Y.S.2d 843 (1944), aff'd, 269 A.D. 662, 53 N.Y.S.2d 465 (1945).

172. See PROSSER, supra note 34, § 115, 785.

173. 360 U.S. 525 (1959) (provision of Federal Communications Act that requires equal opportunities for all political candidates and forbids censorship by publisher grants absolute immunity to publisher).

174. Id. at 535 (quoting Bethlehem Steel Co. v. New York Labor Relations Bd., 330 U.S. 767, 773 (1947)).

175. The privilege attaching to publications made in the interest of the publisher has been analogized to the privilege of self-defense. Thus, it would be unfair to hold a publisher liable for damages in a defamation action where the sole motive for the defamation was the protection of the publisher's reputation. See generally PROSSER, supra note 34, § 115, at 786-87. See also Haycox v. Dunn, 200 Va. 212, 104 S.E.2d 800 (1958) (newspaper editor has right to publish a retort in self-defense to rival newspaper's charge of disreputable conduct if reply made in good faith and without malice or falsity).

176. For example, a privilege exists based on the policy of allowing the reasonable man to speak where, under ordinary social standards, he would feel compelled to warn someone about a third person. The privilege is clearest when some recognizable relationship exists between the publisher and the person on whose behalf he intervenes, such as between employee and employer regarding the character of a prospective employee. See generally PROSSER, supra note 34, § 115, at 787-89.

177. Communications made to the proper authorities in order to protect the public's interest, such as information offered for the prevention or detection of crime, would not be deterred by the threat of a vindication action. These types of communications are in the public interest and should not be discouraged. See Hutchinson v. New England Tel. & Tel. Co., 350 Mass. 188, 214 N.E.2d 57 (1966) (communications made to police are protected by qualified immunity).

178. Id. at 191, 214 N.E.2d at 59.

179. See HARPER & JAMES, supra note 34, § 5.1; PROSSER, supra note 34, § 111, at 739.

180. The origins of the current definition have been traced to Parmiter v. Coupland, 151 Eng. Rep. 340 (1840). *See* RESTATEMENT, *supra* note 37, §§ 569-575.

181. Early libel law was not concerned with a search for the truth but was designed to avoid civil strife: "Every libel has a tendency to the breach of the peace, by provoking the person libeled to break it, which offence is the same (in point of law) whether the matter contained be true or false; and therefore the defendant, on an indictment for publishing a libel, is not allowed to allege the truth of it by way of justification." BLACKSTONE, *supra* note 34, at 125-26 (emphasis in original).

182. If a defendant proves the statement was truthful, he has an absolute defense in a libel action. Criminal libel, at common law, did not allow truth as a defense, but statutes in almost every state have done so. PROSSER, *supra* note 34, § 116, at 796-97.

183. *See supra* notes 35-38 and accompanying text.

184. *See supra* notes 38-46 and accompanying text.

185. If there is no injury to reputation, the plaintiff is nonetheless entitled to nominal damages for an actionable defamation. Denton Publishing Co. v. Boyd, 448 S.W.2d 145, 147 (Tex. Civ. App. 1969), *aff'd,* 460 S.W.2d 881 (Tex. 1970). *See supra* notes 74-79 and accompanying text.

186. Truth or falsity remains the primary issue to be determined in the action. A threshold issue for the court, however, would become whether the plaintiff had satisfied his obligation to bring the offending facts to the attentions of the defendant prior to filing the action and whether the defendant satisfactorily retracted or corrected the offending statement. Typically, the issue could be resolved summarily in advance of trial on the issue of truth or falsity.

187. *See generally supra* note 127 . Rather than creating a major issue for the trier of fact, it is more expedient to allow the court to make this assessment at the conclusion of the case. In those few cases where the challenged statement clearly fails to cast dishonor on the plaintiff, the court may account for this by adjusting the award of attorneys' fees. For example, when the court determines that the alleged false statement was merely a complaint made to the plaintiff, the award of attorneys' fees to the plaintiff can be diminished or denied. This potential sanction should prevent vindication actions being brought for the purpose of harassment. If the plaintiff's conduct was truly unwarranted or outrageous, the court could award attorneys' fees to the defendant, despite plaintiff's successful proof of falsity.

If the use of attorneys' fees as a sanction to deter frivolous litigation is unsuccessful, stronger measures could be considered. Lack of defamatory content could be made an affirmative defense or a necessary element of the plaintiff's case. Either alternative, however, would complicate the vindication action, increase the expense incurred, and delay a final decision; thus, they should he used only if absolutely necessary.

188. The vindication action assumes that plaintiffs will only be willing to file suit if the alleged false statement is also defamatory. In other words, most

parties would not be motivated to file a lawsuit challenging a favorable false statement. Moreover, most parties would be willing to retract or correct a favorable false statement.

189. *See generally* PROSSER, *supra* note 34, § 113, at 766-77.

190. *Id.*

191. *Id.*

192. For example, radio and television broadcast station identification is required regularly. 47 C.F.R. § 73.1201 (1980).

193. *See generally supra* notes 34-66 and accompanying text.

194. *See, e.g.,* Brady v. Hearst Corp., 281 F. Supp. 637 (D. Mass. 1968) (action for libel failed because defamatory article did not identify plaintiff); Velle Transcendental Research Ass'n v. Esquire, Inc., 41 Ill. App. 3d 799, 354 N.E.2d 622 (1976) (complaint failed to state cause of action where plaintiff did not plead fact that he was the object of the alleged defamation).

195. *See* Archibald v. Belleville News Democrat, 54 Ill. App. 2d 38, 203 N.E.2d 281 (1964) (complaint failed to state cause of action when it did not allege that the article was understood by readers to refer to plaintiff).

196. *See, e.g.,* Skeoch v. Ottley, 377 F.2d 804, 807 (3d Cir. 1967) ("identification does not have to be by majority vote. It is enough if some readers reasonably understand that the plaintiff is meant"); Riss v. Anderson, 504 F.2d 188 (8th Cir. 1962) (reference to plaintiff in beginning of telecast reasonably could be understood to identify plaintiff as subject of defamatory remark made later in telecast); Davis v. Macon Tel. Publishing Co., 93 Ga. App. 633, 92 S.E.2d 619 (1956) (test is whether average and reasonable reader could determine that unnamed party referred to in newspaper article was intended to be plaintiff).

197. *See, e.g.,* Washington Post Co. v. Kennedy, 3 F.2d 207 (D.C. Cir. 1925) (article referring to "Harry Kennedy, an attorney, 40-years old," held libelous of Harry F. Kennedy, the only lawyer by that name in the District of Columbia, where person actually arrested was Harry P.L. Kennedy); Larocque v. New York Herald Co., 220 N.Y. 632, 115 N.E. 1042 (1917) (Joseph Larocque granted recovery when libelous article mistakenly named Joseph Larocque when it intended to name John Larocque); Gasperini v. Manginelli, 196 Misc. 547, 92 N.Y.S.2d 575 (1949) (defendant psychiatrist's statement that plaintiff's son was suffering from nervous disorder held to identify father because "Jr." had been omitted from son's name); Laudati v. Stea, 44 R.I. 303, 117 A. 422 (1922) (defamatory circular that mistakenly named the plaintiff sufficiently identified him).

The use of the plaintiff's name in connection with other descriptive material referring to him or her will usually be sufficient identification. *See, e.g.,* Riss v. Anderson, 504 F.2d 188 (8th Cir. 1962) (identification sufficient where reference in defamatory statement at end of television interview was made to earlier mention of plaintiff by name); Michaels v. Gannett Co., 10 A.D.2d 417, 199 N.Y.S.2d 778 (1960) (identification by name and address sufficient).

The question arises regarding how a vindication action will treat the situation in which several plaintiffs claim that they have been identified by the defamatory material. Although the problem is not likely to arise frequently, its occurrence is possible. *See, e.g.,* Washington Post Co. v Kennedy, 3 F.2d 207 (D.C. Cir. 1925); Larocque v. New York Herald Co., 220 N.Y. 632, 115 N.E. 1042 (1917). *See also* the majority opinion and Justice Holmes's dissent in Hanson v. Globe Newspaper Co., 159 Mass. 293, 34 N.E. 462 (1893) (denying recovery for plaintiff, H.P. Hanson, when article mistakenly cited his name instead of A. P. H. Hanson). In the case where several plaintiffs have a legitimate claim for vindication but the defamatory remark was in fact true of one person, the defendant would be required to publish an "elaboration" in lieu of a retraction, thereby explaining which one of the several plaintiffs was referred to accurately by the defamatory language. In the event that the defendant's statement was false as to all plaintiffs, he would be required to publish a retraction of appropriate scope and to clarify the matter with respect to all plaintiffs.

198. *See, e.g.,* Carlisle v. Fawcett Publications, Inc., 201 Cal. App. 2d 733, 742, 20 Cal. Rptr. 405, 411 (1962) (plaintiff identified in allegedly libelous article which used his first name, described him as " 'a tall, handsome fellow, and as a senior' and an athlete in the only high school in the relatively small city."); Klein v. Sunbeam Corp., 47 Del. 526, 94 A.2d 385 (1952), *aff'd,* 47 Del. 575, 95 A.2d 460 (1953) (identification of plaintiff may be established by extraneous evidence showing that the reader understood that the defendant intended to refer to the plaintiff); Brauver v. Globe Newspaper Co., 351 Mass. 49, 217 N.E.2d 736 (1966) (court allowed extrinsic evidence to show third person understood photograph in which facial characteristics were partially obliterated referred to plaintiff); Ward Telecommunications & Computer Serv., Inc. v. New York, 83 Misc. 2d 331, 372 N.Y.S.2d 423 (Ct. Cl. 1975) (although plaintiff corporation not specifically named in audit report alleging the charging of excessive fees, identification was proven because corporation provided the only computer service in the area). *See also* cases cited *supra* note 197.

199. *See, e.g.,* F & J Enter., Inc. v. CBS, Inc., 373 F. Supp. 292 (N.D. Ohio 1974) (insufficient identification shown of plaintiff's product, which was practically identical to that of competitor); Wright v. Rosenbaum, 344 S.W.2d 228, 231-32 (Tex. Civ. App. 1961) (defendant's statement that "[o]ne of the four ladies" had stolen a dress did not identify any of the three plaintiffs about whom the statement had been made).

200. Fowler v. Curtis Publishing Co., 182 F.2d 377 (D.D.C. 1950) (article referring to Washington taxicab drivers generally, with accompanying photograph of plaintiff cab company, held not sufficient identification of any of the sixty individual drivers of that company); Neiman-Marcus v. Lait, 13 F.R.D. 311, 313 (S.D.N.Y. 1952) (statement that "most of the sales staff are fairies" held to have sufficiently identified each of twenty-five salesmen); Ball v. White, 3 Mich. App. 579, 580, 143 N.W.2d 188, 189 (1966) (defamatory statement referring to "someone in your organization" held sufficient for recovery by each of the seven workmen in that organization).

When reference is made to a group, identification and ultimate recovery will depend on the size of the group and the inclusiveness of the statement. The smaller the group, the more likely the impact of the defamatory statement will be felt by each of the members. Vague references to some members of larger groups are less likely to provide grounds for recovery; the individual members would be insulated from the impact of the statements by the size of the group and the consequent anonymity. PROSSER, *supra* note 34, § 111, at 749-51.

201. *See, e.g.,* Ginsburg v. Black, 237 F.2d 790, 793 (7th Cir. 1956) (publication not found where defendant prepared defamatory memorandum but did not authorize its distribution); Colmar v. Greater Niles Township Publishing Corp., 13 Ill. App. 2d 267, 271-72, 141 N.E.2d 652, 656 57 (1957) (defendant who did not participate in preparation, composition, publication, or circulation of libelous statements published by corporation not liable for defamation); Manley v. Greensboro News Co., 241 N.C. 455, 460-61, 85 S.E.2d 672, 676 (1955) (nonsuit entered where no evidence of publication of offered).

202. LeSesne v. Willingham, 83 F. Supp. 918, 923-24 (E.D.S.C. 1949) (transmission and delivery of libelous message by telegraph company is publication); Kelly v. Loew's, Inc., 76 F. Supp. 473, 484 (D. Mass. 1948) (intercorporate communication of defamatory movie script is sufficient publication); Tyler v. Garris, 292 So. 2d 427, 429 (Fla. Dist. Ct. App. 1974) (giving defamatory letter to third person sufficient publication independent of subsequent publication in newspaper); Rickbeil v. Grafton Deaconess Hosp., 74 N.D. 525, 542, 23 N.W.2d 247, 256 (1946) (dictation to stenographer and transcription of notes into letter constitutes publication); Lindley v. Delman, 166 Okla. 165, 167, 26 P.2d 751, 753-54 (1933) (exhibition of defamatory letter regarding deputy county clerk at county political party meeting is sufficient publication). *But see* Gelhaus v. Eastern Airlines, Inc., 194 F.2d 774, 776 (5th Cir. 1952) (publication not shown where alleged defamatory words spoken in office not heard by secretary ten feet away in adjacent office); Lekich v. IBM, 469 F. Supp. 485, 487 (E.D. Pa. 1979) (no publication where not alleged that defamatory letters were shown to third party); Pinkney v. District of Columbia, 439 F. Supp. 519, 527 (D.D.C. 1977) (no action for defamation by employee when not alleged that statement was sent to anyone other than plaintiff, and employer merely retained alleged defamatory statement in files).

203. A person is liable for republication when he voluntarily rereads or otherwise repeats the libelous statement to others. *See* Spears Free Clinic & Hosp. for Poor Children v. Maier, 128 Colo. 263, 266-67, 261 P.2d 489, 491-92 (1953) (fact that death certificate containing alleged defamatory remarks was on file and open to public inspection did not constitute a republication by doctor who wrote defamatory remark).

204. Apportionment of the responsibility for a retraction in a vindication action is illustrated by the following example: A defamatory letter concerning the president of a community civil organization is circulated by its author among the members of the organization. A local newspaper later published the letter. The author of the letter would be ordered to issue a

retraction to the members of the organization and the defendant newspaper would be required to print its retraction in a subsequent edition.

205. A republisher of defamatory material is not relieved of liability even though the original publisher has made a retraction and an apology. Caldwell v. Crowell-Collier Publishing Co., 161 F.2d 333, 336 (5th Cir.), *cert. denied*, 322 U.S. 766 (1947).

206. The nature of the judgment in a vindication action is "dedicated to the search for truth." Pedrick, *supra* note 16, at 604.

207. *See supra* notes 85-92 and accompanying text . Because the plaintiff seeks to have a declaration of the statement's falsity, and the defendant's reasonable retraction and correction is deemed an admission of falsity, the issue would be resolved out of court.

The retraction and correction must meet a standard of reasonableness because defendant could partially retract or clarify the statement, attempting to use an insufficient retraction as an absolute defense. The retraction statutes require that retractions conform to acceptable standards. CAL. CIV. CODE § 48a (West 1954); FLA. STAT. ANN. §§ 770.02, 836.08 (West 1976); OHIO REV. CODE ANN. §§ 2739.13-.14, .16 (Anderson 1954); OR. REV. STAT. §§ 30.160, .165, .170 (1979-80). In order to fully rehabilitate the plaintiff's reputation, the same rules should apply in a vindication action. Thus, the court should decide whether a retraction and correction has adequately stated the truth, thereby providing the defendant with an absolute defense. *See* PROSSER, *supra* note 34, § 116, at 800 (retraction must be full and unequivocal).

208. The U.S. Supreme Court has recently encouraged the use of the summary judgment procedure. *See, e.g.,* Celotex Corp. v. Catrett, 477 U.S. 317, 325 (1986) (finding summary judgment properly regarded not as disfavored procedural shortcut, but rather as measure designed to achieve just, speedy, and inexpensive determination of action); Anderson v. Liberty Lobby, Inc., 477 U.S. 242, 249-50 (1986) (holding no issue for trial unless sufficient evidence favoring nonmoving party exists; mere colorable or insignificantly probative evidence not sufficient to defeat motion for summary judgment); Matsushita Elec. Indus. Co. v. Zenith Radio Corp., 475 U.S. 574, 586 (1986) (nonmoving party must show more than some metaphysical doubt as to material facts). *Cf.* HARPER & JAMES, *supra* note 34, § 5.29, at 463-64 (illustrates circumstances where factual matters may become questions of law for the court).

209. The Uniform Declaratory Judgment Act allows the use of juries where appropriate and necessary for complying with state law. The jury's role is to be limited to the "determination of an issue of fact." UDJAA, § 9. Under the Federal Declaratory Judgment Act, "the right to trial may be demanded" according to the Federal Rules of Civil Procedure governing jury trials in all federal court actions. FED. R. CIV. P. 57.

210. *Cf.* Note, *Vindication of the Reputation for a Public Official,* 80 HARV. L. REV. 1730, 1744 (1967). The limited nature of the judicial inquiry is not far removed from what could prevail under a fault standard where liability is

equated with publishing a false statement. Thus, "[m]edia liability may . . . effectively turn on falsity alone, with little weight given to the defendant's efforts to verify a story before publication." Ashdown, *supra* note 41, at 673.

By eliminating the surpluses in defamation law, the vindication action allows the fundamental issue of truth or falsity to be judged without the intrusion of peripheral considerations. Some issues other than falsity may, however, be relevant in certain vindication actions: whether the statement is one of fact or one of opinion; whether defendant made the statement involved in the litigation; whether the statement refers to plaintiff (similar to common law colloquium doctrine, *see* PROSSER, *supra* note 34, § 111, at 749); and whether a retraction and correction are sufficient, *see supra* notes 207-09; *infra* notes 211-18. Attorneys' fees may be conditioned on plaintiff's good faith in bringing the action and the nature and severity of the statement. This factor would deter some superfluous litigation. *See infra* note 225 and accompanying text.

211. The only possible exceptions would be for a nominal damages award, *see generally* notes 74-79 *supra,* or for fees of the plaintiff's attorney, *see infra* notes 219-25 and accompanying text. As one court has said, "Insofar as the award is intended to compensate for lost reputation rather than to punish the defendant for willful and wanton misconduct, a nominal recovery may be sufficient to vindicate the injury to reputation." Airlie Found. Inc. v. Evening Star Newspaper Co., 337 F. Supp. 421, 431 (D.D.C. 1972). The court noted that the actual injury was "vastly reduced" by the newspaper's immediate publication of a correction and an apology. *Id.*

Professor Anderson is critical of the action for nonmonetary relief because he does not believe that it will protect First Amendment rights. "[I]t creates a danger to self-censorship that is not outweighed by the countervailing state interest in compensating actual losses. In suits for nonmonetary relief, the danger of self-censorship is still real, while the state interest in compensating becomes highly speculative, if not illegitimate." Anderson, *supra* note 127, at 479. Anderson has failed to consider fully the individual's interest in his own reputation, a personal interest, as one of the competing factors at stake. The state's interest may include providing a forum for compensating the victim of defamation. The individual's interest is in obtaining vindication. *See* Pound, *supra* note 35, at 445.

The effectiveness of compelled publication of an adverse judgment has long been recognized in the French law of honorable amends. Under French law, the losing defendant is required to publish, at his own expense, the text of the judgment at a specified place. "In the case of defamation . . . the publicity of the judgment of condemnation will be often the most natural, as well as the most efficacious of indemnities." Garraud, 2 *Droit Penal Francais* § 600 (3d ed. 1914), quoted in Chafee, *supra* note 80, at 14.

212. *See supra* note 128 ; *infra* notes 214-18 and accompanying text.

213. As one commentator observed, "[A] judgment for one libeled can produce far-flung exculpatory results only if it is treated as news, such news can circulate only in the same medium by which retraction is diffused— newspaper." Morris, *supra* note 88, at 39. Strict adherence to this rule, howev-

er, is not an absolute requirement. An alternative medium may be used for the publication. A judgment published in a newspaper may effectively counteract a statement broadcast over a local television station. The parties to the action may work out a suitable publication arrangement or, failing that, the court may choose its own.

214. The judgment must include the basic facts demonstrating that particular statements in the offending article were false. Although Chafee observed that the public would undoubtedly be enlightened as to the truthfulness of the original newspaper article if courts published detailed judgments, he believed such a requirement would be excessively burdensome for the courts to carry out. Chafee, *supra* note 80, at 15. Of course, the length and detail of the judgment would depend on the complexity of the facts and the false statement. In many cases, a very brief statement would suffice. A simple statement could be drafted by the plaintiff, subject to the court's endorsement. Note, *supra* note 210, at 1743, n.88. This would reduce the burden that the proposed remedy might impose on the courts.

215. In some cases the plaintiff's honor may be satisfied simply by the entry of judgment in his or her favor. This is evidenced by the vindicatory effect of nominal damages. *See* Ashdown, *supra* note 41, at 671 n.128; Frakt, *The Evolving Law of Defamation;* New York Times Co. v. Sullivan to Gertz v. Robert Welch, Inc. *and Beyond,* 6 RUT.-CAM. L.J. 471, 499 (1975); RESTATEMENT, *supra* note 37, § 621.

Publication of the judgment should not be permitted to intentionally punish or embarrass the defendant unless absolutely necessary for the vindication of the plaintiff's reputation. Of course, some embarrassment is inherent in the filing of the action. Additionally, any order requiring publication is likely to cause the defendant some embarrassment. "Imagine the effect on the *Chicago Tribune* of being obliged to pay the *Chicago Sun* to print a formal condemnation of the *Tribune* for libel." Chafee, *supra* note 80, at 14. To the extent that this embarrassment lacks any chilling effect or substantial pecuniary loss, it does not offend the First Amendment. *See supra* notes 130-32 and accompanying text.

216. *See generally supra* notes 130-49 and accompanying text. The leading case on the chilling and intrusive effects of forced publication is Miami Herald Publishing Co. v. Tornillo, 418 U.S. 241, 257 (1974), in which the Court concluded that the penalties imposed by the Florida right-of-reply statute might deter editors from publishing politically controversial articles and thus hinder open public debate. An excellent discussion of the constitutional problems in this area may be found in Opinion of the Justices to the Senate, 363 Mass. 909, 298 N.E.2d 829 (1973), in which the court indicated that a proposed statute requiring newspapers to publish political advertisements in response to advertisements previously published would be unconstitutional.

217. *See* Miami Herald Publishing Co. v. Tornillo, 418 U.S. 241, 256, 258 (1974) (choice of material and decision as to what attention or treatment it will receive are strictly within exercise of editorial judgment).

218. If the defendant is a nonmedia entity, or if a media defendant

declines to devote space to the publication, it will be necessary to purchase the requisite space or time in the marketplace. Because there is no compulsion to publish, the problem presented in Miami Herald Publishing Co. v. Tornillo, 418 U.S. 241 (1974), is avoided. *Miami Herald* concerned not only the costs of compelled printing but also the intrusion into editorial discretion. The burden of seeking publication, therefore, is borne by the plaintiff, not by the defendant. The court, however, must be careful to keep the costs of publication down. Otherwise, the vindication remedy could be as expensive as a small damage award.

219. Fleichman Distilling Corp. v. Maier Brewing Co., 386 U.S. 714 (1967) (where statute enumerates available compensatory relief courts may not award attorneys' fees). "The rule here has long been that attorneys' fees are not ordinarily recoverable in the absence of a statute or enforceable contract providing therefor." *Id.* at 717.

Three states have statutes permitting an award of attorneys' fees to the prevailing party in a civil action: ALASKA STAT. § 09:60.010-.060 (1973); OR. REV. STAT. § 20.010 (1973); WASH. REV. CODE § 4.84.010-.030 (1962). The amounts that may be awarded pursuant to the statutes are modest, thereby limiting the burden to the losing party.

220. *See* Newman v. Piggie Park Enter., Inc., 390 U.S. 400 (1968) (counsel-fee provision of Title 11 of the Civil Rights Act of 1964 enacted to encourage individuals to seek judicial relief); Toledo Scale Co. v. Computing Scale Co., 261 U.S. 399, 426 (1923) (statute empowered court of appeals to direct district court to assess attorneys' fees); Note, *Distribution of Legal Expenses Among Litigants*, 49 YALE L.J. 699 (1940).

The Uniform Declaratory Judgment Act contains a provision for the recovery of costs, although few courts have construed this section as permitting an award of attorneys' fees. UDJAA § 10. In any proceeding under the UDJAA, the court may make such award of costs as may seem equitable and just. *Id.* Attorneys' fees have been awarded under the section of the UDJAA governing administrative matters. UDJAA § 1. *See also* Gettings v. Elgin, 16 Or. App. 140, 517 P.2d 686, 687 (1974) (court of equity authorized to award attorneys' fees, absent statute or contract, where derivative suit brought on behalf of an organization, or where equitable relief would be severely inhibited unless a prevailing plaintiff was awarded attorneys' fees).

221. American courts traditionally refuse to award attorneys' fees unless specifically commanded by statute. *See generally* Goodhart, Costs, 38 YALE L.J. 849 (1929); McCormick, *Counsel Fees and Other Expenses of Litigation as an Element of Damages*, 15 MINN. L. REV. 619 (1931); Stoebuck, *Counsel Fees Included in Costs: A Logical Development*, 38 U. COLO. L. REV. 202 (1966).

A bar to the award of attorneys' fees may discourage plaintiffs who wish only to vindicate their reputation rather than seek damages through a traditional defamation suit. The cost of an attorney arguably could make a vindication action appear too expensive. Therefore, a provision that would allow a court to award attorneys' fees to successful plaintiffs acting in good faith would be appropriate in suits for nominal damages or declaratory relief. Allowing an award of attorneys' fees to a successful defendant also would dissuade plaintiffs from instituting groundless vindication actions. Because attorneys' fees constitute a major portion of the proposed vindication action, legislative action would be required to change this firmly entrenched doctrine.

Furthermore, because a reasonable retraction and correction may provide an absolute defense to a vindication action, the only plaintiffs eligible for an award of attorneys' fees would be those who prevail when the defendant refuses to retract the statement. The small amounts involved in pursuing this simplified and expedient remedy would not work a hardship on those few defendants who find themselves in court. The simplified nature of the vindication action would prevent the attorneys' fees from reaching the excessive level of general damage awards or the high defense costs frequently incurred.

Moreover, the vindication action procedure is simple enough to allow some individuals to proceed without an attorney, particularly where the issue of truth is easily established and capable of speedy resolution. A claims counsel for one of the larger libel insurers has stated that "it is the costs of the defense, rather than the judgment losses, that chills [sic] the press." Letter from Chad E. Milton to James H. Hulme (Oct. 31, 1978). Defense costs are rarely less than $1,500 for defamation actions that are dismissed at an early pretrial stage and may range up to $750,000. *Id. See* Ek, *Libel Insurance*, in H. NELSON & D. TEETER, LAW OF MASS COMMUNICATIONS 678 (2d ed. 1973) (review of the costs involved in litigation of defamation claims).

If a large number of vindication actions are filed, one potential problem could be the aggregate effect of several individual awards of attorneys' fees against a single defendant. This problem, however, can be minimized. Because a defendant may successfully avoid an adverse judgment by publishing a reasonable retraction, only those cases involving a sharp dispute should proceed to litigation. Moreover, it is unlikely that prevailing plaintiffs would win an award of attorneys' fees in every case. In some instances the plaintiff may not have an attorney and, thus, would not require an award of fees. Alternatively, the judge may decide that the issue of truth is very close, and therefore, despite the plaintiff's victory, only a small award should be made. Finally, it is possible to limit attorneys' fees to a necessary and reasonable amount. By allowing recovery only for those expenses adjudged "necessary," the British have been successful in reducing the amount of attorneys' fees awarded. *See generally* Mayer & Stix, *The Prevailing Party Should Recover Counsel Fees*, 8 AKRON L. REV. 426, 435 (1975); Comment, *Court Awarded Attorneys' Fees and Equal Access to the Courts*, 122 U. PA. L. REV. 636 (1974).

222. *See supra* note 221 and accompanying text, for a discussion of litigation costs incurred in traditional defamation actions.

223. There are indications that equity courts consider it within their jurisdiction to award reasonable attorneys' fees. *See* Gettings v. Elgin, 16 Or. App. 140, 517 P.2d 686 (1974). One author has pointed out that a rule of discretion may provide the best solution when the award of attorneys' fees is in issue.

It seems a sound assumption that the trial judge who has seen and heard the parties can make a reasonable estimate of their sincerity and the propriety of their methods of conducting the action. Motives may be concealed, sometimes with success, but the margin of error in this matter should be no greater than in other parts of the law where the guiding standard is equally vague and the operative facts as difficult to determine.

Note, *Distribution of Legal Expense Among Litigants*, 49 YALE L.J. 699, 710-11 (1940).

224. *Cf.* Engel v. Ehret, 21 Cal. App. 2d 112, 130 P. 1197 (1913) (upholding state law that permitted court to award attorneys' fees of up to $100 to prevailing party in defamation action).

225. As a matter of fairness, attorneys' fees should be awarded to successful defendants on the same discretionary basis. There is little reason to allow plaintiff free access to the courts to harass defendants with groundless claims. Costs and attorneys' fees should not be awarded to those plaintiffs who appear to pursue their actions in bad faith or without any demonstrable merit to their claims.

It has been argued that the cost of defending a defamation suit may infringe upon First Amendment rights. *See* Anderson, *supra* note 127, at 431-36; Eaton, *supra* note 154, at 1374-75. *But see* Robertson, *supra* note 66, at 261 n.382. "A sense of public duty and professionalism, or conversely, fear of losing public credibility, may often weigh more heavily in publisher decisions than fear of litigation. Libel may simply furnish a rationalization for press timidity." *Id.* This theory has been developed in some courts to include a new practice, the special use of summary judgment to dispose of defamation cases. *See* Wasserman v. Time, Inc., 424 F.2d 920, 922-23 (D.C. Cir.) (Wright, J., concurring), *cert. denied,* 398 U.S. 940 (1970); Martin Marietta Corp. v. Evening Star Newspaper Co., 417 F. Supp. 947, 954 (D.D.C. 1976).

chapter 5

The No-Money, No-Fault Libel Suit: Keeping *Sullivan* in Its Proper Place*

PIERRE N. LEVAL†

In 1964, in *New York Times Co. v. Sullivan,*[1] the Supreme Court changed drastically the U.S. law of libel. Previously, unless the press defendant proved the accuracy of the defamatory statement, the plaintiff won the suit.[2] The *Sullivan* doctrine requires a plaintiff who is a public figure[3] to prove not only that the statement was false but also that the press defendant knew it was false, or proceeded with reckless disregard of probable falsity.[4] This element, mislabeled "actual malice" (in fact, it has little to do with malice), was predictably difficult to satisfy. In the next quarter century, few plaintiffs succeeded. One study concludes that after appeals, only 10 percent of public-figure plaintiffs come out victorious.[5]

Although the *Sullivan* rule is generally assumed to be a boon to press defendants, it also imposes significant costs on them. While protecting them from damage awards, it exposes their integrity to attack, forces them to reveal their investigative and editorial processes (often to their embarrassment), and requires them to expend signifi-

---

*This chapter was originally published in 101 HARV. L. REV. 1287 (1988).
†Judge, U.S. District Court for the Southern District of New York. Judge Leval presided at the trial of Gen. William Westmoreland's libel suit against CBS.

cant sums in defending the issue. The high capacity of the post-*Sullivan* libel law to frustrate the interests of both sides has been noted by several commentators who have offered complex proposals for legislative changes.[6]

I suggest that recognition of a no-damages libel suit, free of *Sullivan*'s actual-malice requirement, would improve the efficiency of the cause of action and reduce its costs and burdens for both defendants and plaintiffs. Such an action exists within the current legal framework without the need for legislation. I argue, first, that given a correct understanding of the *Sullivan* holding, a plaintiff who sues only for a judgment declaring the falsity of the libel and foregoes any claim for a monetary award is exempt from the obligation to prove that the defendant acted with malice. Second, I suggest that a no-money trial on the issue of truth or falsity may be advantageous in some cases to plaintiffs and defendants alike. The principal purpose of a libel suit is the restoration of a falsely damaged reputation;[7] plaintiffs whose prime objective is to vindicate their reputation are more likely to succeed if relieved of the obligation to prove malice. The press defendant will be protected in such a trial from the risk of money liability as well as from the enormous pain, burden, and cost that litigation of the *Sullivan* issue imposes on it. Finally, I suggest, regardless whether I have interpreted the *Sullivan* rule correctly, both the plaintiff and the defendant may find it advantageous in some cases to make an agreement that would relieve both sides of *Sullivan*'s unwelcome burdens, while allocating other advantages as well.

THE *SULLIVAN* RULE AND MONEY DAMAGES

The *Sullivan* ruling was designed to protect free debate from the stifling threat of outsized money awards. The action brought in the Alabama courts by a Montgomery city commissioner against the *New York Times* menaced the future of the press. The *Times* had run a full-page advertisement sponsored by supporters of the Rev. Martin Luther King, Jr.'s movement of civil disobedience and protest. The advertisement, appearing over the names of sixty-four prominent citizens, decried a "wave of terror" unleashed on nonviolent protesters by Montgomery police and urged readers to "join hands with our fellow Americans in the South by supporting . . . the struggle for the right-to-vote."[8] The advertisement did not mention Commissioner Sullivan. The Alabama court asserted jurisdiction over the *New York Times* on the basis of 390 copies of the newspaper sold in Alabama and the presence of a *Times* "stringer" in the state.[9] It found the advertisement libelous per se for tending "to bring the [Commissioner] into public contempt" and entered judgment on the jury's damage award of $500,000.[10] Sullivan's suit was one of five similar actions brought against the *Times* by Montgomery officials. The Supreme Court noted that, at the time of its review of Commissioner Sullivan's suit, the second suit had been tried to a similar $500,000 verdict and the remaining three awaited trial.[11]

The precedent of the Alabama courts threatened the survival of a national press engaged in political reporting and commentary. The intense regional divisiveness of the civil rights movement posed the threat in clearest terms. This example would likely be often repeated, wreaking segregationist vengeance on the Northern and national press. The widespread exclusion of blacks from Southern juries at the time made it likely that libel verdicts in the segregation belt would be rendered by jurors who were hostile to the intrusions of the desegregation movement and of the press. The press could not have absorbed damage awards of *Sullivan* magnitude.

The Supreme Court could have vacated the award of damages to this plaintiff on narrower, more traditional grounds without having to create new constitutional doctrine. In fact, the Court expressly ruled as an alternative ground for reversal that the *Times*'s advertisement did not refer sufficiently to the plaintiff to support a libel judgment.[12] That holding would have saved the *Times* in this instance but would have done nothing about the fundamental problem of the press's vulnerability to crippling awards. Hence the *Sullivan* malice rule.

The purpose of the malice requirement was not to protect falsity from exposure but to protect the press from intimidation or annihilation by money judgments. Justice Brennan's opinion makes clear that the Court's sole concern was for the impact of money judgments on free speech. The opening sentence poses the question as "the extent to which the constitutional protections for speech and press limit a State's power to *award damages* in a libel action brought by a public official."[13] The opinion concludes, "We hold today that the Constitution delimits a State's power to *award damages* for libel . . ."[14] The ruling was not addressed to and has no logical bearing on whether a court might declare a defamatory statement false. Nothing in it suggests that falsely maligned plaintiffs would need to prove malice if they sought no money damages but only a judgment declaring falsity.[15]

The same observation may be made of the lesser fault requirement later imposed by the Supreme Court in *Gertz v. Robert Welch,*

Inc.[16] as a precondition of liability in libel suits brought by private individuals—those who are not public officials or public figures. Such plaintiffs were required to prove some degree of fault, consisting of at least negligence, on the part of the press. This requirement was clearly conceived as a precondition for the imposition of *money* liability on the press. Justice Powell's opinion notes that "punishment of error [by imposition of money damages] runs the risk of inducing a cautious and restrictive exercise of the constitutionally guaranteed freedoms of speech and press."[17] In balancing the interests at stake in libel litigation, the opinion curiously makes no mention of the plaintiff's simple primary interest in correction of the false slander. It identifies the "interest underlying the law of libel" as "the *compensation* of individuals for the harm inflicted on them by defamatory falsehood"[18] and refers repeatedly to the defendant's "liability" as the matter at issue. It concludes that states may not "impose liability without fault."[19] The entire discussion is so expressly directed toward the consequences of monetary awards, it could hardly be thought to express a ruling on questions that would arise in a suit from which monetary awards were explicitly excluded.

The malice element, a constitutional rule established by *Sullivan* to protect press defendants from money awards, has no logical bearing on whether a wronged plaintiff should be entitled to have his* reputation restored by an adjudication of falsity. When a plaintiff agrees to forego recovery of damages, he has given the defendant the very protection for which *Sullivan* was devised. The press and free debate do not need protection from a court judgment that does no more than find falsity.

Thus, in a recent opinion, Justice White argued that the *Sullivan* Court "should not have . . . required [a public official] to satisfy the actual malice standard where he sought no damages but only to clear his name."[20] "Nothing," he added, "in the central rationale behind [*Sullivan*] demands an absolute immunity from suits to establish the falsity of a defamatory misstatement about a public figure where the plaintiff cannot make out a jury case of actual malice.[21] I agree with Justice White that the *Sullivan* Court should not have required proof of malice in a suit that sought no money damages. I argue further that it did not.

The contrary view—that a libel suit may not be maintained without proof of malice, regardless whether it seeks damages—draws

---

*Arbitrarily (and to help clarify the reference of pronouns) this chapter assigns male gender to hypothetical libel plaintiffs and female gender to hypothetical libel defendants.

some oblique support from the Supreme Court's recent decision in *Anderson v. Liberty Lobby, Inc.*[22] The Court there held that the defendant's motion for summary judgment must be granted if a public-figure plaintiff fails to adduce evidence of malice capable of satisfying the clear-and-convincing standard. It might therefore be argued that a public figure may not maintain a libel action, regardless of the type of relief sought, without being able to prove actual malice.

I believe it would be wrong, however, to read *Liberty Lobby* as expressing any view on the need to prove malice in a no-damages libel action, because this question was not argued to the Court. The plaintiff sought money damages. The plaintiff therefore was obliged to prove the *Sullivan* element, and the defendant was entitled to summary judgment if the plaintiff failed to show sufficient evidence to satisfy its burden. That the Supreme Court required the grant of summary judgment in those circumstances does not reliably indicate that it would reach the same conclusion for a plaintiff who pleaded entitlement to a judgment declaring falsity without damages and argued to the Court that *Sullivan* had no application to such a suit.

THE ADVANTAGES TO PLAINTIFFS AND DEFENDANTS OF THE NO-MONEY, NO-FAULT LIBEL SUIT

Does a libel action that seeks no money damages exist? Would plaintiffs be interested in bringing a suit of such limited scope? I think the answer to both questions is yes. Such a form of action, furthermore, offers substantial advantages to defendants as well.

Whether a plaintiff may bring a libel action for a declaration of falsity without money damages is a question of state law, not federal constitutional law. Permitting such an action advances the remedial objectives of the libel law. A libel action differs significantly from other tort actions in which a court redresses the loss only by an award of money damages. Where a plaintiff complains of a broken leg or of having been cheated, a jury's finding that the injury was caused by the defendant's negligence or fraud does nothing to undo the injury or compensate the plaintiff for it. In a libel case, by contrast, where the loss is an injury to reputation caused by the defendant's false statement, the court repairs the damaged reputation to some degree by the mere act of finding that the defamatory statement was false.[23] In fact, were it not for the lapse of time between the publication of the libel and the finding of falsity (during which time the plaintiff's reputation suffers) and the possible failure of the court's finding to reach all the people whose opinion was influenced by the false libel, the finding of falsity would undo the harm and render an award of money damages superfluous. One can well imagine a respectable legal system that would not award money damages for libel—unless, perhaps, a monetary loss was proven (such as a loss of employment)— but would restrict the plaintiff's available relief for intangible harm to a declaration of falsity of the libel.

The finding of falsity should be seen not merely as one of the elements that plaintiffs must prove to make out their case but as part of the relief itself. We would be wrong to regard money as the sole—or even principal—objective of the libel action. At common law, because of the recognition that the correction of a false libel performed a valuable function, a plaintiff was permitted to sue for nominal damages.[24] A plaintiff should be entitled to sue for the entry of a judgment embodying the verdict of falsity.

Important advantages would flow to plaintiffs and defendants from judicial recognition that a libel suit may be maintained solely for a judgment declaring falsity and that the *Sullivan/Gertz* fault rules have no application in such a trial. For the plaintiff concerned primarily with restoring a damaged reputation and willing to forego a claim for money, it permits a vastly cheaper lawsuit limited to the subject of the plaintiff's concern—the truth or falsity of the derogatory press account. It also offers the plaintiff a far greater chance of successfully vindicating his reputation. If he proves the falsity of the libel to the jury's satisfaction, he wins; judgment is entered in his favor. In contrast, under *Sullivan,* even if the plaintiff successfully proves falsity, he would in all likelihood emerge the loser because of his inability to prove "actual malice." Even plaintiffs who, given the choice, would prefer to collect damages might find advantage in such a cause of action because of their recognition that *Sullivan* dooms their quest for damages to failure.

There is reason to believe that a sizable percentage of libel plaintiffs would be interested in pursuing an action for a judgment of falsity without a claim for damages if by doing so they could escape the requirements of *Sullivan.* In a survey conducted by the Iowa Libel Research Project, almost half of all libel plaintiffs cited either restoration of reputation or deterring further publication as the objective of their suit. Fewer than one in four plaintiffs—and even fewer of the public-figure plaintiffs—stated that they were suing to win damages.[25] Many public-figure plaintiffs declare publicly that they are not out for money.[26] Some, such as Gen. William Westmoreland in his suit against CBS,[27] announce their intention to donate any winnings to charity.

Nor is such an action attractive only to wealthy plaintiffs. Tort suits are generally financed either by plaintiffs directly or, as is more commonly the case, by their lawyers in expectation of recovering contingency-fee awards. I believe this is less often true of public-figure libel suits. First, public-figure plaintiffs who are the subject of attacks in the press often have supporters—either of their person or of their cause—who could be tapped to help finance the lawsuit. Gen. Westmoreland's suit, for example, was reportedly financed by wealthy backers. Although I have no idea how Commissioner Sullivan's suit was financed, one can surmise that he would have had no difficulty raising funds through public subscription in Montgomery. Second, and more important, the lawyers who handle libel cases for public-figure plaintiffs on a contingency basis often do not expect to recover fees. Such lawyers have read *Sullivan* and know how unlikely it is that plaintiff will win damages. They take the cases for other reasons—primarily either publicity for the lawyer or loyalty to the plaintiff.

In fact, a no-money, no-fault libel action may be financially more advantageous for the plaintiff than the familiar model. Elimination of the *Sullivan* issue would make the proceeding enormously cheaper for plaintiffs (or for their attorneys), relieving them of the need to pursue evidence of actual malice by deposing all the defendant's personnel who worked on the defamatory piece. Furthermore, if by winning a verdict of falsity, the plaintiff emerges as the winner, rather than the loser, of the lawsuit, he may be entitled to recover costs from the defendant, as opposed to being liable for the defendant's costs.[28]

The press too has much to gain from an action that permits the libel plaintiff to forego damages and avoid the *Sullivan* burdens. *Sullivan* was designed to save the press from the threat of crushing damage awards. Although the medicine has saved the patient, it has had serious side effects.

First, *Sullivan* diverts the focus of the trial to plaintiff's attack on the integrity of the press's defendants. To be the subject of such an attack is at very least unpleasant. I have been told by press sources that several reporters, commentators, and editors who were the subject of such attacks in recent trials have been emotionally marked, sometimes to the point of illness, by the experience.

Second, under *Sullivan,* a plaintiff will intrude significantly into the privacy of the press's investigative, writing, and editing processes. As the Supreme Court recognized in *Herbert v. Lando,*[29] if a plaintiff must prove that the press defendant was aware of the falsity of the report, he must be allowed access to the evidence that would show the defendant's awareness. Thus, plaintiffs have the right to detailed discovery of how the author conducted her investigations, what basis she had for her defamatory assertions, how faithfully she reported her interviews, how the editorial staff altered her copy, whether an editor added unsubstantiated defamations or deleted qualifications to add sensationalism, and what in-house discussions occurred during the process that might have revealed awareness of falsity.

The *Sullivan* standards also expose the press to a high likelihood of public criticism even when it is not merited. Any ambitious piece of journalism will likely contain some factual errors. Even if they are slight and insignificant, these will become a source of embarrassment at trial. It is also a rare piece of accusatory, investigative journalism that cannot, after the fact, be made to look slipshod or biased. Investigative reporter, searching for confirmation of her accusatory sources, will understandably have less interest in speaking to the cadre of loyalists who assure her of the probity of her subject. In an accusatory expose, she may give little or no attention to denials. Also, pressures of time, money, and competition for priority place limits on how far an investigation will be taken before it is considered sufficiently confirmed to justify publication. Whether the exposé was fair depends on the quality of judgment and evaluation employed by the investigative and editorial staffs. But even where fairness and good judgment prevailed, the reporter, editor, and publisher will be vulnerable to the charge that they sought and credited only incriminating sources, that their interpretation of ambiguous facts was biased, that they failed to interview or cite witnesses who would have confirmed the plaintiff's honesty, or that they rushed to publication before completing the investigation.

Finally, litigation of the *Sullivan* issues imposes great expense on the press at both the pretrial and trial stages. Discovery of the reporting and editing processes is likely to involve extensive document review and production as well as numerous and lengthy depositions. In *Herbert v. Lando,* the deposition of a television news producer consumed twenty-six sessions and lasted over a year.[30] In *Westmoreland,* the *Sullivan* discovery included detailed depositions of fifteen reporters, researchers, editors, and production personnel who participated in making the CBS documentary, as well as several of the program's sources to inquire whether they had been influenced in their answers. The cost of this discovery to both sides must have been great.

The trial proper is also made more costly by the *Sullivan* requirement. Trial of the truth or falsity of the libel may be short and simple or long and complex depending on the complexity of the facts at issue. But trial of the *Sullivan* issues—the states of mind of the in-

vestigator, reporter, editor, commentator, producer, and publisher—
is likely in most cases to be complex, time-consuming, and expensive.

A no-money trial may also give the defendant a large hidden cost
saving in the staffing of the litigation. One who faces a $100 million
claim brought by a popular figure may feel obliged to hire a famous
(and expensive) lawyer backed by a large (and expensive) crew. If no
money is at stake, the defendant may see fit to staff the litigation more
economically, notwithstanding the importance to the press of defending its reputation for accuracy. The savings could be large.[31]

Indeed, some defendants might elect not to defend the suit at all,
avoiding completely the expenses of litigation by allowing plaintiff a
judgment of falsity by default. Some could not afford litigation. Some
might follow a "sticks and stones" policy, concluding that a judgment
without money damages is not worth defending; presumably these
would be primarily the scandalmonger press, other organs that have
no interest in cultivating a reputation for accuracy, and organs pro-
fessing a pronounced political bias, which could count on the loyalty
of their readers and the preservation of their reputation notwithstanding the court judgment. Others might default because they
recognize that they cannot demonstrate the truth of their statement,
regardless whether they believe it to be true. The press might have
relied on confidential sources who would not repeat the accusations in
public testimony; alternatively, the evidence supporting the truth of
the defamatory statement might be excludable under the hearsay
rule.[32] Finally, some defendants might default in a losing case to
reduce attention to the plaintiff's suit. The value of the plaintiff's
victory might be somewhat diminished if, as a result of the default, it
received less attention in the press.[33]

Responsible leading press institutions, on the other hand, are
unlikely to default. Defaulting would seriously damage their reputation and would provoke outrage from their journalists whose work
was attacked. The journalists would regard a default as a sacrifice of
their reputation to spare the publisher litigation expenses.

Some press partisans are instinctively suspicious of a proposal
that a plaintiff might eliminate the *Sullivan* issues by foregoing damages. In discussions with journalists, editors, and press lawyers, I have
heard frequent concern that this proposal would encourage plaintiffs
to bring frivolous lawsuits, burdening the press with the distractions
and expense of additional litigation.[34] They argue that *Sullivan*
should be construed to protect the press not only from damages but
from litigation altogether, including the expense and worry of it. This
position comes close to the *New York Times*'s first line of defense in the
Supreme Court in *Sullivan*—that the press should be altogether im-

mune from libel actions brought by public officials.[35] The Supreme Court rejected this argument, presumably because of its perception that false libels are harmful. There is social value in holding the press to account for the accuracy of defamatory statements, so long as it is protected from intimidating damage awards.[36]

The fear of new waves of frivolous lawsuits seems exaggerated. Before *Sullivan,* plaintiffs could bring libel suits free of the *Sullivan* obstacle without even giving up hope for money damages. Even after *Sullivan,* plaintiffs who do not realistically expect damages can bring suit in the hope of winning a favorable verdict on the falsity of the defamatory statement.[37] If the pre-*Sullivan* conditions did not produce floods of frivolous libel suits, there is no reason to suppose there would be floods of litigation under this proposal, which is less advantageous to plaintiffs. It is expensive to bring a lawsuit and even more expensive to carry on with it. It is unlikely that there are large numbers of potential plaintiffs, or plaintiffs' lawyers, who would press frivolous quibbling litigation without the possibility of winning a money award or even recovering legal fees.[38]

Press wariness may also result from divisions within the press establishment. Journalists may fear that their publishers will lose the incentive to back up the staff in litigation if no money is at stake. Also, the disagreeable side effects of *Sullivan* may be less apparent to press personnel before the fact than they will become after a plaintiff develops his attack on their integrity.

The governing question is, of course, not whether the litigation is uncomfortable or expensive for the press. It is whether *Sullivan* was intended, or should be construed, to protect the press not only from damages but also from a suit seeking only a finding of falsity. A declaration of falsity redresses injury without the chilling effect of damage awards. To focus on the possibility that truculent, unreasonable plaintiffs might bring frivolous suits, causing expense and distraction to the press, is to overlook the plight of the reasonable plaintiff who has been harmed by a false defamatory report and asks no money but only a correction—which the press is generally unwilling to give.[39] His injury is serious; his objective—to seek a judgment declaring falsity—is reasonable and relatively cheap. It altogether justifies requiring the press to incur litigation costs if it wishes to defend.

NEGOTIATED AGREEMENTS TO DISPENSE WITH THE *SULLIVAN* RULE

Even if I am wrong in my belief that plaintiffs have the right under existing law to eliminate the *Sullivan* issues by foregoing their claim for money damages, it remains possible for plaintiffs and defendants jointly to achieve the same result by agreement. A plaintiff's willingness to give up his claim for damages is valuable to the defendant; a defendant's willingness to give up her *Sullivan* protection is valuable to the plaintiff. Because the *Sullivan* element was established solely for the defendant's protection, the defendant may agree to dispense with it. As noted above, many libel plaintiffs seek vindication rather than money, and many press defendants should be eager to be saved from the noxious side effects of *Sullivan*. Accordingly, there should be a strong shared incentive to agree to a no-money trial of truth or falsity that banishes the *Sullivan/Gertz* fault element.

The differing interests, objectives, and fears of the plaintiff and the defendant may offer grounds for additional agreements to govern the conduct of a no-damages libel trial. The press defendant often has a great interest in being freed from the restrictions of the hearsay rule because, in many instances, the information on which reporters have relied is hearsay. I do not say this as a criticism. The press, which has neither subpoena power nor the power to place its sources under oath, could not function effectively without relying on hearsay. Whether a reporter's reliance on hearsay is justified depends on whether her sources were trustworthy and well informed. Nonetheless, a defendant whose accusatory report was based on highly reliable (and accurate) hearsay information may be unable to submit a shred of admissible evidence to support the truth of her accusation if she is bound by the hearsay rule.[40]

There is no compelling logic to our Anglo-American evidence rule, which absolutely excludes hearsay (except as to a few formulaic exceptions). It is justified primarily by unavailability of cross-examination, our lack of confidence in jurors' ability to distinguish reliable from unreliable hearsay, the difficulty of defining the differences between reliable secondhand information and rank gossip, and reluctance to send an accused to jail on secondhand evidence. Those propositions do not necessarily justify absolute exclusion of hearsay from all trials.[41] It may well be reasonable to admit hearsay evidence offered by the press defendant in support of the truth of its defamatory publication. In any event, the defendant may have a great incentive to bargain for the right to do so.[42]

An issue of concern to plaintiffs may be their inability to publicize their victory should they win the suit. Unless the suit is widely reported, a plaintiff might win a verdict as to the falsity of the libel but have no way of telling the world about his vindication. In this respect, the defendant possesses an advantage that the plaintiff lacks—access to press space. A willingness on the part of the defendant to guarantee in some manner that a verdict in the plaintiff's favor will receive coverage of a specified prominence may be another valuable bargaining chip.

How to structure such a guarantee is a sensitive issue. If the agreement leaves it to the defendant to report the plaintiff's verdict, the plaintiff may worry that he will be disadvantaged by the defendant's tone and choice of detail. Alternatively, the plaintiff might request that, if he wins, the defendant turn over a specified amount of space to him. My discussions with reporters and editors suggest that the press is highly resistant to such an agreement. It is often stated as an immutable rule that the press will not relinquish control of its column space or air time, especially to a plaintiff in a libel suit. In actual disputes, however, the press might prove more flexible. Newspapers reserve space for syndicated columnists over whom they have little or no control; prime space and time are dedicated to carry important speeches, sight unseen; space is sold to advertisers for the sale not only of soap but also of political candidates and ideas (as *Sullivan* itself attests); many press entities have letter columns or other formats that permit replies by those criticized. Indeed, CBS offered Gen. Westmoreland his own rebuttal program as part of a settlement proposal. And in the 1950s, CBS gave Sen. Joseph McCarthy an unscreened allotment of free time to rebut Edward R. Murrow's exposé.

Whether the press would steadfastly resist ceding space to a plaintiff's control may depend on what is at stake in the particular case and on who makes the decision. This is an issue on which editors and owners may disagree. If the owner can save substantial litigation expenses and avoid the risk of millions in liability merely by promising the plaintiff twelve column inches on the commentary page, she may override the objections of her editor-in-chief.[43]

Another alternative is an agreement to publish the findings of the court, if they are in the plaintiff's favor. This approach sounds simpler than it is. If there is no jury, findings will be written by the court, but the opinion is likely to be ten to fifty pages long—far too long to publish in a newspaper or to read on television. Once again, the plaintiff and the defendant might each be unwilling to trust the other as to how the opinion would be summarized or quoted. If the case is tried by jury, there will be no court opinion. The jury's verdict is in schematic form and does not lend itself to intelligible publication without explanation.

Perhaps a middle-ground solution to both sides' objections would be for the plaintiff and the defendant to agree on a neutral reporter, unaffiliated with either party, who would be commissioned to write an unbiased, fair, and accurate account of the court's finding, to be published by the defendant with the agreed level of prominence.

In some cases, the parties might agree to trial by arbitration.[44] Arbitration generally offers a speedier, simpler, and cheaper trial. Also, it offers the parties greater latitude to tailor the proceeding to their needs. For example, an arbitration agreement could require that the arbitrator prepare a 300-word statement of findings for publication by the defendant. The parties could not impose such a duty on a court. The principal disadvantages of arbitration to a plaintiff or a defendant may be that it does not provide for compulsory discovery and that arbitrations are generally less publicized than court trials. Plaintiffs who wish to attract publicity to their suit would therefore be unlikely to agree to arbitration. The matter could not be heard in arbitration unless both sides agreed.

Thus, the parties might reach a negotiated agreement to try a libel case, either in court or at arbitration, under the following principles, or any acceptable variation:

1. Plaintiff can win no money damages. Plaintiff sue only for a verdict of falsity.
2. Plaintiff need not prove fault on defendant's part, only falsity.
3. Accordingly, there will be neither discovery nor proof on the *Sullivan* issues of the defendant's good or bad faith.

Additional concessions might include:

4. Hearsay evidence will be admitted on the truth or falsity of the libel. (The judge may caution the jury on the possible dangers of reliance on hearsay, which is not subjected to cross-examination.)
5. The defendant guarantees that a finding in the plaintiff's favor will be publicized in some manner. The agreement will specify the space (or time) and prominence of the publication.

I emphatically do not suggest that such a procedure be imposed by either legislation or court rule.[45] A statute or rule would be too rigid and arbitrary to accommodate the needs of the parties in each particular dispute. In my view, the procedure is not of value unless based on a perception of mutual advantage resulting in a negotiated agreement.

Despite all its potential difficulties, such an agreement presents numerous advantages for both the plaintiff and the defendant. For the plaintiff: freedom from the insurmountable obstacle of *Sullivan;* a better chance of winning; a better chance of publicizing his vindication; and a cheaper, simpler proceeding. For the defendant: freedom from unacceptable financial risks; immunity from the frustrating or bitter side effects of *Sullivan;* an improved opportunity to prove the truth of her published accusations through reliable hearsay; and, just as for the plaintiff, a cheaper proceeding.

CONCLUSION

The Supreme Court's ruling in *Sullivan* barred awards of *money damages* unless the plaintiff proved that the defamation was committed with "actual malice." The sole purpose of the ruling was to protect the press from the intimidating threat of a money award. If a plaintiff foregoes money damages and sues only for judgment embodying a verdict of falsity, the defendant receives all the benefit that *Sullivan* confers. Thus, a plaintiff should be entitled to win such a judgment without satisfying the *Sullivan* obstacle. Defendants would benefit as well by being spared the embarrassment, burden, and expense of litigating the *Sullivan* issue. Recognition of a no-money, no-fault suit would enhance the primary objective of the law of defamation: the restoration of a falsely damaged reputation.

NOTES

1. 376 U.S. 254 (1964).
2. Under the common law, truth was an affirmative defense that the defendant had to plead and prove. *See* Rinaldi v. Holt, Rinehart & Winston, Inc., 42 N.Y.2d 369, 379-80, 366 N.E.2d 1299, 1305, 397 N.Y.S.2d 943, 950, *cert. denied*, 434 U.S. 969 (1977); RESTATEMENT (SECOND) OF TORTS § 581A, comment b (1977) [hereinafter RESTATEMENT].
3. Although the *Sullivan* opinion spoke only of public *officials,* it was promptly extended on its logic to public figures. *See* Curtis Publishing Co. v. Butts, 388 U.S. 130 (1967); Pauling v. News Syndicate Co., 335 F.2d 659 (2d Cir. 1964) (Friendly, J.).
4. In Gertz v. Robert Welch, Inc., 418 U.S. 323 (1974), the Court held that the Constitution requires even private plaintiffs to prove fault on the part of the press defendant, leaving state legislatures or courts free to determine the degree of fault required. The reasoning of my argument about the *Sullivan* doctrine applies also to the fault requirement imposed by *Gertz* on private-figure plaintiffs. *See* text discussion, p. 213–14.
5. *See* R. BEZANSON, G. CRANBERG, & J. SOLOSKI, LIBEL LAW AND THE PRESS 122 (1987); *see also* Abrams, *Why We Should Change the Libel*

Law, N.Y. TIMES, Sept. 25, 1985, § 6 (Magazine), at 34, 87 (reporting results of the study). Media defendants are particularly successful at the appellate level. From 1964 to 1982, defendants were victorious in 70 percent of their appeals of findings of actual malice. *See* Brief of the New York Times Co. et al., Amici Curiae, at 17, Bose Corp. v. Consumers Union, 466 U.S. 485 (1984) (No. 82-1246).

6. *See* H.R. 2846, 99th Cong., 1st Sess. (1985) (Schumer bill) (proposing federal cause of action for declaration of falsity without right to damages or need to prove fault at either plaintiff's or defendant's option); Barrett, *Declaratory Judgments for Libel: A Better Alternative,* 74 CALIF. L. REV. 847 (1986) (discussing the Schumer bill); Franklin, *A Declaratory Judgment Alternative to Current Libel Law,* 74 CALIF. L. REV. 809 (1986) (proposing legislation creating a cause of action for restoration of reputation without discovery or award of damages); Franklin, *Good Names and Bad Law: A Critique of Libel Law and a Proposal,* 18 U.S.F. L. REV. 1 (1983) (same); Abrams, *supra* note 5, at 92 (proposing, inter alia, limitation of losses when retraction is published, abolition of punitive damages, limitation of out-of-pocket losses, and broad application of rule immunizing expression of opinion).

7. In the words of Floyd Abrams, probably the nation's most experienced and distinguished libel litigator on behalf of the press, "The sole purpose of libel law is the restoration of unjustly lost reputation." Abrams, *supra* note 5, at 87.

8. New York Times Co. v. Sullivan, 376 U.S. 254, app. (1964).

9. *See* New York Times Co. v. Sullivan, 273 Ala. 656, 665, 666, 144 So. 2d 25, 29, 30 (1962).

10. 376 U.S. at 263 (quoting New York Times Co. v. Sullivan, 273 Ala. at 673, 144 So. 2d at 37 (1962)).

11. *See id.* at 278 n.18.

12. *See id.* at 288.

13. *Id.* at 256 (emphasis added).

14. *Id.* at 283 (emphasis added). The opinion elsewhere stated:

> The fear of *damage awards* . . . may be . . . inhibiting. . . . Whether or not a newspaper *can survive a succession of such judgments,* the pall of fear and timidity imposed upon those who would give voice to public criticism is an atmosphere in which the First Amendment freedoms cannot survive. . . . The constitutional guarantees require, we think, a federal rule that prohibits a public official from recovering damages for a defamatory falsehood . . . unless he proves . . . "actual malice." . . .

Id. at 277-80 (emphases added).

15. An early commentator argued that precisely such a remedy might be available if the public official failed to satisfy the malice requirement. *See* Note, *Vindication of the Reputation of a Public Official,* 80 HARV. L. REV. 1730, 1744 (1967).

16. 418 U.S. 323 (1974); *see also supra* note 4 (discussing *Gertz*).

17. *Gertz,* 418 U.S. at 340.

18. *Id.* at 341, 348 (emphasis added). Compare this formulation to Abrams's view, quoted *supra* note 7.

19. *Gertz,* 418 U.S. at 347.

20. Dun & Bradstreet, Inc. v. Greenmoss Builders, Inc., 472 U.S. 749, 771 (1985) (White, J., concurring).

21. *Id.* at 772.

22. 477 U.S. 242 (1986).

23. *See Greenmoss,* 472 U.S. at 774 (White, J., concurring) (stating that "libel plaintiffs are very likely more interested in clearing their names than in damages"); Abrams, *supra* note 5, at 87. Some would argue that relief would not be complete without an injunction directing the defendant to print an acknowledgment of the court's finding in the plaintiff's favor. Whether such relief is available under existing law, or desirable as an amendment, is beyond the scope of this commentary.

24. *See* RESTATEMENT, *supra* note 2, § 620; F. HARPER, F. JAMES, & O. GREY, THE LAW OF TORTS § 5.30 (2d ed. 1986).

25. *See* BEZANSON, CRANBERG, & SOLOSKI, *supra* note 5, at 79-80.

26. After she won a large libel award against the *National Enquirer,* actress Carol Burnett is reported to have stated, "If they'd given me one dollar plus car fare, I'd have been happy because it was the principle." R. SMOLLA, SUING THE PRESS III (1986).

27. Westmoreland v. CBS, Inc., No. 82 CIV. 7913 (PNL) (S.D.N.Y.). The court's opinion denying summary judgment is reported at 596 F. Supp. 1170 (S.D.N.Y. 1984).

28. *See, e.g.,* Fed. R. Civ. P. 54(d) (providing that "costs shall be allowed as of course to the prevailing party unless the court otherwise directs"). Costs, which include deposition and trial transcripts, fees, and disbursements for printing and witnesses, can run into the hundreds of thousands of dollars in a major litigation.

The suit by former Israeli defense minister Ariel Sharon against *Time* magazine illustrates the problem of costs. *See* Sharon v. Time, Inc., No. 83 Civ. 4660 (ADS) (S.D.N.Y.). Plaintiff had won a verdict of falsity but had lost the lawsuit because he failed to prove *Sullivan* malice. Following the verdict in its favor, the defendant sought, until settlement was reached, to collect sizable costs from the plaintiff. Had plaintiff brought a no-money, no-fault lawsuit, he might have been entitled to recover his costs based on a judgment in his favor declaring the falsity of the libel.

29. 441 U.S. 153 (1979).

30. 568 F.2d 974, 982 (2d Cir. 1977), *rev'd,* 441 U.S. 153 (1979).

31. According to press accounts, CBS's defense of the *Westmoreland* trial cost more than $5 million. *See* Abrams, *supra* note 5, at 90.

32. *See* text discussion, p. 221.

33. Whether a default would cheapen the value of plaintiff's victory is debatable. Plaintiff would have the benefit of an inexpensive certain judgment declaring the falsity of the defamation. On the other hand, the press might treat such a judgment as less newsworthy than a verdict after litigation.

34. *See* Abrams, *supra* note 5; Address by Floyd Abrams, Second Circuit Judicial Conference (Oct. 1987), 120 F.R.D. 160–61.

35. This is the position of Justices Black, Douglas, and Goldberg, *see* New York Times Co. v. Sullivan, 376 U.S. 254, 296 (1964) (Black, J., concurring); *id.* at 298 (Goldberg, J., concurring in the result), as well as of such prominent commentators as Anthony Lewis, *see* Lewis, New York Times v. Sullivan *Reconsidered: Time to Return to "The Central Meaning of the First Amendment,"* 83 COLUM. L. REV. 603, 620-21 (1983).

36. *See, e.g.,* Keeton v. Hustler Magazine, Inc., 465 U.S. 770 (1984) (noting the state interest in protecting nonresidents from libel).

37. In his suit against *Time* magazine, Ariel Sharon achieved a moral victory in this manner by winning a widely publicized special verdict on the issue of falsity, even though he lost the lawsuit on the *Sullivan* element. *See* Sharon v. Time, Inc., No. 83 Civ. 4660 (ADS) (S.D.N.Y.). Under currently prevailing procedures, however, plaintiffs cannot be assured that a special question on the issue of falsity will be put to the jury. Instead, the jury may find for the defendant on the absence of malice and never reach the issue of falsity.

38. Experienced libel counsel inform me that there are plaintiffs who bring an action for cosmetic and emotional reasons but thereafter do not press it. Under the present proposal, this phenomenon might be somewhat increased. It does not represent a great cost to the press.

39. *See* BEZANSON, CRANBERG, & SOLOSKI, *supra* note 5, at 40-44. A 1984 Associated Press survey of 267 newspapers found that more than 60 percent do not apologize for statements that they privately acknowledge to be erroneous. *See id.* at 44.

40. Of course, the defendant may introduce hearsay on which she relied to prove absence of malice, but the hearsay rule bars its use to support the truth of the defamatory statement.

41. *See* Weinstein, *Probative Force of Hearsay,* 46 IOWA L. REV. 331 (1961) (arguing for more liberal admission of hearsay); Note, *The Theoretical Foundation of the Hearsay Rules,* 93 HARV. L. REV. 1786 (1980) (arguing that the hearsay rules should be abolished).

42. It is a commonplace occurrence for litigants to waive valid hearsay objections. Most often this is done by simply not objecting. Sometimes, to avoid confusion, litigants will advise the judge of their intention to forego hearsay objection on a particular issue.

43. A defendant engaged in television or radio broadcasting may worry that plaintiff's production will be amateurish and not up to professional technical standards. This problem is not insurmountable. Under the agreement, the defendant could provide funds to finance the production of a program of professional quality. It could require that the plaintiff's piece be directed and produced by professionals of recognized competence and/or that some neutral industry expert certify that it conforms to professional standards.

44. The Iowa Libel Research Project has pioneered a form of libel dispute resolution in which money damages are not available and the press

defendant's state of mind is not at issue. The experimental program, administered by the American Arbitration Association, is a voluntary alternative to litigation that is available on the agreement of both parties. Under it, a factual hearing is held to determine whether the statement was false and damaging and the remedy is publication of the finding of falsity. *See* Wissler, Bezanson, Cranberg, & Soloski, *Resolving Libel Cases out of Court,* 71 JUDICATURE 197 (Dec.–Jan. 1988) (describing the program); *New Remedy for Libel Claims,* A.B.A. J., Aug. 1, 1987, at 42 (same).

45. A statutory requirement obliging the newspaper to publish the plaintiff's message would raise First Amendment questions. *See* Miami Herald Publishing Co. v. Tornillo, 418 U.S. 241 (1974).

chapter 6

The Annenberg Libel Reform Proposal

RODNEY A. SMOLLA*

In October 1988, at a press conference in the Willard Hotel Office Building in Washington, D.C., the Libel Reform Project of the Annenberg Washington Program in Communications Policy Studies of Northwestern University publicly released a "Proposal for the Reform of Libel Law."[1] Written in the form of a comprehensive model statute, with accompanying commentary, the Annenberg report recommended adoption of an entirely new approach to the law of defamation.

Eleven distinguished experts on libel litigation were brought together by Newton Minow, director of the Annenberg Washington Program, to study modern libel litigation and propose reforms. The members of the reform project represented a spectrum of "constituencies" and were diverse in their politics and professional backgrounds: Sandra S. Baron,[2] Bruce E. Fein,[3] Judge Lois G. Forer,[4] Samuel E. Klein,[5] Anthony Lewis,[6] Roslyn A. Mazer,[7] Chad E. Milton,[8] Anthony S. Murry,[9] Herbert Schmertz,[10] Sichard M. Schmidt, Jr.,[11] and Rodney A. Smolla.[12]

The project was an experiment—as in the words of Oliver Wendell Holmes, "[A]ll life is an experiment."[13] The meetings of the

*Arthur B. Hanson Professor of Law and Director, Institute of Bill of Rights Law, College of William and Mary, Marshall-Wythe School of Law. Professor Smolla is a Senior Fellow of the Annenberg Washington Program, and was Project Director of the Annenberg Libel Project. Portions of this chapter appear, in somewhat different form, in Smolla & Gaertner, *The Annenberg Libel Reform Proposal: The Case for Enactment*, 31 WM. & MARY L. REV. 25 (1989).

eleven project members were intense and vigorous, at times verging on total breakdown. But in the end, the experiment proved to be an extraordinary success. Out of the diversity and extended give-and-take of the group, substantial consensus emerged, ending with the proposed Annenberg Libel Reform Act.

The proposal is in the form of a model statute. The complete statutory text and accompanying section-by-section explanatory analysis form the heart of the report.

THE TEXT OF THE ANNENBERG PROPOSAL

Text of the Proposed Statute

Preamble

The purpose of this Act is to provide an efficient and speedy remedy for defamation, emphasizing the compelling public interest in the dissemination of truth in the marketplace. The provisions of this Act are intended to encourage the prompt resolution of defamation disputes through remedies other than money damages and should be liberally construed to accomplish that purpose.

Section 1. Scope of Coverage

(a) *One Cause of Action.* One cause of action, for defamation, shall exist for all claims based on publication of false defamatory statements. The cause of action for false-light invasion of privacy is abolished.

(b) *Publication Defined.* Publication is the communication of defamatory matter, intentionally or by negligent act, to one other than the person defamed.

(c) *No Distinction Between Media and Nonmedia.* The provisions of this Act shall apply without regard to the media or nonmedia status of the publisher.

Section 2. False Defamatory Statements of Fact Required

(a) *False Statements of Fact Required.* All actions for defamation must be based upon publication of false defamatory statements of fact of and concerning the plaintiff. No action may be based upon statements that are expressions of opinion.

(b) *Defamatory Defined.* A statement is defamatory if, as reasonably construed, it tends to injure the plaintiff's reputation.

(c) *Question for Court.* Whether the statements giving rise to the action are capable of being reasonably understood as defamatory statements of fact is initially a question of law to be decided by the court. If the court determines that the statements are capable of being reasonably understood as defamatory statements of fact, it shall be for the trier of fact to determine whether the statements were actually so understood by recipients of the statements.

(d) *Factors to be Considered.* In determining whether the statements giving rise to the litigation are defamatory statements of fact or statements of opinion, the court and trier of fact shall consider:

(1) The extent to which the statements are objectively verifiable or provable;

(2) The extent to which the statements were made in a context in which they were likely to be reasonably understood as opinion or rhetorical hyperbole and not as statements of fact;

(3) The language used, including its common meaning, and the extent to which qualifying or cautionary language, or a disclaimer, was employed.

Section 3. Retraction or Reply

(a) *Request as Prerequisite to Suit.* No action for defamation may be brought against any defendant, unless the plaintiff shall allege either:

(1) That the plaintiff made a timely and sufficient request for a retraction and the defendant failed to make a timely and conspicuous retraction; or

(2) That the plaintiff made a timely and sufficient request for an opportunity to reply, and the defendant failed to provide the plaintiff with a timely and conspicuous opportunity to reply or to make a timely and conspicuous retraction; or

(3) That the plaintiff made a timely and sufficient request in the alternative for either a retraction or an opportunity to reply, and the defendant failed to make either a conspicuous retraction or provide the plaintiff with a conspicuous and timely opportunity to reply.

(b) *Retraction Defined.* A retraction is a good faith publication of the facts, withdrawing and repudiating the prior defamatory statements.

(c) *Reply Defined.* A reply is the publication of the plaintiff's statement of the facts.

(d) *Timely Request.* A timely request for retraction or reply is a request made within thirty (30) days of the publication of the defamatory statement.

(e) *Requirements for Request.* A request for a retraction or reply must be made in writing and signed by the plaintiff or his authorized attorney or agent. It must specify the statements claimed to be false and defamatory and must set forth the plaintiff's version of the facts.

(f) *Conspicuous Retraction.* A conspicuous retraction is a retraction published in substantially the same place and manner as the defamatory statements being retracted. The placement and timing of the retraction must be reasonably calculated to reach the same audience as the prior defamatory statements being retracted.

(g) *Conspicuous Reply.* A conspicuous reply is a reply written by the plaintiff and published in substantially the same place and manner as the defamatory statements to which the reply is directed. In the case of a broadcast, the defendant may read the reply or permit the plaintiff or his designate to read it. The defendant may require that the reply not exceed the length of the material in which the defamatory statements of and concerning the plaintiff were published, and that its form reasonably accommodate the nature of the medium in which it is to be published. The reply must be concise and limited to rebuttal of the defamatory statements.

(h) *Publication of Retraction or Reply in Customarily Designated Places.* When the defendant customarily publishes retractions, corrections or opportunities to reply in a designated place, publication of a retraction or reply in that place shall be deemed conspicuous if notice of the retraction or reply is published in substantially the same place and manner as the statements to which the reply or retraction is directed.

(i) *Options of Defendant.* Upon receipt of a request for a retraction, the defendant may satisfy the requirements of this section only by publishing a retraction. Upon receipt of a request for an opportunity to reply, or upon receipt of a request in the alternative for either a retraction or opportunity to reply, the defendant may satisfy the requirements of this section by electing either to publish a retraction or to provide the plaintiff with an opportunity to reply.

(j) *Timely Retraction or Reply.* To be timely, the publication of a retraction or reply must be made within thirty (30) days of the request. In the case of a false and defamatory statement about a candidate for public office, however, the retraction or reply shall not be deemed timely unless it is published within a reasonable time under the circumstances prior to the election.

Section 4. Declaratory Judgment

(a) *Declaratory Judgment Action Brought by Plaintiff.* Subject to the requirements of Section 3, a person who is the subject of any defamation may bring an action in any court of competent jurisdiction for a declaratory judgment that such publication was false and defamatory.

(b) *No Damages Permitted.* No damages shall be awarded in such an action, and the filing of such an action for declaratory judgment shall forever bar the plaintiff from asserting or recovering for any other claim or cause of action arising out of the publication which is the subject of the action.

(c) *Proof of Fault or State of Mind Not Required.* Neither the fault nor state of mind of the defendant shall be an element of such an action.

(d) *Burden of Proof.* In any action for a declaratory judgment, the plaintiff shall bear the burden of proving by clear and convincing evidence that the publication was false and defamatory.

(e) *Election of Defendant to Convert Action for Damages to an Action for Declaratory Judgment.* A defendant in an action for defamation shall have the right, at the time of filing its answer or within twenty (20) days from the commencement of the action, whichever comes first, to designate the action as an action for a declaratory judgment. Any action designated by the defendant as an action for a declaratory judgment pursuant to this provision shall be treated for all purposes as if it had been filed originally as an action for a declaratory judgment by the plaintiff, and the plaintiff shall be forever barred from asserting or recovering for any other claim or cause of action arising out of the publication which is the subject of such action.

(f) *Docket Priority.* Actions for declaratory judgments in defamation cases shall be granted priority over other civil actions in setting trial dates, and in all cases must be tried within one hundred twenty (120) days of the filing of the complaint, unless the court makes an explicit finding on the record that such an expedited trial date is impracticable under the circumstances. The court may issue such orders as to discovery as are consistent with the expedited trial required by this Section.

Section 5. Neutral Reportage

No cause of action for either a declaratory judgment or damages may be maintained for the reporting of false and defamatory statements involving matters of public interest or concern made by persons or entities other than the defendant if the persons or entities who made the statements are identified and the statements are accurately reported.

Section 6. Truth or Falsity

(a) *Burden of Proof.* In any action for defamation, whether for declaratory judgment or damages, the plaintiff shall bear the burden of proving by clear and convincing evidence that the defamatory statements of and concerning the plaintiff are false.

(b) *Substantial Truth.* The plaintiff shall not be deemed to have met the burden of proof required by this section if the defamatory statements are substantially true.

Section 7. Minimum Fault Requirements

In all defamation actions for damages, at minimum the plaintiff shall bear the burden of proving, through clear and convincing evidence, that the defendant failed to act as a reasonable person under the circumstances.

Section 8. Privileges

(a) *Absolute Privileges.* Any cause of action for defamation maintained pursuant to this Act, whether for a declaratory judgment or for damages, shall be absolutely barred if the statements were made by:

(1) Judges, attorneys, witnesses, jurors, or other participants in any judicial proceeding;

(2) Legislators, attorneys, aides, witnesses, or other participants in any legislative proceeding; or

(3) Executive and administrative officials, attorneys, witnesses, or other participants in any quasi-judicial or quasi-legislative executive or administrative proceeding.

(b) *Conditional Privileges Abolished in Declaratory Judgment Actions.* All conditional privileges are abolished in actions for declaratory judgment maintained pursuant to Section 4.

(c) *Conditional Privileges in Damages Actions.* In actions maintained for damages, the defendant shall be given a conditional privilege for statements made:

(1) In the self-defense of the defendant's own legitimate interests;

(2) In furtherance of the legitimate interests of others;

(3) To protect a common interest between the defendant and the recipient of the communication; or

(4) To persons officially charged with the duty of acting in the public interest.

(d) *Abuse of Conditional Privilege.* No cause of action based upon statements encompassed by a conditional privilege may be maintained unless the plaintiff proves that the defendant abused the privilege. The privilege shall be deemed abused and forfeited if the defendant deliberately communicated the defamatory matter to persons other than those to whom communication was necessary to serve the interests giving rise to the privilege. If the communication was not made to persons other than those necessary to serve the interest giving rise to the privilege, then the privilege shall be deemed abused and forfeited only if the defendant published the defamatory statements with the knowledge of falsity or reckless disregard for truth or falsity.

Section 9.   Damages

(a) *Libel and Slander Distinctions Abolished.* All distinctions among libel, slander, libel per se, libel per quod, slander per se and slander per quod are abolished.

(b) *Recovery Limited to Actual Injury.* In any action for damages, recovery shall be limited to reasonable compensation based on proof of actual injury. Presumed damages are abolished. Proof of special damages (specific, pecuniary, out-of-pocket damages) shall not, however, be required. Proof of damage to reputation is a prerequisite to any recovery of damages. If proof of reputational injury is established, the plaintiff may additionally recover damages for personal humiliation, anguish or emotional distress.

(c) *All Factors Considered.* In awarding compensatory damages for actual injury the trier of fact may take into account all factors relevant to the impact of the defamatory statement, including whether it was in written or oral form.

(d) *No Punitive Damages.* No punitive damages shall be permitted in any action for defamation.

Section 10.   Attorneys' Fees

(a) *In Litigating the Sufficiency of a Retraction or a Reply.* The defendant may move to dismiss any action for defamation on the grounds that the plaintiff failed to comply with the requirements for a request for a retraction or reply set forth in Section 3, or on the grounds that the defendant either published a retraction or provided an opportunity to reply, in compliance with the requirements of Section 3. If the action is so dismissed, the defendant shall be awarded reasonable attorneys' fees. If the action is not so dismissed, attorneys' fees shall be awarded as otherwise provided in this section.

(b) *In Declaratory Judgment Actions.* In any action brought as a declaratory judgment or converted to an action for a declaratory judgment, the court shall award the prevailing party reasonable attorneys' fees. The court shall have discretion to deny or reduce the award of attorneys' fees to any prevailing party who litigated vexatious or frivolous claims or defenses.

(c) *In Damages Actions.* In any action for damages, each side shall bear its own attorneys' fees, subject to the applicable general rules of the jurisdiction for civil litigation.

Section 11. Limitations Period: One Year

Any action for defamation must be commenced no later than one (1) year after the first date of publication.

Section 12. Single Publication Rule

An action brought pursuant to this Act shall be the exclusive remedy for all injury in all jurisdictions arising from the defamatory statement upon which the action is based.

Section 13. Severability

The provisions of this Act are severable, and any judicial decision declaring any provision of this Act invalid shall not be deemed to invalidate other provisions of the Act.

Section 14. Preemption and Jurisdiction

Alternative A—Federal Statute

The provisions of this Act shall be preemptive of all applicable state laws governing defamation or false-light invasion of privacy. A cause of action pursuant to this Act may be brought in any state or federal court of competent jurisdiction.

Alternative B—State Statute

Except as otherwise provided herein, the provisions of this Act are preemptive of applicable prior law governing defamation or false-light invasion of privacy. A cause of action pursuant to this Act may be brought in any state or federal court of competent jurisdiction.

Text of the Section-by-Section Analysis

Preamble

The Preamble should be read in conjunction with this section-by-section analysis to illuminate the principal legislative purpose of this statute: to encourage the speedy and efficient resolution of defamation disputes through remedies other than money damages, emphasizing the compelling public interest in the dissemination of truth in the marketplace. The retraction, reply, declaratory judgment, and attorneys' fees provisions of this Act are designed to work together in an integrated system of checks and balances. They aim to create incentives for both plaintiffs and defendants to resolve defamation disputes through mechanisms other than prolonged and costly suits for damages. All provisions of this Act should be liberally construed to accomplish that legislative purpose.

Section 1.   Scope of Coverage

1. This section abolishes the common law cause of action for false-light invasion of privacy. It should be construed in conjunction with Section 9(a), which abolishes the distinctions between libel and slander. The Act creates one cause of action, defamation, for all claims based on false defamatory statements.

2. The creation of one cause of action simplifies the law and prevents parties from evading the coverage of this Act by attempting to recast a cause of action for defamation as an action for false-light invasion of privacy.

3. The common law causes of action for defamation and false-light invasion of privacy are largely duplicative. Technically, the common law cause of action for false-light invasion of privacy did not require proof of injury to reputation, but was meant instead to redress injury to the peace of mind of the plaintiff who wishes to be left alone. In practice, however, the overlap between the two torts resulted primarily in needless confusion and duplication. The abolition of the false-light tort should also be construed in light of Section 9(c), which instructs the trier of fact to take into account all factors relevant to the impact of the defamatory statement in awarding compensatory damages.

4. This Act covers only actions based on false defamatory statements of fact. It does not encompass or affect actions existing at

common law other than libel, slander, or false-light invasion of privacy. Actions such as infliction of emotional distress or invasion of
privacy actions based on intrusion, publication of private embarrass-
ing facts, or appropriation of name or likeness are thus not covered
by this Act. Nevertheless, it is the purpose of this Act to preempt all
common law causes of action based on false defamatory statements of
fact. The Act does not permit causes of action such as infliction of
emotional distress or invasion of privacy to be used as surrogates for
defamation to avoid the coverage of the Act.

5. "Publication" as defined in this section adopts the common
law position requiring intentional or negligent communication to a
third person other than the publisher and the person defamed.
Publication is a term of art referring to any form of dissemination of
information to a third person. It may include writings, spoken words,
symbols, electronic transmissions, or any other form of communication.

6. This Act rejects any distinction between media and nonmedia
defendants, and encompasses all actions for defamation. The provisions of this Act would thus apply to defamation spoken from one
private person to another as well as defamation in a newspaper article
or television broadcast. The provisions of this Act are to be flexibly
interpreted to accommodate the wide variety of contexts in which
defamation may occur. A retraction, for example, may take one form
in a newspaper, another in a radio broadcast, and yet another in the
context of correcting a credit report or employment letter of reference. The statutory purpose in media and nonmedia cases, however,
remains the same: encouraging prompt resolution and correction of
the record in lieu of prolonged suits for damages. No matter what the
context of the defamation, therefore, the Act is to be construed to
accomplish that overriding legislative goal.

Section 2.   False Defamatory Statements
of Fact Required

1. This section requires that all actions for defamation be based
on false defamatory statements of fact. The common law evolved
many colorful pejoratives to define "defamatory," employing such
terms as "hatred," "contempt," "ridicule," or "obloquy." This section
employs a simplified, commonsense formulation: A defamatory statement is one that tends to injure the plaintiff's reputation.

2. With respect to the language giving rise to the action, the
words are to be given a reasonable construction in light of the context
of the communication. The court must determine in the first instance

whether the words are capable of being reasonably understood as defamatory statements of fact. This is an issue of law for the court. Whether, in the actual circumstances of the case, recipients of the statements in fact understood the statements as defamatory statements of fact remains a fact issue for resolution by the trier of fact. One of the most perplexing problems in defamation law is the concept of defamatory implications. Suits often involve accurately reported facts that are alleged to carry a false and defamatory implication. There is a conflict among judicial decisions as to whether defamation actions may be maintained by public officials and public figures solely on the basis of implications. It is possible for a valid defamation action to be maintained on the basis of allegedly false and defamatory implications alone, but such an action may be maintained only when the implications alleged to be communicated may reasonably be drawn from the actual statements made. In all instances, of course, the implication must be a false and defamatory factual statement and not an expression of opinion. The "reasonableness" of a defamatory implication drawn from accurate facts depends on such factors as the omission or inclusion of other relevant facts, the use of suggestive language hinting at other implications, and the drawing of conclusions from ambiguous facts. The reasonable construction requirement, in the context of defamatory implications, should be read in conjunction with the retraction provisions of the Act. As set forth below in the analysis of provisions dealing with retractions, in cases in which the action for defamation is grounded in what the words imply, rather than what they actually state, a retraction in compliance with the Act may be perfected by a statement indicating that the alleged defamation was not intended either to state or imply the meaning ascribed to it by the plaintiff.

3. Statements of opinion are never actionable in a cause of action for defamation. This principle is now entrenched in federal constitutional law. This section draws on the rich constitutional and common law traditions in establishing the factors to be considered in determining whether a statement is one of fact or opinion. The first factor is the extent to which the statements are objectively verifiable or provable. If they cannot be objectively proved they are not statements of fact. The second factor emphasizes the general context of the communication: Statements made in a work of fiction, as part of satire or parody, or in the context of artistic, athletic, literary, academic, culinary, theatrical, religious, or political review or commentary should be presumptively construed as opinion. Letters to the editor, editorials, and editorial cartoons should be presumptively construed as opinion. Statements made in a straight news story should be pre-

sumptively construed as factual, unless qualifying language is employed to indicate otherwise. Mere colorful exaggeration, rhetorical hyperbole, verbal abuse, name calling, ridicule, or jest should be presumptively construed as opinion. In all instances, however, the emphasis must be on the overall context of the communication and on how the statements were reasonably understood in that context. The final factor emphasizes the nature of the language giving rise to the communication, including the extent to which qualifying, cautionary, or disclaiming language was employed. In a work of fiction, the use of a disclaimer shall presumptively establish that the statements giving rise to the action were reasonably understood as imaginary and not factual.

Section 3.　Retraction or Reply

1. This section establishes, as an absolute prerequisite to the maintenance of any suit for defamation, that the plaintiff first demand a retraction or opportunity to reply, and that such demand be refused by the defendant. The rationale for this section is that the simplest, most efficient remedy for defamation is a prompt and reasonable retraction or reply. This section should be read in conjunction with the attorneys' fees provisions of Section 10, which include provisions for the awarding of attorneys' fees in cases in which the sufficiency or reasonableness of a retraction or opportunity for reply is litigated.

2. Along with the declaratory judgment provisions of Section 4 and the attorneys' fees provisions of Section 10, this section establishes a system of checks and balances in which each party has incentives to self-critically assess its own version of the facts and its willingness to litigate disputes over those facts. A defendant who refuses a demand for a retraction or an opportunity to reply may be forced to litigate under penalty of paying the plaintiff's attorneys' fees if the plaintiff's version of the facts prevails. Conversely, a plaintiff who chooses to commence an action after refusal of a demand for a retraction or reply may be penalized by being forced to pay the defendant's attorneys' fees if that action does not prevail in court. The overall effect of these sections is to encourage the parties to negotiate and settle the dispute prior to litigation.

3. This section establishes a hierarchy of options for plaintiffs and defendants in choosing between the retraction and reply alternatives. The plaintiff always has an absolute right to demand a retraction in the first instance. (This provision is not to be a trap for the unwary plaintiff. If there is ambiguity as to whether the plaintiff has requested a retraction or a reply, the request is to be construed as one for a retraction.) A plaintiff who specifically demands a retraction,

not an opportunity to reply, is entitled to a retraction before litigation is barred. Therefore, a defendant faced with such a plaintiff may not avoid litigation merely by offering an opportunity to reply. The rationale for this provision is that the plaintiff has a right to a full repudiation of the defamation by the defendant, instead of the mere opportunity to reply, before the plaintiff is stripped of any litigation remedy. Conversely, however, when the plaintiff asks specifically for an opportunity to reply, the defendant may avoid litigation either by providing an opportunity to reply or by publishing a retraction. A retraction, in short, always bars litigation. The rationale for this different treatment is that the plaintiff has no persuasive grounds for insisting on reply time or space when the defendant has voluntarily repudiated the defamation. Similarly, in the case of a plaintiff who demands a retraction or opportunity to reply in the alternative, the defendant has the option of choosing either option.

4. To be sufficient, a retraction must withdraw and repudiate the prior defamatory statements and publish the corrected facts. An equivocal, hypothetical or halfhearted retraction will not suffice. When the allegedly false and defamatory statement giving rise to the plaintiff's demand for a retraction is not a statement actually made by the defendant, but rather an implication allegedly communicated by the actual statements, the defendant may satisfy the retraction requirement by publishing a statement that the defendant did not intend either to state or to imply the meaning ascribed by the plaintiff.

5. To be conspicuous the retraction must be published in substantially the same place or manner as the defamatory statements being retracted. The retraction must be reasonably calculated to reach the same audience as the prior defamatory statements.

6. A reply must also be published in a conspicuous manner—that is, in substantially the same place and manner as the defamatory statements to which the reply is directed. The reply submitted by the plaintiff must be concise and limited to rebuttal of the defamatory statements. Gratuitous statements irrelevant to rebuttal of the facts alleged to be false and defamatory may not be included. No obscene language or material may be included. The precise form and placement of a conspicuous reply may differ, depending on the nature of the medium. So long as the defendant offers the plaintiff an opportunity to reply that is reasonably calculated to reach the same audience as the original defamatory statements, the defendant may require reasonable accommodations in placement or timing of the reply.

7. In some cases the defendant may by custom have designated a particular place or time for the publication of corrections or retractions. A newspaper may customarily print retractions on the first

inside page, for example. In a nonmedia context, there may be a particular bulletin board or display area within an office that is customarily set aside for important notices. Publication of a retraction or reply in such a location will satisfy the requirement that the retraction or reply be conspicuous, so long as notice of that placement is published or "flagged" in substantially the same place and manner as the defamatory statements to which the reply or retraction is directed.

8. The defendant may require that the length of the reply not exceed the length of the material in which the defamatory statements were published. The phrase "length of the material" refers to that portion of the prior communication in which the allegedly defamatory statements of and concerning the plaintiff were made. This length may be as great as that of an entire story or broadcast segment, for example, but only if the entire story or segment contained defamatory material of and concerning the plaintiff. Indeed, the reply will normally be longer than the single sentence or sentences in which the actual defamatory statements were made, if the story or segment included other material that could have been reasonably understood as supporting or explaining the defamatory statements. An entire ten-paragraph article, for example, may be completely devoted to defamatory material of and concerning the plaintiff, even though only three sentences contain the actual defamatory language giving rise to the plaintiff's complaint. In such a case, the plaintiff would be entitled to reply space equal to the length of the entire article. On the other hand, a ten-paragraph article may contain three sentences actually defamatory of the plaintiff, within three paragraphs elaborating on those sentences. The rest of the article may not concern the plaintiff. In such a case, the length of the reply could be limited by the defendant to three paragraphs.

9. Most retractions or replies must be made within thirty (30) days of the request. In the unique context of elections, however, the retraction or reply must take place within a reasonable time under the circumstances, prior to the election. In determining the reasonableness of the timing of the retraction, the court shall consider the promptness or the delay of the plaintiff in making a demand and the promptness or delay of the defendant in responding, all in light of the strong public interest in accurate information concerning candidates for public office.

Section 4.   Declaratory Judgment

1. This section permits either the plaintiff or the defendant to dictate that the lawsuit be tried as a declaratory judgment action over

the truth or falsity of the defamatory statements, with no damages permitted. It must be construed in light of Section 10's provisions for shifting attorneys' fees to the prevailing party in such actions.

2. In a declaratory judgment action the only issue litigated is the truth or falsity of the defamatory statement. All questions of fault or state of mind are eliminated. The plaintiff bears the burden of proving with clear and convincing evidence that the publication was false and defamatory.

3. The court is to expedite trials of declaratory judgment actions. Normally such trials must be set no later than one hundred twenty (120) days after the filing of the complaint. The plaintiff in declaratory judgment cases receives no monetary remedy and therefore in fairness is entitled to a speedy trial.

4. A prompt trial on the issue of truth or falsity in which the plaintiff prevails and is awarded attorneys' fees pursuant to Section 10 will normally make the plaintiff whole. In such a case, the plaintiff will have received an expedited judicial declaration that the defamatory facts published were false. Although plaintiffs forfeit any opportunity for money damages in a declaratory judgment action, that loss is offset by the provision for the award of attorneys' fees, by the speed and efficiency of the declaratory judgment remedy and by the elimination of the burden of establishing fault on the part of the defendant.

Section 5. Neutral Reportage

1. This section adopts the emerging absolute privilege for neutral reportage. The common law employed a fiction that in republishing a defamatory statement the republisher "adopted" the statement as his own. Thus, a defendant could be successfully sued for defamation for merely quoting some other person's defamatory statement, even when the original speaker's very making of the defamatory statement was itself newsworthy.

2. This section absolutely bars any liability for merely reporting the defamatory statements of others, when the statements involve issues of public interest or concern. The plaintiff's recourse in such event is to pursue the remedies provided in this Act against the person who made the defamatory statements that were reported. Statements made by others include statements accurately reported and identified in documents such as correspondence or the complaint or pleadings filed in litigation. To qualify as neutral reportage, the publication must disclose the identity of the persons or entities that actually made the defamatory statement and those statements must be

accurately reported. The phrase "persons or entities" is used to make clear that in addition to statements directly made by natural persons, the privilege encompasses statements made in identified documents such as committee reports, law enforcement records, exhibits in administrative, legislative or judicial proceedings, and the like. The statement need not be quoted verbatim to satisfy the accuracy requirement; a paraphrase or summary is sufficient. In all cases, however, the report must correctly characterize the gist or sting of the other person's defamatory statement.

3. The neutral reportage privilege does not encompass statements that do not merely report the defamatory statements of others, but instead incorporate such statements into an independent defamatory accusation by the defendant. If the defendant states, for example, that the police chief took a bribe, and that the proof comes from a public statement by the chief's secretary that the chief took a bribe, the neutral reportage privilege would cover the publication of the secretary's statement (assuming it was accurately reported), but not the defendant's separate assertion that the chief took a bribe.

4. The neutral reportage privilege will automatically encompass accurate reports of statements made by identified persons in judicial, legislative or executive branch proceedings, or statements from identified documents in those proceedings; therefore, no separate absolute privileges covering such proceedings are set forth in this Act.

Section 6. Truth or Falsity

1. Constitutional decisions already place the burden of proof on the plaintiff in many defamation cases. This section establishes that rule as a uniform requirement in all defamation actions. Putting the burden of proof on the plaintiff serves the compelling interest of providing breathing space for the free flow of information. It brings defamation into line with most other tort actions in which the plaintiff normally has the initial burden of proving all elements of the prima facie case.

2. The substantial truth test codified in this section has long been an element of the common law. Minor inaccuracies in terminology or detail do not invalidate the substantial truth of a statement if its gist or sting is true. The test is whether those aspects of the communication that are false are the same aspects that tend to injure the reputation.

Section 7. Minimum Fault Requirements

1. This section establishes negligence as the minimum level of fault that the plaintiff must prove, with clear and convincing evi-

dence, in all defamation actions for damages. Under the First Amendment, actions for damages brought by public officials or public figures are subject to the higher requirement that the plaintiff prove through clear and convincing evidence that the defendant published the defamatory statements of fact with knowledge of falsity or reckless disregard for truth or falsity. This fault requirement, imposed by the United States Constitution, may not be amended through statute. This section therefore establishes negligence as a universal minimum statutory fault level but does not attempt to codify through statute the higher levels of fault required by Supreme Court decisions, nor does it affect present or future decisions by state courts in jurisdictions that chose to evolve higher fault standards through judicial decisions. Minimum constitutional fault requirements may be set only by the judiciary, through constitutional adjudication; this section makes no attempt to interfere with that process. Accordingly, under this Act, fault levels for defamation above the minimum negligence standard are free to move with the evolution of constitutional and common law.

2. This section should be construed in conjunction with Section 4, which gives either party the right to avoid a damages suit altogether by electing the declaratory judgment alternative.

Section 8. Privileges

1. Absolute privileges are intended to completely immunize defendants from any legal action for statements made in certain narrowly defined circumstances. Absolute privileges thus bar any action under this Act, including both actions for declaratory judgment and actions for damages.

2. This section does not include a separately defined privilege of fair report for reportage by journalists and other nonparticipants about judicial or other governmental proceedings or activities, because such reports are automatically encompassed by the absolute neutral reportage privilege established in Section 5.

3. This section establishes an absolute privilege for statements made by participants in judicial and legislative proceedings. The privilege is also extended to executive and administrative proceedings that are quasi-judicial or quasi-legislative in character. Public hearings before administrative agencies such as school boards, power commissions, or environmental agencies, for example, are within the scope of the privilege. The rationale for these absolute privileges is that in certain narrowly defined settings the public interest in totally unfettered freedom of speech is so powerful that no action for defamation arising from these settings should be permitted. Statements made in these settings are subject to the truth-seeking devices of the

judicial or legislative processes, and those devices serve to vindicate the public interest in the dissemination of truth in the marketplace, diminishing to at least some degree the need for defamation actions to serve that function. Of overriding significance, however, is the conviction that in judicial or legislative proceedings and quasi-judicial or quasi-legislative executive or administrative proceedings, the public need for complete candor and openness by participants must prevail over any private interest in the vindication of reputation.

4. Conditional privileges function differently from absolute privileges. They provide only qualified protection for defamatory statements and traditionally have been regarded as defeated when the privilege has been abused through the fault of the defendant. Since conditional privileges place the fault of the defendant in issue, they are inappropriate for declaratory judgment actions maintained under Section 4, in which a no-fault standard is employed.

5. In suits for damages, however, conditional privileges remain applicable. The privileges codified in this section are the four conditional privileges traditionally recognized at common law. They pertain to certain recurring-fact situations in which the interest in free and open communication is particularly high, requiring enhanced legal protection. Although this section embraces those conditional privileges recognized by current law, it is not intended to freeze or stultify their evolution through judicial interpretation.

6. The privilege of protecting one's own interest is analogous to the privilege of self-defense against physical attack, and covers such communications as statements made in connection with the retrieval of stolen property or the recovery of a debt. The privilege of protecting the interest of others includes such communications as a doctor's statements to protect a patient or an attorney's statement on behalf of a client. Statements made to protect a common interest typically include statements made within an organization or enterprise in which information is exchanged in furtherance of the group's conduct or activities, such as intracorporate communication or communication within religious, political, professional, fraternal, labor, educational, or social organizations.

7. The privilege of communicating information to public officials or others charged with actions in the public interest embraces a wide spectrum of communications, including reports to law enforcement officials concerning prevention or detection of crime and complaints about the performance of public officials or institutions. This privilege is particularly important in protecting the speech of whistleblowers who report alleged wrongdoing in public or private institutions or organizations.

8. Current law recognizes a wide variety of circumstances in which a conditional privilege would be deemed abused and forfeited, including excessive publication, ill will or spite, negligence, and knowing or reckless falsity. This Act, however, recognizes only two grounds for defeating a conditional privilege: excessive publication and publication with knowledge of falsity or reckless disregard for truth or falsity.

9. When the communication is deliberately spread by the defendant to persons other than those with a legitimate need for the information in light of the interests being served by the privilege ("excessive publication"), the rationale for the privilege dissolves and the privilege should be forfeited.

10. Since this Act establishes negligence as a minimum fault standard in all defamation actions, the notion that a privilege could be forfeited through the mere negligence of the defendant is obsolete, for the privilege would then provide nothing to the defendant not already required by the prima facie case.

11. This section rejects the view that a conditional privilege may be lost simply because a communication is motivated by "common law malice," in the sense of spite or ill will. A communication motivated by spite may nonetheless serve the purposes advanced by the privilege and be made in the sincere belief that it is true. A tainted motive does not of itself reduce the social value of the communication and should not cause the privilege to be forfeited.

12. This section accepts the knowledge of falsity or reckless disregard for truth or falsity standard as the only level of fault that will operate to defeat a conditional privilege when no excessive publication exists. This provides such communications with the breathing space that the privileges are designed to ensure, and it advances the additional interest in simplification of defamation rules, by synchronizing the definition of the fault standards applicable to conditional privileges with the prevailing constitutional fault rules.

Section 9.   Damages

1. The traditional common law distinction between libel and slander is antiquated and can no longer be justified. Modern forms of technology—such as radio, television, and computer communication—have blurred the distinction between oral and written communication. The confusing and arbitrary rules for slander per se and per quod, pursuant to which some forms of slander require proof of special damages while others are actionable without special damages, work in a haphazard and irrational way, increasing or decreasing

the protection for the statements in a manner bearing no logical relation to the actual balance of reputational and speech interests involved. Similarly, the rules of libel per se and libel per quod impose the burden of proving special damages on the plaintiff in a manner different from the slander rules but no less confusing and arbitrary. Finally, the doctrinal quagmire of current law is further complicated by the imposition of constitutional damages rules, rules that generally bear no relation to the common law libel/slander and per se/per quod distinctions.

2. This section eliminates the entire set of confusing distinctions in current law and replaces it with a simple, unified set of damages rules.

3. There is no longer any distinction between libel or slander, but the trier of fact may take the nature of the communication into account in assessing damages. Special damages, in the sense of out-of-pocket pecuniary losses, are never required as a prerequisite to recovery. In any action for damages, recovery is limited to proof of actual injury, which necessarily involves proof of some damage to reputation. Presumed damages, in which no proof of injury is required, are abolished. Once damage to reputation is proved, the plaintiff may enhance the recovery of damages with proof of injury in the form of personal humiliation, anguish, or emotional distress. Recovery for such emotional harm is only permitted when reputational injury is first established.

4. This section absolutely bars the award of punitive damages in all defamation actions. Punitive actions act as an excessive chill on free expression and may be devastating to the defendant. In addition, such awards often bear no relation to reality, sometimes serving to vent distaste for the nature or character of the defendant instead of fulfilling any rational interest in deterrence. Compensatory damages for defamation are already highly subjective and may even contain a hidden punitive component. To permit additional punitive damages, therefore, may punish the defendant twice and provide the plaintiff with a windfall grossly out of proportion to actual injury.

Section 10. Attorneys' Fees

1. This section serves to ensure that the defendant's attorneys' fees incurred in the process of getting a suit dismissed for failure by the plaintiff to make a proper demand for retraction or reply will be paid by the plaintiff. This section further ensures that when the defendant does retract or provide an opportunity to reply, and the plaintiff files suit anyway, on the grounds that the retraction failed to

meet the standards of Section 3 (such as conspicuousness or timeliness), that the defendant's attorneys' fees be paid if the court determines that the retraction or reply was sufficient under Section 3.

2. The plaintiff's interests in this situation are fully protected under the other fee-shifting rules in this section. In cases in which the court determines that the defendant's retraction or offer of opportunity to reply was not adequate under Section 3, and the plaintiff goes on to prevail in a declaratory judgment action, this section provides for an award of plaintiff's attorneys' fees, which would include fees incurred in the process of litigating the adequacy of the defendant's retraction or opportunity to reply.

3. The party who prevails in a declaratory judgment action will ordinarily recover reasonable attorneys' fees as a matter of course unless that party has prolonged the litigation through the maintenance of vexatious or frivolous positions. The intent of this section is to encourage prompt resolution of defamation disputes by establishing a balance of incentives for both parties to self-critically evaluate their versions of the truth and to be forthcoming in providing the evidence upon which their versions are based to the other side. A prevailing party who is guilty of "sandbagging," by not coming forward with evidence that would have ended the litigation promptly if revealed, may in the discretion of the court be penalized for having litigated in a vexatious or frivolous manner.

4. The fee-shifting provisions of this Act do not apply when neither side elects to pursue the declaratory judgment option and the suit is tried for damages.

Section 11. Limitations Period One Year

This provision should be construed in light of the single publication rule in Section 12.

Section 12. Single Publication Rule

This section adopts the single publication rule, which prevails under current law in most American jurisdictions. The purpose of the section is to bar a multiplicity of actions filed in separate states for the same publication.

Section 13. Severability

In the event that any court should declare invalid any provision of this Act, all other provisions shall continue to be of full force and effect.

Section 14.　Preemption and Jurisdiction

1. The Act is intended to preempt current law with regard to those issues addressed by it and to leave untouched those issues not addressed by it, such as the rules governing disclosure of confidential sources. If enacted as a federal law, the Act will preempt all existing applicable state laws. If enacted as a state law, the Act will preempt current common law rules except where provisions in the Act indicate otherwise.

2. If enacted as federal law, state and federal courts shall have concurrent jurisdiction.

3. If enacted as state law, actions may be brought pursuant to the Act in state courts of competent jurisdiction or federal courts in which diversity and other jurisdictional requirements are met.

AN ANALYSIS OF THE ANNENBERG PROPOSAL

The Perils of Reform

Reform is always difficult, Machiavelli cautioned:

> Because the innovator has for enemies all those who have done well under old conditions, and lukewarm defenders in those who may do well under the new. This coolness arises partly from fear of the opponents, who have the laws on their side, and partly from the incredulity of men, who do not believe in new things until they have a long experience of them.[14]

Reaction to the Annenberg Proposal was extraordinary in its breadth and intensity.[15] The Annenberg recommendations apparently struck a number of responsive chords—not always harmonious[16]—generating a cacophony of public discourse ranging from euphoric praise to excoriating criticism. Virtually every major newspaper in the United States carried stories about the report;[17] many publications ran editorials commenting upon it;[18] a virtual cottage industry of symposia and conferences sprang up in its wake to discuss it.[19] Legislators, bar associations, press organizations, and other groups with influence on public policy took up the report for serious consideration and study.[20]

If nothing else, the Annenberg project has substantially advanced public discussion of libel law, and helped focus debate.[21] The thoughtfulness and drafting clarity of the report drew "bipartisan" praise, even from those skeptical of its substantive recommendations.

Floyd Abrams, a preeminent media attorney, called the report an "exquisitely toned balance."[22] Henry Kaufman described the report as the "most elegant"[23] of all recent libel reform proposals.

The composition of the eleven-member group that participated in formulating the proposal is, to say the least, striking. How could consensus be reached by persons as ideologically diverse as Anthony Lewis, Bruce Fein, Richard Schmidt, and Herbert Schmertz?[24] How could one of General Westmoreland's former lawyers, Anthony Murry, and ardent defense attorneys like Samuel Klein, Roslyn Mazer, and Sandra Baron agree?[25] When one adds to the mix the very different experiences of a distinguished trial judge and libel author, Lois G. Forer,[26] and a leading media insurance expert, Chad Milton,[27] the sweeping agreement of the group seems even more remarkable.

The end product the group produced is not a series of watered-down compromises, a string of lowest common denominators. The group members were not shrinking violets. The debate was rigorous but thoughtful. This was no labor negotiation in which people came to the table willing to treat the First Amendment like a bargaining chip. It was, rather, a conscientious exercise in problem solving. As Milton put it:

> Many of us have adapted to the status quo, such that we may have a financial or emotional attachment to it, and there is always reluctance to try unknown paths. In that regard, this proposal urges us to set aside self-interest and expediency in favor of what is, in my view, the right thing to do.[28]

The Basic Structure and Philosophy of the Proposal

Why is it "the right thing to do?" The Annenberg Libel Reform Project had its genesis in the hypothesis that the current law of libel is not working well for anyone. Plaintiffs, defendants, judges, lawyers, and academics have all criticized the modern law of libel; in practice, it neither adequately protects First Amendment values nor provides plaintiffs with an efficient, meaningful forum for vindicating reputational damage.[29] The Annenberg Libel Reform Act proceeds from the premise that traditional libel suits for money damages are poor vehicles for resolving modern defamation disputes. If one strives to look at the current system objectively and neutrally, without a pro-plaintiff or pro-defendant bias, the case for reform is overpowering.

A society starting from scratch to design the "perfect" legal mechanism for handling libel disputes would never arrive at the current system. It is costly and cumbersome and fails to vindicate either free speech values or the protection of reputation.[30] The enormous defense costs of protracted litigation exert a chilling effect on the press,[31] while plaintiffs are left with no meaningful legal remedy for reputational injury.[32] Libel suits tend to drag on interminably, are enormously costly for both sides, and very rarely end in a clear-cut resolution of what ought to be the heart of the matter: a determination of the truth or falsity of what was published.[33]

If the indictment of the current system is relatively familiar, however, and the theoretical case for reform fundamentally sound, the debate generated by the Annenberg Proposal clearly demonstrates that moving from abstract discussion to concrete proposals is extremely difficult. The question posed by the Annenberg Washington Program's reform proposal is not whether libel law should be reformed but whether the proposal contains the *right* reforms. The Annenberg plan cannot please all the people all the time, but can it please enough of the people enough of the time? As historian Arthur M. Schlesinger, Jr. puts it: "Change is threatening. Innovation may seem an assault on the universe."[34]

The Annenberg report sets forth a comprehensive model Libel Reform Act, designed to encourage the dissemination of truth in the marketplace by emphasizing remedies other than money damages to facilitate the prompt and efficient resolution of defamation disputes. The driving philosophy behind the proposed Libel Reform Act is the conviction that the First Amendment's guarantee of freedom of speech and the law of defamation should function in harmony to serve the compelling public interest in the discovery of truth. The Act sets forth a three-stage process for the resolution of disputes over allegedly defamatory statements, providing incentives for the parties to evaluate their positions early in the controversy and seek a mutually satisfactory resolution of the dispute.

Stage I of the Act imposes a forceful retraction and reply mechanism, requiring every potential plaintiff[35] to seek a retraction or an opportunity to reply from the defendant before filing suit.[36] The plaintiff must seek the retraction or opportunity to reply within thirty days of publication of the defamatory statement;[37] failure to do so bars the plaintiff from later bringing a defamation action against the defendant.[38] If the defendant honors the plaintiff's request within thirty days,[39] no suit may be brought.[40] The plaintiff has the option of choosing to demand a retraction or a reply. If the plaintiff insists on a retraction, the defendant cannot satisfy the demand by offering an opportunity to reply instead. Because the retraction and reply mechanisms in the Act are so powerful—they can instantly end the litigation—and because past experience under such statutory provisions indicates great potential for breakdown on matters of detail, such as timing, length, or placement, the Act and commentary contain a great deal of elaboration governing the specifics of the retraction and reply devices.[41]

Stage II takes effect if the plaintiff and defendant fail to resolve the dispute through the retraction or opportunity to reply provisions of Stage I. If the defendant refuses to grant the plaintiff's request for a retraction or opportunity to reply, the plaintiff may file suit. In Stage II, either the plaintiff or defendant can elect that the suit be tried as an action for declaratory judgment.[42] If either party exercises that option, the plaintiff forfeits the opportunity to pursue money damages,[43] while the defendant loses the protection of constitutional fault requirements (negligence or actual malice, as the case may be).[44]

The only question decided at the declaratory judgment trial is whether the statement at issue was true or false.[45] The burden of proof on this issue is on the plaintiff, and falsity must be established by clear and convincing evidence.[46] The defendant's knowledge, recklessness, negligence, or malice is irrelevant.[47] The final element of the declaratory judgment option is a fee-shifting provision: The losing party must pay the attorneys' fees of the winner.[48]

If neither the plaintiff nor the defendant selects the declaratory judgment option under Stage II, the dispute proceeds to Stage III. Under Stage III, the plaintiff may proceed with an action for damages, which in most respects resembles the traditional defamation action. In an action for damages, the plaintiff must show by clear and convincing evidence that the statement was false and defamatory.[49] Since legislation cannot, of course, modify constitutional doctrines,[50] the Act does not attempt to codify existing First Amendment fault rules. Rather, it sets as a minimum floor a universal requirement of negligence in all cases, leaving to judicial development the imposition of higher fault standards, such as actual malice, in appropriate cases.[51] If successful, the plaintiff may recover only actual damages;[52] the Act eliminates presumed and punitive damages.[53] No fee-shifting provision exists in Stage III; in a damage suit each party must pay its own attorneys' fees.[54]

In addition to the three-stage process for the resolution of libel disputes, the Annenberg Proposal contains a number of other important reforms. The Act eliminates the distinction between media and nonmedia defendants,[55] as well as the distinction between libel and slander.[56] It curtails the use of alternative causes of action, such as infliction of emotional distress and invasion of privacy.[57] The Act strives to clarify the always elusive distinction between fact and opinion by employing a flexible multifactor test for defining opinion, presumptively classifying certain genres of speech, such as "editorials, letters to the editor, editorial cartoons, reviews, parody, satire, and fiction as opinion.[58] Finally, the Act creates a broad "neutral reportage" privilege that protects a defendant who merely quotes another's defamatory statements; if the statements involve matters of public concern, the source is identified and the statements are accurately quoted.[59]

If libel reform is a zero-sum game, then plaintiffs and defendants cannot both be winners under the Annenberg plan. But reform is not always a stark zero-sum exercise—the legal system may get so out of kilter that correctives can actually make life better for both sides.

Do plaintiffs get a fair shake under the Annenberg Proposal? Are the retraction and reply mechanisms fair to plaintiffs, or do they create traps for the unwary? Does the provision eliminating any suit for money damages in the event that the defendant honors, in a timely fashion, the request for a retraction or opportunity for reply, unfairly strip the plaintiff of an entitlement to compensation for reputational injury suffered in the interregnum between the publication of the libel and the issuance of the retraction? Similarly, is it fundamentally unfair to allow the defendant, rather than only the plaintiff, to opt for the declaratory judgment remedy, thereby foreclosing, against the plaintiff's will, any monetary relief other than possible recovery of attorneys' fees? At the very least, could not the Annenberg Proposal have offered a somewhat less harsh compromise for plaintiffs, permitting them to recover special damages—provable, pecuniary, out-of-pocket losses—even when the declaratory judgment procedure is invoked?

Judge Pierre N. Leval, the thoughtful and highly respected federal district judge who presided over the trial between Gen. William Westmoreland and CBS,[60] emerged as the leader of the attack on the Annenberg Proposal from the plaintiff's side. (The Annenberg project included one of General Westmoreland's lawyers among its members,[61] and General Westmoreland himself, at a program examining the Annenberg plan, endorsed the proposal, though he doubted it would have changed events in his case against CBS.[62])

The intensity of Judge Leval's critique caught the members of the Annenberg project by surprise. Judge Leval had authored an article in the *Harvard Law Review*[63] that made precisely the same attack on the regime of *New York Times Co. v. Sullivan* that had driven the Annenberg project members toward their recommendations. Judge Leval had also offered what at first glance appeared to be a solution very similar to the Annenberg plan—the use of a declaratory judgment suit in lieu of a suit for money damages. Where, then, was the disagreement among these two apparent allies?[64]

Judge Leval perceived a number of critical differences between his proposal and the Annenberg plan. In Judge Leval's scheme, resort to a declaratory judgment would be purely voluntary on the plaintiff's part and could not be foisted on the plaintiff against his or her will (an issue discussed in the next section).[65] The judge's most pointed attack, however, was directed toward the Annenberg Proposal's retraction and reply mechanisms, which he characterized as creating a trap for unwary plaintiffs.[66]

The Act bars plaintiffs from bringing suit if they fail to demand a retraction or opportunity to reply within thirty days.[67] Judge Leval found this provision "quite unreasonable."[68] He stated two reasons. First, unschooled plaintiffs may be unaware of the law and thus inadvertently find themselves barred from bringing suit because they failed to demand a retraction or opportunity to reply within the mandated thirty-day period.[69] Second, plaintiffs may only feel the effects of the libel, or only discover the existence of the defamatory statement, after the thirty days has expired.[70] As a result, plaintiffs may not deem it necessary to pursue a retraction or opportunity to reply until after the thirty-day period. In either case, the speaker is not only excused from granting a retraction or opportunity to reply but is immune from suit.[71]

Criticism was also made of the Act's limit on the length of the opportunity to reply. The Act limits the reply to "the length of the material in which the defamatory statements of and concerning the plaintiff were published."[72] Judge Leval harshly faulted the opportunity to reply as "inadequate to plaintiff's needs and . . . unjustifiably unfair to plaintiff."[73] Judge Leval stated four reasons for his objections. First, the Act limits the reply to the plaintiff's own statement; the plaintiff is unable to append supporting statements of knowledgeable third parties. Second, Judge Leval thought that the restriction on the length of the reply is unreasonable.[74] Third, the Act limits the plaintiff's reply "to rebuttal of the defamatory statements."[75] As a result, the plaintiff would be unable, for example, to demonstrate the publisher's malicious intent. Finally, Judge Leval challenged the defendant's right to choose who shall read the plaintiff's statement, in cases involving a radio or television defendant,[76] as denying the public the opportunity "to see and hear the plaintiff's impassioned, moving, personal statement, rather than a perfunctory reading of a denial."[77]

As admirable as Judge Leval's articulate compassion for the interests of plaintiffs surely is, his attacks on the Annenberg Proposal partake of a rhetorically hyperbolic flair that at times distort the Act's provisions. There is nothing in the Act that prohibits a plaintiff from using the normal tools of persuasion and argument in his or her reply, and garnering whatever evidence is available, including citations or quotes from third parties. Nor is the plaintiff prohibited from establishing the defendant's malicious intent, when that proof is probative of truth or falsity.

Written rebuttals, of course, will be in the plaintiff's own words. Judge Leval is right in pointing out that in the case of broadcasts, the Act does not entitle the plaintiff to appear on the air personally. But some concessions to the nature of the medium were necessary if the reply provisions were to have any practical chance of being utilized in the real world.

Judge Leval is also absolutely correct in pointing out that the proposal forces a plaintiff to move swiftly by demanding a retraction or opportunity to reply within thirty days of publication of the libel. The unfairness the judge complains of, however, is functionally indistinguishable from the inherent "unfairness" in any statute of limitations: the law toughmindedly leaves behind plaintiffs who fail to sue within the prescribed period. The debate, then, must be narrowed to the shortness of the deadline, not its existence.

The Annenberg Proposal forces the plaintiff to move fast—but for important reasons. If the Annenberg Proposal were enacted, the tremendous public attention it would receive would make the speedy timetable common knowledge among members of the bar and public alike. Public interest in the prompt resolution of libel disputes justifies the short demand period. Since a central driving philosophy of the proposal is the prompt disposition of libel disputes when the controversy is alive and matters, through resort to counterspeech remedies whenever possible, it makes perfect sense to put both plaintiffs and defendants on a fast track for the pursuit of such remedies. The plaintiff is *not* forced to file suit in this period but merely to demand a retraction or reply—a demand that starts an equally fast clock ticking against the defendant.

Judge Leval's arguments do illuminate one easily corrected oversight in the Annenberg retraction and provisions, however. Either through judicial construction or amendment of the Act's provisions, an exception should be made for plaintiffs who could not, through the exercise of reasonable care, have known about the publication. This would in effect toll the thirty-day period in situations analogous to "latent condition" cases in products liability or medical malpractice litigation. It will be a rare case when the plaintiff is not very quickly aware of a libelous publication, but when such lack of knowledge does exist and is not the plaintiff's fault, Judge Leval's point is well taken.

On a broader level, Judge Leval's critique of the retraction and reply mechanisms fail to take into account the fact that plaintiffs have an absolute option to choose which of those two demands they will insist on, and in the event of any ambiguity, the request will be construed as a demand for a retraction. As the official commentary to the Act explains:

> The plaintiff always has an absolute right to demand a retraction in the first instance. (This provision is not to be a trap for the unwary plaintiff. If there is ambiguity as to whether the plaintiff has requested a retraction or a reply, the request is to be construed as one for a retraction.) A plaintiff who specifically demands a retraction, not an opportunity to reply, is entitled to a retraction before litigation is barred. Therefore, a defendant faced with such a plaintiff may not avoid litigation merely by offering an opportunity to reply. The rationale for this provision is that the plaintiff has a right to a full repudiation of the defamation by the defendant, instead of the mere opportunity to reply, before the plaintiff is stripped of any litigation remedy.[78]

Most fundamentally, however, many of Judge Leval's criticisms of the reply and retraction mechanisms fail to take into account the ultimate intention and assumption of the drafters: that the reforms will work. The whole point of these provisions is to defuse and derail libel litigation at an early stage by resort to retraction and reply remedies whenever possible. The Annenberg project members had to ask, Why don't retraction and reply remedies seem to work today, and what can be done to make them work?

First, many states have no retraction or reply laws in place. Second, the provisions are often shot full of confusing loopholes and exceptions.[79] Third, the provisions do not end litigation but merely diminish the amount or types of damages recoverable.[80] Fourth, and perhaps most critical, the provisions are so general and ill defined in substance and procedure that the parties inevitably dissemble into disputes over timing, sufficiency, and placement.[81]

Retraction and reply remedies are paper tigers unless they really count for something, like an end to litigation, and are drafted to anticipate most of the squabbles and objections that plaintiffs and defendants are likely to put forward. They must provide balanced and clear language establishing the rules of the game. A meaningful reply provision simply must have a clearly delineated "who, what, when, and where."

Take, for example, the question of length—one of Judge Leval's principal points of attack. There is simply no avoiding this issue. If the law is to provide for a reply, then the question must be addressed: How long can it be? Is it to be limited to a length confined to the few damning phrases that actually contain the "smoking gun" language on which the dispute is based? Or should there be no limitation— should plaintiffs be entitled to all the print space or broadcast time they want to rebut the defamatory charges?

Judge Leval is too uncharitable in his characterization of Annenberg to answer this question, acting as if the drafters chose the first option, unduly crimping the opportunity for a meaningful response. In fact, however, the proposal takes an intermediate position precisely because an intermediate position is most likely to actually be palatable to, and invoked by, both sides. The proposal then takes great care to define the contours of this middle position. The Act states that the "defendant may require that the reply not exceed the length of the material in which the defamatory statements of and concerning the plaintiff were published, and that its form reasonably accommodate the nature of the medium in which it is to be published."[82] The Act further requires that the reply "must be concise and limited to rebuttal of the defamatory statements."[83] The official commentary to this provision meets all of Judge Leval's concerns head on:

> The phrase "length of the material" refers to that portion of the prior communication in which the allegedly defamatory statements of and concerning the plaintiff were made. This length may be as great as that of an entire story or broadcast segment, for example, but only if the entire story or broadcast segment contained defamatory material of and concerning the plaintiff. Indeed, the reply will normally be longer than the single sentence or sentences in which the actual defamatory statements were made, if the story or segment included other material that could have been reasonably understood as supporting or explaining the defamatory statements. An entire 10-paragraph article, for example, may be completely devoted to defamatory material of and concerning the plaintiff, even though only three sentences contain the actual defamatory language giving rise to the plaintiff's complaint. In such a case, the plaintiff would be entitled to reply space equal to the length of the entire article. On the other hand, a 10-paragraph article may contain three sentences actually defamatory of the plaintiff, within three paragraphs elaborating on those sentences. The rest of the article may not concern the plaintiff. In such a case, the length of the reply could be limited by the defendant to three paragraphs.[84]

This provision, of course, is a compromise. But it is a fair compromise and a practical one. Like many other provisions of the Act, it will force both sides in a defamation dispute to give a little. That, however, is exactly the point: With each side forced by the law to give a little, both sides, and the public, gain a lot.

Among the Annenberg Proposal's most dramatic features are its provisions entirely eliminating any recovery for money damages. This can occur two ways: if the defendant honors the plaintiff's request for a retraction or reply or if either the plaintiff or the defendant opts for the declaratory judgment.

Criticism of these features exists on two levels. Some strenuously object to the whole idea of ever stripping a plaintiff of the right to sue for money.[85] Others concede that it may be sound public policy to limit, or abolish altogether, monetary recovery in some defamation cases. These critics make a much more subtle and discriminating argument. In cases in which there is a retraction or opportunity to reply offered, or in which a declaratory judgment remedy is obtained, there should be limited special damages recovery. This recovery should be for the plaintiff's pecuniary out-of-pocket losses suffered prior to the date of the retraction, reply, or declaratory judgment.[86]

To reveal a bit of the "legislative history" of the Annenberg report, this issue was among the most hotly debated and painstakingly explored questions taken up by the project members. After great wailing and gnashing of teeth, the group reached surprising unanimity, voting unanimously to permit defendants to opt for the no-damages declaratory judgment procedure even against the will of plaintiffs, and voting 10–1 (with Judge Lois G. Forer the only dissenter) not to permit "interregnum" special damages—damages accumulated prior to the issuance of the retraction or reply or the declaratory judgment. The Annenberg group's thought processes on this issue provide an important key to understanding the entire Annenberg report. Certainly, there will be some plaintiffs who will suffer demonstrable damages and nonetheless be shut out by a defendant who opts for the declaratory judgment procedure. Reforms, however, must be designed for the large run of cases,[87] and there are reasons for believing that most plaintiffs will be much better off under the proposal.[88] Plaintiffs who get a speedy judicial declaration that the defamatory statements leveled against them were false, and who get attorneys' fees, are better off under the proposal than under current law.[89] Most plaintiffs will in fact be made whole by such a declaratory remedy. After all appeals are exhausted, most plaintiffs lose under existing law. Under the proposal, those with meritorious claims on the issue of truth or falsity will at least have a fighting chance.

But why not permit plaintiffs who prevail at the declaratory judgment stage to still recover for special damages—provable pecuni-

ary loses? The answer is fundamental to the entire debate over the
Annenberg plan: Under current constitutional rules, making this
concession would cause the whole structure of the Annenberg Proposal to unravel.

At least when the speech concerns matters of public interest, the
First Amendment rules emanating from the *Sullivan,*[90] *Gertz,*[91] and
Greenmoss[92] decisions preclude the awarding of money damages without fault. Money damages may only be awarded on a finding of actual
malice in public-figure and public-official cases, and on a finding of
negligence in private-figure cases. These rules have a profound impact on the options available for reform. Any libel legislation that
allows money damages to be awarded must include a trial over the
defendant's fault. If the Annenberg Proposal allowed the plaintiff to
elect to sue on a no-fault basis and still recover some damages, it
would thus be plainly unconstitutional under existing cases. (The
Annenberg Proposal does permit recovery of attorneys' fees under
the no-fault declaratory judgment procedure. The question whether
recovery of attorneys' fees without fault is constitutional is explored
later in this chapter.)[93]

It would be possible, however, to construct a hybrid declaratory
judgment procedure in which, following the no-fault trial on truth or
falsity, there would be a separate trial on special damages. This trial
could be, as constitutionally mandated, predicated on fault. But this
would be a disaster, undermining the entire Annenberg plan and
defeating the whole purpose of the declaratory judgment innovation.
It would open up every case to a minitrial on special damages and
fault, eviscerating the streamlining purpose of the declaratory judgment procedure.

This may well be what some critics want, at least if their real
objection is to the whole notion of eliminating money damages. We
have been conditioned for two centuries to think reflexively of money
damages as the appropriate legal remedy for all tortuous harms,
including libel. For those who cannot escape that mind-set, there is no
hope of conversion to the Annenberg plan, or any plan remotely like
it. If one is willing to realize, however, that the traditional suit for
money damages has proven to be an exceptionally poor vehicle for
meaningful reputational redress, then one must be willing to roll up
the sleeves and push the pencil in attempting to devise a balanced
alternative. As tempting as a special damages exception is, there does
not appear to be any way out of the box posed by First Amendment
fault requirements and the resulting minitrial dilemma.

There is a final possibility to be explored. Should special damages
still be permitted in those cases in which the *defendants* have chosen

the declaratory judgment option? Should the Annenberg Proposal have provided for a special damages recovery only in those cases? It may be that it is constitutionally mandated that a no-fault trial be a no-damages trial when the no-fault trial comes at the plaintiff's election. Plaintiffs cannot have their cake (not even that part of the cake represented by special damages) and eat it too; they cannot recover money damages and still opt out of all First Amendment fault burdens.

In those cases in which the defendant chooses the declaratory judgment option, however, the policy call is much closer, for the constitutional dimension drops out. When the plaintiff has sued for money damages and it is the defendant who plays the declaratory judgment trump card, the defendant has voluntarily waived its First Amendment protection. In such cases the defendant could have obtained a traditional suit governed by *Sullivan* or *Gertz* merely by not exercising the declaratory judgment option.

The Constitution should not be challenged by putting it to the defendant to agree that, if the declaratory judgment option is chosen, the defendant will also be exposed to special damages liability on a no-fault basis. Presumably, defendants confident that no special damages exist (and they almost *never* do exist, really[94]) would still be willing in many cases to choose the declaratory judgment option and take their chances on special damages. (Note that a plaintiff who makes frivolous claims for special damages might be penalized under the provisions of the Act governing the shifting of attorneys' fees.[95]) On the other hand, when special damages do indeed exist, the defendant can always stay away from the declaratory judgment option and stick with a traditional damage suit, with its constitutional fault provisions.[96]

This modification of the Annenberg plan as originally written would only require plaintiffs to forfeit all damage recovery when plaintiffs have chosen the declaratory judgment procedure. When the choice is exercised by defendants, plaintiffs would still have a special damages "loophole" available.

The Annenberg project did not elect this alternative, primarily on the policy judgment that the net gains for those few plaintiffs with genuine out-of-pocket damages are dwarfed by the net social losses (including all plaintiffs, defendants, and the costs to the legal system) in creating any exceptions to the no-damages rule at the declaratory judgment stage. Defendants, it was thought, would not exercise the declaratory judgment option for fear that the definition of "special damages" would prove too elastic a restraint on a plaintiff's recovery. Defendants would fear exposing themselves to strict-liability risks for what are really traditional nonpecuniary reputational injuries. This concern was further augmented by other values that were influential on the Annenberg project members: simplicity, symmetry, and streamlining. If the very complexity of libel law is one of the major indictments against the current system, then simplicity should be an important "tie breaker" when all other considerations are in rough equipoise.

This is, however, one of the several judgments in the Annenberg Proposal on which it is not merely true that "reasonable persons could differ" but also that a different conclusion could be reached without upsetting the entire structure of the plan. Thus, a "modified Annenberg," so to speak, that granted special damages on a no-fault basis when the defendant exercises the declaratory judgment option, might still be feasible—though, on balance, inferior.

From the perspective of the press, does the pursuit of libel reform make any sense? Even the simple proposition that libel law *needs* reform is controversial. From the defense viewpoint, certainly, a case may be made for the status quo. Many media lawyers, pointing to the declining number of libel suits and the increasing success rate of the media in combatting libel actions, question any need for libel reform.[97]

Several years ago, an air of crisis existed within the defense bar. Suits against the press were increasing, and so were multi-million-dollar damage awards. The libel insurance market was rapidly deteriorating. Supreme Court Justices were hinting that *Gertz v. Robert Welch, Inc.*,[98] and perhaps even *New York Times Co. v. Sullivan*,[99] should be reexamined.[100] And the *Sharon v. Time, Inc.*[101] and *Westmoreland v. CBS*[102] suits were in full swing, seeming to symbolize the escalating libel threat.

The crisis, however, ran its course. Most media defendants have recently experienced an easing in the number of libel suits they are facing.[103] Insurance markets have adjusted. The siege on the citadel has abated. The Supreme Court in *Hustler Magazine Inc. v. Falwell*,[104] through none other than Chief Justice William Rehnquist, went out of its way to endorse the basic principles of *Sullivan* and *Gertz*. And the failure of either Defense Minister Ariel Sharon or Gen. William Westmoreland to prevail in their suit illustrated to plaintiffs (and to the plaintiff's bar) the apparent futility of bucking the First Amendment in a libel action. Defendants had reached the winter of their discontent.

The case for libel reform, however, was no less compelling in 1989 than it was in 1986. Indeed, the time for reform is never in the heat of a crisis but after it, in the quiet between storms. Defendants may not feel threatened at the moment, but there is no reason whatsoever to think that the libel crisis of 1986 could not suddenly reappear. Trends in litigation come and go. Underlying conditions have not changed. Plaintiffs are still quite capable of suing, often for hidden agendas. Judges are still quite capable of denying defense motions for summary judgment. Juries are still prone to return large verdicts. Some of these megaverdicts may still be affirmed on appeal.[105] And even though defendants have every reason to expect that their excellent record at the appellate level will continue, so will the high litigation costs of a system that provides most of its defense protection at the back end, rather than the front end, of the litigation. Even if utterly unmoved by any feelings of sympathy for plaintiffs, the press thus has every reason to thoughtfully explore reform.

Many members of the press, it should be said, are not unwilling to pursue reform. They are, however, unwilling to leave their fate in the hands of either state legislatures or the U.S. Congress.[106] The press fears that the political process of legislative enactment could distort the Annenberg Proposal and thus upset the delicate balance of the Annenberg Libel Reform Act as written.[107] The media also worries that legislators will seek intentionally to add repressive features to the Act.[108] On balance, many press representatives prefer a methodical, deliberate, case-by-case approach to reform.[109] The current system may be the best indictment of this argument. The sweeping structural changes contemplated by the Annenberg plan, such as the retraction-and-reply provision, simply could not be accomplished by judicial decision. More significant, case-by-case development could never create the mechanism at the heart of the Annenberg plan, the declaratory judgment procedure. Debate over that element of the Annenberg plan emerged as the primary battleground over the proposal.

Many defense representatives voiced fears concerning the declaratory judgment provisions of the Annenberg Proposal. The Act's removal of the defendant's First Amendment safeguards in a declaratory judgment trial creates a frightening Faustian bargain, and many press lawyers are understandably wary about surrendering the constitutional protections that have provided them an effective shield from libel judgments for the last twenty-five years.[110] Feeling safe under the present law, they are unwilling to venture into the Act's unknown legal world.[111] According to C. Thomas Dienes, a highly respected media lawyer and academic, for most media defendants, "the potential savings in litigation costs from a declaratory judgment alternative [are not] worth the loss of the constitutional privilege, with the high probability of a media win."[112]

The press critique has centered on three themes: (1) the proposal would generate an increase in frivolous litigation; (2) the proposal places an unrealistic and antispeech emphasis on litigation over "truth"; and (3) the shifting provisions for attorneys' fees entail liability without fault in violation of the First Amendment.

Would the statute trigger an increase in frivolous litigation? This fear is grounded in the suspicion that plaintiffs will file suits and immediately opt for the declaratory judgment option in which they no longer face the impediment of proving actual malice (or negligence, in private-figure cases) and may receive the bonus of attorneys' fees if they prevail. Abrams warned: "The main danger of the proposal is that it could lead to an explosion of new libel litigation in which people seek declarations that something said about them was not true."[113] Others claimed that the focus of litigation would shift merely from the defendant's fault under current law to other contentious points under the proposed Act.[114] Some critics believe "suits are just as likely to be fought over a journalist's viewpoint, or opinion, or over the plaintiff's interpretation of the facts presented."[115] Other commentators point to the current litigation involving state retraction statutes as evidence of the Act's potential for increased litigation.[116] Many plaintiffs under the current libel system "assert legally suspect claims [in an effort to] put pressure on the defense to settle a legally meritless action."[117] By removing the media protections established in *Sullivan,* the Act thus arguably encourages plaintiffs to file frivolous suits to harass the media.

These fears are reasonable. They present the types of questions that can never be satisfactorily resolved until the statute is actually enacted somewhere and tried for several years. There are, however, reasons to believe that many of these fears are ungrounded. First, it must be remembered that every would-be plaintiff must, within thirty days of the publication of the defamatory statement, file a demand for a retraction or opportunity to reply as a prerequisite to filing suit.[118] This request "must specify the statements claimed to be false and defamatory and must set forth the plaintiff's version of the facts."[119] The defendant then has thirty days to respond and may absolutely bar litigation by honoring the plaintiff's request.[120] This is a powerful defense option, for the defendant who has in fact been "caught redhanded" in a mistake now has the ability to completely eliminate exposure to litigation. More significantly, when the plaintiff's only complaint is that the published story contained defamatory implications, the defendant may avoid suit simply by retracting the implication.[121]

Second, even in the absence of a retraction or reply barring the suit, the plaintiff faces downside risks that work to deter frivolous suits. The declaratory judgment mode is not a perfectly level playing field but rather has a bias designed to protect First Amendment interests. The plaintiff has the burden of proving falsity and must meet that burden with "clear and convincing" evidence.[122] Much more significantly, plaintiffs must deal with the risk that they will be forced to pay the defendant's attorneys' fees if they do not prevail.[123]

Third, the statute very carefully circumscribes the range of statements that qualify as defamatory. No statute will ever completely solve the intractable problem of separating statements of fact from statements of opinion.[124] The Annenberg Proposal, however, contains an elaborate definition of opinion that goes a long way toward insulating certain genres of speech by presumptively classifying them as opinion, including fiction; satire or parody; artistic, athletic, literary, academic, culinary, theatrical, religious, or political commentary; letters to the editor; editorials; and editorial cartoons.[125]

Fourth, if no statute will ever eliminate all problems of separating fact from opinion, a statute may come close to eliminating exposure to suit for neutral reportage.[126] The proposal contains a broad neutral reportage privilege. The Act bars liability for the mere repetition of the defamatory statements of others, provided the quote is accurately reported, involves a matter of public interest, and the source is identified.[127]

Finally, the fear of frivolous suits is mitigated by the fact that the Annenberg Proposal requires plaintiffs to "put up or shut up." Plaintiffs must be able to articulate prior to suit what the facts are and must have confidence in their ability to prove them.[128] Under the current system, plaintiffs have their own ability to "hide" behind *Sullivan*. They can file suit and then blame their failure to recover on the First Amendment. Under the proposal, the nuisance suit carries the risk of deeper embarrassment and liability for attorneys' fees.[129]

The opening sentence of the Annenberg Libel Reform Act Preamble states, "[T]he purpose of this Act is to provide an efficient and speedy remedy for defamation, emphasizing the compelling public interest in the dissemination of truth in the marketplace."[130] This bold assertion sets the philosophical tone for the entire proposal. There is no doubt where the Annenberg statute is coming from, but in truth, it carries some heavy baggage.

Perhaps Emily Dickinson had it right when she admonished to "Tell all the truth but tell it slant":

> Tell all the truth but tell it slant—
> Success in Circuit lies

> Too bright for our infirm Delight
> The Truth's superb surprise
> As Lightning to the Children eased
> With explanation kind
> The truth must dazzle gradually
> Or every man be blind—[131]

The Annenberg Proposal has been criticized for *not* "telling it slant," for elevating "truth" on a pedestal that is both unrealistic and unconstitutional. This attack on the Annenberg proposal proceeds on two levels: (1) that the proposal is naive, assuming that "truth" is determinable (or that it exists at all); and (2) that it is "Orwellian," contemplating a "truth trial" that is antithetical to the Holmes/Brandeis First Amendment tradition of a marketplace of ideas.

The Annenberg Proposal has thus been criticized as forcing "judicial determinations of the often-elusive concept of truth,"[132] and for "grossly underestimating the difficulty of determining truth/falsity."[133] To make matters worse, proving "truth" is typically the most costly part of a libel defense.[134] George Vrandenberg III, vice president and general counsel of CBS, views the proposal "as anti-speech," one that "strikes at the heart of the concept that speakers are not guarantors of truth."[135] Chicago press lawyer Don Reuben agrees, charging virulently that the Act would discourage aggressive reporting. "If the publisher abandons all the constitutional defenses accorded to him by the [First] Amendment to avoid paying damages," Reuben argues, "It becomes easier for plaintiffs to prevail and thus more likely that there will be harm to the reporter's professional reputation and standing."[136] According to Reuben, the media will be less willing to fight for its reporters if the threat of large damage awards no longer exists. As a result, he predicts, the Act "will likely chill the hell out of the working press, the reporter, and the editor."[137]

In answering these critiques, one must separate serious philosophical objections from rhetorical hyperbole. The "truth" attacks are, unfortunately, often misleading, for they are often attacks not really aimed at the Annenberg Proposal's method of litigating truth but rather at the possibility of liability without fault as part of the declaratory judgment scheme. It is not so much truth as liability without fault that is the sore point. The proof of this is quite straightforward: The Annenberg Proposal contains *nothing* in its mechanism for determining truth more onerous to the press than existing law. Indeed, the Annenberg proposal is in several respects more generous than existing law.

First, The Annenberg Proposal adopts the "substantial truth" concept—if the "gist" or "sting" of the defamatory charge is accurate, the plaintiff may not prevail merely by demonstrating minor inaccuracies of detail.[138] Second, the Act requires the plaintiff to fear the burden of proof on the issue of truth or falsity in all cases—going beyond current constitutional requirements.[139] Finally, through its expansive protections for opinion and neutral reportage,[140] the Annenberg proposal narrows the range of actionable dispute over truth or falsity far more than existing law.

That the attack on the "truth-centricity" of the Annenberg Proposal is disingenuous is further demonstrated by the inexorable logical force of one elemental proposition: It is impossible to design any libel system that does not include truth or falsity as an issue for litigation. Libel is, at base, a lie. If it is to be litigated, courts must determine who is a liar and who is not. To assault the Annenberg plan for placing truth on a "pedestal" is thus misleading and deflects debate from a far more serious concern. For, it is not the Annenberg Proposal's mechanism for litigating truth that ought to be debated but its mechanism for determining truth without regard to fault.

The various provisions of the proposal are meant to work together, to create a matrix of incentives that encourage both sides to examine their position self-critically and seek to settle in the early stages of the dispute. Philosophically, these incentives combine to make the prompt dissemination of truth in the marketplace the central driving purpose of the reform, and the elimination of fault at the declaratory judgment stage is indeed integral to that scheme. But this is no reason to characterize the Annenberg plan as having some sort of perverse preoccupation with truth in which the First Amendment has been sacrificed on truth's altar.

In the final analysis, the only test of truth is the market, and government has no business declaring it, in the Annenberg libel reform statute or anywhere else. Nothing in the Annenberg Proposal, however, diminishes the classic dictum that "[i]f there is any fixed star in our constitutional constellation, it is that no official, high or petty, can prescribe who shall be orthodox in politics, nationalism, religion, or other matters of opinion."[141]

There are some who treat the dictum prohibiting governmental declarations of orthodoxy as prohibiting any governmental determinations of truth. This argument, however, proves too much. For if followed to its logical end, it would unravel even the current law of libel in which the judicial system does, after all, purport to pass on truth or falsity as part of the litigation. Truth, under the Annenberg Proposal, is made to stand naked in the declaratory judgment procedure, without the protective clothing of *Sullivan*. But freedom of speech is not left more exposed by this statute. When all of the proposal's provisions are taken in combination, free speech values are enhanced while worthy plaintiffs are offered a meaningful remedy. This net effect is the ultimate question posed by the Annenberg Proposal. It is a question wrapped up in what some have called the Achilles heel of the entire Annenberg plan, the constitutionality of the fee-shifting provision of the declaratory judgment procedure.

Is it constitutional to expose a defendant to liability for attorneys' fees without the benefit of the actual malice or negligence fault protections of *Sullivan* and *Gertz*?[142] The argument against the constitutionality of the Act is a straightforward syllogism:

1. The First Amendment principles of *Sullivan* and *Gertz* bar liability for damages without fault.
2. Liability for attorneys' fees cannot be distinguished from liability for money damages.
3. The Annenberg proposal's imposition of liability for attorneys' fees without fault is unconstitutional.

Abrams, whose reaction to the Annenberg Proposal was generally (but guardedly) favorable, questions the constitutionality of the declaratory judgment provision on these grounds.[143] Richard Winfield, another prominent press attorney who reacted positively to most of the Annenberg Proposal, similarly questioned this element of the declaratory judgment mechanism, calling it the plan's "Achilles heel."[144]

The defense of the fee-shifting device in the declaratory judgment stage contains two principal arguments: (1) historically a distinction has been made between substantive legal rules governing immunity and rules governing litigation costs and attorneys' fees; (2) the fee-shifting provision must not be examined in isolation from the rest of the Annenberg proposal. If the "net chilling effect" of all of the Act's provisions on free speech is less than existing law under *Sullivan* and *Gertz*, then as a package the entire plan, including the fee-shifting provision, is constitutional.

Only legal minds would elevate the distinction between "substance" and "procedure" to roughly the importance of the law of gravity in the world of physics.[145] Yet there is a powerful tradition of distinguishing rules of substance from rules of procedure, and part of that tradition includes the legitimacy of subjecting litigants who have been given a substantive law litigation advantage to procedural rules that are neutral in operation.[146] The First Amendment area has long been a fertile ground for litigation on this point. At times, special procedural rules more protective of free speech interests have been imposed on litigation, to reinforce substantive constitutional principles.[147] At other times, however, First Amendment litigation has been held subject to whatever procedural rules would otherwise apply, on the theory that the substantive law provisions provide sufficient constitutional protection, and that additional procedural safeguards would be an overprotective form of "double counting."[148] This notion of procedural neutrality has been invoked a number of times by the Supreme Court in the libel area.[149]

As is so often the case, in the few instances in which the distinction between substance and procedure really matters, it proves to be an illusive distinction to apply. How should the fee-shifting provision of the Annenberg plan be characterized?

It would be facile to dismiss it as "merely procedural." Money is money, and if a defendant writes a check for $200,000 at the end of the case, how can it make a constitutional difference that the check is for attorneys' fees rather than compensatory or punitive damages? More important, the fee-shifting provision is included in the Annenberg plan as part of the overall *substantive* balance. It would be duplicitous to tout the fee-shifting device as part of the Act's carefully constructed balance of interests and then to turn around and pretend as if it doesn't count when the constitutionality of the Act is assailed. How, then, should this use of an attorneys' fees rule that is "procedural," but designed to affect the substantive balance, be analyzed?

The closest existing analogy is the experience under the Civil Rights Attorneys' Fees Awards Act of 1976.[150] The Civil Rights Attorneys' Fees Awards Act allows recovery for prevailing parties in actions brought under various federal civil rights acts.[151] In many civil rights actions, however, governmental entities and public-official defendants often enjoy either qualified or absolute immunity from liability for damages.[152] Even in situations in which the defendant enjoys immunity from damages, the plaintiff is nevertheless permitted to sue for declaratory and injunctive relief.[153]

In current federal civil rights practice, this from time to time presents a situation analogous to the Annenberg declaratory judgment mechanism: A defendant immunized from liability pursuant to substantive law immunity rules is nevertheless a losing party for the purposes of declaratory or injunctive relief. May such a defendant be saddled with attorneys' fees? In *Supreme Court of Virginia v. Virginia Consumers Union*,[154] the Supreme Court said yes. Notwithstanding the substantive law immunities cloaking the defendants (Justices on the Supreme Court of Virginia) with protection against money damages liability, they could still be subjected to the fee-shifting provisions of the Civil Rights Attorneys' Fees Awards Act.

The analogy here is tighter than it might at first appear. The substantive law immunities in federal civil rights practice are almost identical in jurisprudential function to the immunities created under *Sullivan* and its progeny. Like the actual malice requirement of *Sullivan*, the prevailing doctrine for official immunity under *Harlow v. Fitzgerald*[155] exists to permit adequate breathing space for the performance by executive officiants of their discretionary functions. Indeed, the Supreme Court has been consistently more concerned with reducing "chilling effects" on governmental officiants than on members of the press. In discussing the balance of interests posed by qualified official immunity, the Court has included as among the social costs "the expenses of litigation, the diversion of official energy . . . [and] the danger that fear of being sued will 'dampen the ardor of all but the most resolute, or the most irresponsible [public officials] in the unflinching discharge of their duties.' "[156]

This exceptional sensitivity to the "self-censorship" by officials is all the press has always hoped for after *Sullivan* for itself, but never received. The substantive law doctrines created by the Supreme Court today make it harder to sue a public official and win damages than to sue a newspaper and win damages. But *despite that,* the Court has also permitted attorneys' fees against such officials, even when the plaintiff's victory is merely declaratory or injunctive.[157]

Analogies are indispensable to legal argument but seldom dispositive. The experience under the Civil Rights Attorneys' Fees Awards Act should be enough to defeat mechanical reliance on the simplistic syllogism equating attorneys' fees to damages as establishing an open and shut case against the Annenberg Proposal. The matter proves to be rather more open.

The analogy to the federal civil rights practice, however, only proves that it is possible to treat attorneys' fees differently from money damages. It does not prove that the balance of interest struck by the Annenberg Proposal makes it an appropriate candidate for such treatment.

On this point, everything discussed in this article comes full circle. It is as elementary as *Marbury v. Madison*[158] that no act of legislation may modify the Constitution. The First Amendment has been interpreted by the Supreme Court as outlawing money damages without fault in most libel cases. If damages include attorneys' fees, the game is over for this provision of the Annenberg plan, pure and simple. In making that interpretation, however, thoughtful reviewing courts will be forced to look at how this fee-shifting rule fits into the overall matrix of criss-crossing incentives in the Annenberg plan. The plaintiff, after all, also bears the risk of paying the defendant's attorneys' fees.[159] Many other provisions of the Annenberg Proposal similarly exert restraining pressures on the plaintiff[160] or provide mitigating relief for defendants.[161] The best question to ask of the Annenberg Proposal's fee-shifting rule is thus a question of wider focus: Taken as a whole, does the Act increase or decrease the chilling effect on defendants? If in combination the provisions of the plan advance rather than retract the First Amendment principles of *Sullivan*, the plan should be declared constitutional.

Constitutional principles cannot be applied with such stilted, stagnant lack of imagination that all innovative legislative alternatives are doomed. *Sullivan* applied one set of correctives to one mode of dealing with libel disputes. The Court said, in effect, "If your libel system is going to be constructed this way (traditional tort suits for damages) then you must add these fault rules." The Court did not say, however, that the libel system *must* be constructed in the traditional way, nor did it say what rules it would impose on imaginative alternatives.

What is the "net chilling effect" of the Annenberg Proposal? For the reasons detailed throughout this chapter, the conviction of the project membership is that as a package it is more generous to free speech values than the existing system, even under *Sullivan*. In the end, however, that judgment rests on empirical assumptions about the behavior of plaintiffs and defendants that will never be convincingly proved or disproved until the statute is tested for a number of years in action. And for that, some bold and innovative legislature must give it a try.

Commentary from the defense perspective on the Annenberg Proposal has been dominated largely by mainstream corporate media interests. The Annenberg Proposal, however, applies to small media outlets and to nonmedia suits every bit as much as the corporate press, and attention is owed to their concerns.[162]

Smaller press outlets have tended to be more enthusiastic about the Annenberg Proposal than the larger, more powerful media voices. This is the same pattern that was observed by Rep. Charles E. Schumer (D-N.Y.), in reaction to the declaratory judgment bill he introduced in Congress, a bill that contained several provisions picked up in the Annenberg package.[163] For small media outlets—college or "alternative" radio stations, the neighborhood newspaper, flyers, newsletters and magazines distributed by public interest groups, churches, or neighborhood organizations, and the rich and diverse collection of underground and avant garde "readers" and "voices" distributed free of charge throughout U.S. cities, the Annenberg Proposal offers many improvements on the existing libel system. The Annenberg Proposal's emphasis on nonmonetary remedies may be particularly helpful in alleviating the special chill on First Amendment freedoms that the existing system places on small media. These small media outlets may be much more intimidated by the threat of punishing damage awards than their larger corporate counterparts and are far less able to absorb the costs of attorneys' fees and the drain on staff resources that accompany protracted litigation.[164] In combination, the retraction, reply, and declaratory judgment devices offer small media significantly less exposure to catastrophic loss.

From the beginning of the modern First Amendment era in libel law there has been considerable debate over whether principles enunciated in cases such as *Gertz v. Robert Welch, Inc.*[165] should be deemed applicable to nonmedia defendants.[166] When the plaintiff was a public official or public figure, decisions generally held that the actual-malice standard governed even against nonmedia speakers.[167] When the plaintiff was a private figure, however, some states specifically held *Gertz* inapplicable to nonmedia defendants.[168]

The Supreme Court has never clearly resolved the issue,[169] but there are indications that a majority of the Court believes that the same First Amendment rules should govern all libel cases, without regard to the media or nonmedia states of the defendant.[170] In *Dun & Bradstreet, Inc. v. Greenmoss Builders, Inc.*,[171] none of the Justices chose to rely on the media/nonmedia distinction,[172] and the opinions of Justice White[173] and Justice Brennan[174] (joined by Justices Marshall, Blackmun, and Stevens) rejected the distinction outright.[175]

The Annenberg Proposal similarly rejects any distinction between media and nonmedia defendants.[176] All provisions of the Annenberg Libel Reform Act apply to private-figure nonmedia defamation actions every bit as much as defamation suits brought by a powerful government official against the *New York Times.*

The Annenberg Proposal nevertheless recognizes that nonmedia defamation disputes may often present circumstances quite distinct from typical media cases.[177] Defamation arising from employees suing former employers after termination provide perhaps the best example of a burgeoning area of defamation practice involving fact patterns substantially different from the standard libel suit aimed against the press. Rather than carve a separate law of libel for such cases, however, the Annenberg Proposal instructs courts to construe the Act flexibly and liberally so as to vindicate the Act's purposes in the wide variety of different factual circumstances in which defamation may occur. In this respect, the Annenberg project proceeds from the conviction that the defamation system in the private, nonmedia context also has a great deal to gain from an emphasis on nonpecuniary, counterspeech remedies. In the context of workplace defamation, for example, the employee wronged by a libelous letter of recommendation may utilize the retraction or declaratory judgment remedies to secure a correction of his or her work record when it is most important—quickly after termination when the employee is seeking a new job. Employers, on the other hand, are relieved somewhat from the burden of libel suits brought as a substitute for wrongful discharge actions, largely for their nuisance value.

POSTSCRIPT

The material contained in this chapter has been maintained essentially as I initially wrote it, to preserve the integrity of the "historical record" on the Annenberg plan. I have now come to the view, however, that the Annenberg Proposal, as originally written is a "dog that won't hunt," and that a "modified Annenberg" proposal is preferable.

From the beginning of the libel reform debate, the notion of some form of declaratory judgment or "truth trial" mechanism has been a sore point. I have now come to the conclusion that if any meaningful libel reform package is ever to be adopted, this mechanism must not be included. The only declaratory judgment device that I now support is one that is voluntarily agreed to by both sides.

I have come to this view for several reasons. The first is pragmatic. It is now clear to me that the institutional press will never be convinced that this mechanism is either wise policy or constitutional. Any reform package that includes some form of involuntary truth trial will be virulently opposed by most of the media bar and mainstream press organizations. The opposition would be intense and organized. If I were overwhelmingly confident that the declaratory judgment mechanism is "the right thing to do," I would not shy away from a cataclysmic battle. I continue to believe that, as structured in the Annenberg Proposal, the overall balance struck in that proposal would have produced a level of protection for the press *greater* than that of *Sullivan,* while still improving the lot for plaintiffs.

I understand, of course, that many people whom I respect and regard as friends have criticized Annenberg from both the defense's and the plaintiff's perspectives. But I think that debate is now beside the point. I am now convinced that we tried to do too much at once in the Annenberg plan, and that as a practical matter, no legislature will enact that entire plan "as is." And so one must have the intellectual flexibility and practical judgment to assess the debate as it now stands.

Finally, I have come to the conclusion that the ultimate empirical question whether the declaratory judgment device will or will not excessively chill free speech cannot be separated from the question of psychological perception. There is a self-fulfilling quality to the phenomenon of chilling effects: If reporters *perceive* the declaratory judgment as oppressive, they will act as if it is oppressive. Chill, if you will, is in the mind of the beholder. Because so many journalists instinctually blanch at any version of involuntary "truth trial," as a practical matter such a regime would tend to chill free expression.

I thus believe that the declaratory judgment device contained within the Annenberg plan should be modified so that it is activated only on the mutual consent of both parties. This will not, in my view, render the proposal meaningless—for it remains chock full of other advances that in my view dramatically improve the rationality and fairness of defamation law. Furthermore, the mere existence of this declaratory judgment option, formalized in a statute, will in my view encourage some parties to go down this route and will provide leverage and legitimacy to judges like Leval, who may wish to entice the parties to experiment with it.

In the end, it proves that Machiavelli had it right: Reform is always difficult.

NOTES

1. THE ANNENBERG WASHINGTON PROGRAM, PROPOSAL FOR THE REFORM OF LIBEL LAW (1988) [hereinafter Annenberg Proposal]. The report is available at no charge from the Annenberg Washington Program in Communications Policy Studies of Northwestern University, The Willard Office Building, 1455 Pennsylvania Ave., NW, Suite 200, Washington, D.C. 20004.

2. Sandra S. Baron is managing general attorney in the National Broadcasting Company Law Department. Baron is responsible for legal matters involving NBC News and the NBC Television Stations Division news operations, as well as libel, privacy, copyright, trademark, and other content-related issues for NBC news and other program divisions of NBC. She has held this position since 1985, having joined NBC in March 1983 as a general attorney. Before that she was with the Educational Broadcasting Corporation, operators of WNET, which she joined in May 1979 as an attorney. Like all other members of the Annenberg project, Baron participated in the project as a citizen interested in reform and not as an official spokesperson for her institution, the National Broadcasting Company.

3. Bruce E. Fein is a leading conservative constitutional scholar. He served in 1983–84 as General Counsel to the Federal Communications Commission, has been a Visiting Fellow for Constitutional Studies at the Heritage Foundation, and the Supreme Court Editor of *Benchmark Magazine,* of the Center for Judicial Studies.

4. The Hon. Lois G. Forer retired in 1987 as a judge of the Court of Common Pleas in Philadelphia, Pennsylvania, where she had served since 1971. She has been a prolific writer, authoring five books and many scores of articles in journals and magazines, including writings on libel. Her latest book is A CHILLING EFFECT: THE MOUNTING THREAT OF LIBEL AND INVASION OF PRIVACY ACTIONS TO THE FIRST AMENDMENT (1987).

5. Samuel E. Klein has represented media clients for many years, including major metropolitan newspapers, national magazines, television and radio stations, local and weekly newspapers, and a coalition of Pennsylvania publishers and broadcasters organized to preserve and defend First Amendment rights. Klein has been actively engaged in all phases of First Amendment litigation, has tried numerous defamation and invasion of privacy cases throughout the United States, and has handled major cases before trial and appellate courts involving access to information, reporters' rights to shield disclosure of sources, and numerous other press-related issues. Mr. Klein received the Sigma Delta Chi First Amendment Award from the Society of Professional Journalists in 1980 and 1984, and is the author of MEDIA SURVIVAL KIT, now in its fourth edition.

6. Anthony Lewis, twice winner of the Pulitzer Prize, is a columnist for the *New York Times.* Lewis joined the Washington Bureau of the *Times* in 1955, to cover the Supreme Court, the Justice Department, and other legal subjects. In 1956–57 he was a Nieman Fellow at Harvard, where he studied law. In the following years he reported on, among other things, the Warren Court and the federal government's responses to the civil rights movement. He won his second Pulitzer Prize in 1963 for his coverage of the Supreme Court. He is the author of two books: GIDEON'S TRUMPET, about a landmark Supreme Court case, and PORTRAIT OF A DECADE, about the great changes in American race relations.

7. Roslyn A. Mazer has spent her entire legal career at the Washington, D.C., law firm Dickstein, Shapiro & Morin, where she has been a litigation partner since 1982. A substantial amount of her recent trial practice has been devoted to first amendment cases. She recently represented *The New Yorker Magazine* in a libel suit arising from Renata Adler's article on the *Westmoreland* and *Sharon* libel trials, Rushford v. The New Yorker Magazine, 846 F.2d 249 (4th Cir. 1988). She also represented the Association of American Editorial Cartoonists, the Authors Guild of America, and satirist Mark Russell as amici curiae in Hustler Magazine, Inc. v. Falwell, 485 U.S. 46 (1988), the recent Supreme Court case involving the First Amendment protection of satiric works.

8. Chad Milton is one of the most knowledgeable press attorneys in the United States. He has, since 1978, been responsible for managing insured

litigation for all types of communications media, in his capacity as vice president and assistant general counsel for Media/Professional Insurance, Inc., the nation's largest underwriter of media insurance.

9. Anthony S. Murry served as staff attorney (in 1982–87) and (in 1986–87) vice president of the Capital Legal Foundation, a public interest law firm that advocated free enterprise on behalf of small businesses. Murry played a key role as principal deputy to lead counsel Dan Burt in the *Westmoreland v. CBS* libel trial. He has lectured at college campuses and appeared on television regarding public policy issues involving the *Westmoreland* case. In 1987, Murry engaged in private practice in the Virgin Islands and is now an attorney with the United States Department of Justice, Civil Rights Division. (He participated in the Annenberg libel reform project as a private citizen with expertise in the libel area, particularly from his experience in the *Westmoreland* case, and not as a representative of the Department of Justice.)

10. Herbert Schmertz is president of the Schmertz Company, a public affairs counseling company in New York City. He was director and vice president of Mobil Corporation, involved with public affairs, corporate public relations, domestic and international government relations, and investor relations. He retired from Mobil in 1988. He became particularly interested in libel issues through his role at Mobil in the *Tavoulareas v. Washington Post* litigation. *See* Tavoulareas v. Washington Post Co., 817 F.2d 762 (D.C. Cir.) (en banc), *cert. denied,* 484 U.S. 870 (1987).

11. Richard M. Schmidt, Jr. is a partner in the law firm Cohn & Marks in Washington, D.C., specializing in communications law. Schmidt served as general counsel and congressional liaison for the United States Information Agency and Voice of America in Washington, D.C., from 1965 to 1968. He has been the general counsel for the American Society of Newspaper Editors since 1969, and has been the Washington counsel for the Association for American Publishers, Inc. since 1969. Schmidt's contributions to the journalism profession have been recognized by awards and a fellowship in the Society of Professional Journalists (Sigma Delta Chi).

12. See biographical entry at beginning of this article.

13. Abrams v. United States, 250 U.S. 616, 630 (1919) (Holmes, J., dissenting).

14. N. MACHIAVELLI, THE PRINCE, ch. vi., at 29-30 (W.K. Marriot, trans., J.-M. Dent & Sons, eds., 1958).

15. *E.g., Review of Libel Law Suggests Big Changes,* IOWA CITY PRESS-CITIZEN, Oct. 17, 1988, at 1, col. 1; *"No-fault" Cases Proposed in Lieu of Libel Laws Suits,* BALTIMORE SUN, Oct. 18, 1988, at 6, col. 6; *Libel-Law Plan Could Eliminate Damage Awards,* WALL ST. J., Oct. 18, 1988 [on the law page]; *Libel-Law Plan Urges "No-Fault" Trials,* CHICAGO TRIBUNE, Oct. 19, 1988, § 1, at 17, col. 1; *Panel Proposes Eliminating Damage Awards in Libel Suits,* PUBLISHERS' AUXILIARY, Oct. 31, 1988, at 1; *Building a Better Libel Law,* BROADCASTING, Nov. 7, 1988, at 54; *"Model" Libel Law Would Substitute Retractions for Money Damages,* PUBLISHER'S WEEKLY, Nov. 11, 1988, at 12; *Libel Reform Proposal Gets Mixed Reviews,* PUBLISHING NEWS, Feb. 1989, at

22; *Libel Law Under Scrutiny,* (WILLIAMSBURG) DAILY PRESS, Feb. 13, 1989, § B, at 2, col. 1.

16. See Reuben, *Libel-Law Reform that Would Chill the Working Press,* CHICAGO TRIBUNE, Dec. 2, 1988, § 1, at 19, col. 2; *see also,* Bush *After 25 Years, Change Is Liable for Libel Law,* (LOS ANGELES) DAILY J., Mar. 9, 1989, at 1, 11, col. 6 (quoting Jerome Baron) (the Act " 'would eviscerate libel law in the United States' "); *"Model" Libel Law Debated at Annenberg Washington Seminar,* BROADCASTING, Feb. 27, 1989, at 44 (quoting George Vrandenberg) (the proposal is " 'antispeech' ").

17. See *supra* notes 15, 16; *infra* note 19.

18. See Bush, *After 25 Years, Change Is Liable for Libel Law,* (LOS ANGELES) DAILY J., Mar. 9, 1989, at 1, 11, col. 6. (quoting David Anderson); Smolla, *A Streamlined, Rational Way to Handle Libel Disputes,* CHICAGO TRIBUNE, Jan. 2, 1989, § 1 at 11, col. 2; Fein, *How to Promote Fact Over Fiction,* WASH. TIMES, Nov. 15, 1988, at F3, col. 1; Mazer, *It's Time to Change Libel Law,* WASH. POST, Oct. 24, 1988, at A3, col. 4. *See also* Cooper, *Connecticut Bill Would Offer Alternative to Libel Suits,* DALLAS MORNING NEWS, Mar. 7, 1989, at C9, col. 1 (supporting adoption of the Connecticut bill based on the Libel Reform Act).

19. Among the programs were a forum in New Brunswick, New Jersey, "Alternatives to Libel Litigation," a Nassau conference sponsored by the New Jersey Press Association and Bench/Bar Media/Dialogues (transcript copy on file with author); "A 25th Anniversary Commemoration of New York Times Co. v. Sullivan," (featuring a panel on the Annenberg Proposal) in New York City sponsored by the New York State Bar Association; "Forum on Alternatives to Libel Litigation," Chicago, Illinois, sponsored by the Northwestern University Medill School of Journalism, the Illinois Bar Association, and the Northwestern Law School; "Alternatives to Libel Litigation," Honolulu, Hawaii, sponsored by the American Bar Association Section on Communications Law; "The Annenberg Proposal," New Orleans, Louisiana, Program of the Proposed Section on Defamation and Privacy, Association of American Law Schools Annual Meeting; "Is This the Way Out of the Libel Dilemma?: A Roundtable on the Proposal of the Annenberg Libel Reform Project," Washington, D.C., Feb. 13, 1989 [herinafter Roundtable], sponsored by the Annenberg Washington Program, the Institute of Bill of Rights Law of the College of William and Mary's Marshall-Wythe School of Law, and the Frances Lewis Law Center of Washington and Lee University. For a summary of the participants' reactions to the Washington program, *see e.g., "Model" Libel Law Debated at Annenberg Washington Seminar,* BROADCASTING, Feb. 27, 1989, at 44; Warren, *"Corrections and Clarifications" on Libel Reform,* CHICAGO TRIBUNE, Feb. 19, 1989, § 4 at 1, col. 2; *Libel Reform Proposal Gets Mixed Reviews,* PUBLISHING NEWS, Feb. 1989, at 22.

20. A bill based on the Annenberg program was introduced in the Connecticut legislature. *See* Cooper, supra note 18; *No-fault Libel Law Proposed in Conn.,* EDITOR & PUBLISHER, Feb. 4, 1989, at 23; *Libel Bill Would Soften Impact of Lawsuits,* MANCHESTER (CONN.) J. INQUIRER, Jan. 21, 1989, at 12, col. 2. Rep. Charles E. Schumer (D-N.Y.) is considering introduction of a

bill based on the report. Schumer had introduced a bill in 1985 with a no-fault declaratory judgment provision similar to the provision that was incorporated in part in the Annenberg Proposal. *See* H.R. 2846 99th Cong., 1st Sess. (1985).

21. The report was universally praised for its clarity and craftsmanship, even by those opposed to its substance. *See* Johnston & Kaufman, *"Annenberg, Sullivan at 25, and the Question of Libel Reform,* 7 COMM. LAW. 4 (1989).

22. Remarks of Floyd Abrams, Roundtable, *supra* note 19.

23. Johnston & Kaufman, *supra* note 21.

24. See *supra* notes 6, 3, 11, 10.

25. See *supra* notes 9, 5, 7, 2.

26. See L. G. FORER, A CHILLING EFFECT: THE MOUNTING THREAT OF LIBEL AND INVASION OF PRIVACY ACTIONS TO THE FIRST AMENDMENT (1987).

27. See *supra* note 8.

28. Annenberg Proposal, *supra* note 1, at 31.

29. *See generally* R. BEZANSON, G. CRANBERG, & J. SOLOSKI, LIBEL LAW AND THE PRESS: MYTH AND REALITY (1987); R. SMOLLA, SUING THE PRESS: LIBEL, THE MEDIA, AND POWER (1986).

30. *See* Smolla, *supra* note 29.

31. *See* Lewis, New York Times v. Sullivan *Reconsidered: Time to Return to "The Central Meaning of the First Amendment,"* 83 COLUM. L. REV. 603 (1983).

32. *See* Bezanson, et al., *supra* note 29; Forer, *supra* note 26; Smolla, *supra* note 29.

33. *See* Bezanson, et al., *supra* note 29.

34. A. SCHLESLINGER, THE CYCLES OF AMERICAN HISTORY 424 (1986).

35. For simplicity, throughout this chapter "plaintiff" also includes "would-be plaintiffs" and refers to every defamed person who feels that he or she has been libeled, regardless of whether that person has brought suit.

36. Annenberg Libel Reform Act § 3(a) [herinafter Act].

37. Act § 3(d).

38. Plaintiffs may not bring a defamation action against any defendant unless the plaintiffs allege that they made a timely request for a retraction or opportunity to reply and the defendant refused that request. Act § 3(a).

39. Act at § 3(j). "In the case of a false and defamatory statement about a candidate for public office, however, the retraction or reply shall not be deemed timely unless it is published within a reasonable time under the circumstances prior to the election." *Id.*

40. A defendant can always satisfy the requirements of Stage I if he or she grants a retraction, even if plaintiffs request an opportunity to reply. Act § 3(i).

41. Act § 3.

42. Act §§ 4(a), 4(e).

43. Act § 4(b).

44. Act § 4(c).

45. *Id.* Plaintiffs bear the burden of proving by clear and convincing evidence that the statement was false and defamatory. Act §§ 4(d), 6(a).

46. Act § 4(d).

47. Act § 4(c).

48. Act § 10(b). While the Act contemplates that the loser will pay the winner's attorneys' fees as a matter of course, there is a safety-valve provision allowing the court to deny or reduce awards to any prevailing party who litigated "vesatious or frivolous claims or defenses." *Id.*

49. Act § 6(a).

50. Marbury v. Madison, 5 U.S. (1 Cranch) 137 (1803).

51. *Id.*

52. Act § 9(b).

53. Act §§ 9(b), 9(d).

54. Act § 10(c).

55. Act § 1(c).

56. Act § 9(a).

57. Act § 1(a).

58. Annenberg Proposal, *supra* note 1, at 20 (Section-by-Section Analysis [hereinafter "Commentary,"], § 3, para. 3). *See* Act § 2.

59. Act § 5.

60. *See* Westmoreland v. CBS, Inc., 596 F. Supp. 1170 (S.D.N.Y. 1984).

61. The member was Anthony Murry. See *supra* note 9.

62. General Westmoreland made his remarks at the Washington, D.C., conference on the proposal, which was broadcast live on C-SPAN. See *supra* note 19.

63. Leval, *The No-Money. No-Fault Libel Suit: Keeping Sullivan in Its Proper Place,* 101 HARV. L. REV. 1287 (1988).

64. Judge Leval's critiques, it should be stressed, have been pointed but always collegial and constructive.

65. See *infra* notes 85–101 and accompanying text.

66. Letter from Pierre N. Leval to Rodney A. Smolla (Sept. 6, 1988). Judge Leval's critiques of the Annenberg plan were delivered publicly at a luncheon address at a conference sponsored by the Annenberg program in February 1989.

67. Act §§ 3(a), 3(d).

68. Letter from Pierre N. Leval to Rodney A. Smolla (Sept. 6, 1988); *see also* Letter from Richard N. Pearson to Rodney A. Smolla (Feb. 16, 1989) (supporting Judge Leval's criticism to the Act's thirty-day period for demanding a retraction or reply).

69. *Id.*

70. *Id.*

71. See *supra* note 37 and accompanying text.

72. Act § 3(g).

73. Letter from Pierre N. Leval to Rodney A. Smolla (Sept. 6, 1988).

74. *See also* Letter from Richard N. Pearson to Rodney A. Smolla (Feb. 16, 1989) (Prof. Richard Pearson argued that the plaintiff may often find this length inadequate to explain his or her position or dispel the innuendo of the libelous piece.).

75 Act § 3(g).

76. *See* Act § 3(g).

77. Letter from Pierre N. Leval to Rodney A. Smolla (Sept. 6, 1988).

78. Annenberg Proposal, *supra* note 1, at 21 (Commentary, § 3, para. 3).

79. *See* Smolla, supra note 29, at 241.

80. *See, e.g.,* CAL. DIV. CODE § 48a(1) (West 1954); CONN. GEN. STAT. ANN. § 52, 237 (West 1960); LA. CIV. CODE ANN. art 2315.1 (West 1979); ME. REV. STAT. ANN. tit. 14, § 153 (1965); N.C. GEN. STAT. § 99.2(a) (1979); OKLA STAT. ANN. tit. 12, § 1446u (West 1961).

81. *See* Burnett v. National Enquirer, Inc., 144 Cal. App. 3d 991, 193 Cal. Rptr. 206 (1983), *appeal dismissed,* 465 U.S. 1014 (1984).

82. Act § 3(g).

83. *Id.*

84. Annenberg Proposal, *supra* note 1, at 21–22 (Commentary, § 3, para. 8).

85. *See* Reuben, *Reform Libel Law,* A.B.A J., April 1989, at 43.

86. *E.g.,* Bush, *After 25 Years. Change Is Liable for Libel Law,* (LOS ANGELES) DAILY J., Mar. 9, 1989, at 1, 11, col. 6 (the Act's "major flaw" is that plaintiffs cannot receive damages) (quoting Marc A. Franklin).

87. *See* Letter from Anthony Murry to Rodney A. Smolla (Mar. 1, 1989) ("[I]t is absurd to make social policy and skewer the whole system to allow for the rare case. You just can't run the railroad that way."); Letter from Richard N. Pearson to Rodney A. Smolla (Feb. 16, 1989) ("In framing what the best law is, we always have to take account what happens at the fringes, but law cannot always be drafted to protect the farthest out case. Law pretty much has to take account what we want to happen in the vast bulk of cases.").

88. *See* Letter from Richard N. Pearson to Rodney A. Smolla (Feb. 16, 1989) ("Judge Leval presented a compelling case, but one that by no stretch of the imagination of even the media baiters could be said to be typical.").

89. *See* Smolla, *Let the Author Beware: The Rejuvenation of the American Law of Libel,* 132 U. PA. L. REV. 1–14, 92-94 (1983).

90. New York Times Co. v. Sullivan, 376 U.S. 254 (1964).

91. Gertz v. Robert Welch, Inc., 418 U.S. 323 (1974).

92. Dun & Bradstreet, Inc. v. Greenmoss Builders, Inc., 472 U.S. 749 (1985).

93. *See infra* notes 142–162 and accompanying text.

94. *See* Smolla, *supra* note 30.

95. Act § 10b.

96. Note that the Act currently abolishes all of the old per se and per quod rules on special damages. Act § 9a.

97. Scardino, *Panel Backs Libel Law Shift,* N.Y. TIMES, Oct. 18, 1988, at 24, col. 3 (quoting George Freeman, a lawyer for the New York Times Company); DeVore, *The Annenberg Libel Proposal* (unpublished manuscript; copy on file with author). The estimates of the decline in libel litigation vary. *See generally,* Stille, *Libel Law Takes On a New Look,* NAT'L L.J., Oct. 24, 1988, at 1 (libel-suit filings have decreased between 25 and 40 percent since 1985); Scardino, *Libel Suits Wane, Press Study Finds,* N.Y. TIMES, Dec. 3, 1988, § 1, at 52, col. 4 ("Since 1985, the number of libel suits has declined 17 percent compared to the average number filed from 1981 through 1985.").

98. 418 U.S. 323 (1974).

99. 376 U.S. 254 (1964).

100. *See* Dun & Bradstreet, Inc. v. Greenmoss Builders, Inc., 472 U.S. 749, 767-74, (1985) (opinion of White, J.); *id.* at 764, (opinion of Burger, C.J.).

101. 599 F. Supp. 538 (S.D.N.Y. 1984).

102. 596 F. Supp. 1170 (S.D.N.Y. 1984).

103. *See supra* note 97.

104. 485 U.S. 46 (1988).

105. *See* Brown & Williamson Tobacco Corp. v. Jacobson, 827 F.2d 1119 (7th Cir. 1987), *cert. denied,* 108 S. Ct. 1302 (1988).

106. *E.g.,* Johnston & Kaufman, *supra* note 21, at 6–7; Bush, *After 25 Years, Change Is Libel for Libel Law,* (LOS ANGELES) DAILY J., Mar. 3, 1989, at 1, col. 6 (quoting Floyd Abrams); *Libel Law Under Scrutiny,* (WILLIAMS-BURG) DAILY PRESS, Feb. 13, 1989, § 84, at 2, col. 1 (quoting Donald Reuben); *New Proposal to Deal With Libel,* A.B.A. J., Jan. 1989, at 34 (quoting Henry Kaufman); DeVore, *The Annenberg Proposal* (unpublished manuscript; copy on file with author); C.T. Dienes, *Libel Reform: An Appraisal,* Remarks at the Detroit Media Law Conference, March 8, 1989, at 16 (copy on file with author).

107. *Libel Reform Proposal Gets Mixed Reviews,* PUBLISHING NEWS, Feb. 1989, at 22 (quoting Harry Johnston).

108. Bush, *After 25 Years, Change Is Liable for Libel Law,* (LOS ANGELES) DAILY J., Mar. 9, 1989, at 1, col. 6 (quoting Floyd Abrams).

109. *E.g., New Proposal to Deal With Libel,* A.B.A. J., Jan. 1989, at 34 (quoting Henry Kaufman).

110. *E.g., Study Urges Law Be Changed to Reduce Libel Litigation,* WASH. POST, Oct. 19, 1988, at A3, col. 5 (quoting Henry Kaufman).

111. *Libel Law Under Scrutiny,* (WILLIAMSBURG) DAILY PRESS, Feb. 13, 1989, § B, at 2, col. 1 (quoting C.T. Dienes). Dienes stated bluntly the media viewpoint: " 'We know we're safe under the present law; we don't know what this would do. . . . Why should we take the chance?' " *Id.*

112. Dienes, *supra* note 106, at 15.

113. *Panel Proposes Eliminating Damage Awards in Libel Suits,* PUB. AUX-ILIARY, Oct. 31, 1988 (quoting Floyd Abrams); *see also* Warren, *Westmore-land, CBS Oppose Libel Law Plan,* CHICAGO TRIBUNE, Feb. 14, 1989, at C5, col. 1 (citing George Vrandenburg) (the Act " would make filing suits easier").

114. C.T. Dienes, Remarks at the Detroit Media Law Conference 16 (date) (copy on file with WM. & MARY L. REV.).

115. *A Stem Toward Common Sense on Libel,* CHICAGO TRIBUNE, Oct. 29, 1988, § 1, at 10, col. 1; *see* Dienes, *supra* note 106, at 16; *Libel-Law Plan Urges "No-Fault" Trials,* CHICAGO TRIBUNE, Oct. 19, 1988, § 1, at 17, col. 1.

116. *Libel Reform Proposal Gets Mixed Reviews,* PUBLISHING NEWS, Feb. 1989, at 22 (quoting Harry Johnston). " 'It's very easy to say 'retraction,' but as long as there are lawyers to fight issues, there will be fights.' " *Id.*

117. Johnston & Kaufman, *supra* note 21, at 7–8.

118. Act § 3(a).

119. Act § 3(e).

120. Act §§ 3(a), (3)(j).

121. Annenberg Proposal, *supra* note 1, at 21 (Commentary, § 3, para. 3). This is an extremely significant provision. Many modern cases are based not on what was said in an article on broadcast, but what was left unsaid. This provision of the Annenberg proposal allows a defendant to avoid liability by renouncing defamatory implications.

122. Act § 6(a).

123. Act § 10(b).

124. *See* R. SMOLLA, LAW OF DEFAMATION §§ 6.01–6.12 (1986).

125. Annenberg Proposal, *supra* note 1, at 20 (Commentary, § 2, para. 3).

126. The common law rule followed in most jurisdictions prior to 1977 rendered a person liable for "republication" of libelous statements originated by others. *See* Smolla, *supra* note 124, § 4.13. The common law employed the fiction that the republisher "adopts" the defamatory statement as his own. *Id.* This rule tends to hamstring the press when the original speaker's *very making of the defamatory statement* is newsworthy. Id., § 4.14. In Edwards v. National Audobon Soc'y, 556 F.2d 113 (2d Cir.), *cert. denied sub nom.*, Edwards v. New York Times, 434 U.S. 1002 (1977), the Second Circuit adopted what has come to be known as the "neutral reportage" privilege. Under it, the press is privileged to republish defamatory statements of another when the very making of the statements is newsworthy, the charges are made by a responsible public figure, official, or organization, the charges are made about a public figure, official, or organization, and the press coverage of the statements is "neutral." *See, e.g.,* Cianci v. New Times Publishing Co., 639 F.2d 54, 67-69 (2d Cir. 1980); Dixon v. Newsweek, 562 F.2d 626, 630-31 (10th Cir. 1977); Edwards v. National Audobon Soc'y, 556 F.2d 113 (2d Cir.), *cert. denied sub nom.*, Edwards v. New York Times, 434 U.S. 1002 (1977); Barry v. Time, Inc., 584 F. Supp. 1110, 1126-27 (N.D. Cal. 1984); Smolla, *supra* note 124, § 4.14. The neutral reportage concept has gained increasing judicial acceptance, but it is still far from being a majority rule among the states. See Smolla, *supra* note 124, § 4.14[4]. The Annenberg Proposal adopts a broader neutral reportage privilege than existing case law by not requiring that the person quoted be "responsible." The rationale for this extension is that often individuals who might well be deemed "irresponsible" by most persons may nevertheless make public charges that are newsworthy and deserve to be reported. The quid pro quo under the Annenberg Proposal is that the source of the quote must be identified—preventing the press from hiding behind "anonymous sources."

127. Act § 5.

128. Act § 3(e).

129. Act § 10.

130. Act at Preamble.

131. E. Dickinson, *Tell All the Truth but Tell It Slant,* in THE COMPLETE POEMS OF EMILY DICKINSON 506 (Thomas N. Johnson ed. 1960).

132. *Libel Law Plan Urges "No-fault" Trials,* CHICAGO TRIBUNE, Oct. 19, 1988, § 1, at 17, col. 1.

133. Dienes, *supra* note 106, at 15.

134. DeVore, *The Annenberg Libel Proposal* (copy on file with author).

135. *"Model" Libel Law Debated at Annenberg Washington Seminar,* BROADCASTING, Feb. 27, 1989, at 44 (quoting George Vrandenberg).

136. Reuben, *Libel-law Reform That Would Chill the Working Press,* CHICAGO TRIBUNE, Dec. 2, 1988, § 1, at 19, col. 2.

137. *Id. See also New Proposal to Deal with Libel,* A.B.A. J., Jan. 1989, at 34 (quoting Don Reuben) (" 'there will be a chilling effect' "); Reuben, *Reform Libel Law?: No,* A.B.A. J., April 1989, at 43.

138. Act § 6(b); Annenberg Proposal, *supra* note 1, at 23 (Commentary, § 6, para. 2).

139. *See* 'Philadelphia Newspapers, Inc. v. Hepps, 475 U.S. 767 (1986).

140. Act §§ 2, 5.

141. West Va. State Bd. of Educ. v. Barnette, 319 U.S. 624, 642 (1943).

142. For a review of these rules, *see* Smolla, *supra* note 124, §§ 2.01–.04, 3.01–.05.

143. *New Proposal to Deal with Libel,* A.B.A. J., Jan. 1989, at 34 (quoting Floyd Abrams); *see also Study Urges Law to Be Changed to Reduce Libel Litigation,* WASH. POST, Oct. 19, 1988, at A3, col. 5 (quoting Floyd Abrams) (" 'there is a very live issue as to whether the proposal is constitutional in the first place' ").

144. Remarks of Richard N. Winfield at [the Annenberg Washington Program] 2 (Feb. 13, 1989).

145. *See, e.g.,* Guaranty Trust Co. v. York, 326 U.S. 99 (1945); Erie R.R. Co. v. Tompkins, 304 U.S. 64 (1938); Ely, *The Irrepressible Myth at Erie,* 87 HARV. L. REV. 693 (1974); Friendly, *In Praise of Erie—And of the New Federal Common Law,* 39 N.Y.U.L.REV. 383, 400 (1964).

146. *See, e.g.,* Hanna v. Plumber, 380 U.S. 460 (1965).

147. *See* Bose v. Consumers Union of United States, Inc., 466 U.S. 485 (1984).

148. *See* Keeton v. Hustler Magazine, Inc., 465 U.S. 770 (1984); Calder v. Jones, 465 U.S. 783 (1984); Smolla, *supra* note 124, § 12.07[2].

149. *See* Smolla, *supra* note 89, §§ 12.02[3][b], 12.07[2].

150. 42 U.S.C. § 1988 (1976).

151. *See* City of Riverside v. Rivera, 477 U.S. 561 (1986).

152. *See, e.g.,* Penhurst State School & Hosp. v. Halderman, 465 U.S. 89 (1984); Imbler v. Patchman, 424 U.S. 409 (1976); Scheurer v. Rhodes, 416 U.S. 232 (1974); Edleman v. Jordan, 415 U.S. 651 (1974); P. SHUCK, SUING GOVERNMENT: CITIZEN REMEDIES FOR OFFICIAL WRONGS (1983).

153. *See* Pulliam v. Allen, 466 U.S. 522 (1984).

154. 446 U.S. 719 (1980).

155. 457 U.S. 800 (1982).

156. *Id.* at 314 (quoting Gregoire v. Biddle, 177 F.2d 579, 581 (2d Cir. 1949), *cert. denied,* 339 U.S. 949 (1950)).

157. Supreme Court of Va. v. Virginia Consumers Union, 446 U.S. 719 (1980).

158. 5 U.S. (1 Cranch) 137 (1803).

159. Act § 10.

160. *See supra* notes 118–29 and accompanying text.

161. *See supra* notes 118–29 and accompanying text .

162. *See generally* T. LITTLEWOOD, COALS OF FIRE: THE ALTON TELEGRAPH LIBEL CASE (1988).

163. *See supra* note 20.

164. *See* Littlewood, *supra* note 162.

165. 418 U.S. 323 (1974).

166. *See generally* Brosnahan, *From* Times v. Sullivan to Gertz v. Robert Welch: *Ten Years of Balancing Libel Law and the First Amendment*, 26 HASTINGS L.J. 777 (1975); Christie, *Injury to Reputation and the Constitution: Confusion Amid Conflicting Approaches*, 75 MICH. L. REV. 43, 50 (1976); Lange, *The Speech and Press Clauses*, 23 U.C.L.A. L. REV. 77 (1975); Nimmer, *Is Freedom of Press a Redundancy: What Does It Add to Freedom of Speech?* 26 HASTINGS L.J. 639, 649 (1975); Shiffrin, *The First Amendment and Economic Regulation: Away from a General Theory of the First Amendment*, 78 VA. L. REV. 1212, 1268 (1983); Shiffrin, *Defamatory Non-Media Speech and First Amendment Methodology*, 25 U.C.L.A. L. REV. 915 (1978); Smolla, *supra* note 29, at 29–33, 90; Stewart, *Or of the Press*, 26 HASTINGS L.J. 631 (1975); Watkins & Schwantz, *Gertz and the Common Law of Defamation: Of Fault, Nonmedia Defendants, and Conditional Privileges*, 15 TEX. TECH. L. REV. 823, 831-63 (1984).

167. *See, e.g.,* Avins v. White, 627 F.2d 637, 649 (3d Cir.), *cert. denied*, 449 U.S. 982 (1980); Davis v. Schuchat, 510 F.2d 731, 734 n.3 (D.C. Cir. 1975); Woy v. Turner, 533 F. Supp. 102, 104 (N.D. Ga. 1981); Antwerp Diamond Exch. v. Better Business Bureau, 130 Ariz. 523, 637 P.2d 733, 731 (1981); Rodriguez v. Nishiki, 653 P.2d 1145, 1150 (Haw. 1982); Michaud v. Inhabitants of Livermore Falls, 381 A.2d 1110, 113 (Me. 1978).

168. *See, e.g.,* Rowe v. Metz, 195 Colo. 424, 579 P.2d 83 (1978); Stvempages v. Parke, Davis & Co., 297 N.W.2d 252 (Minn. 1980); Wheeler v. Green, 286 Or. 99, 593 P.2d 777 (1979); Harley-Davidson Motorsports, Inc. v. Markley, 279 Or. 361, 568 P.2d 1359 (1977); Denny v. Mertz, 106 Wis. 2d 636, 318 N.W.2d 141, *cert. denied*, 459 U.S. 883 (1982); Calero v. Del Chem. Corp., 68 Wis. 2d 487, 228 N.W.2d 737 (1975).

169. The Supreme Court seemed to eschew the media/nonmedia distinction in Dun & Bradstreet. Inc. v. Greenmoss Builders, Inc., 472 U.S. 749 (1985). *See infra* notes 170–173 and accompanying text. But in Philadelphia Newspapers, Inc. v. Hepps, 475 U.S. 767 (1986), the Court conspicuously articulated its holding as limited to media defendants. *Id.* at 779 n.4.

170. *See* Smolla, *supra* note 89, § 3.02[2].

171. 472 U.S. 749 (1985).

172. The plurality opinion of Justice Powell noted that the *Gertz* First Amendment protections "were not 'justified solely by reference to the interest of the press and broadcast media in immunity from liability.' " *Id.* at 756

(opinion of Powell, J.) (quoting Gertz v. Robert Welch, Inc., 418 U.S. 323, 343 (1974).

173. 472 U.S. at 773 (White, J., concurring) ("Wisely, in my view, Justice Powell does not rest his application . . . on a distinction between media and nonmedia defendants. On that issue, I agree with Justice Brennan that the First Amendment gives no more protection to the press in defamation suits than it does to others exercising their freedom of speech.").

174. *Id.* at 774 (Brennan, J.).

175. Justice Brennan wrote that the media/nonmedia "distinction is irreconcilable with the fundamental First Amendment principle that '[t]he inherent worth of . . . speech in terms of its capacity for informing the public does not depend upon the identity of its source.' " *Id.* at 781 (quoting First Nat'l Bank of Boston v. Belloitti, 435 U.S. 765, 777 (1978)).

176. Act § 1c.

177. Act § 9.

chapter 7

Resolving Libel Disputes out of Court: The Libel Dispute Resolution Program

ROSELLE L. WISSLER
RANDALL P. BEZANSON
GILBERT CRANBERG
JOHN SOLOSKI
BRIAN MURCHISON *

There seems to be a growing consensus among legal scholars, media attorneys, journalists, and judges that current libel law does not serve the interests of the media, the plaintiffs, or the public. The high degree of dissatisfaction with the existing libel litigation system has led a number of legal scholars to offer proposals to reform libel law.[1] The Iowa Libel Research Project (ILRP) set out to explore a different approach: to investigate the feasibility of a voluntary alternative process for resolving libel disputes outside the courts. In 1987, the ILRP, in cooperation with the American Arbitration Association, implemented the Libel Dispute Resolution Program (LDRP).[2] The LDRP is

*The authors are members of the Iowa Libel Research Project. Roselle L. Wissler is research director of the Iowa Libel Research Project. Randall P. Bezanson is dean of the School of Law at Washington and Lee University. Gilbert Cranberg is George H. Gallup Professor of journalism and mass communication at the University of Iowa. John Soloski is head of graduate studies and professor of journalism and mass communication at the University of Iowa. Brian Murchison is professor of law at Washington and Lee University.

a voluntary alternative program available nationwide for resolving media libel disputes with the aim of providing a more efficient, inexpensive, and satisfactory resolution outside the courts. The alternative process was developed based on the findings of the ILRP's empirical study of the functioning of the libel litigation system,[3] on consultation with editors and with attorneys who specialize in libel and media law, and on a review of alternative dispute resolution methods. This chapter explains why the program was developed, describes how it works, and discusses the findings of the research phase of the program. Although the research component and the ILRP's involvement have ended, the American Arbitration Association is continuing to provide mediation and arbitration procedures for resolving libel disputes out of court.[4]

PROBLEMS WITH THE LIBEL LITIGATION SYSTEM

Beginning in 1964, the U.S. Supreme Court decided a series of cases that protect the media from liability for inadvertently publishing false information by requiring a showing of "fault." To prevail in a libel suit today, plaintiffs need to show not only that the information published about them is false and harmed their reputations, but also that the media published the information negligently, with actual knowledge of its falsity, or with reckless disregard of the truth.[5] It was thought that the negligence and actual-malice standards (referred to as "constitutional privileges") would diminish the risk of the media's having to pay large money judgments by making it more difficult for plaintiffs, especially public plaintiffs, to win a libel suit. This would, in turn, reduce the "chilling effect" that the fear of large damage awards has on the media's willingness to report controversial news stories.[6]

The constitutional privileges have generally succeeded in protecting media defendants from large money judgments. The media win most of their cases[7] and, when they do lose, the final damage award is generally reduced to less than 10 percent of the trial award.[8] Thus, the main economic impact of libel on the media today is the high cost of defending a seriously litigated suit.[9] To defend such a suit through trial typically costs the media $150,000;[10] the legal fees in the *Sharon* and *Westmoreland* cases ran about $6 million.[11] Even the cost of ending a case at the summary judgment stage can easily run between $20,000 and $80,000.[12] Attorneys' fees comprise 80 percent of the cost of defending a libel suit; damage awards, settlements, and administrative fees make up only 20 percent of the cost.[13]

The major reason for the high cost of defending a libel suit is that the constitutional privileges have made libel litigation more complex by requiring plaintiffs to show the media were at fault. As a consequence, the primary focus of libel litigation is on the defendants' investigative and editorial processes in order to ascertain how the journalists did the disputed story and their state of mind as they did their work. Time-consuming and expensive depositions of journalists, examination of journalists' notes and other papers, and exhaustive scrutiny of newsroom procedures are normal parts of libel suits. The process of gathering and presenting this evidence not only has made libel litigation more protracted and expensive[14] but also disrupts the media organization and places its journalistic integrity under attack.[15] The chilling effect of libel suits today is due more to litigation costs and intrusion into the editorial process than to adverse judgments.

From the plaintiffs' perspective, libel litigation's focus on fault does not always address what plaintiffs say they care most about: the underlying falsity of the alleged libel and restoring their reputation.[16] Even in cases in which the truth or falsity of the statements is determined, the slowness of the litigation process (on average, four years) means the decision comes long after the time it can effectively repair the plaintiff's reputation. The majority of plaintiffs (64 percent) said that they had suffered solely emotional or reputational harm. Twenty-two percent reported both emotional and financial harm, and 14 percent reported solely financial harm.[17] Lacking any other way of responding to the alleged libel, plaintiffs resort to the legal system in an effort to obtain public vindication. Not surprisingly, 65 percent of the plaintiffs interviewed expressed dissatisfaction with their litigation experience, mainly due to frustration with the judicial system's unresponsiveness to their claimed harm.[18]

Plaintiffs' actions immediately following publication of the alleged libel are consistent with a primary concern for restoring their reputation. Half of the plaintiffs interviewed contacted the media before contacting a lawyer, and nearly 90 percent of the plaintiffs said that they, on their own, through their attorney, or with their attorney, had contacted the media prior to filing suit in an attempt to resolve the dispute.[19] Seventy-eight percent of these plaintiffs said they had asked the media to run a retraction, correction, or apology, 6 percent said they had asked the media to discuss the story with them, and 3 percent said they had asked the media to provide space or air time for them to respond to the alleged libel.[20] Seventy-three percent of the plaintiffs said that they would have been satisfied if the media had run a retraction, correction, or apology immediately after the alleged libel had appeared. In all, less than 4 percent of the plaintiffs said that they would have been satisfied only if the media had paid them money damages.[21] Interestingly, even those plaintiffs who reported that the libel had caused them financial harm said that they would have been satisfied if the media had immediately retracted or corrected the alleged libel.

But once the decision to sue was made, the objectives of many plaintiffs underwent a not unexpected change. Although reputational repair remained the objective of some plaintiffs, nearly 29 percent said they had sued in order to punish the media and 22 percent said they had sued in order to win money damages.[22] The latter group of plaintiffs tended to be those who had suffered real economic loss because of the alleged libel.[23] Although an immediate correction or retraction of the alleged libel might have mitigated the financial damages suffered by these plaintiffs, by the time suit had been filed, any economic harm caused by the alleged libel could no longer be remedied by correction or retraction alone. Also contributing to the change in plaintiff objectives was the high level of frustration and anger many plaintiffs felt after their contact with the media. This resulted not simply from the media's rejection of the plaintiffs' request for a retraction, correction, or apology but also from the media's treatment of them during their postpublication contact. Most plaintiffs said that the nature of the media's response or their lack of response was a factor in their decision to sue.[24]

DEVELOPING AN ALTERNATIVE PROCESS FOR RESOLVING LIBEL DISPUTES

The disjunction between the goals of libel law and the real interests of the parties, their dissatisfaction with the litigation process, and the expense and delay of litigation suggest that a more effective method for resolving libel disputes is needed.[25] From the perspective of libel litigants, a dispute resolution mechanism should take into consideration the plaintiffs' interest in a prompt determination of the truth or falsity of the defamatory statements and the media's interest in avoiding large damage awards and high litigation costs. We assume that a timely finding on falsity and publication of that finding can minimize any monetary loss resulting from the alleged libel and can be more helpful in repairing the reputational harm already suffered than the remote chance of recovering money damages in a libel suit. If the plaintiffs relinquish their monetary claims and seek only a judgment on falsity, the media defendants would be protected from the economic loss that would result if they should lose a libel suit in court. Accordingly, the media would not need the protection of constitutional privileges[26] or the heavy commitment of resources to litigation.

By making irrelevant the behavior and state of mind of the journalists at the time of publication, the amount of discovery and the scrutiny of journalistic practices would be significantly reduced. Although the complexity of the facts at issue will influence the length of the hearing and the amount of discovery needed, the proceeding is likely to be simpler, less expensive, and less protracted. The plaintiff, freed from having to establish negligence or actual malice, has a better chance to have the falsity issue addressed and to publicize any possible vindication. Such a resolution would give plaintiffs what they want (an authoritative determination of truth or falsity) and spare the defendants what they fear (large damage awards and high litigation costs).

Several solutions to the problems of the current libel litigation system have been proposed,[27] the majority of which involve substantive reform of the laws governing libel or intervention in other aspects of the litigation process. One proposal is the expanded use of a special verdict in which the jury reaches a separate verdict on the issues of whether the challenged statements are defamatory, whether they are false, and whether the defendants acted negligently or with actual malice.[28] Although a special verdict allows the truth or falsity of the statements to be addressed, it does so only at the end of the trial, after a great deal of energy, time, and money have been expended to obtain and present evidence on the privilege issues, and it does nothing for the majority of plaintiffs whose cases are dismissed on privilege grounds before trial.[29] Proposals to establish an alternative cause of action for a declaratory judgment that the statement is false and defamatory in lieu of money damages improve on this by allowing discovery and the trial to focus solely on issues of falsity and reputational harm.[30] Such proposals are likely to reduce significantly the expense and intrusion involved in traditional litigation, although some do not address the issue of pretrial delay.[31] A declaratory judgment is not an available option, however, until legislation establishing that cause of action is enacted[32] or until a case tests Judge Pierre N. Leval's contention that this opportunity exists under current law.[33]

Our approach to developing a quicker and less expensive method for resolving libel disputes involves an out-of-court alternative process rather than legal reform. There are several reasons to focus on alternative processes[34] for resolving libel disputes. First, alternative dispute resolution programs have been used in other civil disputes to address problems similar to those observed in libel litigation: the failure of the courts to address the real issues involved in the dispute, the limited range of remedies available, high cost and delay, and the tendency of court processes to increase the conflict between the parties and to reduce communication and cooperation.[35] In addition, implementing an alternative process permits the evaluation of different procedures without changing the current legal system.

Moreover, legislated reform may not provide sufficient flexibility to meet the needs of the parties in a particular case.[36] In a voluntary process, both parties have a voice in selecting many of the procedural aspects of the process, in choosing a neutral third party to assist in resolving the dispute, in controlling the range of issues to be resolved in the hearing, and in determining the remedy. In addition, a voluntary program leaves in the hands of both parties the decision regarding the appropriate forum for resolving a given dispute.[37] Although many plaintiffs do not suffer substantial financial harm from the alleged libel, those who do can pursue the case in court for money damages. Similarly, though many libel cases do not involve novel legal issues or threaten First Amendment principles, the media can choose to defend a particular case in court or to seek a motion to dismiss a frivolous action.

Many libel litigants, though not all, should find an alternative process to be an attractive option. Seventy percent of the interviewed libel plaintiffs said that if they could have obtained a quick, fair, and public finding on the dispute without going to court, they might have chosen this means rather than a lawsuit. The features of the process that plaintiffs listed as most attractive were having the outcome made public, avoiding suit, achieving a more just outcome, and reducing time and cost. Another 13 percent said they would have considered such a process under certain conditions; most of these plaintiffs said the process would need to provide money damages.[38] Fourteen percent of the plaintiffs interviewed, however, stated that they would not have used a nonlitigation alternative. Litigants who are unlikely to be interested in using an alternative process include plaintiffs whose objective is to punish the defendant, either through the litigation process or through a large verdict; parties who are engaging in the tactical use of litigation (e.g., plaintiffs more interested in publicity than in the accuracy of the story; defendants interested in delaying liability); parties who want a court decision to establish a new rule of law; or media defendants who think that aggressive litigation will prevent future suits.[39]

The case of *Kadet v. Daytona (Fla.) Times* illustrates the potential benefits of an out-of-court alternative for resolving libel disputes.[40]

The case had been in litigation for three and one-half years, at an estimated cost to the newspaper defendant of $100,000 in donated legal fees, when the parties agreed to dismiss the suit and submit the dispute to a six-person panel. The panel had the authority to determine the truth or falsity of the alleged libel but could not award damages. The panel found unanimously that the newspaper had accurately reported the statements of a community leader, but that those statements were false. The panel split as to whether the statements were published with malice and whether they had harmed the plaintiff's reputation. The plaintiff was pleased with the finding on falsity and with the newspaper's publishing the finding. The paper also was pleased with the outcome because of the time and money saved.

Several processes for resolving libel disputes out of court have been suggested. The Center for Public Resources proposed an arbitration hearing that could be either binding or nonbinding and that would focus on a determination of the truth or falsity of the statements and the harm caused, with the remedy being some type of corrective publication or broadcast.[41] Robert Ackerman has proposed binding fact-finding on the issue of the truth or falsity of the statements, in which the plaintiff agrees to drop the claim and the medium agrees to publish a retraction phrased by the fact-finder.[42] Neither proposal has been implemented. In 1989, Robert Chandler developed a form of simplified arbitration in which the complainant agrees to waive litigation and the editor agrees to print the arbitrator's decision on whether the media organization "has made significant error which reflects adversely upon the aggrieved party."[43] Chandler's proposal has been adopted by his own and several other newspapers.

THE PROCEDURES OF THE LDRP

The LDRP represented the first formal effort to apply systematically alternative dispute resolution methods to libel cases. The components of the program were developed based on information concerning problems with the libel litigation system, the interests of the litigants, and the characteristics of dispute resolution processes.[44] The LDRP was designed to be flexible, with the parties negotiating many of the specifics of the process. The LDRP is described briefly here; the procedures are reprinted in full in the appendix to this article.

The LDRP is geared toward resolving the questions of the truth or falsity of the challenged factual statements and the existence of reputational harm. Fault-related questions such as negligence and actual malice are not relevant. The complainant has the burden of defining the specific statements that are alleged to be false, showing that the challenged statements have caused reputational harm, and proving they are false. The remedy is subject to negotiation but is likely to consist of the media respondent's agreeing (1) to publish or broadcast in full the arbitrator's brief written finding on the falsity issue or (2) to pay to have the finding published or broadcast. The parties may include a provision to award reasonable attorneys' fees to the prevailing party; otherwise, each party bears its own costs. The LDRP emphasizes a resolution of the dispute in sixty to seventy-five days through a combination of strict scheduling of the process plus cooperative and limited discovery.

The parties may proceed directly to a hearing. Many parties, however, may find a prehearing settlement conference to be useful. The goals of the settlement conference include reducing the scope of the dispute, encouraging stipulations of uncontested facts, and facilitating settlement discussions. All admissions, proposals, and statements made in the course of the conference are confidential and inadmissible in the hearing or in any other proceeding. Parties may choose between a settlement conference that involves mediation or one that involves assessment by a special master. The role of the mediator and special master is advisory; neither can make a finding on the dispute. The mediator guides the parties' discussion about relevant information, helps to clarify issues, helps the parties analyze their dispute, and encourages them to consider how they might be able to reach a mutually satisfactory settlement. The special master helps the parties identify areas of agreement, assesses the relative strengths and weaknesses of each side's evidence and arguments on contested issues, helps the parties explore settlement options, and, if an agreement is not reached, provides the parties with an evaluation of the likely outcome of the dispute in arbitration.

Any issues not resolved at an earlier point are submitted to an evidentiary hearing before an arbitrator. The hearing is informal, with relaxed rules of procedure and evidence, and is public unless both parties agree that it should be closed. Within ten days of the hearing, the neutral issues a brief written finding stating the factual questions at issue; the existence of reputational harm; the truth, falsity, or indeterminacy of the facts as found; and the basis on which the finding has been made.

Either party to a media libel dispute or their counsel, as well as judges and insurers, may ask program staff to ascertain whether the parties are willing to submit the dispute to the program. The dispute should be one that is likely to be seriously litigated and that involves statements of a factual nature that have damaged the complainant's reputation. The program staff explains the procedures available and assists the parties in fashioning the process. After the parties have decided to use the program to resolve their dispute and have negotiated the details of the process, they complete a submission agreement. In this document, the parties specify the components of the process they plan to use and agree to submit the dispute to the LDRP under its rules, to abide by the agreed-on remedy, and to waive further legal action.[45] After the submission agreement is signed, the American Arbitration Association schedules the process, appoints a neutral to conduct the settlement conference, and provides a list of arbitrators from which the parties select the person to conduct the hearing. Sessions may be held at any location convenient for the parties.

THE EXPERIENCE OF THE LDRP

During the three years of the research phase of the program, LDRP staff members were in contact with lawyers in 128 libel disputes. Disputes were referred by a variety of sources, including defense attorneys (9 percent), plaintiffs or their attorneys (10 percent), libel insurers (20 percent), and third parties (e.g., a friend of the plaintiff) (5 percent). We supplemented these cases with media libel cases we identified (56 percent) through searches of NEXIS, through articles in newspapers and trade journals, and through a clipping service covering daily and weekly newspapers. After learning about a dispute, we attempted to contact both attorneys by telephone in addition to mailing them information about the LDRP. Because in most instances we were in contact with cases involved in ongoing litigation, we spoke about the LDRP with the attorneys rather than the parties. We were able to reach 86 plaintiffs' attorneys (67 percent) by telephone and contacted an additional 27 (21 percent) by mail only. We spoke with 105 defense attorneys (82 percent) by telephone and reached 4 (3 percent) by mail only. Both the plaintiff and defense attorneys in the same case were contacted by telephone or mail in 94 cases (73 percent).

When we reached the attorneys, we described the LDRP and its potential benefits compared to litigation. We followed up with subsequent telephone calls to answer any questions about the LDRP, to determine the parties' willingness to resolve the dispute through the program, and to ascertain whether the dispute met the LDRP's criteria (i.e., that it was likely to be seriously litigated and involved statements of a factual nature that had caused apparent reputational harm). If both sides to a case indicated they might be interested in using the LDRP, we would offer to hold a conference call with the lawyers to facilitate their discussion of the program and to assist their negotiating the details of the process.

From the conversations with the attorneys, we learned a good deal about the dispute, the lawyers' and parties' reactions to the LDRP, and the reasons they were or were not interested in using the program. Structured telephone interviews exploring these and additional issues in more detail were conducted with attorneys who had given the LDRP some thought and, thus, were better able to provide a meaningful evaluation of its pros and cons as an alternative to litigation.[46] Attorneys who used the LDRP were asked additional questions about their assessments of the process and the outcome. Telephone interviews were completed with forty plaintiffs' attorneys and forty-two defense attorneys. Partial interviews or responses to a mailed questionnaire were obtained from nine plaintiffs' attorneys and five defense attorneys.

We attempted to interview a sample of the plaintiffs and media defendants. Many attorneys would not consent to our contacting their clients while the case was still in litigation (and even near the end of the research phase, many cases were not resolved); others denied consent for unspecified reasons. Some of the defense attorneys said there was no one to speak to at the media organization because they (the lawyers) had made all the decisions regarding the LDRP. Interviews were completed with fourteen plaintiffs and eleven defendants. The plaintiffs' interviews addressed their reaction to the alleged libel and their decision to sue, discussions with their attorney about the alternative process, their understanding of and reactions to the program, and their assessments of their experience with libel litigation. Comparable information was obtained from editors, publishers, and news directors.

Because we spoke with the attorneys in our initial case contacts and conducted most of our interviews with them, the attorneys were our primary source of information about the disputants' reactions to the LDRP. However, it was frequently difficult to ascertain whether the attorneys were indicating their own views and interests or those of their clients. In many instances, the attorneys would clearly talk about their own interests or would speak in terms of "our" interest. In addition, some attorneys told us they did not tell their clients about the LDRP, and others rejected use of the LDRP before they had discussed it with their clients. Many of the responses reported here, therefore, may be more an indication of the attorneys' interest than the clients'.[47] The following quote from an interview with a plaintiff's attorney is illustrative. "The remedy is not adequate [because] we need money. I'm a tort attorney on contingency [and] I get paid when I win. I only take a client if he can win money; I don't take a client if he just wants vindication. I didn't tell my client [about the LDRP]. I knew he wouldn't want to use it."

Case Characteristics[48]

Plaintiffs in 106 of the 128 cases (83 percent) contacted about the LDRP were individuals, whereas 22 (17.2 percent) of the plaintiffs were businesses or corporations. At the time the alleged libel appeared, 34 plaintiffs (29 percent) were candidates for or were holding public office (both elected and appointed).[49] Twenty-eight plaintiffs (24 percent) were professionals or white-collar employees and 22 (19 percent) were business managers or business owners. Six plaintiffs (5 percent) were entertainers and 6 (5 percent) held a variety of other jobs. The content of the alleged libel in 52 percent of the cases involved the plaintiff's business or professional activity, 26 percent involved public or political activity, 11 percent involved personal or private activity, and 11 percent involved criminal activity.

Defendants in 82 of the 128 cases (66 percent) were media organizations; in 18 cases (14 percent), the defendants were nonmedia entities; and in 25 cases (20 percent), both media and nonmedia entities were named as defendants.[50] In 64 of the cases (60 percent) involving a media defendant, the media organization was a newspaper; in 19 cases (18 percent), a television or radio station; in 15 cases (14 percent), a magazine, trade, or scholarly journal; and in 8 cases (7 percent), the media defendant was a book publisher, wire service, movie company, or other publication. In 58 of the cases (55 percent) involving a media defendant, the medium had a local circulation area, 12 (11 percent) had state or regional circulation, and 20 (19 percent) had national or international circulation. In 15 cases (14 percent), the media defendant had a specialized circulation (e.g., a legal newspaper, a scholarly journal, a university or high school newspaper).

Most of the cases had been filed less than three months before our first contact with them. One hundred and four cases (81 percent) had been filed before our first contact and 24 (19 percent) had not been filed.[51] Of the filed cases for which we had an approximate filing date, we contacted 34 cases (39 percent) less than a month after filing, 32 (37 percent) between one and three months, 9 (10 percent) between three and twelve months, and 12 cases (14 percent) more than a year after filing. Of the filed cases for which we had information about discovery and pretrial activity that had occurred prior to our first contact, 22 cases (30 percent) had conducted substantial discovery and 15 cases (16 percent) had already had pretrial judicial action.

Plaintiffs' Reactions to the Alleged Libel

The fourteen plaintiffs who were interviewed gave responses consistent with those of plaintiffs interviewed in the ILRP's prior study. What had upset them most about the story was that it was false. All fourteen plaintiffs reported reputational harm. Several commented that the alleged libel had affected every part of their public and private lives: Their children were harassed, their families received threatening phone calls, and they and their families were constantly asked about the story by acquaintances. Two plaintiffs said the alleged libel caused them to lose an election, and one said the story played a substantial role in his removal from public office. Three plaintiffs reported suffering financial harm as a result of the alleged libel: One plaintiff said his grant funding was cut substantially, another reported a temporary drop in business, and a third said he experienced a dramatic drop in business income and had to sell his business at a substantial loss. "It was a crime to lose the business . . . one day [the business] was there, the next day it was gone. The business we created and cared very much about was destroyed." Comparing the responses of the plaintiffs we interviewed with their lawyers' responses, the plaintiffs seemed to focus more on the way the story harmed them personally, even if it dealt with their performance in a business or professional sphere, whereas the lawyers seemed to focus more on the harm to their clients' professional reputation.

Both plaintiff and defense attorneys indicated a majority of plaintiffs had contacted the media about the story prior to suit, and most of these plaintiffs had asked the defendant to correct, retract, or clarify the story or to apologize. A few plaintiffs had noted problems with the story but had requested no specific action, several had requested that the media publish letters from them or from others taking issue with statements in the story, and a few had asked the media to delay publication while the plaintiffs gathered evidence to prove that the statements were false. Only one plaintiff was reported to have asked the media organization to pay money damages.

Almost all of the fourteen plaintiffs interviewed said that they would have been satisfied if, immediately following the story, the media had published or broadcast a correction or retraction. One plaintiff said, "My reputation is worth far more to me than money"; another noted, "I could care less whether we got a dollar back. It was a matter of strictly fairness, and that was it." Several plaintiffs specified that the correction had to be substantial and detailed and receive as much coverage as the original story.

Only two plaintiffs indicated that they would have sought money damages even if the media had immediately corrected the story. One of these plaintiffs lost many customers after the alleged libel and felt a retraction would not have been enough to change people's minds or to make up for the money he had lost. The other plaintiff wanted to punish the defendant financially because "I faced great uncertainty over the effect of the broadcast, and it caused me a lot of worry. I felt they should pay for that aggravation."

The following comments illustrate how the objectives of some plaintiffs had changed by the time they decided to sue.

> Originally, I would have been satisfied if the stations had "come clean," said "we all make mistakes, our sources were wrong, we apologize." Once it got nasty, then I became defensive and started to be concerned about punishing the stations monetarily for what they did.

> I finally got to the point where I felt "somebody's got to pay me for this." Later, I didn't care about the money; I wanted the station to suffer embarrassment.

> After the dispute had dragged on and on with no apology, no nothing, then I wanted money for the aggravation.

> Now my client wants compensation for his lost employment prospects. Early on, he would have wanted something that would have prevented or stopped the damage to his reputation. Now he needs compensation.

According to their attorneys, six plaintiffs (18 percent) sued in order to receive financial compensation, three (9 percent) wanted money damages in order to punish the defendant, and two (6 percent) wanted to stop further publication. Nonetheless, almost half of the plaintiffs' attorneys interviewed (16 or 47 percent) said their clients sued in an effort to restore their reputation and have the record set straight, and seven (20 percent) said their clients wanted to have the record set straight as well as to receive monetary compensation for financial harm.

When the plaintiffs themselves were asked why they had decided to sue, seven of twelve said they filed suit in order to clear their name, to show that the statements were false, to get the story corrected, or to restore their reputation. One plaintiff said, "I sued to set the record straight"; another said, "I sued to show that the statements were false." Some of these plaintiffs said suit was a last resort, something they felt they had to do in order to prevent this from happening to others or not to let a blatant falsehood go without a response. Two additional plaintiffs reported that their primary goal was to clear their name and show that the story was false; recovering financial damages was secondary. For instance, one of these plaintiffs said, "I sued to clear my name and make up for the great financial damages I've incurred." One plaintiff said he wanted to stop publication and to redress damages; another said he sued to punish the defendant financially.

Interest in the LDRP

Before discussing the extent of interest in the LDRP based on our initial case-contact conversations with the attorneys (i.e., not the interviews), we must note a number of cautions about using this measure as an indication of interest. The measure reflects the level of interest in the LDRP the attorney expressed during the conversations, which may or may not be the true interest of the attorney (let alone of the client).[52] An attorney's indication of interest or noninterest during a given telephone call is highly dependent on what is happening with the case in the litigation process, on the other side's interest, and on the timing of the contact.[53] Thus, our measure of interest is affected by the relative timing and nature of our contact with the attorney.

Of the attorneys reached by telephone and thus able to express an initial reaction, the majority of plaintiffs' attorneys (80 percent) and defense attorneys (86 percent) were at least willing to consider using the LDRP to resolve the case. In the remaining cases, one or both of the lawyers rejected the process almost immediately. Of the cases in which an attorney was contacted by telephone or mail about the LDRP, forty-six plaintiffs' attorneys (41 percent of 113) and twenty-eight defense attorneys (26 percent of 109) reported their clients were not interested in using the LDRP; fifteen plaintiffs' attorneys (13 percent) and twenty-seven defense attorneys (25 percent) had not expressed a clear opinion or had said they might be interested "later" (e.g., after doing some discovery or after a ruling on a summary judgment motion); and twenty-two plaintiffs' lawyers (20 percent) and thirteen defense lawyers (12 percent) had expressed no opinion. Thirty plaintiffs' lawyers (26 percent) and forty-one defense lawyers (38 percent) reported their clients were interested in using the LDRP. In only fifteen cases were both parties in the same case interested in using the LDRP; in nine of these cases, both parties expressed serious interest. In some of these cases, both sides were not interested in using the LDRP at the same point in time.

In all, five of the 128 cases[54] agreed in principle to use the LDRP to resolve their disputes. Two of the five cases settled before formally submitting their disputes to the LDRP. In one of these cases, the defense attorney had assumed that the plaintiff wanted substantial money damages and, thus, did not seriously consider the LDRP as a option for resolving the case. During a subsequent conference call with program staff and both attorneys, the plaintiff's attorney said his client was interested in vindicating his reputation, not in money damages, and was willing to use the LDRP. In the process of discussing the program, the attorneys decided to try to write a joint clarification. They succeeded in producing a statement that both sides found satisfactory and settled the case. In the other case, both parties had agreed to use the LDRP, but before they entered the program, the defendant received a favorable ruling on a discovery motion that made a defense win at trial certain. At that point, the defendant refused to enter the program, the plaintiff decided not to pursue the dispute, and the case was resolved by a confidential settlement.

The three other cases each used a somewhat different version of the LDRP procedures. One of the cases had a settlement conference with a mediator. The defendant had agreed that the statement was false and had published a correction in the next issue of the newspaper. Although there was no issue of truth or falsity to be arbitrated, the parties were interested in seeing whether mediation could facilitate a settlement of the case. We agreed to modify the usual procedure and to let the parties use only the mediation component of the LDRP. The mediator explored each party's interests and proposals for resolving the dispute, but the parties were unable to agree on what further corrective measures were appropriate or acceptable.

A second case had a settlement conference with a special master after efforts to negotiate a correction had reached an impasse. The newspaper's editor did not want to participate in a binding process but was willing to have a respected journalist hear both sides, decide whether there were problems with the story, and suggest the wording of a correction. The plaintiff was interested in a correction, had no interest in money damages, and was agreeable to the editor's suggestions. A mutually chosen journalist served as the special master and helped to break the deadlock in the negotiations by identifying weaknesses in the position of each side and suggesting possible phrasing of a correction for several of the items. The attorneys drafted a correction that was acceptable to both sides, and its publication resolved the dispute. Parties in the third case signed an agreement to arbitrate and dismissed the suit but have not yet gone through arbitration.

The lawyers and their clients who used the LDRP said it was faster, less disruptive, and less expensive than litigating the case at trial.[55] The parties and attorneys felt the process was fair and that the neutral had understood the issues in dispute and had made good efforts to help them reach an agreement. Satisfaction was somewhat lower in the case that did not settle, precisely because it had not been resolved. Nonetheless, both sides felt mediation had been useful in providing them with information on how the other side viewed the issues in the case and what each party's motives and objectives were.

The lawyers in two additional cases attributed settlement to the LDRP, saying that it provided the context in which the parties began to discuss the dispute and their real interests. In one case, the attorneys said their discussions about the program and the form the remedy might take had stimulated settlement talks. In another case, the prospective plaintiff was interested in a correction rather than money damages and wanted to use the LDRP. The news organization did not want to use the LDRP but, through talking with program staff, became convinced of the plaintiff's interest in a correction and his willingness to pursue litigation if the LDRP was not used. Subsequently, a senior editor agreed to meet with the plaintiff, and, as a result, the newspaper published a correction satisfactory to both sides and averted a suit. In these cases, the program facilitated settlement by opening lines of communication and acting as an intermediary through individual contacts and conference calls. As one attorney said, "The program was an excuse for the two parties to speak to one another about settlement. It got the wheels moving, got us talking."

Reactions to the LDRP

Plaintiffs' attorneys who said their clients wanted to use the LDRP gave as reasons that it would be a cheaper and faster way of getting what the plaintiff wanted (i.e., to get a correction and clear his or her reputation), that it would save the emotional cost of a long trial, and that it would provide an impartial assessment and allow a simple determination of the truth or falsity because there would be no constitutional defenses. A number of plaintiffs said they had felt they had no choice but to file suit in order to get a response from the media organization. These plaintiffs felt an advantage of the LDRP was that by indicating their willingness to use the program, they could let the media know they were serious about the dispute while showing they were acting in good faith by not suing for money damages.

> The LDRP provides an alternative route if one just wants to be vindicated and just wants to clear stuff up. It allows both sides to be less

defensive. It is a simpler and easier process. The defendant is less defensive and may be more willing to correct the statements because there is no threat of big money damages.

My client did not want money. He felt that he had been wronged and he wanted to do something about it, but he didn't have enough money to survive a legal battle. He was not looking for a million dollars; he just wanted to have his name cleared, and have it cleared quickly. Time was very important: A quick retraction could prevent damage to his reputation.

Plaintiffs' attorneys in cases that were not interested in using the LDRP most frequently cited the lack of money damages as a problem. The attorneys gave different reasons why money was needed: to compensate economic loss, to compensate the harm suffered more effectively than a retraction or apology alone could, to pay attorneys' fees and litigation expenses, or to punish or send a message to the media. Other plaintiffs' attorneys said the case was too far along to use the LDRP: too much money had already been spent, the parties were too dug in and were determined to go to court, or things had become too polarized and there was too much acrimony between the parties. Some plaintiffs' attorneys felt that publication of the arbitrator's finding would not restore the plaintiff's reputation because it might repeat the libel or it might not get as much coverage as the original story or as a trial. A few plaintiffs' attorneys indicated they would have been interested in using the LDRP if the media would have agreed to let the arbitrator award some money damages.

The program does not accomplish anything . . . without the award of money damages. I didn't want money for myself—I would be willing to give it to charity—but to make a difference, the defendant has to suffer monetarily. An award for monetary damages shows the public that the defendant was wrong. The program doesn't have consequences sufficient to satisfy the harm done to the plaintiff and to make the parties "even."

When I heard about the program, I wasn't interested—I said "now I'm going for broke" [for the money]. I have nothing to lose. My reputation is already destroyed. People have to know about your program before irreparable damage has been done to the plaintiff and before both sides have sunk much money into it. Once both sides have spent a lot of money, it is hard for them to put aside the litigation and throw away the money they have spent. In this case, the damage had already been done and there was no way publication after mediation would restore the plaintiff's reputation.

My client feels he has been too severely harmed to be satisfied with the publication remedy. He wants to put the defendant on the same hot seat of uncertainty of outcome and threat of losing a lot of money. He wants to make the defendant suffer as much as he suffered, feel what he felt.

My client wants revenge, a pound of flesh, which he can get best through money. He feels what was done to him was very wrong. The process would not provide him with that.

Defense attorneys whose clients were interested in using the LDRP most frequently mentioned that it was likely to be faster and less expensive and would eliminate the threat of money damages. Other advantages cited included that the process would be simpler, both in terms of discovery and presenting the case at the hearing, and that a more knowledgeable neutral might produce a more fair outcome.

I was interested . . . because it would enable us to avoid economic damages and shorten the already lengthy process, saving us time and trouble. It would help us get it over with. It would end the case. Libel cases take a toll in distraction with the editorial staff and journalists. It becomes the focal point of the newsroom and takes many person-hours.

We think we can win the lawsuit and that we could also win in your program. We believe we can show that it was true or that we had reason to believe it was true. . . . So we thought we might as well save some money in litigation costs and some time and use the program. It would also eliminate any exposure to monetary damages.

I would have liked to get the hassle out of my life, to get the case over. In court, we're all going to die before this case is resolved.

The LDPR is simple, less expensive, gets the job done, and the parties foreswear financial gain. The civil courts have lost all touch with reality.

The biggest advantage would be that it would have gotten the parties to the table and discussing the matter. The real value is that the program is an outside force that could bring the parties together. . . . It would remove us from the atmosphere of being concerned about appearing to be weak. Everyone is afraid to resolve a case peaceably, even for nuisance value, because it would look like a sign of weakness.

The most frequent reasons given by defense attorneys for not wanting to use the LDRP included that the case was likely to be dismissed or settled and that the media did not want to give up their constitutional privileges. Additional reasons included that they had too much invested in litigation, they always take an "all-out-war" approach to libel litigation to prevent future suits, and an arbitrator might be more likely to compromise than a judge would in ruling on motions to dismiss or for summary judgment.

We do not want to compromise or settle on even the small, nuisance cases because the First Amendment considerations involved are too important. Saving money is secondary; in the long haul, the money is justified in preserving the principles.

We don't believe that any of the three defendants in the case deserve to be sued. As such, we want to file a Rule 11 motion to recover our legal fees. If we succeed in your program, we can't recover our legal fees unless the plaintiff agrees to it. . . . You can't give us a quick summary judgment resolution like we get in court.

A majority of both plaintiff and defense attorneys interviewed thought the program would provide a hearing that would be as fair or fairer than a trial, would save their clients time and money, and would produce an outcome favorable to their client. One attorney estimated it would save 60 to 75 percent of the cost of a trial; others focused on the time that would be saved and the backlog in the courts. Several attorneys commented that the neutral's knowledge of libel issues and familiarity with the editorial process would permit an easier and shorter presentation and would likely result in a more sophisticated outcome than at trial.

Eighty-one percent of the defense attorneys thought that they would have a very good or pretty good chance of getting a favorable outcome in the LDRP. Virtually the same percentage (79 percent) predicted a good outcome at summary judgment, but even more (95 percent) predicted a good outcome at trial. The plaintiffs' attorneys had less optimistic views of the likely outcome of both the alternative process and trial than did the defense attorneys. Fifty-nine percent of plaintiffs' attorneys predicted a favorable outcome in the LDRP, and 43 percent predicted a favorable outcome at trial. A majority of defense attorneys said using the LDRP would have no effect on the number of libel actions filed against their clients. Some of these attorneys noted that the outcome of one case would have very little impact on future cases because so few plaintiffs' lawyers specialize in libel and follow how the media resolve cases. Others commented that even though the LDRP makes it easier and less expensive for plaintiffs to bring a dispute to the program, it would not greatly increase complaints because it does not involve money damages.

Plaintiffs were asked whether publication of an arbitrator's finding in their favor would have restored their reputation if they had used the LDRP shortly after the story had appeared. Six of eight plaintiffs said it would have, particularly if the statement were detailed, clearly worded, and received the same kind of coverage as the original story. Two plaintiffs, however, said it would not have restored their reputation, even shortly after publication. One of these plaintiffs said the damage had already been done; the other said the second story either would not reach the same audience or would not change the opinions people had formed as a result of the first story, making a monetary damage award necessary to show the public that the defendant had been wrong.

The plaintiffs' attorneys were asked whether publication of the neutral's finding that the story was false and defamatory would restore the plaintiff's reputation. Twelve of forty (30 percent) said it would, twenty-one (52 percent) said it would not, and seven (18 percent) said it would depend. Those who said such publication would restore their client's reputation noted that the plaintiff could mail or give the finding to specific people, such as prospective employers, who the plaintiff wanted to be sure saw the determination that the statements were false. One attorney said the LDRP would have been good for his client, who needed to have his name cleared fast in order to prevent harm to his reputation. Another attorney noted that the trials of "small" plaintiffs would not receive substantial publicity anyway.

Plaintiffs' attorneys who said that publication either would not or might not restore the plaintiff's reputation gave a number of reasons. Many felt that publication never restores reputation because it is impossible to correct the impression created by the first story; a few expressed concern that publishing the finding would repeat the libel and do more harm than good. Others said the finding would not reach the same audience, it would not get as prominent coverage as the original, or it would not receive as much publicity as a trial. Several attorneys said that publication without money damages was either inadequate compensation for the plaintiff or insufficient punishment for the defendant. When asked specifically whether publication of the finding would have provided enough publicity to satisfy the plaintiff, over two thirds of the plaintiff's attorneys interviewed said it would not. Two thirds of the defense attorneys said publication of the neutral's finding that the statements were true and not defamatory would vindicate their clients.

FACTORS AFFECTING INTEREST IN THE LDRP

What factors seemed to determine whether a plaintiff or defendant in a given case would be interested in using the LDRP? Our analyses point to the following: the attorneys' familiarity with alternative dispute resolution processes and their recommendations to their clients, the parties' motives or objectives for the litigation, the intensity of the conflict, and the stage of litigation when considering the program. We are continuing to examine how these interrelated factors interact in a given case and to explore the effects of other potentially relevant factors.

The Role of the Attorneys

Consistent with the findings of other studies, the attorney's recommendation and encouragement was a key factor in whether the party was interested in using an alternative process.[56] Attorneys serve as gatekeepers generally, and even more so in the present study because they were the people we spoke to about the LDRP. The attorneys had total control over whether they told their clients about the program and, if so, whether they explained it accurately and whether they characterized it positively or negatively. Several plaintiff and defense attorneys told us they did not tell their clients about the program, and almost one fifth rejected use of the LDRP before they had discussed it with their clients. Several defense attorneys said that they had mentioned the program to their clients but that they make all the litigation decisions.

Lawyers' resistance to using alternative dispute resolution programs has been attributed to a lack of familiarity (which can produce misjudgment or contempt), a concern that they might make less money or lose control, a fear that doing anything short of all-out litigation might be viewed as a "sign of weakness," and an adversarial perspective that constricts the way lawyers function in settings in which a problem-solving approach might be more appropriate.[57] In the present study, the attorneys' familiarity with and attitudes toward alternatives influenced their recommendations regarding the LDRP. The majority of both plaintiffs' attorneys and defense attorneys said they previously had been involved in mediation or arbitration.[58] Those who had previously used alternatives were more likely to say they had recommended that their client use the LDRP. Attorneys who had previously had a bad experience in arbitration or who had a general negative perception of the process (e.g., feeling that arbitrators tend to "split the baby") were less likely to be interested in using the program. Thus, the attorneys were a major factor in determining whether the LDRP would be used.

The Parties' Objectives

Media organizations have different policies regarding libel litigation. Some litigate everything and settle nothing in order to send a message to potential plaintiffs that suit will be long and expensive. Thus, their concern for preventing future suits often overrides their interests in a given case. These defendants were rarely interested in using the LDRP. In other instances, the case involved certain legal issues on which the defendant wanted a court decision. Defendants who viewed the dispute solely in terms of legal rights and First Amendment principles were less likely to be interested in the LDRP.[59] Organizations with a limited circulation were more likely to be interested in using the LDRP than were media with national or international circulation. Perhaps these organizations are more interested in an alternative because they are less able financially to afford litigation or damage awards.[60]

Plaintiffs who wanted to have their name cleared or to have the record set straight were more likely to be interested in using the LDRP than were plaintiffs who wanted to recover money, either to compensate for economic harm or to punish the defendant. A few plaintiffs did not appear to want a determination regarding the accuracy of the statements but were using the libel suit to denounce publicly the alleged libel, to deter further publication, and to get publicity. The more the dispute had escalated, the more likely plaintiffs were interested in punishing the defendant and the less likely they were interested in the LDRP.[61] In cases where there was a long-standing animosity between the parties, neither party was likely to be interested in using the LDRP.

The objectives of some parties may help to explain why the lower transaction costs of the LDRP did not seem to be an important factor in their decision about the program. Although most plaintiff and defense attorneys viewed the LDRP as likely to be faster, less expensive, and less disruptive for their clients, this was apparently not enough to persuade them to use the program. Perhaps because the LDRP would not enable their clients to accomplish their objectives (e.g., to punish the defendant financially or to uphold their constitutional rights), the likely time and cost savings of the LDRP appeared to receive little weight. As one publisher said, "Money is not really a consideration to us. We're concerned with the operation of our business, saying what we do is right. The end thing is to be declared right." Another noted, "Saving money is secondary. In the long haul, the money is justified in preserving the [First Amendment] principles." From the media's perspective, because the outcome of litigation is fairly predictable and usually in their favor, they may need a greater incentive than incurring lower costs to prompt them to use the LDRP. Not surprisingly, both plaintiff and defense attorneys were more likely to be interested in using the LDRP in cases where they saw little chance of a satisfactory outcome at trial or at summary judgment.

The Stage of Litigation

The stage of litigation during which we contacted the cases seemed to affect their interest in the program. Those who had not yet filed suit were more likely to be interested in using the program than those who had already filed. This may be because they had not yet decided to pursue litigation or had not yet adopted an adversarial perspective and, thus, were more responsive to a different way of repairing their reputation. Plaintiffs were least interested in the LDRP shortly after filing. Others have noted that "by the time clients have decided to litigate, they are too angry to consider an alternative to litigation."[62] "Emotions run high at the outset of litigation," and people "tend to start out with a very one-sided view of their case."[63] Plaintiffs became more interested three to twelve months after the suit was filed and were also more likely to be interested if there had been some pretrial activity. It is possible that they began to see the weaknesses in their case or began to realize the burden of litigating a libel case and the resources that suit would require. Plaintiffs' interest declined later, presumably because they or their lawyers had too much money invested in litigation at that point or because the dispute had escalated too far to consider a process that required some level of trust and goodwill.

Defendants showed greater interest if there had been discovery or pretrial activity. This could be because defendants know that many libel complaints never become suits and that many suits are not pursued; thus, they have little incentive to act until they know the plaintiff intends to litigate the case seriously. Another explanation could be that information obtained in discovery or a decision on a pretrial motion had indicated that their cases were not as strong as they had earlier thought. Like the plaintiffs, defendants were more interested in using the LDRP between three to twelve months after the suit was filed than they were in the first three months. We are continuing to explore the factors underlying changes in interest in the LDRP over time.

CONCLUSION

The low rate of utilization of the LDRP is typical of voluntary mediation and arbitration programs in contexts ranging from farmer–creditor mediation to medical malpractice arbitration.[64] Most disputes that use alternative dispute resolution procedures do so because they are required to by law (e.g., court-annexed arbitration of claims below a certain amount, mandatory child custody mediation), by preexisting contractual agreement, or because one party, usually an insurance company, has decided to resolve a given segment of its disputes through mediation or arbitration. Programs that depend on the willingness of both parties to agree to their use after a dispute has arisen attract relatively few cases, even when offered on a low- or no-cost basis.[65] Low usage of voluntary programs has been attributed to the lack of public awareness and understanding of alternatives and the negative or ambivalent attitude of the legal community.[66] At present, we can make several recommendations that may increase the use of an alternative process in libel disputes and may also have implications for the use of declaratory judgment options.[67]

Attorneys and litigants need to change their perception that expressing interest in using an alternative dispute resolution process is a sign that their case is weak. Cases that are likely to settle anyway might be settled sooner with the help of mediation. Cases in which parties want a determination by a third party can go to arbitration for a faster and less expensive adjudication. Thus, the processes of settlement and adjudication that occur in litigation also occur in alternative programs, just in a slightly different form.

If media organizations are interested in resolving libel suits quickly and inexpensively, and in averting some suits altogether, they may have to take the initiative to propose the use of an alternative process. Because few plaintiffs' attorneys specialize in media law and there is no organized plaintiffs' libel bar, it is difficult to inform attorneys who may become involved in libel cases about an alternative program. Similarly, there is no way to inform potential plaintiffs across the country about an alternative program in advance of their contemplating litigation. However, many media lawyers already know about the LDRP, and reaching other attorneys in the media defense bar as well as media personnel is comparatively easy.

In addition, it is in the media's interest to recommend using the program early in the dispute. Plaintiffs' interest in obtaining a nonmonetary resolution of a dispute is highest immediately following publication of the alleged libel, while any harm they have suffered can still be mitigated by a correction or clarification and before they have decided to file suit. If plaintiffs are informed of a process resulting in a nonmonetary remedy before they hire a lawyer, they may be more likely to seek an attorney who is willing to use an alternative program and to agree to an hourly fee arrangement. After the plaintiff has hired a lawyer (often with a contingency-fee arrangement) and has decided to file suit, it is more difficult to interest the plaintiff (and his or her lawyer) in using an alternative program. Moreover, the earlier the parties get involved in an alternative program, the more time and money they can save. A quick resolution can be achieved only if the process is entered early; the benefits are considerably reduced if substantial discovery and trial preparation have been conducted or if the case has been sitting around for a year.

It is important that an alternative program have a range of dispute resolution options in order to accommodate the varying interests of parties in different cases. Some media organizations may want to ensure a final resolution of the dispute outside the courts and would want to use only binding arbitration with a litigation waiver. Other media defendants, however, may be reluctant to have a third party make findings about the story but would participate in a nonbinding process in an effort to try to settle the case. Similarly, some plaintiffs may be willing to use a nonbinding process in the hope of negotiating a correction but would be unwilling to give up their ability to pursue the dispute in court if a satisfactory correction is not obtained. An alternative program, therefore, should provide binding arbitration for those who want a final resolution out of court as well as nonbinding options ranging from mediation to arbitration for those who are seeking the opinion of a neutral person to help settle the case. In addition, a range of people to serve as neutrals should be available, as some parties may prefer a retired judge and others may want someone with journalistic experience.

APPENDIX: LIBEL DISPUTE RESOLUTION PROGRAM PROCEDURES

1. Eligibility Criteria

1.1   The dispute should be one that is expected to be seriously litigated.

1.2   Disputes will not be eligible for consideration if they are determined by the Libel Dispute Resolution Program [hereinafter the Program] to involve (a) challenged statements of a nonfactual nature or (b) the absence of reputational harm.

1.3   For research purposes, the parties and attorneys must be willing to be interviewed and to have the proceedings observed and recorded by the Program. All information collected for research purposes shall be strictly confidential and the parties will remain anonymous. The research will be reported in such a way that the parties will not be identifiable.

2. Issues to Be Adjudicated

2.1   The complainant shall have the burden of defining the specific pub-
      lished/broadcast statements that are alleged to be false, must show that
      the challenged statements have caused reputational harm, and, unless
      the parties agree otherwise, shall have the burden of proof on the issue
      of falsity.

2.2   The issues to be adjudicated shall be (a) the existence of reputational
      harm and (b) the truth or falsity of alleged and defined factual state-
      ments or assertions published/broadcast by the responding publisher/
      broadcaster. Whether the challenged statement is one of fact will be
      determined by the words published or inferences reasonably implied by
      the publication, even though not expressed explicitly in the text.

2.3   In cases where the publisher republished information alleged to be
      false, every effort should be made to have the original source included
      as a party to the proceeding. Regardless of whether the source's inclu-
      sion is possible, the issue to be adjudicated shall be the truth or falsity of
      the underlying facts. The finding may also indicate (a) that the respon-
      dent had obtained the information from another party who was unwill-
      ing to cooperate in the proceedings; or (b) whether the respondent had
      accurately reported what the source had said.

2.4   The finding will contain a statement that no determination of the
      publisher's/broadcaster's fault or the reasonableness of its procedures
      has been made, nor should such a conclusion be drawn from the find-
      ing.

3. Remedy

3.1   If the neutral decides that the dispute involves factual statements and
      that reputational harm has occurred, the neutral shall make a written
      finding on the falsity issue. If the neutral decides that no reputational
      harm has occurred, the neutral's written finding shall so state and the
      falsity issue need not be addressed.

3.2   The finding of the neutral shall be available for publication.

3.3   The respondent shall agree to publish/broadcast the neutral's finding in
      full or, in lieu of such agreement, shall agree to pay the other party to
      have the findings published/broadcast by the respondent or in other
      comparable media such that the finding is likely to reach the same
      audience as the original publication/broadcast. The specifics of the
      remedy shall be subject to the negotiation of the parties.

3.4   The parties, by agreement, may depart from the remedy outlined in
      Section 3.3 and determine any other remedy.

3.5   Attorneys' fees may be available on terms agreed to by the parties.

4. Submission Agreement to Initiate Process

In order to initiate the alternative process, parties must file a signed copy of a written submission agreement to proceed under these rules. It shall include the following points.

4.1   The parties agree to submit the dispute to this alternative process under its rules. The rules shall be effective unless the parties have specified otherwise. The rules will be supplemented by the Mediation and Arbitration Rules of the American Arbitration Association [hereinafter the administrator].

4.2   The parties agree to abide by the agreed-on remedy and to waive further legal action.

4.3   In the absence of an agreement otherwise, each party agrees that it shall bear the cost it incurs in connection with preparation for the proceedings (e.g., legal costs and fees, travel, photocopying, and witnesses).

4.4   The parties agree that neither the Program, the administrator, nor the neutrals shall be liable to any party for any act or omission in connection with any action under the rules.

4.5   The Program, the administrator, and the neutrals shall not divulge any information produced in these proceedings and shall not testify in regard to the dispute in any adversary proceeding or judicial forum.

4.6   The submission agreement shall include the names, addresses, and phone numbers of all parties, their representatives and counsel, and a brief statement of the nature of the dispute, including the specific factual statements that are alleged to be false, or the procedure by which they are to be determined.

4.7   The parties shall determine the elements of the process which are negotiable (remedy, information exchange, type of settlement conference, formality of the hearing, location of the hearing, etc.) within the general parameters of the alternative process.

5. Scheduling

5.1   Schedule:
Day (on or before)
1   sign submission agreement
7   neutrals selected/appointed
21   information exchange
30   settlement conference
50   hearing
60   receive finding

5.2   The parties may agree to change these times, but the schedule they establish should ensure that the dispute will be resolved within seventy-five (75) calendar days.

5.3 The administrator will help the parties set a date and time for the exchange, conference, and hearing that is convenient for both parties and the neutral.

5.4 Any request to extend an agreed-on deadline must be presented to the administrator and may be granted only for good cause.

6. Selection of the Neutrals

6.1 Immediately after the filing of the submission agreement, each party simultaneously will be given an identical list of five neutrals from which one neutral shall be appointed to conduct the hearing. Each party shall have the right to strike two names from the list on a peremptory basis and an unlimited number with cause. If the list is not returned within seven (7) days, all persons named therein shall be deemed acceptable. From among the persons who have been approved on both lists, the administrator shall appoint a neutral. The parties shall be given notice by telephone of the appointment of the neutral.

6.2 The administrator shall appoint the neutral for the settlement conference.

6.3 Each party is responsible for promptly (within seven (7) days) disclosing to the administrator and to the other party any circumstances known that would cause reasonable doubt regarding the impartiality of any individual appointed.

6.4 The neutrals shall disclose to the administrator any circumstances likely to affect impartiality, including any bias or any financial or personal interest in the result of the process or any past or present relationship with the parties or their counsel. On showing of cause, the administrator will determine whether the neutral shall be disqualified and replaced.

6.5 Administrative and settlement matters will not be heard by the same person selected to conduct the hearing unless the parties agree otherwise.

6.6 The neutrals shall follow their respective codes of ethics.

6.7 There shall be no ex parte communication between the parties and the neutrals other than at the proceedings. Any oral or written communications from the parties to the neutrals shall be directed through the administrator.

7. Information Exchange

7.1 In lieu of discovery, there shall be a structured exchange of information (either by meeting or by conference call; if desired, in the presence of a neutral). If both parties agree that a more formal process is needed, they shall agree on a plan for strictly necessary, limited, expeditious discovery aimed at determining the essential facts.

7.2   Any conferences needed to resolve or clarify informational issues will be held by telephone conference call between the attorneys and the administrator or neutral. These conferences will be of an informal nature.

7.3   the information to be exchanged is subject to the agreement of the parties, but may include:

a.   The identification of witnesses and a summary of the testimony they are expected to give;

b.   a description of any physical evidence;

c.   copies of documents;

d.   summary statements of claims or defenses and the facts underlying them; and

e.   offers of admission and stipulation.

7.4   The neutral, during the hearing, shall have the authority to limit information that was not presented during the information exchange.

8. Settlement Conference

8.1   The parties shall choose (a) to participate in a settlement conference with either a mediator or a special master (see Sections 8.A and 8.B), or (b) to proceed directly to a hearing. If the parties cannot agree, the Program will assign them randomly to either the mediation or special master conference.

8.2   The goals of the settlement conference include (a) reducing the scope of the dispute by defining and simplifying the issues and by identifying and stipulating to uncontested facts, and (b) encouraging settlement discussions.

8.3   Parties who choose to go directly to a hearing will hold a telephone conference call with a neutral, before the hearing, in order to resolve any remaining questions or conflicts concerning information needed for the hearing.

8.A. Mediation

A.1   The mediator may, but need not, request that the parties submit, a week before the conference, a brief statement that identifies any issues whose resolution might reduce the scope of the dispute or contribute significantly to the productivity of settlement discussions, and their position on these issues.

A.2   The mediation session shall be private and informal.

A.3   The parties as well as counsel must be present during the mediation.

A.4   The mediator does not have authority to impose a settlement upon the parties but will attempt to help them reach a satisfactory resolution of their dispute.

A.5   The mediator is authorized to conduct joint and separate meetings with the parties and to make oral and written recommendations for settlement.

A.6   The mediator is authorized to end the mediation whenever, in the judgment of the mediator, further efforts at mediation would not contribute to a resolution of the dispute between the parties.

A.7   Confidential information disclosed to a mediator by the parties or by witnesses in the course of the mediation shall not be divulged by the mediator.

A.8   The parties shall not rely on or introduce as evidence in any other proceeding, any and all aspects of the mediation effort, including, but not limited to: (a) views expressed or suggestions made by the other party with respect to a possible settlement of the dispute; (b) admissions made by the other party in the course of the mediation proceedings; (c) proposals made or views expressed by the mediator; and (d) the fact that the other party had or had not indicated a willingness to accept a proposal for settlement made by the mediator.

A.9   The mediator shall be disqualified as a hearing or trial witness, consultant, or expert for any party in any pending or future action relating to the subject matter of the mediation, including those between persons not parties to the mediation.

8.B. Special Master

B.1   The special master may, but need not, request that the parties submit, a week before the conference, a brief statement that identifies any issues whose resolution might reduce the scope of the dispute or contribute significantly to the productivity of settlement discussions, and their position on these issues.

B.2   The conference shall be private and informal.

B.3   The parties as well as counsel should be present at the conference unless otherwise agreed to in advance.

B.4   Each attorney will make a brief presentation of his or her side of the case (focusing on the apparently disputed areas), explaining his or her view of the facts and describing the supporting evidence.

B.5   The special master will identify areas of substantial agreement and encourage stipulations. He or she also will note areas of disagreement, probing the support for differing views of the facts. The special master then will offer his or her assessment of the relative strengths and weaknesses of key evidence and arguments.

B.6   If the parties and counsel are interested, the special master will help them explore settlement options.

B.7   If the parties have no interest in exploring settlement, or if they try but fail to reach an agreement, the special master will provide them with an evaluation of the likely outcome in a hearing and the reasoning behind it.

B.8   All offers, promises, conduct, and statements, whether oral or written, made in the course of the settlement conference by the special master or by any of the parties, their witnesses, or attorneys are confidential and are inadmissible and not discoverable for any purpose in the hearing or in any other litigation.

B.9   The special master shall be disqualified as a hearing or trial witness, consultant, or expert for any party in any pending or future action relating to the subject matter of the settlement conference, including those between persons not parties to the conference.

9. Hearing

9.1   The neutral may, but need not, request that the parties submit a brief prehearing memo seven (7) to ten (10) days before the hearing in order to familiarize the neutral with the facts and issues in dispute.

9.2   The hearing shall be public unless both parties agree that it shall be closed. The hearing shall be informal.

9.3   The neutral shall require witnesses to testify under oath.

9.4   Starting with the complainant, each party shall present its claims and proofs and witnesses, who shall submit to questions or other examination. The neutral has discretion to vary this procedure but shall afford full and equal opportunity to all parties for the presentation of any material or relevant proofs.

9.5   The neutral shall be the judge of the relevance and materiality of the evidence offered and conformity to legal rules of evidence shall not be necessary. (The Federal Rules of Evidence may be used as a guide in determining the admissibility of evidence.) Except as probative on the question of truth or falsity, the neutral may rule that evidence relating to procedures, decisions, discussions, documents, or any other materials relating to the reasonableness of publication/broadcast decisions, or fault of the publisher/broadcaster, shall neither be admissible nor relevant.

9.6   The parties shall produce such additional evidence as the neutral may deem necessary for an understanding and determination of the dispute. The neutral, when authorized by law to subpoena witnesses or documents, may do so upon the neutral's own initiative or upon the request of any party. All evidence shall be taken in the presence of all the parties, except where any of the parties is absent in default or has waived the right to be present.

9.7 The proceedings shall be recorded for research purposes; the parties may obtain a copy of the recording of the hearing if they wish.

9.8 The neutral shall be empowered to take whatever steps seem appropriate for noncompliance with the procedures.

9.9 If a party fails to be present or fails to obtain an adjournment, after due notice, that party shall be declared in default and a finding may be made. The finding of the neutral would include an indication that the party had failed to appear to present or respond to the claim.

9.10 The failure of a witness to appear, when requested, may, if appropriate, be considered by the neutral in reaching a finding.

9.11 To end the hearing, the neutral shall inquire of all parties whether they have any further proofs to offer or witnesses to be heard; if not, the neutral shall declare the hearing ended.

9.12 The neutral shall make a finding within ten (10) days of the close of the hearing.

9.13 The written findings of the neutral shall be concise but of sufficient detail to identify the factual question(s) at issue; the existence of reputational harm; the truth, falsity, or indeterminacy of the facts as found; and the basis on which the finding has been made. The neutral's finding shall also indicate, if the statement is found to be false, the time within which the publisher/broadcaster must comply with the agreed-on remedy.

NOTES

1. *See infra* note 30 and accompanying text.

2. Major funding for the program was provided by the John and Mary R. Markle Foundation, with additional funding from the Prudential Foundation, the National Institute for Dispute Resolution, and the University of Iowa Interdisciplinary Research Program.

3. The ILRP conducted a detailed empirical analysis of the libel litigation process based on over 700 reported libel cases decided between 1974 and 1984; interviews with 164 plaintiffs, selected media organizations, and attorneys involved in libel litigation; and information from the claim files of a major media libel insurer. R. BEZANSON, G. CRANBERG, & J. SOLOSKI, LIBEL LAW AND THE PRESS: MYTH AND REALITY (1987) [hereinafter LIBEL LAW AND THE PRESS].

4. Questions about the findings of the research phase of the program should be directed to the authors. Referrals and requests for information about using the LDRP should be addressed to Robert Meade, American Arbitration Association, 140 West 51st Street, New York, New York 10020-1203 ((212)-484-4060).

5. New York Times Co. v. Sullivan, 376 U.S. 254 (1964); Gertz v. Robert Welch, Inc., 418 U.S. 323 (1974).

6. *Sullivan*, 376 U.S. at 279.

7. LIBEL LAW AND THE PRESS, *supra* note 3, at 112. Marc A. Franklin's studies of reported libel cases also found media defendants had a high rate of success. Franklin, *Winners and Losers and Why: A Study of Defamation Litigation*, 1980 AM. B. FOUND. RES. J. 457; Franklin, *Suing Media for Libel: A Litigation Study*, 1981 AM. B. FOUND. RES. J. 795.

8. Johnston & Kaufman, *Annenberg, Sullivan at 25, and the Question of Libel Reform*, 7 COMM. LAW. 4, 8 (1989).

9. "The greatest problem in libel today is almost certainly the cost of litigation." Kaufman, Johnston, & Sackler, *Tort Reform and Libel*, 10 COMM. & LAW. 15, 25 (1988) [hereinafter Kaufman].

10. Garbus, *The Many Costs of Libel*, 230 PUBLISHERS WEEKLY, Sept. 5, 1986, at 34; Kaufman, *supra* note 9, at 25; Weber, *Editors Surveyed Describe Half of All Libel Cases as "Nuisance Suits,"* ASNE BULL., Jan. 1986, at 38. Litigation costs increased with the paper's circulation size. Legal fees averaged $10,000 per libel suit for papers with a circulation under 20,000. Papers with a circulation greater than 400,000 spent an average of $542,000 per suit on attorneys' fees. Id. at 38.

11. Stille, *Libel Law Takes on a New Look*, NAT'L L.J., Oct. 24, 1988, at 1, 32. These sums are relatively rare, although defense fees of $200,000 to $300,000 per case are not uncommon. Goodale, *Survey of Recent Media Verdicts, Their Disposition on Appeal, and Media Defense Costs*, 1985 MEDIA INS. & RISK MGMT. 69, 87.

12. Garbus, *supra* note 10, at 37; Genovese, *Libel Update: Issues Remain Heated in Legislatures, Courtrooms*, 8 PRESSTIME, April 1986, at 37.

13. Garbus, *supra* note 10, at 34; Massing, *The Libel Chill: How Cold Is It Out There?*, COLUM. JOURNALISM REV., May/June 1985, at 31, 34.

14. Stille, *supra* note 11, at 33.

15. The litigation process "can destroy a newsroom." Garneau, *Libel Law Reform*, EDITOR & PUBLISHER, Oct. 22 1988, at 36, 37 (quoting Richard Schmidt, attorney for the American Society of Newspaper Editors). In describing his experience in General Westmoreland's suit against CBS, Mike Wallace commented, "When a reporter goes on trial for libel, you're going to his gut. You're going to his soul because you are calling him a cheat." Hall, *The Frustrations of Tough Guy Mike Wallace*, L.A. TIMES, Sept. 26, 1990, § F, at 4. *See also* Leval, *The No-Money, No-Fault Libel Suit: Keeping Sullivan in Its Proper Place*, 101 HARV. L. REV. 1287 (1988).

16. LIBEL LAW AND THE PRESS, supra note 3, at 21.

17. *Id.* at 22.

18. *Id.* at 155-56.

19. *Id.* at 25.

20. *Id.* at 26.

21. *Id.* at 24.

22. *Id.* at 79.

23. *Id.* at 81.

24. *Id.* at 83.

25. "An effective dispute resolution mechanism is one that is inexpensive, speedy, and leads to a final resolution of the dispute. At the same time it should be procedurally fair, efficient (in the sense of leading to optimal solutions), and satisfying to the parties." S. GOLDBERG, E. GREEN, & F. SANDER, DISPUTE RESOLUTION 7 (1985).

26. Leval, *supra* note 15, at 1289-91.

27. Perhaps the best solution is to prevent suits from being filed through more systematic and sensitive complaint-handling practices by the media. LIBEL LAW AND THE PRESS, *supra* note 3, at 53. Such changes have been instituted by some media organizations and have been credited as partly responsible for a recent decline in the number of newly filed libel suits. Society of Professional Journalists, MEDIA LITIGATION '88, Nov. 4, 1988, at 1, 6-7. Nonetheless, a mechanism is still needed to resolve those disputes that reach a stalemate or become a lawsuit.

28. Ackerman, *Defamation and Alternative Dispute Resolution: Healing the Sting*, 1986 MO. J. DISPUTE RESOLUTION 1, 10. In the *Sharon* case, the jury found that the statement was defamatory and false but that the defendants had not acted with actual malice and, consequently, were not responsible for paying damages. Both Sharon and *Time* proclaimed victory. Kaplan, *The Judge's Postmortem of the Sharon Libel Trial*, NAT'L L.J., Mar. 18, 1985, at 27.

29. LIBEL LAW AND THE PRESS, *supra* note 3, at 130-131.

30. *See* Barrett, *Declaratory Judgments for Libel: A Better Alternative*, 75 CALIF. L. REV. 847 (1986); Franklin, *A Declaratory Judgment Alternative to Current Libel Law*, 74 CALIF. L. REV. 809, 812 (1986); Hulme, *Vindicating Reputation: An Alternative to Damages as a Remedy for Defamation*, 30 AM. U. L. REV. 375 (1981); Ingber, *Defamation: A Conflict Between Reason and Decency*, 65 VA. L. REV. 785 (1979); THE ANNENBERG WASHINGTON PROGRAM, *Proposal for the Reform of Libel Law* (1988) [hereinafter ANNENBERG PROPOSAL]; National Conference of Commissioners on Uniform State Laws, DEFAMATION ACT (draft of December 6, 1991).

31. Both the Annenberg Proposal and Franklin's POLRA have a provision that declaratory judgment trials be granted priority over other civil actions. ANNENBERG PROPOSAL, *supra* note 30, at 16; Franklin, *supra* note 30, at 813. It remains to be seen whether the courts will be willing to give defamation actions such priority.

32. To date, none of the bills introduced in Congress or in state legislatures has passed (e.g., H.R. 2846, 99th Cong., 1st Sess. (1985); H.B. 5932, General Assembly, Connecticut (1989); S.B. 1393, General Assembly, California (1989)).

33. Leval, *supra* note 15, at 1294. Judge Leval argues "that, given a correct understanding of the *Sullivan* holding, a plaintiff who sues only for a judgment declaring the falsity of the libel and forgoes any claim for a monetary award is exempt from the obligation to prove that the defendant acted with malice." *Id.* at 1288, 1298.

34. Although often referred to as "alternatives to litigation," most of

these processes have been used in conjunction with litigation in various types of civil cases. Under Rule 16 (c)(7) of the Federal Rules of Civil Procedure, parties in any case can explore the use of procedures other than litigation to resolve their dispute.

35. E. JOHNSON JR., V. KANTOR, & E. SCHWARTZ, OUTSIDE THE COURTS: A SURVEY OF DIVERSION ALTERNATIVES IN CIVIL CASES (1977); Pearson, *An Evaluation of Alternatives to Court Adjudication,* 7 JUST. SYS. J. 420 (1982).

36. Leval, *supra* note 15, at 1301.

37. This is in contrast to declaratory judgment options, which can be used even if only one of the parties wants to use it. In all proposals, if the plaintiff chooses a declaratory judgment option instead of traditional litigation for damages, the defendant must participate in that forum. In some proposals, the media defendant can also elect to use a declaratory judgment option and, thus, can override the plaintiff's desire to sue for money damages. ANNENBERG PROPOSAL, *supra* note 30, at 16; Franklin, *supra* note 30, at 833.

38. LIBEL LAW AND THE PRESS, *supra* note 3, at 159-62.

39. Cole, Hanson & Silbert, *Mediation: Is It an Effective Alternative to Adjudication in Resolving Prisoner Complaints?,* 65 JUDICATURE 481 (1982); Merry & Silbey, *What Do Plaintiffs Want? Reexamining the Concept of Dispute,* 9 JUST. SYS. J. 151 (1984); *Vidmar, Justice Motives and Other Psychological Factors in the Development and Resolution of Disputes,* in THE JUSTICE MOTIVE IN SOCIAL BEHAVIOR: ADAPTING TO TIMES OF SCARCITY AND CHANGE 195 (M. Lerner & S. Lerner eds., 1981).

40. *Libel Dispute Ended by Stipulation for Expert Panel Resolution,* 1 ALTERNATIVE DISPUTE RESOLUTION REPORT 5 (1987).

41. Center for Public Resources, *An Alternative to the Courthouse for Libel Disputes* (draft of April 26, 1985).

42. Ackerman, *supra* note 28, at 1, 19-23. Ackerman has also proposed a nonbinding fact-finding process in which the parties decide whether to accept the fact-finder's advisory opinion on falsity and what action should be taken as a result of the finding. *Id.* at 23-24.

43. Chandler, *Controlling Conflict,* Gannett Center Working Paper at 11 (1989).

44. We reviewed studies of the general effectiveness of scheduling and discovery-management practices, settlement strategies, and third-party decision-making procedures in reducing cost and delay, facilitating settlement, achieving a final resolution, and providing a forum that the participants regard as fair and satisfying.

45. During the research phase of the program, members of the ILRP handled case contacts and referrals. Presently, American Arbitration Association (AAA) staff are available to discuss the range of mediation and arbitration services they can provide.

46. We decided not to continue interviewing attorneys who had declined to use the LDRP on the first telephone call or who were involved in cases that settled or were dismissed shortly after our contact. Initial interviews

with attorneys in these types of cases indicated that because they had not given the LDRP much consideration, they were unable to provide thoughtful answers to many of the questions.

47. This study relied on very different data sources than the prior ILRP study, in which virtually all of the information came from plaintiff interviews and most of the interviews were conducted after the cases had been resolved. LIBEL LAW AND THE PRESS, *supra* note 3, at 241-42.

48. For ease of discussion, we use the terms "plaintiff," "defendant," and "case" throughout the chapter, even though some of the disputes did not involve a filed lawsuit. *See* discussion *infra*.

49. Of the plaintiffs for whom we had information on whether they had held public office prior to the appearance of the alleged libel, thirty-three (45 percent) had previously held public office and forty (55 percent) had not.

50. We were interested in focusing on media defendants; we have some cases with nonmedia defendants because we learned only on making contact in the case that a media organization had not been named as a defendant. In cases involving only nonmedia defendants, the plaintiff's harm was caused by some type of publication, such as campaign literature or a news release picked up by the media. In cases involving both media and nonmedia defendants, the nonmedia entity was typically the source of the allegedly defamatory statements.

51. Of the twenty-four cases that had not been filed at our first contact, five were later filed, four were settled before filing, eight were not filed, and the filing status of seven cases could not be determined.

52. *See supra* note 47 and accompanying text for a discussion of the difficulty of assessing the interest of the parties.

53. For instance, a lawyer may not have expressed a clear opinion about the use of the LDRP in several conversations before the case was dismissed or before the other side declined to use the LDRP. Once one of these events had occurred, no further effort was made to gauge their interest. Had one more conversation with the lawyer taken place, however, he or she might have expressed an interest in using the LDRP or, conversely, might have indicated that the client was not interested in the program.

54. At least 25 of the 128 cases did not use the LDRP because the case was dismissed or settled shortly after our contact, the plaintiff decided not to pursue any action against the defendant, or the LDRP staff determined that the case did not involve factual issues.

55. Both settlement conferences took place within three weeks of the time the parties agreed to use a conference. The administrative and neutrals' fees, which were paid by the LDRP during the research phase, totaled $800 in one case and $500 in the other. Under the AAA's management, the administrative fees will be set in accordance with the AAA's Commercial Arbitration and/or Mediation Rules. The neutrals' fees will be set on a case-by-case basis, varying with the region of the country and the type of expertise the parties request.

56. *Medical Malpractice: Few Claims Resolved Through Michigan's Voluntary Arbitration Program*, GAO REPORT, Dec. 1990, at 8; Pearson, Thoennes, & Vaderkooi, *The Decision to Mediate*, 6 J. DIVORCE 17 (1982).

57. Millhauser, *The Unspoken Resistance to Alternative Dispute Resolution* 3 NEGOTIATION J. 29 (Jan. 1987); L. RISKIN & J. WESTBROOK, DISPUTE RESOLUTION AND LAWYERS 53, 54 (1987); Volpe & Bahn, *Resistance to Mediation: Understanding and Handling It,* 3 NEGOTIATION J. 297 (Oct. 1987).

58. One defense attorney had been involved in two libel cases that had been resolved by court-annexed arbitration. The most frequent contexts in which the attorneys had been involved in alternative dispute resolution procedures include court-annexed arbitration of civil cases; commercial, contract, construction, labor, or personal injury arbitration; and family mediation.

59. *See* Merry & Silbey, *supra* note 39, at 151; Vidmar, *supra* note 39, at 195.

60. *See* Wilkinson, *ADR: Valuable Tool Is Often Misunderstood,* 10 NAT'L L.J., November 2, 1987, at 19.

61. *See* Merry & Silbey, *supra* note 39, at 151; Vidmar, *supra* note 39, at 195.

62. Burch, *ADR in the Law Firm: A Practical Viewpoint,* 1987 MO. J. DISPUTE RESOLUTION 149, 161 (1987). See also LIBEL LAW AND THE PRESS, *supra* note 3.

63. Wilkinson, *supra* note 60, at 19.

64. Goldberg, Green, & Sander, *supra* note 25, at 485; Kressel & Pruitt, *Themes in the Mediation of Social Conflict,* 41 J. SOCIAL ISSUES 179, 183 (1985); Pearson, *supra* note 35, at 427; Roehl & Cook, *Issues in Mediation: Rhetoric and Reality Revisited,* 41 J. SOCIAL ISSUES 161, 179 (1985). For example, a study of Michigan's voluntary arbitration program for medical malpractice claims found that over its thirteen-year history, 811 claims were filed with the arbitration program out of a total of 20,000 claims filed in that time period (4 percent of all claims). *Medical Malpractice, supra* note 56, at 7.

65. Kressel & Pruitt, *supra* note 64, at 183.

66. Goldberg, Green, & Sander, *supra* note 25, at 485-89; Pearson, *supra* note 35, at 427-28. For a discussion of factors affecting lawyers' attitudes toward alternatives, *see supra* note 57 and accompanying text.

67. Getting parties to use an alternative process may be more difficult in libel disputes than in other civil cases. Compared to general civil litigation, libel cases are characterized by a lower incidence of settlement, more pre- and posttrial appeals, and a greater percentage of cases going to trial. LIBEL LAW AND THE PRESS, *supra* note 3, at 145, 283 n.76.

chapter 8

Uniform
Defamation Act*

NATIONAL CONFERENCE
OF COMMISSIONERS ON
UNIFORM STATE LAWS

The National Conference of Commissioners on Uniform State Laws (the Conference)[1] was organized in 1892 to "promote uniformity by voluntary action of each state government." As one of the oldest state organizations whose purpose is to encourage interstate cooperation, the Conference over its 100-year history has drafted over 200 uniform laws on numerous subjects and in various fields of law, many of which have been widely enacted in the states. The Conference's central purpose is the drafting and enactment of uniform state legislation on subjects where uniformity is desirable and practicable.

The Conference is composed of commissioners from each state, the District of Columbia, and Puerto Rico. With an average of four commissioners per state appointed by the governors of each state, the Conference consists of distinguished lawyers, judges, legislators, and law school professors. The Conference is nonpartisan, and in their efforts to procure consideration and enactment of uniform acts, the commissioners represent no special interest.

The Conference meets annually to consider drafts of proposed uniform legislation. Proposals that uniform acts be drafted by the

---

*The ideas and conclusions herein set forth, including drafts of proposed legalization, have not been passed on by the National Conference of Commissioners on Uniform State Laws. They do not necessarily reflect the views of the committee, reporters, or commissioners. Proposed statutory language, if any, may not be used to ascertain legislative meaning or any promulgated final law.

The draft Act is dated December 6, 1991.

Conference are received from many sources. Acts deemed potentially appropriate for drafting are selected from such proposals and submitted, first, to a study committee, which determines whether a drafting project is consistent with the purposes of the Conference and recommends, when appropriate, the appointment of a formal drafting committee. If the Conference decides to undertake the drafting of an act, a special committee (called a drafting committee) composed of commissioners from various states is appointed to prepare a draft of an act. The drafting process is extended and exacting, and may span two or three years before a draft is first presented to the Conference.

A draft act must be discussed and considered section by section by the entire Conference at no fewer than two annual meetings before the Conference may decide, by a vote of states, whether to promulgate the draft as a uniform act. In the final vote by states, each state is entitled to one vote only, and an act is not promulgated as a uniform act unless a majority of states represented at the annual meeting and at least twenty jurisdictions have approved the draft. Once promulgated, uniform acts are submitted for consideration to the American Bar Association. The drafting committees of the Conference establish liaison with the American Bar Association and other interested groups throughout the drafting process.

The time period from beginning to end of the drafting process is usually three to five years. During the course of the year, drafting committees will meet on two or more separate occasions, refining and shaping the act and consulting with interested parties who serve formally or informally as liaison to the committee. It is not uncommon for an act to have gone through ten or more formal redrafts during the course of consideration by the committee and formal readings and debate before the Conference as a whole. Because of the care and attention to policy and detail, the Conference's drafts are widely respected for their quality in the legal profession and in the chambers of government.

UNIFORM DEFAMATION ACT
(DECEMBER 6, 1991, COMMITTEE DRAFT)

Prefatory Note

Since the U.S. Supreme Court recognized the First Amendment limitations on the common law tort of defamation, courts have struggled to find the proper balance between the constitutionally protected guarantees of free expression and the need to protect citizens from reputational harm. In addition, new technologies for information distribution have caused tension within the traditional rules of the defamation tort. The Scope and Program Committee recognized, as have other commentators, that the state of the law is in chaos and that some issues may not be fit for judicial resolution.

The central question that animates this draft is whether there is a way to provide additional protection for reputation without interfering with legitimate First Amendment concerns. There is empirical evidence to suggest that many targets of defamatory statements would be satisfied with vindication, that is, with a determination that the statement was false. A fair reading of Supreme Court jurisprudence suggests that the constitutional privileges accorded speakers in defamation cases are designed to ensure that the threat of monetary awards for potentially defamatory statements will not chill speech.

The draft attempts to balance these concerns by affording plaintiffs an option of seeking vindication alone rather than money damages. In addition, incentives are created throughout the Act to encourage plaintiffs to accept vindication as a complete remedy. The draft also attempts to provide defamation defendants with incentives to respond with retractions or corrections when their published statements are in error.

Finally, and within the framework of still-evolving constitutional doctrine, the draft reflects an effort to bring an important measure of clarity and consistency to the adjudication of defamation actions and to effect needed changes in such areas as compensatory and punitive damages, privileges, and retraction.

The Act

Section 1. Definitions

In this [Act]:

(1) "Defamation" means a statement tending to harm reputation.

(2) "Pecuniary damage" means provable economic loss.

(3) "Person" means an individual, corporation, business trust, estate, trust, partnership, association, joint venture, or other legal or commercial entity, but does not include a government or governmental subdivision, agency, or instrumentality.

(4) "Publication" means an intentional or negligent communication to a person other than the person alleging reputational harm from the communication.

Comment to Section 1

By the definition of "person," which does not include products or services, and by the requirement in Section 2 that a publication harm the reputation of a "person," the Act is made inapplicable to product disparagement or trade libel claims, as well as to the increasing variety of defamation-like false or misleading advertising claims. The definition also excludes from liability under the Act libels of government or governmental bodies, which are constitutionally immune from liability under the First Amendment (as distinguished from libels of public officials, which are not excluded and with respect to which actions may be brought under the Act).

The concepts of public figure and public official, which are of constitutional origin, are not defined. Instead, the Act relies on the contours of the Supreme Court definitions, which will apply because of their constitutional basis. As the Court stated in *Gertz v. Robert Welch, Inc.,*[2] "[P]ublic officials and public figures have voluntarily exposed themselves to increased risk of injury from defamatory falsehood concerning them." In *Gertz,* the Court also noted the possibility, although rare, that "public figure" could include someone who was swept involuntarily into the vortex of a public issue. Because the definitions are of constitutional origin, and because they will likely continue to evolve, a set of fixed definitions in the Act was deemed inadvisable.

Under subsection 1(4), "publication" is defined as an intentional or negligent communication to a person other than the person alleging reputational harm from a communication. This definition is consistent with Section 577 (1) of the *Restatement (Second) of Torts.*[3] By the requirement that a communication be "intentional or negligent," the definition excludes communications to a third person that are the result of mistake or inadvertence, as long as the mistake or inadvertence is nonnegligent. The Act, like the *Restatement,* includes this qualification as part of the definition of publication, rather than as a defense to liability, thereby making clear that the concepts of intentional or negligent communication go to the act of communicating, not, as with the privileges contained in Sections 9 (negligence) and Sections 17 and 18 (malice), to the content of a communication.

Section 2. Elements of Claim

A person who causes the publication of a false and defamatory factual statement about another person which harms that person's reputation is subject to liability to that person in an action under this [Act].

Factual statement means a communication that is reasonably understood by recipients to be of a factual nature and is objectively provable or disprovable.

Comment to Section 2

A number of features of the Act should be noted in connection with Section 2, which sets out the elements of the legal wrong. First, no distinction is made between slander and libel. The distinction is now largely anachronistic, and the rules of liability per se and related requirements for proof of harm and damage that turned on the distinction are not retained in the Act. All defamations are made subject to the same rules.

Second, no distinction is drawn on the basis of the medium employed in the publication, or the media or nonmedia identity of the offending publisher. Differences in the impact of a given medium can, of course, be relevant on a case-by-case basis under such headings as audience interpretation of meaning, reputational harm, and damage. The media/nonmedia distinction, generally employed as a means of distinguishing press or mass communication from private individual communication, is not used in the Act because, while occasionally of analytical utility, it is difficult to define and was considered unnecessary. Private speech is protected equally with public speech under the Act.

The use of the term "factual statement" protects statements of opinion from liability, although not in so many words. By requiring as a condition of liability that a communication be a factual statement, based on reasonable interpretation of the recipient, and that it be disprovable and disproven by the injured party (see Section 3), statements of an evaluative, judgmental, or general and open-ended character, as well as statements not reasonably understood as factual, are fully protected.[4]

The definition contained in Section 2 follows the approach taken by the Court in *Milkovich v. Lorain Journal Co.*[5] This approach is consistent with, although a somewhat different formulation of, the position taken in Section 566 of the *Restatement,* which provides that "[a] statement in the form of an opinion . . . is actionable . . . if it implies the allegation of undisclosed defamatory facts as the basis for the opinion." In a related fashion, Section 563 of the *Restatement* provides that "[t]he meaning of a communication is that which the recipient correctly, or mistakenly but reasonably, understands that it was intended to express." Both of these ideas have been incorporated in the definition of "fact."

By using "factual statement" to mean information that is "reasonably understood by recipients to be of a factual nature and that is objectively provable or disprovable," the Act avoids the need to define "opinion," or to provide a separate privilege for opinion. The Act therefore departs from the approach taken by many courts prior to the *Milkovich* case, in which a four- or five-factor analysis was used to define opinion as a matter of law. Many of the same considerations (such as whether the context of the statement is one ordinarily associated with satire, hyperbole, or pure opinion) will still apply, but they will be more fact based and dependent on the particular circumstances of each case and not on presumptive categories of statement.

The Act rests liability on the reasonable understanding or interpretation given a statement. For example, the statement that "it is rumored that X is a thief" could not escape liability simply because the fact of rumors is true. If in its context the statement is interpreted reasonably as implying that X is a thief, that will be the relevant issue in an action under the Act, not simply the correctness of the assertion that rumors exist.

Section 3. Burden of Proof

In an action under this [Act]:

(1) The plaintiff bears the burden of proving by a preponderance of the evidence:

(i) Publication

(ii) Defamation

(iii) Harm to reputation

(iv) Falsity

(2) The plaintiff bears the burden of proving by clear and convincing evidence:

(i) Abuse of privilege

(ii) Negligence

(iii) Knowledge of falsity or reckless disregard for truth

(3) The plaintiff bears the burden of proving the amount of damages with reasonable certainty.

(4) The defendant bears the burden of proving by a preponderance of the evidence the facts necessary to establish a privilege.

Comment to Section 3

In *Bose Corp. v. Consumers Union of United States, Inc.*,[6] the Supreme Court held that issues of *constitutional fact*, such as actual malice and, presumably, negligence, must be proved by clear and convincing evidence. Because abuse of privilege issues, such as common law malice or publication beyond the protected scope of a privilege, are of similar character and importance, the higher standard is applied to these issues, as well.

In outlining the burden of asserting and proving privilege, the Act is intended to reflect the common rule that one who seeks privilege has the burden of raising it and, if questions of fact are involved, of proving them by a preponderance of the evidence . The Act does not, however, purport to allocate factual issues involved in privilege matters between the judge and jury, but rather leaves these issues to local practice.

The Act adopts the *Restatement* requirement that the amount of damages be proved with reasonable certainty. This requirement applies, of course, not only to pecuniary and economic damages, but also to damages flowing from harm to reputation.

Section 4. Pleadings; Expedited Proceeding

(a) In addition to other matters required by [the rules of procedure for civil actions], the complaint [petition] must:

(1) Identify with particularity the publication and the specific statements alleged to be false and defamatory;

(2) State the alleged defamatory meaning and identify the specific circumstances giving rise to it if the defamatory meaning arises from an implication of the publication rather than or in addition to its ordinary meaning, or from innuendo, sarcasm, or conduct;

(3) State that the alleged defamatory meaning is false;

(4) Include a copy of each retraction and each request for retraction; and

(5) Identify whether the action brought is one for damages under Section 9 or for vindication under Section 5.

(b) If upon motion by the plaintiff the court finds that the plaintiff is likely to suffer significant additional reputational harm from repetition of the publication, the court may expedite the proceeding.

Comment to Section 4

Section 4 provides that a plaintiff filing a complaint under the Act must describe the subject communication in sufficient detail adequately to inform the defendant of the subject of the suit. This section imposes special requirements in defamation actions that extend beyond the requirements generally imposed for all pleadings under state laws. Although some states require particularity of pleading in libel actions,[7] current law is largely silent on how particularly a cause of action for defamation must be pled. Consequently, in some states a plaintiff may append a copy of a book or a lengthy article to the complaint, accompanied by very generalized allegations, thus forcing the defendant to deduce the part of the publication that is objectionable to the plaintiff. Particularity of pleading makes the defendant immediately aware of the subject of the suit and thus promotes efficiency and facilitates early steps to retract the communication or to settle the suit.

Subsection 4(a) requires that the exact offending words or conduct be set out in the complaint. A plaintiff may not give a general description of the communication limited by terms such as "to the effect" or "substantially." Furthermore, if only a portion of a communication is actionable, the plaintiff must specify in the complaint the actionable portion.

If the ordinary meaning of the subject communication does not give rise to a cause of action under the Act, but the circumstances surrounding the communication imply a meaning to the communication other than the ordinary meaning, the plaintiff must plead the specific circumstances. In a case involving innuendo, sarcasm, or a statement accompanied by conduct, the plaintiff must state the alleged implicit meaning.

Subsection 4(b) provides that a plaintiff who alleges continuing injury from a communication that is being repeatedly published may seek to have the proceeding expedited. At least one state currently provides for an expedited proceeding.[8] Inclusion of this subsection reflects a judgment that plaintiffs, who are not eligible for injunctions but who nonetheless are being injured by a continuous publication, should have an opportunity to obtain relief earlier than normal litigation procedures would provide. The court, however, is given full discretion in the matter.

Section 5. Action for Vindication: Required Proof; Exclusive Remedy

A person bringing an action under this [Act] may elect, at the time of filing a complaint [petition], to limit the action to an action for vindication. If the election is made:

    (1) The plaintiff must prove the elements stated in Section 2;

    (2) The publisher may not assert absence of fault or claims of conditional privilege;

    (3) Damages may not be awarded; and

(4) Except as provided in Section 7(b), the plaintiff may not bring an action for damages for reputational or dignitary injury caused by publication of the false statement.

Comment to Section 5

Section 5 provides an alternative cause of action to the traditional action for damages. The cause of action is one for vindication, by which a successful plaintiff can obtain a written and published finding of fact on the question of falsity but without the opportunity for any form of money damages. Defenses to the action are likewise limited. Claims of absolute privilege can be raised and, if successful, will defeat an action for vindication, but claims of conditional privilege, including constitutional privileges based on negligence or actual malice, may not be raised.

Section 6. Action for Vindication: Termination by Defendant

If at any time before ninety (90) days after service of process in an action for vindication a defendant by motion stipulates on the record that it does not assert the truth of the publication or did not intend to assert its truth at the time of publication, or both, and agrees to publish, at the plaintiff's request, a sufficient retraction, the court shall, after the required publication, dismiss the action against the defendant making the motion.

Comment to Section 6

Section 6 provides, in substance, a counterpart to the offer of termination provision contained in Section 12, which is applicable only to actions for damages. The purpose of Section 6 is to permit— indeed, to encourage—the termination of a vindication action if the defendant is willing to disclaim any assertion of truth and to publish that disclaimer. It is important to note that the defendant need not concede falsity. That is something that defendants are rarely willing to do and are rarely in a position to do. A clear disclaimer of the assertion of truth, however, was judged to provide both significant and realistic relief for a plaintiff.

A plaintiff whose vindication action is terminated by action of the defendant under Section 6 is not a prevailing plaintiff. Therefore such a plaintiff would not be able to receive attorneys' fees under Section 8.

Section 7. Action for Vindication: Findings of Fact; Default by Defendant

(a) Except as provided in subsection (b), if the plaintiff prevails in an action brought pursuant to Section 5, the court shall enter judgment which shall include written findings of fact on falsity and an order requiring the defendant, at the defendant's option:

(1) To publish the findings in conformance with Section 15(b)(1); or

(2) To pay the plaintiff an amount sufficient to secure their publication in conformance with Section 15(b)(1).

(b) If the defendant makes a motion pursuant to Section 6, but fails within a reasonable time to publish a sufficient retraction at the plaintiff's request, the plaintiff may:

(1) Amend the complaint to assert a claim for damages against the defendant under Section 9; or

(2) Introduce evidence of falsity and, upon adequate proof of falsity, the court shall enter judgment which shall include written findings of fact on falsity and order the defendant to pay an amount sufficient to secure publication of the findings in conformance with Section 15(b)(1).

Section 8. Attorneys' Fees and Expenses in an Action for Vindication

(a) In an action brought under Section 5, reasonable expenses of litigation, including attorneys' fees, shall be awarded:

(1) To a prevailing plaintiff upon proof that the defendant was provided sufficient grounds for retraction in the plaintiff's request for retraction, and that a timely retraction was unreasonably refused; or

(2) To a prevailing defendant upon proof that the plaintiff had no reasonable basis upon which to allege falsity.

(b) An award of expenses and attorney's fees to a prevailing party under this section may not be disproportionate to the amount incurred by the other party for its own expenses and attorney's fees, or to the reasonable value thereof.

Comment to Section 8

Subsection 8(a)(2) is the only provision in the Act that permits defendants to receive reasonable expenses of litigation, including attorneys' fees. Awarding fees in cases in which plaintiffs have no reasonable basis on which to allege falsity in a vindication action seemed appropriate in view of the fact that defendants in such cases are precluded from claiming any but absolute privileges. The potential award of fees was also seen as an effective deterrent against plaintiffs bringing frivolous vindication actions.

The term "expenses of litigation, including attorneys' fees" is intended to be inclusive of all costs of litigation and therefore to be broader than the recovery of attorneys' fees and costs. Recoverable expenses could include, for example, the costs of witnesses, experts, travel, and the like.

The amount of recoverable expenses is effectively limited by the requirement that the award be proportionate to the expenses of the party from whom recovery is made. In most cases this will result in setting the amount awarded at a level no higher than the actual expenses of the other party, although the possibility of pro bono representation, for example, led to the use of "reasonable value" in order that free services to one party not defeat a reasonable award to the other party.

Section 9. Action for Damages

(a) A plaintiff may recover damages in an action under this Act if the plaintiff proves the elements of a cause of action stated in Section 2 and also proves:

(1) In a case involving a conditional privilege, that the defendant published the statement with knowledge of its falsity or reckless disregard for its truth, or

(2) In all other cases, that the defendant knew or reasonably should have known the publication was false.

(b) A plaintiff entitled to recover damages under subsection (a) may recover:

(1) Damages for harm to reputation and resulting emotional distress; and

(2) Pecuniary damages caused by the publication.

Comment to Section 9

Section 9 requires a showing of negligence or, for public-official and public-figure cases as well as for other cases in which conditional privilege is successfully established, of actual malice, in all cases in which damages are sought. Under current law, strict liability still applies to certain, although highly limited, settings of purely private libel.[9] The Act reflects the judgment that all speech should be equally protected irrespective of context, that in any event distinctions between fault-based and strict liability are unnecessarily confusing and conducive to litigation, and that the remaining instances of strict liability under the U.S. Supreme Court's decisions are so narrow as to be of doubtful utility as a matter of policy.

It should also be noted that general or presumed damages are foreclosed under the Act. Moreover, by requiring that damages for emotional distress result from harm to reputation, the Act is intended to foreclose recovery for "pure" emotional distress, and to limit the scope of emotional distress damages recoverable.

The Act uses the term "pecuniary damages," defined in subsection 1(2), to describe provable economic or out-of-pocket losses caused by a publication. The term is intended to include the types of damage described variously in state common law as "pecuniary damage," "special damage," "economic loss," or "out-of-pocket loss."

Alternative A (Committee Alternative)
[Section 10. Punitive Damages Prohibited

Punitive damages may not be recovered under this (Act).]

Alternative B
[Section 10. Punitive Damages

A plaintiff may recover punitive damages under this (Act) only upon a showing by clear and convincing evidence that the defendant published the challenged statement with knowledge of its falsity and with ill will toward the plaintiff. The provisions of (States should insert a reference to such provisions generally applicable to punitive damages as are appropriate) apply to the award of punitive damages under this section.]

Comment to Section 10

Pursuant to the Conference's action in 1991, a punitive damage provision has been drafted in order that a narrow alternative to complete prohibition of punitive damages will be available at the time of final reading. The provision limits punitive damages very strictly to cases in which the plaintiff can prove knowledge of falsity (not reckless disregard for truth) *and* ill will or intent to harm.

Notwithstanding the limited nature of the punitive damage provision, the Committee remains convinced that punitive damages should not be available in any cases. The punitive damage provision is therefore presented as an alternative to the committee's recommendation. The action of the Committee of the Whole in 1991 did not amend the Act to require punitive damages but rather required that an alternative provision allowing punitive damages be drafted for possible consideration at the time of final reading.

Section 11. Attorneys' Fees and Expenses in an Action for Damages

In an action brought under Section 9, reasonable expenses of litigation, including attorneys' fees, may be awarded to a prevailing plaintiff who:

(1) Made an adequate request for retraction within sixty (60) days of publication; and

(2) Proves that the challenged statement was published with knowledge of its falsity or reckless disregard for its truth.

Section 12. Offer of Termination in an Action for Damages

(a) Any time before trial of an action for damages under this [Act] a defendant, by motion, may make a termination offer. In the motion, the defendant shall stipulate on the record that the defendant does not assert the truth of the publication or did not intend to assert its truth at the time of publication, or both, and the defendant shall agree:

(1) To pay the plaintiff's reasonable expenses of litigation, including attorneys' fees, incurred prior to the filing of the motion; and

(2) To publish, at the plaintiff's request, a sufficient retraction.

(b) If the plaintiff accepts the offer, the court shall dismiss the action against the defendant after the defendant fully complies with its terms. A plaintiff who does not accept the termination offer is limited to pecuniary damages and may not recover from the defendant making the offer the expenses of litigation, including attorneys' fees.

Section 13. Request for Retraction

(a) To be adequate, a request for retraction must:

(1) Be made in writing and signed by the requester or by the requester's authorized agent;

(2) Identify with particularity the publication and the specific statements alleged to be false and defamatory;

(3) State the alleged defamatory meaning and identify the specific circumstances giving rise to it if the defamatory meaning arises from an implication of the publication rather than or in addition to its ordinary meaning, or from innuendo, sarcasm, or conduct; and

(4) State that the alleged defamatory meaning is false.

(b) If an adequate request has not previously been made, service of a [summons and complaint [petition]] in conformance with Section 4 constitutes an adequate request for retraction and the time for filing a responsive pleading is suspended during the period provided in Section 15 for responding to the request.

Comment to Section 13

The retraction provisions of the Act (Sections 13–15) should be read as a whole. These sections represent a careful balancing of the interests of plaintiffs and defendants and are designed to encourage the prompt informal settlement of defamation claims

Section 13 contains the general requirement that a retraction be sought as a precondition to suit. Subsection 13(b), however, provides that in all cases a complaint shall constitute such a request, thus avoiding the preclusive effect of an inadequate earlier request or a failure to seek a retraction for any other reason. A retraction serves to limit or eliminate the damages caused by a communication. Unlike many current retraction statutes, Section 13 does not require a party to seek a retraction within a certain time period following publication.[10] A party may seek a retraction at any time prior to the expiration of the statute of limitations. Sections 11 and 14, however, are designed, respectively, to encourage an early request for retraction, and a favorable response.

Subsection 13(b) provides that the complaint shall constitute a request for retraction if no adequate retraction has been sought before the action is filed. This provision relieves the plaintiff of the obligation to request a retraction at some point before filing, although the Act is not intended to encourage that procedure. Indeed, Section 11 provides an incentive for an early request, as will, presumably, the plaintiff's own interest in reputational vindication. The principal reason for subsection 13(b) is to provide a cure in all cases for potential claims that the request for retraction was deficient in form or content and for the attendant difficulties such claims might needlessly pose under the statute of limitations.

A publisher who has received a request for retraction prior to the filing of an action, and who considers that request to have been deficient, should therefore consider the complaint to constitute a new request for retraction requiring the publisher's response. Failure to give due notice of the publisher's intent to consider the complaint a request for retraction in such circumstances and, if necessary, to suspend the time for response, should constitute a waiver of any objections to the prior retraction request.

Section 14. Effect of Retraction

If a timely and sufficient retraction is published, a person may not bring an action for vindication based on the challenged publication under Section 5, and a person who brings an action for damages under Section 9 may recover damages only for pecuniary loss caused before the date of the retraction.

Comment to Section 14

Section 14 is designed to encourage parties to grant a request for retraction by providing that a retraction forecloses an action under Section 5, and that in an action for damages the requesting party may seek only pecuniary damages in the event of the publication of a retraction. Additionally, by refusing the request, a publisher is subject under Section 11 to a possible award of attorneys' fees if the requesting party thereafter prevails in an action, proves actual malice, and has sought the retraction promptly.

Consideration was given to a section prohibiting introduction of evidence on the granting or refusal of a retraction in subsequent proceedings. Such a provision was not included because such information should rarely if ever be relevant—particularly on questions of falsity, negligence, or malice at the time of publication—under current law, and an absolute ban even for exculpatory uses or extreme cases was deemed unwise.

In limiting recovery of damages for pecuniary loss to those "caused before the date of the retraction," the Act attempts to cut off damage that arises after or is caused after the retraction, but not to prevent the recovery of damages caused prior to the retraction, but which may extend beyond the date of retraction. For example, if a physician is defamed and a retraction thereafter made, the physician should be able to recover damages for economic loss stemming from the loss of patients prior to the date of the retraction, even though that loss may continue for some period after the retraction. On the other hand, economic losses resulting from patients who changed doctors after the date of a retraction should not be recoverable, even though their decision was based on the original defamation. At a trial of an action in which the defendant has published a retraction in accordance with Section 14, the plaintiff will bear the burden of proving damages caused by the publication before the retraction.

It should be noted that under Section 14, a publisher may unilaterally retract and limit damages to pecuniary loss. This feature is designed to encourage publishers quickly to correct mistakes and thereby avoid much of the harm that may flow from the publication.

Section 15. Timely and Sufficient Retraction

(a) A retraction is timely if it is published before or within thirty (30) days after receipt of a request pursuant to Section 13.

(b) A retraction is sufficient if it:

(1) Is communicated in writing to the requester, is published in a manner and medium reasonably calculated to reach substantially the same audience as the publication complained of, and, if the retraction is published in another medium to conform to the thirty (30)-day period required by subsection (a), is also published in the next practicable issue or edition, if any, of the original publication; and

(2) Refers to the challenged statement and:

(i) Corrects the challenged statement;

(ii) In the case of a statement implied by a publication, or arising from innuendo, sarcasm, or accompanying conduct, disclaims any intent to communicate or to have communicated the implied meaning or to assert its truth; or

(iii) In the case of a statement attributed to another person, identifies that person and disclaims any intent to assert or to have asserted the truth of the statement.

(c) Notwithstanding subsection (b), a retraction is sufficient if the plaintiff states in writing that it is sufficient.

Comment to Section 15

Section 15 sets out the requirements for a timely and sufficient retraction. A "timely" retraction must be published within thirty days of a request for retraction. A "sufficient" retraction must be published in substantially the same manner and medium as the original communication unless publication in some other manner and medium is reasonably calculated to reach the same audience as the original communication.

The important factors in determining whether a retraction is sufficient are reasonableness and whether the efforts are directed at reaching the same audience. Where publication is frequent, the retraction question is not likely to be problematic. Given the scope of the [Act], however, the obligation to retract will apply to all forms of communication, some of which will be narrowly focused, infrequent, and even one time only. In many of these settings, the [Act's] focus on reasonable efforts to reach the same audience will be important.

Newspapers and other frequent publications have been the principal subjects of retraction statutes throughout the country. Ordinarily, retractions are required to be placed in similar locations to those in which the original story occurred, although even this rule depends on a number of factors, including the nature and scope of the original story as well as the newspaper's practices concerning reserved space for corrections. Such alternatives, as well as others presented in different types of media, such as radio and broadcast, should be addressed in terms of the Act's requirement that the retraction, in its location and prominence, should be reasonably calculated to reach substantially the same audience as the original publication.

With other media and in other contexts, however, the rule will yield different results. For example, retraction of a defamatory employee reference or evaluation may require no more than contacting those persons or firms to whom the defamatory statement was communicated. If the statement has made its way into permanent files or broader audiences, however, reasonable efforts to have the material removed from such files or to communicate the retraction to identifiable members of the broader audience should be attempted.

For a book currently being sold, with no next edition in sight, reasonable efforts to retract might involve several measures: Make necessary corrections in any future editions; notify persons who have purchased the book if that information is available, or instead attempt through a notice at bookstores or a press release to reach this group; and provide through an insert or other warning notice to those persons who will, in the future, buy the current edition. The latter step assumes, of course, that future reputational harm can be avoided by such an insert rather than by recalling and correcting books that are on the shelf but unsold.

In the case of an oral defamation to friends or colleagues—a classic slander—a letter to those persons retracting the defamation (ungrudgingly, of course) might suffice, on the assumption that word of the apologetic retraction would spread as rapidly in the channels of gossip as did the original defamation.

Under subsection 15(b)(2), a "sufficient" retraction must also correct the original communication. An equivocal retraction will not satisfy this requirement. But where the alleged defamation was the result of an implication contained in a communication or a statement attributed in the publication to another person, a sufficient retraction need only contain a statement that the party making the communication did not intend the implication and disclaims it, or that in publishing the attributed statement of another person the publisher disclaims any intent to attest to the truth of the facts contained therein. This will allow the publisher to disavow the alleged implication and yet stand behind the "facts" of the story.

It is important to note that in the case of statements attributed to another person, the retraction must identify that person even if the original publication did not do so.

Section 16. Absolute Privileges

An action may not be maintained under this [Act] based on:

(1) A statement made:

(i) In and pertaining to a judicial proceeding by a judge, attorney, witness, juror, or other participant;

(ii) In and pertaining to a legislative proceeding by a legislator, attorney, aide, witness, or other participant; or

(iii) In and pertaining to any quasi-judicial or quasi-legislative executive or administrative proceeding by an executive or administrative official, attorney, witness, or other participant;

(2) A statement that constitutes a fair and accurate report of an official action or proceeding of a governmental body, including an order or opinion of a court, or of a meeting of a governmental body which is open to the public;

(3) A statement published with the consent of the person harmed;

(4) A statement communicated between husband and wife; or

(5) A statement required by law to be published.

Comment to Section 16

In listing the absolute privileges applicable to defamation actions, it is intended that Section 16 contain a statement of all such privileges. This is consistent with the desire to make uniform the basic practices applicable to the defamation tort. Two caveats should, however, be noted. First, the privileges are stated in very general terms, and therefore are intended to allow for minor differences in scope and interpretation that exist from state to state. Such differences would exist, for example, in the specific application of the privileges pertaining to judicial, legislative, and quasi-judicial or quasi-legislative proceedings, as well as interpretations of the particular individuals who may be able to claim protection under the privilege.[11] Second, the absolute privileges are not stated in the exclusive, and therefore the section is not designed to foreclose the development of further absolute privileges at common law or as a matter of constitutional requirement. The statement of privileges does, however, constitute a full listing of absolute privileges generally recognized in current law.

Subsection 16(4) provides an absolute privilege for communications between husband and wife. At common law there has not been, historically speaking, such a privilege, although such statements have not been subject to liability on the ground that there was no publication. The more common view today is that the publication rule in such cases was an artifice, and that the better approach would be to privilege such statements directly. That is the approach taken in the current draft.

The absolute privileges stated in Section 16 are not intended to exclude other absolute privileges that may stem from other sources of law. For example, privileges stemming from the federal speech and debate clause, U.S. Const. Art. 1, § 6, ch. 1, their counterparts at the state level and other legislative, executive, and judicial privileges are available even though not mentioned in the Act. The source of these privileges is generally to be found in statutory or constitutional provisions not specifically applicable only to defamation claims.[12]

Claims of absolute privilege, whether listed in Section 16 or based on other law, may be raised in actions for vindication under Section 5.

Section 17. Conditional Privileges

(a) A person may not be held liable for damages based on a statement that is:

(1) Reasonably necessary to protect the publisher's legitimate interests;

(2) Reasonably necessary to protect the legitimate interests of others;

(3) Reasonably necessary to protect or foster a common interest between the publisher and the recipient of the communication; or

(4) Made to a person officially charged with the duty of acting in the public interest and in relation to that person's official responsibilities.

(b) The privileges under subsection (a) are not available if the plaintiff proves that the publisher:

     (1) Unreasonably published the statement to persons other than those to whom publication was necessary to serve the interests giving rise to the privilege; or

     (2) Published the statement with knowledge of its falsity or reckless disregard for its truth.

Comment to Section 17

As with the statement of absolute privileges in Section 16, the Act provides a listing in Section 17 of the conditional privileges at common law. The statement of privileges is general so as to comprehend minor differences in interpretation in the various states, and the privileges are not listed as exclusive in order that additional privileges recognized in various states, or which might arise in the future, not be foreclosed. The privileges are drawn generally from the *Restatement*.[13]

     The Act treats publications protected by conditional privilege (i.e., the scope of publication comports with the requirements of a privilege) in the same manner as statements falling within the public-figure and public-official constitutional privileges. Actual malice applies in both contexts. This reflects a judgment that there is little policy justification for treating common law and constitutional privileges differently, and that much confusion can be avoided by simplifying the standards for various privileges.

     The fair comment privilege, formerly recognized in the *Restatement* and still recognized in most jurisdictions, has not been included, nor is it currently included in the *Restatement*.[14] The reason for not including the fair comment privilege is twofold. First, given that statements of opinion are not, by virtue of the definition of factual statement in Section 2, actionable, the privilege is not necessary. Second, the other privileges in the Act, including specifically the constitutional privileges outlined in Section 18, were deemed to make the fair comment privilege redundant, as those privileges would provide overlapping, and often greater, protection.

     It should be noted that the fair report privilege, which applies to accurate and fair reports of official actions or proceedings open to the public, is included in the listing of absolute privileges in subsection 16(2). This privilege is sometimes considered a qualified privilege, but the better practice seems to be to consider it an absolute one, subject to its qualifications of "accuracy" and "fairness."

     Similarly, the protection of a person who provides a means of publication for a privileged publisher, often described as a "wire service" privilege, is not included in the Act, as the constitutional privileges have made it unnecessary.

Section 18. Conditional Privilege for Statements Concerning Public Officials and Public Figures

A person may not be held liable for damages based on a statement about a public official or a public figure unless the plaintiff proves that the statement was:

(1) Unrelated to the person's status as a public official or public figure; or

(2) Made with knowledge of its falsity or reckless disregard for its truth.

Comment to Section 18

Section 18 reflects the constitutional privileges applicable to statements concerning public officials and public figures. The statements must be related to the person's status as a public official or public figure and can be overcome only upon a showing of actual malice. Section 18 is intended fairly to reflect current law. The section does not affect future developments except insofar as they might be less protective than current law.

It should be noted that the negligence privilege established for "private" libel plaintiffs in *Gertz v. Robert Welch, Inc.*,[15] and its progeny is not reflected in Section 18 but is instead contained in Section 9 as a precondition to recovery of damages. Because negligence was deemed an appropriate precondition to recovery of damages in any type of defamation action, including purely private ones not covered by *Gertz,* and because negligence is not required to be proven in vindication actions under Section 5, the requirement was placed in the damage section rather than stated as a privilege.

The Act does not define "public official" and "public figure" but instead relies on the Supreme Court's still-evolving approach to the meaning of those terms. Under the Court's current approach, the category of public officials includes essentially all public employees, and public figures include those persons, whether public employees or not, "who are . . . intimately involved in the resolution of important public questions or, by reason of their fame, shape events in areas of concern to society at large."[16] In both cases, the constitutional privilege afforded a publisher only applies to "a defamatory falsehood relating to [a public official's] official conduct," or to the public figure's relationship to a public issue.[17]

Section 19. Liability of Republisher

A person who republishes a statement is subject to liability under this [Act] as if the person were an original publisher.

Comment to Section 19

Section 19 states the long-standing rule that persons who republish information are subject to liability as if they were the original publisher. Consideration was given to placing conditions on liability for republication, such as the foreseeability of harm, the reasonableness of reliance on the original publisher, and the like, but it was concluded that the various privileges contained in the Act would, taken together, provide adequate protection for republishers in such circumstances.[18]

Section 20. Liability for Republication by Another

A publisher is subject to liability for harm caused by a reasonably foreseeable republication by another person unless:

(1) The publisher made a sufficient retraction prior to the republication;

(2) The publisher did not publish with knowledge of falsity or reckless disregard for truth, and requested the republisher, before the republication, not to publish; or

(3) The republication was made or caused by the party harmed.

Comment to Section 20

Unlike the relatively straightforward way that liabilities of republishers have been dealt with in Section 19, the Act provides a more specific outline of potential liability of publishers for subsequent republication. Under Section 19, a republisher is in a greater measure of control over its liability and has a full panoply of privileges available to it as it makes a publication judgment. In contrast, Section 20 imposes liability on a former publisher for subsequent publications over which that publisher may have no control and little, if any, information. Accordingly, Section 20 limits earlier publishers to liability only for reasonably foreseeable republications, and even with respect to such publications provides a safe harbor against liability for the former publisher if a sufficient retraction has been made or if the former publisher requests a republisher not to publish and if the former publisher did not publish with actual malice.

It is assumed with respect to Sections 19 and 20 that local law and existing third-party practice in various jurisdictions will deal with questions of joint and several liability, indemnification as between an original publisher and a republisher, and the ability to join such parties in an action.

Section 21. Information Retrieval Services

A library, archive, or similar information retrieval or transmission service providing directly or through electronic or other means access to information originally published by others is not subject to liability under Section 19 or 20 if the library, archive, or similar information retrieval or transmission service:

(1) Is not reasonably understood to assert in the normal course of its business the truthfulness or reliability of the information maintained or transmitted; or

(2) Takes reasonable steps to inform users that it does not assert the truthfulness or reliability of the information maintained or transmitted.

Comment to Section 21

Section 21 is designed to provide protection for the increasing number of library-type information retrieval or data base sources of information, such as Lexis, Westlaw, Nexis, and the like. Data bases are increasingly serving as principal sources for historical as well as contemporaneous information, much like the traditional library or archive. The provision of access to information through such library-type services is protected under Section 21 if the person using a service would not reasonably believe that the maintenance or provision of access to the information carries any connotation as to its truthfulness or reliability. In other words, as long as there is reasonable notice in the ordinary course of business that the truthfulness or reliability of the information is not asserted by virtue of its maintenance and accessibility, the information retrieval or transmission entity will bear no liability for subsequent republication. Subsection 21(2) provides a "safe harbor" by which the maintainer of such information may notify those using it of the fact that the material's truthfulness or reliability is not asserted and should not be relied on. The provision of such notification by, for example, a warning or disclaimer must be reasonable in order to qualify for protection from liability.

It is assumed by the drafters that such traditional facilities as public libraries, for example, would generally be exempt from liability by virtue of subsection 21(1), as it is normally understood in the course of business that a public library does not attest to the truthfulness of all of the material and information contained within its collection.

The term "information . . . transmission service" used in the Act is intended to cover not only pure transmission services but also computer bulletin boards. Such bulletin boards, however, must be of such a nature that the users do not understand the transmitting service to attest to the truthfulness or reliability of the information transmitted, or the service should so inform the customers. In excluding such transmission services from liability, the Act does not preclude liability against the person or persons who originate a defamatory message which is carried on the transmission service.

Section 22. Single and Multiple Publications

(a) Except as provided in subsections (b) and (c), each publication is a separate publication.

(b) A publication simultaneously received by more than one person is a single publication.

(c) An aggregate and reasonably contemporaneous publication is a single publication.

(d) As to any single-publication damages for all resulting harm to a plaintiff must be recovered in a single action under this [Act].

Comment to Section 22

The single-publication rule under subsections 22(a)-(c) is drawn, although with significant drafting changes, from the *Restatement.*[19] The Act treats "aggregate and reasonably contemporaneous" publications as single publications. This differs in approach from the *Restatement,* which uses the term "aggregate" but also specifies that any "edition of a book or a newspaper, a radio or television broadcast, and an exhibition of a motion picture" is a single publication. Given technological change, these particularized categories are both incomplete and outdated. In their place, the twin ideas of aggregation and contemporaneous publication were used. The Act is not intended to change the rule with respect to motion pictures, books, newspaper, radio, and TV, nor is it intended to change the basic underlying approach reflected in the Restatement as it will in the future be applied to new technologies, such as rental and home movies, pay TV, and the like.

Subsection 22(d) departs from the Restatement in that it concerns only the recovery of damages from all jurisdictions in the action and puts that provision in mandatory, rather than permissive, terms. Section 577A (4)(c) of the *Restatement* also bars recovery of damages between the same parties in all jurisdictions. Such a provision was not included in the Act because of its doubtful enforceability in other jurisdictions and because doctrines of issue preclusion and res judicata would likely address many of the problems.

Section 23. Survivability of Claims; Defamation of Deceased Person

(a) A claim arising under this [Act] survives the death of the harmed individual, but only to the extent that the claim is for vindication under Section 5 or for the recovery of pecuniary damages. This section does not affect the survivability of other claims arising from the publication.

(b) A person who publishes a statement concerning a deceased person is not liable under this [Act] to the estate of the deceased person or the deceased person's relatives.

Comment to Section 23

Section 23 departs from the common law rule of non-survivability of defamation claims, as well as the common practice in state survival statutes to exclude defamation claims from their reach.[20] Under the Act, defamation claims that arise before the death of a plaintiff survive that person's death. A rule of nonsurvivability was considered unfair, as it would require the termination of litigation, for example, upon the death of the plaintiff and would foreclose the recovery of damages for pecuniary harm experienced by the deceased plaintiff or the vindication of that person's reputation. It is noteworthy in this connection that defamation actions are not uniformly nonsurvivable, depending instead on the survival statute in particular states, and that in some states survivability is restricted to pecuniary damages (on the ground that recovery of emotional damage would represent a windfall to the estate) or excludes exemplary or punitive damages. Given the Act's limitation on recoverable damages, the survivability provision was deemed to be a reasonable compromise of the competing interests.

Section 23 does not, however, change the general rule that a deceased person cannot be defamed. The provision dealing with defamation of deceased persons is drawn from the Section 560 of the *Restatement*.

Section 24. Exclusive Remedy; Other Actions

This [Act] provides the exclusive remedy for reputational or dignitary harm to a person caused by the publication of a false statement.

Comment to Section 24

Section 24 is intended to foreclose all other claims based on reputational or dignitary harm arising from and based on the falsity of a

published statement. This would foreclose such claims as emotional
distress, negligence, and false-light privacy, but not claims based, for
example, on privacy invasion for which the falsity is irrelevant. The
preclusive effect of Section 24 is limited to causes of action that
depend on the publication of false fact, and in which the injury is at
least in part attributable to the falsity. Thus, a claim arising in privacy,
for example, which involves published falsity but which does not
depend on that falsity for proof of the claim or of injury, would not be
precluded. But when such a claim does depend upon falsity, the Act
precludes it even if the remedy provided in such a claim is for
dignitary (e.g., privacy) harm rather than harm to reputation.

Section 25. Limitation of Actions

(a) A claim under this [Act] is barred unless an action is commenced in a court of competent jurisdiction within five (5) years after
the publication or, in the case of a claim against a publisher based on a
subsequent republication by another publisher, within ten (10) years
after the publication from which the republication was derived.

(b) Within the period of limitations established by subsection (a),
a claim is barred one (1) year after the plaintiff knew or should have
known of the publication or republication.

(c) The limitation periods of this section are suspended during
the period provided in Section 15(a) for responding to a request for
retraction.

(d) For purposes of this section, the date of publication printed
on or contained within a publication is the date of publication, unless
later publication is proved.

Comment to Section 25

Section 25 contains two provisions addressing limitations on actions.
First, it balances the interests of both parties to a suit under the Act by
adopting a rule based on plaintiff's discovery of the publication but
strictly limiting the period for filing suit once discovery is or should
have been made and precluding all suits after five years of the
publication. Second, it provides a ten-year limitation for suits based
on republication covered by Section 20.

Subsection 25(b) provides that a plaintiff must commence a suit
under the Act within one year of the plaintiff's actual or constructive
knowledge of the publication. Although most states provide a one-
year statute of limitations on libel actions, state statutes vary as to
when the limitations period begins. Some states provide that a libel

cause of action accrues when the publication is made,[21] while other states provide that a libel cause of action does not accrue until the plaintiff learns of the publication.[22] Basing the statute of limitations on the point of the publication has the advantage of providing a definite limitation on a publisher's liability. The Act departs from this approach in recognition of the fact that a person can be injured by a publication of which he is unaware.

A principal reason that a one-year "discovery" statute of limitations is used is that the Act covers private as well as media defamation. With a media defamation, such as one that occurs in a local newspaper, a discovery provision should have no significant effect in most cases, as it should be interpreted as justifying the conclusion that the plaintiff "should have known" of the story at the time of its publication in the newspaper. Purely private defamations, however, are more often unknown to the defamed individual until a later time, such as at the time of a subsequent job evaluation or at the point of an adverse job decision. It is in view of these problems arising in the private setting that a discovery provision was used.

Subsection 25(a) provides that a publisher's potential liability is terminated after five years of the publication. The five-year limit on liability represents a balance struck between fairness to plaintiffs and fairness to defendants. The Act protects the unaware plaintiff, but only for five years. Accordingly, a publisher will not have to defend a suit more than five years after the publication.

Subsection 25(a) also limits the original publisher's liability for foreseeable future republications to ten years.

Subsection 25(c) provides that the statute of limitations is tolled while the plaintiff awaits a defendant's reply to a request for retraction. Although Sections 12 and 15 require a defendant to respond to a request for a retraction within thirty days, if the request comes within thirty days of the running of the statute of limitations, a defendant should not be able to delay his answer to permit the running of the statute.

[Note to revisers]

[All or part of the statue of limitations provision can, if appropriate, be inserted in a statutory chapter of the state Code, which sets forth general statutes of limitations. The state's general chapter on statutes of limitations may include a period of limitations for libel and slander, which will need to be repealed and replaced by Section 25 or portions of it. By placing the provisions of Section 25 in the general statute of limitations provision, the ordinary tolling provisions applicable to general statutes of limitations, such as absence of a defendant, the minority of a plaintiff, and the like, will be made applicable.]

Section 26. Uniformity of Application and Construction

This [Act] shall be applied and construed to effectuate its general purpose to make uniform the law with respect to the subject of this [Act] among states enacting it.

Section 27. Short Title

This [Act] may be cited as the Uniform Defamation Act.

Section 28. Severability

If any provision of this [Act] or its application to any person or circumstance is held invalid, the invalidity does not affect other provisions or applications of this [Act] which can be given effect without the invalid provision or application, and to this end the provisions of this [Act] are severable.

Section 29. Effective Date

This [Act] takes effect _____.

Section 30. Application to Existing Relationships

This [Act] applies to all publications made on or after its effective date.

NOTES

1. This description of the National Conference of Commissioners on Uniform State Laws is drawn from the 1990-91 REFERENCE BOOK OF THE NATIONAL CONFERENCE OF COMMISSIONERS ON UNIFORM STATE LAWS.

2. 418 U.S. 323, 344–45 (1974).

3. RESTATEMENT (SECOND) OF TORTS § 577(1) (ALI 1977) [hereinafter RESTATEMENT].

4. *See* Hustler Magazine, Inc. v. Falwell, 485 U.S. 46 (1988).

5. 110 S. Ct. 2695 (1990).

6. 466 U.S. 485 (1984).

7. *See* N.Y. CIV. PRAC. L. & R. LAW § 3016(a) (McKinney 1974).

8. CAL. CIV. PROC. CODE § 460.5 (West 1973).

9. *See* Gertz v. Robert Welch, Inc., 418 U.S. 323 (1974); Dun & Bradstreet, Inc. v. Greenmoss Builders, Inc., 472 U.S. 749 (1985).

10. *Cf.* N.C. GEN. STAT. § 99-1 (1985); WIS. STAT. ANN. § 895.05 (West 1983).

11. For a sense of some of the variations, see W. PROSSER & P. KEETON, THE LAW OF TORTS § 115 (5th ed. 1984); RESTATEMENT, Supra note 3, §§ 582-92A.

12. *See* Barr v. Mateo, 360 U.S. 564 (1959).

13. RESTATEMENT, *supra* note 13, §§ 594-98A.

14. *See id.* §§ 606–10.

15. 418 U.S. 323 (1974).

16. Curtis Publishing Co. v. Butts, 388 U.S. 130 (1967), quoted in Gertz v. Robert Welch, Inc., 418 U.S. at 336–37; Milkovich v. Lorain Journal Co., 110 S. Ct. 2695, (1990).

17. Milkovich v. Lorain Journal Co., 110 S. Ct. at (quoting New York Times Co. v. Sullivan, 376 U.S. 254, 279–80 (1964)).

18. *See generally* RESTATEMENT, *supra* note 3, §§ 578, 581.

19. *Id.* § 577A. *See also* Uniform Single Publication Act (1952), which while different from the Act and the *Restatement,* is similar in substance.

20. *See* PROSSER & KEETON, *supra* note 11, § 126.

21. *See* N.Y. CIV. PRAC. L. & R. LAW § 215 (McKinney 1974); ILL. ANN. STAT. ch. 110, para. 13-201 (Smith-Hurd 1934).

22. CAL. CIV. PROC. CODE § 340(3) (West 1982).

chapter 9

Legislative Efforts to Reform Libel Law

JOHN SOLOSKI*

While legal scholars, media attorneys, and, to a lesser extent, journalists have been debating the pros and cons of the various proposals for reforming libel law, there have been numerous attempts to legislate reform at the state level. Since 1989, over sixty-five bills have been introduced in state legislatures to modify libel and defamation laws.[1] Nearly all of these bills died in committee. Most of the attempts to modify libel and defamation laws can be divided into two categories: (1) attempts to provide relief for special categories of plaintiffs and defendants and (2) attempts to establish a declaratory judgment action for defamation in suits filed against the media.

SPECIAL CATEGORIES OF PLAINTIFFS AND DEFENDANTS

The bills introduced in state legislatures to provide protection from libel for certain types of businesses and individuals take a wide variety of forms. In a number of states, bills have been introduced to protect insurance companies, their agents, and employees from being sued for libel.[2] The purpose of the bills is to provide immunity from liability for defamatory statements that might appear in private reports (e.g., medical reports, accident records, and credit reports) furnished to an insurer.

*Professor of journalism and mass communication, University of Iowa.

Bills have been introduced in New York to allow actions for declaratory judgment by the family of a deceased person within five years of the person's death.[3] A bill that would have allowed recovery of damages for libel of a deceased individual passed the New York Senate but was withdrawn by its sponsor after it was opposed by the news media.[4] The news media argued that it would be very difficult to defend such a suit, presumably because of jury sympathy and because the deceased "plaintiff" could not be deposed or subjected to cross-examination.[5] The media also believed that the bill would encourage suits by people primarily interested in punishing the media for publishing stories critical of a deceased individual.[6] The film industry was concerned that libel suits would be used to prevent the showing of docudramas about deceased famous persons.[7]

One of the more recent attempts to modify state laws relating to libel and defamation deals with libel suits brought for the purpose of stifling the speech of private citizens. These lawsuits, labeled "strategic lawsuits against public participation" (SLAPP),[8] often involving a defamation claim, have been used to intimidate and harass private citizens who opposed commercial development, changes in zoning laws, and the dumping of waste. Most SLAPPs are won by defendants, but at such a high cost in litigation expense that they are likely to have a chilling effect on the willingness of private citizens to engage in discussion of public issues.[9] Just the threat of a SLAPP often is enough to silence vocal critics.[10]

Bills to limit or prohibit SLAPPs have been introduced in a number of state legislatures.[11] Some of the bills would make plaintiffs in such actions limited-purpose public figures who would have to prove actual malice in order to prevail in a libel suit. Legislation introduced in New York,[12] for example, would classify any plaintiff who applies for a permit, lease, license,[13] certificate, or other entitlement from any governmental agency as a limited-purpose public figure who must prove actual malice by clear and convincing evidence in a suit brought against a person challenging or opposing the permit, lease, license, or certificate. One purpose of such bills is to make it easier for defendants to prevail at summary judgment, thus reducing the cost of litigation. The New York legislation would also permit a defendant to recover attorneys' fees upon a demonstration that the suit was frivolous. And if a defendant proved that the action was brought to harass, intimidate, or punish the defendant, the court could award compensatory and punitive damages.

Bills introduced in California to limit SLAPPs have been even more encompassing and would erect additional procedural obstacles to such suits.[14] Plaintiffs would be required, prior to filing suit, to file a petition and affidavits with the court stating the facts of the claim. The defendant could file opposing affidavits. The plaintiff could sue only if the court determines that there is a substantial probability that the plaintiff will prevail. If the court finds that the plaintiff is not likely to prevail, the plaintiff would be barred from filing suit and the defendant would be entitled to recover attorneys' fees.

In 1990, the California state legislature passed such a bill, but it was vetoed by Governor Deukmejian.[15] In his veto message, Deukmejian said the bill was unnecessary because there already existed ample protection from frivolous lawsuits.[16] The bill was reintroduced in 1991. It was passed by the legislature and was again vetoed.[17]

Bills have been introduced in a number of state legislatures to provide relief for candidates who are libeled or defamed by an opponent during an election campaign.[18] Most of the bills would impose liability on a winning candidate who made or authorized others to make libelous statements about an opponent.[19] If a court determines that the libelous statements were made with knowledge of their falsity or with reckless disregard as to their truth, the winner of the election would forfeit the seat if the court found that the libelous statements were a major contributing factor to the defeat of the opponent.[20]

Some of these bills would require candidates to sign a statement promising not to defame opposing candidates.[21] A 1990 California law requires every person running for public office be given a copy of the "Code of Fair Campaign Practices."[22] Section 2 of the Code states: "I shall not use or permit the use of character defamation, whispering campaigns, libel, slander, or scurrilous attacks on any candidate or his or her personal or family life."[23] Candidates are asked to sign the Code, but they are not obligated to abide by it, nor are they legally liable if they violate it.[24]

DECLARATORY JUDGMENT ACTIONS

A number of bills have been introduced in Congress and in state legislatures to establish a declaratory judgment action for defamation in suits brought against the media. These libel reform bills take a number of forms and will be summarized briefly in the following pages.

The Schumer Bill

Perhaps the best-known declaratory judgment bill was introduced by Rep. Charles E. Schumer (D-N.Y.) in the U.S. House of Representatives in 1985.[25] Public hearings on the Schumer bill were held before the Subcommittee on Courts, Civil Liberties, and the Administration of Justice on June 27 and July 18, 1985.[26]

While the Schumer bill did not pass, it had a major influence on legislative efforts to reform libel law. All of the bills introduced in state legislatures to modify libel law contain most of the key elements of the Schumer bill. The Schumer bill generated a great deal of reaction from the media, media attorneys, and legal scholars. The bill and the criticisms of it will be briefly summarized here. Marc A. Franklin and David A. Barrett examine the bill in depth in Chapters 2 and 3 of this volume.[27]

Under the Schumer bill, a public official or public figure could bring an action for a declaratory judgment that a broadcast or publication was false and defamatory. No proof of the defendant's state of mind (actual malice) would be required in an action for declaratory judgment, and no money damages could be awarded.

The Schumer bill would also permit a defendant to designate a libel action brought by a public official or public figure as an action for declaratory judgment. This election would have to be made within ninety days from the commencement of a libel action . If the media defendant designates a libel action as a declaratory judgment action, it would be treated as if it were originally an action for declaratory judgment and the plaintiff would be barred from bringing any other claim or cause of action arising out of the publication or broadcast. The bill would prohibit the awarding of punitive damages in any libel action brought against the media.

In a departure from common U.S. practice, the bill would award attorneys' fees to the prevailing party unless the court determines that there is an overriding reason not to do so. Attorneys' fees could not be awarded to the prevailing plaintiff if the defendant exercised reasonable effort to determine that the publication or broadcast was true or if the defendant published or broadcast a retraction within ten days after the action was filed.

The Schumer bill proved controversial on a number of grounds.[28] One was whether the bill was fair to public officials and public figures. A public figure or public official who suffered actual financial loss because of a libelous statement would be barred from recovering damages if the media defendant were to unilaterally designate the libel action as an action for declaratory judgment. Supporters of the bill pointed out that under current libel law, the constitutional privileges make it very difficult for public officials and public figures to win a libel suit. From a financial perspective, then, public officials and public figures would not be any worse off under the Schumer bill than they are under current libel law. Moreover, because public officials and public figures would be more likely to prevail on the falsity issue, if only by virtue of the less complex proof required, the bill would allow them to clear their name and to set the record straight. This would help to minimize any financial loss they experience.

Another concern raised by the bill was that by eliminating the penalty of money damages, the bill would encourage the media to be less responsible. The concern was that unscrupulous media would designate a libel action by a public official or public figure as an action for declaratory judgment to escape financial liability for their recklessly publishing libelous statements. Supporters of the bill pointed out that the integrity of the media is critical to the media's ability to maintain the public's trust. If a media defendant were to lose a number of declaratory judgment actions, the defendant's journalistic integrity and public trust would be eroded. Fear of being adjudged to have published false information would encourage the media to be more responsible.

Media attorney Floyd Abrams believed the Schumer bill would likely result in an increase in the number of libel suits filed against the media, which would not lead to any decrease in the total amount of money and time spent by the media to defend libel suits.[29] And he was concerned that under the bill, the media would find themselves defending "truth" suits. Abrams also questioned whether modifying libel law at the federal level was the most appropriate way of proceeding with libel law reform. He suggested, instead, that one or two states experiment with a declaratory judgment action before it is adopted at the federal level.

State Legislative Reforms

Beginning in 1986, a number of bills have been introduced in state legislatures to establish a declaratory judgment action for defamation. Most of the bills would limit the action to suits involving the mass media. No money damages could be awarded in a declaratory judgment action. Rather, the issue to be decided is the truth or falsity of the allegedly libelous statements and reputational harm to the plaintiff. The bills are premised on the idea that for many plaintiffs, especially those who are public officials or public figures, quickly repairing their reputation is more important than the unlikely prospect of winning money damages. The purpose of the bills is to provide a legal recourse for public officials and public figures who are libeled by the media but unable to prove that the media acted with actual malice.

Maryland

A bill to establish a declaratory judgment action for public officials and public figures was introduced in the Maryland House of Delegates in 1986.[30] It was one of the first attempts to experiment with the use of a declaratory judgment action for defamation. The bill did not pass.

The bill would allow public officials and public figures to bring a declaratory judgment action against the media in circuit court. A plaintiff who brought an action for declaratory judgment would be barred from asserting any other claim or action arising from the publication or broadcast of the allegedly libelous statements. To succeed, plaintiffs would be required to prove by clear and convincing evidence that the publication was false and that it had damaged their reputation.

Like the Schumer bill, the Maryland proposal would permit media defendants to designate any libel action brought by a public official or public figure as an action for declaratory judgment. If a media defendant elected to designate a libel action as an action for declaratory judgment, the plaintiff could not be awarded damages and would be barred from asserting or recovering from any other claim arising from the publication or broadcast.

The bill would award attorneys' fees to the prevailing party. However, the court could not award the prevailing plaintiff attorneys' fees if the media defendant exercised reasonable effort to ascertain that the publication was not false and defamatory or if the media defendant published or broadcast a retraction within ten days after the libel action was filed.

Illinois

A 1987 attempt in Illinois to establish a declaratory judgment action for defamation came closer to being enacted than any other state effort.[31] The bill was passed by the Illinois House of Representatives but did not survive in the senate.[32]

Robert J. Steigmann, a circuit court judge, drafted the bill.[33] His purpose was to provide an alternative cause of action for restoration of reputation. His stated goal was to provide a means of getting at the underlying truth or falsity of the allegedly libelous statements without subjecting the media to the possibility of paying money damages.[34] The bill made no distinction between private individuals and public officials or public figures. Any libel plaintiff could bring an action for declaratory judgment. Steigmann relied heavily on the work of Franklin in drafting his bill.[35]

The bill would require media defendants to furnish to plaintiffs copies of the material alleged to be false. If the defendant were a broadcaster, the defendant would have to furnish copies of tapes, films, or transcripts of the statements alleged to be false. Failure of a broadcaster to furnish the plaintiff with the material alleged to be false would result in the payment of $5,000 to the plaintiff.

Discovery could take place only with the approval of the court. Prior to granting approval, a hearing would be held at which the party requesting discovery would have to demonstrate to the court's satisfaction a compelling need for the information sought. No discovery would be permitted relating to whether the media acted negligently or with actual malice.

The outcome of the declaratory judgment action would be a court determination of the falsity of the published statements. The remedy could take two forms. The first would be for the media defendant to publish the judicial finding that the statements were determined to be false. The finding would have to be published at a time and manner so that the greatest number of people who saw or heard the false statements would see or hear it. A media defendant that declines to publish the finding would have to pay to have the finding published in another mass medium approved by the court. The alternative mass medium would have to be similar in form and content to the medium in which the false statements appeared.

The bill would award reasonable attorneys' fees, not to exceed $10,000, to the prevailing plaintiff. If the court found that the plaintiff's suit was frivolous, attorneys' fees, not to exceed $10,000, would be awarded to the defendant.

Opposition to the bill came from the Illinois State Bar Association, the Illinois American Civil Liberties Union, the Illinois News Broadcasters Association, and the Illinois News Association.[36] A Libel Task Force, composed of publishers, media attorneys, and educators, was formed to study the bill.[37] The task force found that the bill suffered from a number of problems, the most significant being:

1. The bill would result in a proliferation of nuisance lawsuits against the media.[38]
2. The bill would "create a new tort of 'falsehood,' which would stifle uninhibited, aggressive news gathering and reporting, and free and open debate of public issues."[39] And it would be very difficult for courts to determine whether the challenged statements are actually true or false.[40]
3. The bill was unconstitutional because it put the courts in the

position of dictating media content and because it allowed public officials and public figures to recover attorneys' fees without having to prove fault on the part of the media defendant.[41]

In a letter to the *Chicago Daily Law Bulletin*, Steigmann responded to these criticisms.[42] Steigmann argued that the bill would not encourage nuisance suits because media defendants could recover up to $10,000 in attorneys' fees from plaintiffs who brought frivolous suits. Steigmann argued that the bill was constitutional because it would not require media defendants to publish the court's finding. The media defendant would have the option of paying to have the finding published in comparable media. And Steigmann argued that the bill would have no greater chilling effect on the media than does current libel law. As to the difficulty of determining whether the challenged statements are true or false, Steigmann wrote:

> Is it really that much more momentous for a jury to decide whether some newspaper had published a statement referring to the plaintiff which was both damaging to the plaintiff's reputation and false than it is for the same jury to decide whether someone is guilty of murder and should be executed? . . . The bottom line, it seems, is that the media do not want anyone who can slap their wrist with moral authority even when the press has been found to have wrongly damaged someone's reputation by printing false statements about that person.[43]

Steigmann's bill was reintroduced in 1989. The one major change in the bill was that the ceiling on attorneys' fees was lowered from $10,000 to $5,000 for both plaintiffs and defendants. The bill was opposed by the same organizations that had opposed the 1987 bill. David L. Bennett, executive director of the Illinois Press Association, called the bill "the most dangerous and damaging bill to newspapers introduced in the Illinois legislature in several years. . . . The ultimate danger is the real possibility that enemies of a free press will use this bill as a weapon to intimidate the working press."[44] The bill did not pass.

Iowa

A bill to establish a declaratory judgment action for libel was introduced in the Iowa Senate in 1989.[45] The bill was not reported out of the Judiciary Committee.

One of the purposes of the bill is to attempt to resolve libel disputes prior to the filing of a lawsuit. The bill would bar plaintiffs from bringing a libel suit seeking money damages until they received a mediation release. To obtain this release, a plaintiff would have to file a request for mediation with the attorney general's office. Once a request was filed, a mediation meeting would be held within fourteen days of the issuance of notice to the parties. To obtain a mediation release, the plaintiff or the plaintiff's representative would be required to attend the mediation meeting. Failure of the defendant to attend the meeting would result in the immediate issuance of a mediation release. If the parties were unable to settle the dispute, a mediation release would be issued to the plaintiff.

The bill would establish a declaratory judgment action for libel. Plaintiffs seeking a declaratory judgment would have to prove that the statements were false and had damaged their reputation. The sole remedy would be the issuance by the district court of a declaratory judgment. The media defendant would not be required to publish the finding. Publication or broadcast of a retraction, in a manner similar to the original publication, would be an absolute defense to a declaratory judgment action.

The bill would also establish an action for setting the record straight. A plaintiff could bring such an action in district court, with the sole issues to be decided being falsity and harm to the reputation of the plaintiff. If the plaintiff prevailed, the defendant would be required to publish the results of the fact-finding process in a manner similar to the original publication or to pay to have the results published in a comparable medium.

If both the plaintiff and the defendant agree, either an action for declaratory judgment or an action to set the record straight could be submitted to arbitration. This would facilitate quick resolution of the dispute. A decision by an arbitrator would be issued within twenty-eight days of the date of filing a request for arbitration.

The bill would award attorneys' fees in certain circumstances. If the plaintiff were a public official or public figure, attorneys' fees would be awarded to the prevailing plaintiff only if the plaintiff proved that the false information was published with actual knowledge of its falsity or with reckless disregard of the truth. If the plaintiff were not a public official or public figure and the challenged statements did not relate to an issue of public concern, attorneys' fees would be awarded to the prevailing plaintiff if the defendant negligently published the false statements. The defendant would be awarded attorneys' fees on a finding that the plaintiff's suit was frivolous.

Connecticut

Legislation to revise libel law in Connecticut was introduced in 1989.[46] The bill was based on the Annenberg Libel Reform Proposal.[47] The bill died in the Judiciary Committee.

The bill would require a libel plaintiff to seek a retraction or an opportunity to reply from the defendant prior to filing an action for defamation. If the defendant honored the plaintiff's request within thirty days, whether by retracting or affording the plaintiff an opportunity to reply, no action for defamation could be brought against the defendant. A plaintiff who failed to receive a retraction or an opportunity to reply could file a defamation suit, and either the plaintiff or the defendant could designate the action as an action for declaratory judgment. In an action for declaratory judgment, the only issue to be decided would be the truth or falsity of the allegedly libelous statements.

Only if neither party requests a declaratory judgment action could an action for money damages be brought. Money damages would be limited to reasonable compensation for actual injury (including harm to reputation, which is difficult to limit or measure). No punitive damages could be awarded.

The bill would eliminate any distinction between media and nonmedia defendants. And it would bar a plaintiff from filing a libel suit against a defendant who accurately quoted defamatory statements made by others, provided that the statements involved issues of public concern and that the source of the statement was identified. The bill also would bar any action based on statements that constitute expressions of opinion.

California

A bill to modify libel law in California was introduced by Sen. Bill Lockyer in 1986.[48] The bill would establish an action for a declaratory judgment in libel suits brought by public officials or public figures against the media. The two issues to be decided in an action for declaratory judgment would be the truth or falsity of the allegedly libelous statements and reputational harm to the plaintiff. The bill would not require a media defendant to publish the findings of the declaratory judgment action or to pay to have them published in comparable media. The only remedy would be a determination by the court that the statements are false and defamatory.

The bill would award attorneys' fees to the prevailing party, but the exceptions are large enough to swallow the rule. Fees could not be awarded to a prevailing plaintiff if the defendant could prove that reasonable efforts had been made to determine that the statements were not false and defamatory prior to publication. Moreover, attorneys' fees could not be awarded to a prevailing plaintiff if the defendant had published a correction or retraction within ten days of the filing of the action. Attorneys' fees could be awarded to a prevailing defendant only on proof that the action was brought without a reasonable chance of success.

The California Newspaper Publishers Association formed an Ad Hoc Libel Reform Committee to study and make recommendations about the bill.[49] The committee identified a number of potential problems with the bill.

The committee believed that the bill would encourage public officials and public figures to sue the media for libel because it relieved them of the heavy burdens imposed by current libel law.[50] The subsequent increase in the number of suits, the committee believed, would result in the media's spending as much if not more on litigation as they do now.[51] The committee was also concerned that as more libel suits are filed, a libel plaintiff's bar would develop. With plaintiffs' attorneys becoming more adept at suing the media for libel, the cost of defending libel suits would increase and more suits would be lost by the media.[52]

The committee also believed that the bill would result in more libel suits going to trial, which, in turn, would result in more litigation expense for the media.[53] Determining the truth or falsity of an allegedly libelous statement, according to the committee, would be neither easy nor inexpensive.[54] And the committee noted that "the track record of newspapers losing the vast majority of libel trials is not encouraging."[55]

The committee objected to the way the bill would award attorneys' fees to plaintiffs. The bill would permit a plaintiff to recover attorneys' fees only if it was proved that the media defendant had not exercised reasonable care when publishing the libelous statements. In order to determine whether the media had exercised reasonable care, trials would have to focus on the way the media did the disputed story. This led the committee to conclude that the same elements considered in trials under current law would be considered under the proposed declaratory judgment action, except that the media are protected by a higher fault standard under current law.[56]

Consequently, the committee believed that the bill would result in the media's having to spend large sums defending their journalistic performance. And the media would suffer greater disruption of newsrooms than they do under current law. "As more libel suits are filed and more trials result editors and reporters will increasingly be called to defend their editorial decisions and to testify at depositions and trials. . . . Under the Lockyer approach newsrooms would find themselves more immersed than ever in the libel litigation business."[57]

Finally, the equity of the bill was brought into question. The bill would apply only to public officials and public figures; private plaintiffs would have to pursue traditional libel litigation. And it would not prevent a public official or public figure from suing the media for money damages. The committee concluded that the bill would provide public officials and public figures with a new remedy without replacing the existing one.[58]

The bill was not passed by the legislature. Sen. Barry Keene reintroduced it in 1989 with one major change.[59] Keene's bill would not allow public officials or public figures to bring an action for declaratory judgment until after a demand for a correction had been made. If a correction were not published in a manner similar to that of the publication of the allegedly libelous statements within ten days after service of the notice, the plaintiff could bring an action for declaratory judgment. If a correction were published within ten days, the plaintiff would be barred from bringing an action for declaratory judgment.

During the Senate Judiciary Committee's debate, Keene added two amendments in response to criticisms of the bill.[60] The first would make each party responsible for paying his or her attorneys' fees.[61] And if the media defendant proved that the plaintiff brought the action without a reasonable chance of success, the plaintiff would have to pay the defendant's attorneys' fees. Keene's second amendment would prohibit public officials from using campaign funds to bring libel suits.[62] The bill was defeated on a 3–6 vote.[63] Lockyer, who sponsored the 1986 bill, voted against the bill.[64]

Opposition to the Keene bill came from media attorneys, the California Newspaper Publishers Association, and the Radio and Television News Association of Southern California.[65] Michael Dorias, lobbyist for the California Newspaper Publishers Association, said the bill would "have a chilling impact on aggressive reporting."[66] The Keene bill was reintroduced in 1990 by Sen. Ed Davis and, like its predecessors, it did not pass.[67]

CONCLUSION

There are a number of important lessons to be learned from the legislative efforts to reform libel law. First, all of the attempts to legislate reform have been opposed by the media. The media have opposed even those bills that are highly favorable to them. Bills that would permit the media to designate any libel suit brought by a public official or public figure as a declaratory judgment action have been either actively opposed by the media or ignored, with the hope that the bills would eventually die. No legislative proposal to systematically reform libel law has been supported by the media.

A second lesson is that there is no politically influential group that supports reform of libel law. Libel plaintiffs are unorganized, so it is not possible for them to form a politically influential group. And because the number of libel suits filed in any jurisdiction is small, there are few plaintiffs' attorneys who specialize in libel law. Consequently, there is no organized plaintiff's bar that could marshall support for libel law reform. On the other hand, both the media and the libel defense bar are well organized and are an effective political force.

A third lesson is that libel law reform seems to be caught in a *Catch-22*. On the one hand, there seems to be widespread belief among media attorneys, journalists, and legal scholars that libel law does not work and that the law needs to be changed. There is support among some media attorneys to experiment with legislative reform in one or two states.[68] But, on the other hand, all attempts to enact legislation in states have been opposed by media attorneys and media organizations in those states. Libel law reform seems to suffer from a NIMBY (not in my backyard) attitude on the part of the media. Everyone thinks something needs to be done about libel law, but no one seems to want it done in his or her own state.

And until legislation is enacted, it is not possible to address the major criticisms of many of the libel reform proposals. These criticism can be briefly summarized: (1) a concern that a declaratory judgment action will encourage the filing of more libel suits, especially by public figures and public officials; (2) a concern that determining the truth or falsity of the allegedly libelous statements is neither an easy nor an inexpensive task; (3) a concern that a declaratory judgment action will undermine the credibility of the media; (4) a concern that the availability of a declaratory judgment action will have a chilling effect on the media's willingness to report controversial news; and (5) a concern that a declaratory judgment action will not result in any decrease in the media's litigation cost. These criticisms cannot be assessed until there is empirical evidence about the use of declaratory judgment actions to resolve libel disputes.

The strong media opposition to legislative reform of libel law has led Rodney A. Smolla, director of the Annenberg Libel Reform Project, to reconsider the viability of a mandatory declaratory judgment action for libel.[69] He believes that a mandatory declaratory judgment action would have a chilling effect on media because journalists perceive such an action as being a "truth trial." Smolla now believes that a declaratory judgment action should be strictly voluntary.[70]

Opposition to legislative reform has led David A. Anderson to conclude that the best hope for reforming libel lies not with legislatures but with the Supreme Court.[71] Anderson may well be correct. But if the Court were to alter current libel law even by a minor degree, the howls of protest from the media will be heard clearly and loudly by members of Congress. It is likely that legislation would be introduced to nullify any changes made in the law by the Supreme Court.

Where does libel law reform go from here? The short-term answer is probably nowhere. Libel suits are not that big a problem today for the media. There is evidence to suggest that the number of libel suits filed against the media has declined in recent years.[72] But there is no reason to assume that this is a long-term trend. The problems with current libel law have not changed, but because the libel atmosphere is rather calm, this may be the most propitious time to reform libel law.

The Uniform Defamation Act of the National Conference of Commissioners[73] is the latest and possibly the most comprehensive libel law reform proposal. The proposal has all but been ignore by the press,[74] but it has drawn harsh criticism from the Libel Defense Resource Center.[75] If libel law is to be reformed through legislation, the media in one or two states may be well advised to closely study the proposed act. There may be some media organizations willing to get over their inherent fear of legislative reform and endorse the act. The media could even hedge their bets by having a three-year sunset clause added to the legislation. Unless the media within a state support legislation to reform libel law, there is almost no chance legislation will be enacted even on an experimental basis.

NOTES

1. 1990 ARIZ. H.B. 2215; 1991 CAL. A.B. 435; 1991 CAL. A.B. 436; 1991 CAL. S.B. 860; 1991 CAL. S.B. 999; 1989 CAL. A.B. 2024; 1990 CAL. A.B. 3517; 1989 CAL. S.B. 1393; 1990 CAL. S.B. 1797; 1988 CAL. A.C.A. 4; 1990 FLA. S.B. 1458; 1990 GA. H.B. 1551; 1989 GA. S.B. 239; 1991 HAW. H.B. 215; 1990 HAW. H.B. 2360; 1990 HAW. H.B. 2821; 1989 HAW. S.B. 103; 1990 HAW. S.B. 2296; 1991 IND. S.B. 1163; 1989 ILL. H.B. 1391; 1989

ILL. S.B. 1002; 1989 IOWA S.B. 40; 1990 IOWA S.B. 2404; 1991 ME. S.B. 677; 1991 MD. H.B. 464; 1989 MICH. H.B. 5056; 1990 MISS. H.B. 834; 1990 N.J. A.B. 3903; 1991 N.J. A.B. 4404; 1990 N.J. A.B. 675; 1991 N.M. S.B. 533; 1991 N.Y. A.B. 1117; 1991 N.Y. A.B. 1691; 1991 N.Y. A.B. 2544; 1991 N.Y. S.B. 716; 1991 N.Y. S.B. 1575; 1989 N.Y. A.B. 1593; 1989 N.Y. A.B. 1832; 1989 N.Y. A.B. 2528; 1989 N.Y. A.B. 2765; 1989 N.Y. A.B. 5267; 1990 N.Y. A.B. 8897; 1990 N.Y. A.B. 10624; 1990 N.Y. A.B. 12204; 1989 N.Y. S.B. 1081; 1989 N.Y. S.B. 1246; 1989 N.Y. S.B. 4164; 1990 OHIO H.B. 915; 1990 OKLA. S.B. 615; 1991 ORE. H.B. 2884; 1990 PA. H.B. 2831; 1989 R.I. H.B. 6427; 1991 S.C. H.B. 3004; 1991 S.C. S.B. 202; 1991 S.C. S.B. 609; 1989 S.C. H.B. 3021; 1989 S.C. S.B. 31; 1989 S.C. S.B. 294; 1989 S.C. S.B. 407; 1990 TENN. H.B. 1650; 1990 TENN. H.B. 2497; 1991 TEX. H.B. 68; 1990 TEX. S.B. 27; 1990 TEX. S.B. 58; 1990 TEX. S.B. 76; 1991 UTAH H.B. 356; 1991 VA. H.B. 1878; 1991 W.VA. H.B. 2594; 1991 WIS. A.B. 241.

2. *See, e.g.,* 1991 CAL. S.B. 860; 1990 ARIZ. H.B. 2215.

3. 1991 N.Y. A.B 1691; 1991 N.Y. S.B. 716; 1990 N.Y. A.B. 8897; 1989 N.Y. S.B. 4164.

4. *See* Winfield, *Bill Granting Publicity Rights to Heirs Threatens 1st Amendment,* MANHATTAN LAW., April 12–18, 1988, at 12.

5. *Id.*

6. *Id.*

7. *Id.*

8. *See* Canan & Pring, *Studying Strategic Lawsuits Against Public Participation: Mixing Quantitative and Qualitative Approaches,* 22 LAW & SOC'Y REV. 387 (1988). McEvoy, *"The Big Chill": Business Use of the Tort of Defamation to Discourage the Exercise of First Amendment Rights,* 17 HASTINGS CONST. L.Q. 503 (1990).

9. Pell, *The High Cost of Speaking Out,* CALIFORNIA, Nov. 1988, at 142. *See also* McEvoy, *supra* note 8.

10. *Id.*

11. *See, e.g.,* 1989 N.Y. A.B. 2765; 1991 N.Y. S.B. 1575, 1990 CAL. S.B. 2313.

12. 1991 N.Y. S.B. 1575.

13. Driver's licenses and fishing and hunting licenses would be exempt from the legislation.

14. 1990 CAL. S.B. 2313; 1991 CAL. S.B. 341.

15. Sotero, *Governor Vetoes Bill to Quell "SLAPP" Suits,* Gannett News Service, Sept. 27, 1990.

16. *Id.*

17. *See* 1991 CAL. A.B., California Bill Tracking Statenet, Information for Public Affairs.

18. *See, e.g.,* 1989 CAL. A.B. 2024; 1989 N.Y. A.B. 2765; 1989 R.I. H.B. 6427; 1990 ARIZ. H.B. 2215; 1991 HAW. H.B. 215; 1991 IND. S.B. 1163; 1989 ILL. S.B. 1002; 1990 N.J. 3903; 1990 N.J. A.B. 4404; 1990 N.J. A.B. 675; 1990 OHIO H.B. 915; 1990 PA. H.B. 2831; 1990 TENN. H.B. 2497; 1990 TEX. S.B. 27; 1990 TEX. S.B. 58; 1990 TEX. S.B. 76.

19. *See* bills at note 18.

20. *See e.g.*, 1991 IND. S.B. 1163; 1989 N.Y. A.B. 675; 1989 R.I. H.B. 6427.

21. *See, e.g.*, 1990 ME. H.B. 802; 1991 N.J. A.B. 4404; 1990 OHIO H.B. 915.

22. 1990 Cal. Adv. Legis. Serv. 1470.

23. *Id.*

24. *Id.*

25. H.R. 2846, 99th Cong., 1st Sess. (1985).

26. *Libel Law and the First Amendment: Hearings on H.R. 2846 Before the Subcomm. on Courts, Civil Liberties, and the Administration of Justice of the House Committee on the Judiciary*, 99th Cong., 1st Sess. (1985).

27. *See* Franklin, *A Declaratory Judgment Alternative to Current Libel Law*, and Barrett, *Declaratory Judgments for Libel: A Better Alternative*, in THE LIBEL LAW REFORM MOVEMENT (J. SOLOSKI & R. BEZANSON eds., 1992).

28. For an in-depth discussion of the criticism of the bill, see Franklin and Barrett, *supra* note 27.

29. Abrams, *Why We Should Change the Libel Law*, N.Y. TIMES, Sept. 29, 1985, §6 (Magazine), at 34.

30. 1986 MD. H.B. 1255.

31. 1987 ILL. H.B. 950.

32. *See News Notes*, Bureau of National Affairs (on file with author).

33. *See* Anderson, *Creator's Rebuttal Seeks "Restoration of Reputation" of Legislative Proposals*, CHICAGO DAILY LAW BULL., April 13, 1987, at 2.

34. Steigmann, *An Alternative to the Illinois Libel Hodge Podge* (on file with author).

35. *Id.*

36. *See* Golden, *ISBA Votes to Oppose Libel Legislation*, CHICAGO DAILY LAW BULL., April 1, 1987, at 1.

37. *See* Anderson, *Vindication for Some at the Expense of Too Many*, CHICAGO DAILY LAW BULL., March 30, 1987.

38. *Id.*

39. *Id.*

40. *Id.*

41. *Id.*

42. *See* Anderson, *supra* note 33.

43. *Id.*

44. *See News Notes*, *supra* note 32.

45. 1989 IOWA S.F. 40.

46. 1989 CONN. H.B. 5932.

47. Smolla, *The Annenberg Libel Reform Proposal*, in THE LIBEL LAW REFORM MOVEMENT (J. SOLOSKI & R. BEZANSON eds., 1992).

48. 1986 CAL. S.B. 1979. A similar bill was passed by the Hawaiian House of Representatives in 1990. *See* 1990 Hi. H.R. 2360.

49. *See* Ad Hoc Libel Reform Committee, *Declaratory Actions in Libel Litigation* (on file with author).

50. *Id.*

51. *Id.*

52. *Id.*

53. *Id.*

54. *Id.*

55. *Id.*

56. *Id.*

57. *Id.*

58. *Id.*

59. 1989 CAL. S.B. 1393.

60. Simons, *Bill Making It Easier for Politicians to Sue Is Defeated,* United Press International, May 23, 1989.

61. *Id.*

62. *Id.*

63. *Id.*

64. *Id.*

65. *Radio/TV News Association Opposes State Senate Bill SB 1393,* United Press International, May 16, 1989.

66. Simons, *supra* note 60.

67. 1990 CAL. S.B. 1797.

68. *See* Abrams, *supra* note 29; Smolla, *supra* note 47.

69. *See* Smolla, *supra* note 47.

70. *Id.*

71. Anderson, *Is Libel Law Worth Reforming,* in THE LIBEL LAW RE-FORM MOVEMENT (J. SOLOSKI & R. BEZANSON eds., 1992).

72. *See* Society of Professional Journalists, *Media Litigation '88,* Nov. 4, 1988, at 1, 6–7.

73. *Uniform Defamation Act,* in THE LIBEL LAW REFORM MOVE-MENT (J. SOLOSKI & R. BEZANSON eds., 1992).

74. A search of NEXIS revealed that only two stories have been published about the Uniform Defamation Act. *See* Samborn, *ULC to Meet—for 100th Time; Shadow Super-Legislature,* NAT'L L.J., July 29, 1991, at 3; and COMM. DAILY, July 23, 1990, at 10.

75. The Libel Defense Resource Center has written two reports critical of the Uniform Defamation Act (on file with author.)

chapter 10

A Concluding Note

JOHN SOLOSKI
RANDALL P. BEZANSON

It is difficult to find anyone who has much good to say about current libel law. It is unworkable, frustrating, and a threat to freedom of the press and speech. There seems to be widespread agreement that the law needs to be changed, but there is little agreement on how it should be changed. The proposals discussed in this book take different approaches to reforming libel law. Some would require wholesale changes in the law; others would modify only specific aspects.

Despite significant differences in the reform proposals, there is agreement on the major problems with current libel law. For plaintiffs, libel law provides little opportunity to repair reputation. Plaintiffs who can prove that the information published about them is false and that it harmed their reputation cannot succeed in a libel suit unless they can prove that the media published the information with some degree of negligence, with actual knowledge of its falsity, or with reckless disregard of the truth. Few plaintiffs are able to surmount this hurdle of libel law.

All of the reform proposals in this book would provide the opportunity for plaintiffs quickly to repair their reputation. Most of the reform proposals would permit an action for vindication based strictly on truth or falsity of the allegedly libelous statements. Plaintiffs would not be required to prove fault and no money damages would be available. The premise underlying a vindication action is that for many plaintiffs repairing reputation is more important than the prospect of winning money damages.

The reform proposals vary on the exact nature of the vindication action. The Annenberg Proposal and many of the legislative bills would leave the decision to pursue a no-fault, truth or falsity approach completely in the hands of the defendant. Plaintiffs would be permitted to bring suit for money damages only if the defendant declined to declare the suit an action for declaratory judgment. The Uniform Defamation Act, on the other hand, allows plaintiffs to sue for money damages, but provides financial disincentives for them to do so.

A related problem with current libel law is the size of money damages awarded to plaintiffs. Plaintiffs who prove that the media were at fault in publishing the libelous statements can expect to win huge money awards. Often these awards far exceed the actual financial loss experienced by plaintiffs. While punitive damages are not the exclusive reason for this, they represent a large part of the problem and pose a real threat to the media. Most of the reform proposals would eliminate them, permitting plaintiffs to recover damages only for real economic harm caused by the libel.

The reform proposals offer substantial protections to the media from the dangers of being sued for libel. In many of the proposals, these protections are greater than those provided by current libel law. The most obvious protection is the elimination of punitive damages. But the media would also be better protected from the pernicious effects of costly litigation. By permitting and encouraging plaintiffs to bring an action for vindication, the media would not be required to spend large sums defending their journalistic performance. In addition, many of the reform proposals provide for some fee shifting which would protect the media from frivolous libel suits. The proposals do not lessen any of the media's current common law and constitutional protections.

AVENUES FOR REFORM

How should libel law be reformed? Some believe that legislation is the most appropriate way to reform libel law; others believe that the courts offer the best, and possibly the only realistic, opportunity for reform. The Iowa Libel Research Project experimented with a voluntary alternative dispute resolution process. All of these approaches have their advantages and disadvantages.

Alternative Dispute Resolution

The Dispute Resolution Program showed that the use of a voluntary process for resolving libel disputes is not likely to be successful in the current libel-litigation climate. Media attorneys are reluctant to surrender their constitutional privileges even in exchange for a process in which no money damages could be awarded. Despite the high cost of defending a libel suit and the prospect of having to pay large money damages if they should lose, media attorneys are more comfortable with the current libel-litigation system. The media lose very few libel cases under current libel law, no matter that the cost of victory is very high.

Plaintiffs also do not appear very willing to participate—at least in the present environment of huge damage awards and contingency fees—in a voluntary process such as the Dispute Resolution Program, though most expressed interest in the program and in a prompt vindication remedy unaccompanied by damages. Once plaintiffs commit to suing the media for libel, it is difficult to convince them to use a process that provides no money damages. And plaintiff's attorneys, who often are on a contingency fee arrangement, may have a vested interest in the legal system, even though the prospect of winning money damages is remote.

The best chance for programs like the Dispute Resolution Program to work lies in the hands of journalists. Journalists need to recommend the use of an alternative dispute resolution program at the outset of the dispute. There is every reason to believe that such a step would meet with some success, as both plaintiffs and defendants recognize the advantages of a non-litigation alternative and have expressed broad-based interest in it.

Once suit is filed, however, it is very difficult to move the dispute out of the legal system. Costs have begun to mount at that point, consideration of strategic advantages in litigation have set in, and lawyers, not their clients are really calling the shots. Moreover, it is not likely that many journalists would recommend the use of alternative dispute resolution programs. Media organizations are accustomed to receiving and dealing with complaints, most of which do not result in a libel suit. Identifying complaints that are serious enough to recommend the use of programs such as the Dispute Resolution Program is difficult. And if journalists recommend the use of such programs for a large number of disputes, there may be no savings in litigation costs to the media organization. Rather than court trouble, it may be easier for media organizations to wait until a complaint ripens into a libel suit before expending resources to resolve the dispute.

Unless there is a sea change in how libel cases are litigated, it seems unlikely that alternative dispute resolution programs will play a major role in resolving libel disputes, despite the fact that these programs provide the most flexible and quickest way of dealing with libel disputes.

Judicial Reform of Libel Law

The courts can quickly and readily reform libel law. As David A. Anderson and Judge Pierre N. Leval argue, the courts can implement a declaratory judgment action immediately. The Supreme Court could encourage state courts to experiment with various reforms and, based on the outcome of the experiments, decide which reforms should be incorporated into law. The Supreme Court created the law; it can change it.

The problem with court reform is that it may never occur. There is no reason to believe that the Supreme Court is interested in modifying libel law. On the contrary, the Court seems committed to the current course of libel law. Its recent decisions have clearly and loudly affirmed the actual malice standard in libel cases. This does not mean that reforms initiated elsewhere would be rejected by the Court. Instead, it may simply reflect the Court's view that further judicial reform of libel law raises a troubling issue: Are the courts the most appropriate body to modify the law or should it be done by legislatures, where changes in the law can be publicly debated?

A related issue is whether libel law should be the subject of continuous modification by the courts and whether courts are suitably equipped to make the types of changes required. Libel law is a patchwork; it demands clear and coherent reexamination, for the problems are diverse and so also are the solutions. Despite the substantial barriers to suit erected by the Supreme Court, plaintiffs continue to sue the media for libel, and libel cases continue to be appealed to the Supreme Court. The Court is called on regularly to interpret new questions about libel law. And each year lower courts wrestle with difficult questions about the nuances of the law. Until libel law is made clearer and simpler, it will continue to consume judicial resources, and the Supreme Court will continue to be called on to decided difficult questions about the law. It may be difficult for the courts to make the reforms necessary to resolve the serious problems with libel law. To put it differently, the courts may be unable to make the kind of wholesale changes in the law that might be needed.

Legislative Reform

Most of the reform proposals favor legislation to change libel law. As with court reform of libel law, legislative reform has its advantages and disadvantages.

The advantages of legislative reform include:

1. Through legislative reform, clarity of law and procedure can be achieved.

2. Uniformity of treatment on a national level can only be achieved through legislation. A broad array of substantive and procedural differences exist from state to state and present significant problems for publishers in national and regional markets. These differences can only be resolved through legislation.

3. Legislative reform can achieve analytical and theoretical coherence in libel law. Current libel law is, in the view of many, theoretically incoherent, consisting of little more than a patchwork of rules and procedures.

4. A uniform and useful retraction system can only be accomplished through legislation. Current retraction statutes have largely proved to be failures because they do not reflect the media's needs and they are often little more than procedural traps for plaintiffs. An effective retraction system can prevent litigation—clearly the ideal solution.

5. Only by legislation can changes be made in the litigation process that encourage settlement and informal resolution of disputes. Currently, the media rarely settle libel suits, believing that settlement will encourage more suits.

6. Legislation will permit wholesale rethinking of damages in defamation cases, with limits based on a more rational understanding of the nature of the dispute and the harm caused by libels.

7. Legislation provides the opportunity systematically and rationally to clarify potential liabilities in the developing areas of database and computer technology.

8. Legislation can provide assurance that current levels of protection for the media are maintained, without foreclosing greater protections in accordance with federal and state constitutional requirements.

The disadvantages of legislative reform are:

1. Legislative reform will retain and make more permanent the libel tort. This is a clear disadvantage for those who wish to eliminate the tort.

2. Legislative change requires enactment, and enactment in each of the 50 states risks the introduction of legislative changes in the enacting process that might significantly alter the proposed reform, and might in any event defeat the interest in uniformity.

3. Legislative enactment may be unattractive because of substantive objections to particular features of a specific proposal.

4. Legislation presents the risk that current libel law will become "locked in," thus precluding or discouraging future favorable developments.

5. Legislation that moves to simplify the libel tort and includes opportunities for vindication without money damages may cause an increase in libel disputes.

Notwithstanding its disadvantages and cumbersomeness, legislative reform is, at least as of now, occupying center stage in the libel reform debate.

CONCLUSION

The libel reform issue is one of critical importance. Libel represents the most dramatic and frequent conflict at the intersection of law and journalism, and it thus involves the judicial system in a surprisingly broad array of questions, ranging from the meaning of reputation in an organized society, the modes of interpreting words and symbols, and the very idea of falsity, on the one hand, to the mundane facts of journalistic existence, such as the reliability of sources, the confidentiality of sources, and the limits of acceptable misquotation. Libel law, therefore, is effectively a prism through which the entire journalistic enterprise is explored.

In this respect, libel law is also symbolic of a much broader array of issues dealing with freedom of the press and freedom of speech. Since the beginning of its constitutionalization in 1964, the Supreme Court's approach to libel law has served as the fountainhead of a broader jurisprudence dealing with freedom of the press. Questions of public versus private expression, the core objects of political speech, and the application of contract principles to assurances made by the press have all been directly influenced by the Supreme Court's jurisprudence.

The approach taken to the reform of libel law, therefore, is of importance not just for the libel tort, but for freedom of expression itself. The libel reform question, therefore, is understandably subtle and complex. At the present time, most questions are open. There is, of course, disagreement about the problems posed by libel law, and even greater disagreement about how, or even whether, they should be addressed. And the problems are not only large in number, but different in quality. Some of the problems require systematic solutions; others might be susceptible to more limited and focused attention.

But even were we able to achieve consensus on the diagnosis of the problems and the appropriate treatments they require, we would confront difficult issues about the very nature of the approach to be taken. Some would prefer voluntary and extralegal approaches, believing that the risks of formal governmental intervention, whatever its form, could thus be avoided. Others, of course, would agree with such aspirations, but conclude that they are unrealistic. Yet another group would favor judicial solution, recognizing that it is by necessity limited in scope, but nevertheless perhaps more achievable. And yet a final group would urge legislative reform, notwithstanding its complexities, believing that the problems posed by the libel tort are too profound and complex to address in piecemeal fashion.

These are but the first two layers to be peeled away in the discussion of legislative reform of libel. Many other issues lie beneath and are addressed in specific provisions of legislative proposals, or the nuances of other methods of reform.

All of this is perhaps enough to discourage, if not depress, anyone approaching the libel law reform question. But the problems should also, in the end, excite and challenge. For they are real problems, and they portend real solutions. Many of the legal scholars who have proposed reforms base their proposals on important empirical studies of libel litigation. These studies have yielded valuable insights into the dynamics of libel litigation and have uncovered important and unsettling facts about the way libel law works. The system of U.S. libel law is broken, and broken badly. It may not be repaired tomorrow, but anyone gaining an understanding of current libel law and the difficulties it presents will, in the end, have no doubt about the inevitability of change.

Index